edexcel
advancing learning, changing lives

Further Pure
Mathematics 3

Edexcel AS and A-level Modular Mathematics

Greg Attwood
Bronwen Moran
Laurence Pateman
Keith Pledger
Geoff Staley
Dave Wilkins

Contents

About this book

This book is designed to provide you with the best preparation possible for your Edexcel FP3 unit examination:

- This is Edexcel's own course for the GCE specification.
- Written by senior examiners
- The LiveText CD-ROM in the back of the book contains even more resources to support you through the unit.

Finding your way around the book

Brief chapter overview and 'links' to underline the importance of mathematics: to the real world, to your study of further units and to your career

Every few chapters, a review exercise helps you consolidate your learning

Detailed contents list shows which parts of the FP3 specification are covered in each section

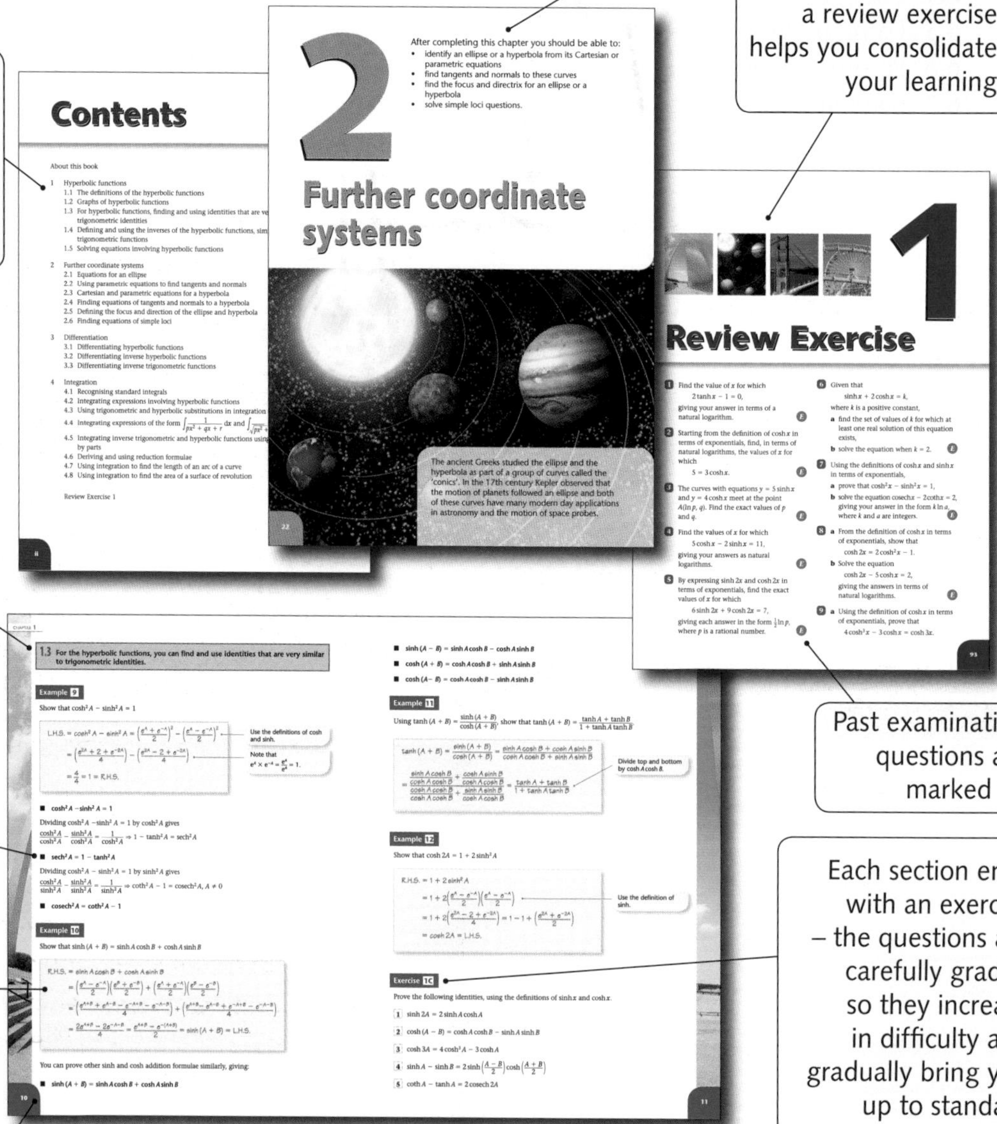

Each section begins with a statement of what is covered in the section

Concise learning points

Step-by-step worked examples – they are model solutions and include examiners hints

Past examination questions are marked 'E'

Each section ends with an exercise – the questions are carefully graded so they increase in difficulty and gradually bring you up to standard

Each chapter has a different colour scheme, to help you find the right chapter quickly

Each chapter ends with a mixed exercise and a summary of key points.

At the end of the book there is an examination-style paper.

LiveText software

The LiveText software gives you additional resources: Solutionbank and Exam café. Simply turn the pages of the electronic book to the page you need, and explore!

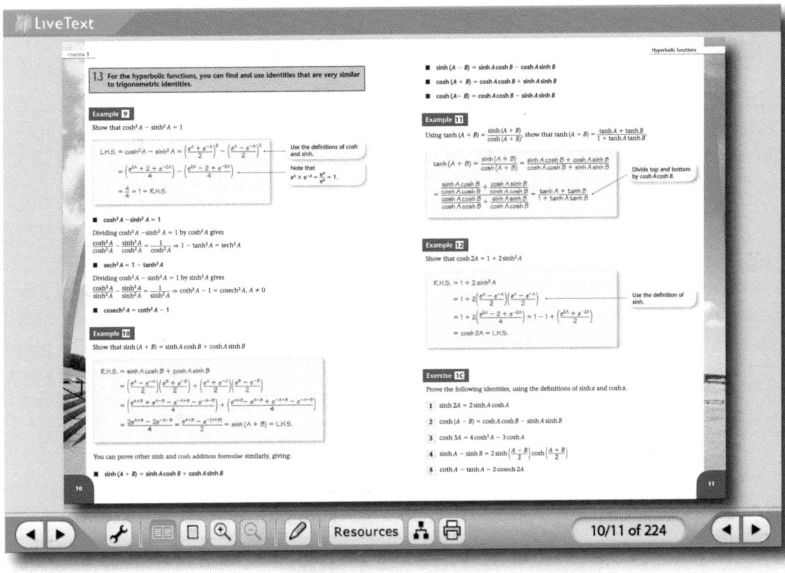

Unique Exam café feature:

- Relax and prepare – revision planner; hints and tips; common mistakes
- Refresh your memory – revision checklist; language of the examination; glossary
- Get the result! – fully worked examination-style paper with chief examiner's commentary

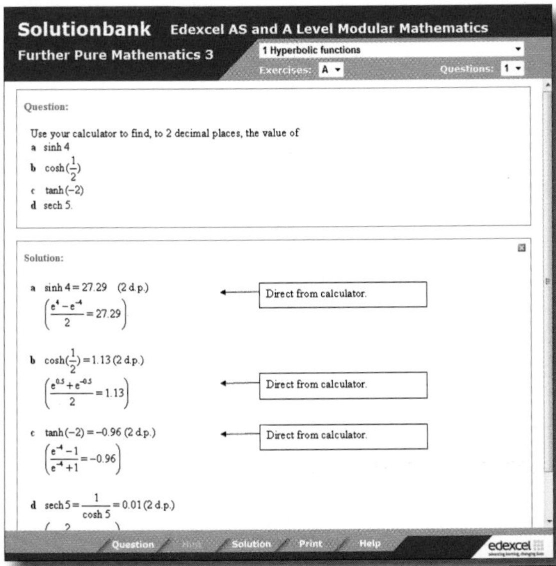

Solutionbank

- Hints and solutions to every question in the textbook
- Solutions and commentary for all review exercises and the practice examination paper

Published by Pearson Education Limited, a company incorporated in England and Wales, having its registered office at Edinburgh Gate, Harlow, Essex, CM20 2JE. Registered company number: 872828

Edexcel is a registered trademark of Edexcel Limited

13 12 11 10 09
10 9 8 7 6 5 4 3 2

British Library Cataloguing in Publication Data
A catalogue record for this book is available from the British Library on request.

ISBN 978 0 435519 22 3

Edited by Susan Gardner
Typeset by Tech-Set Ltd
Illustrated by Tech-Set Ltd
Cover design by Christopher Howson
Picture research by Chrissie Martin
Cover photo/illustration © Edexcel
Index by Indexing Specialists (UK) Ltd
Printed in Great Britain by Scotprint

Acknowledgements
The author and publisher would like to thank the following individuals and organisations for permission to reproduce photographs:

Shutterstock/Dmitry Zaltsman **p**1; Shutterstock/Christos Georghiou **p**22; Shutterstock/Stas Volik **p**46; Shutterstock/Rafael Franceschini **p**55; Rex Features/CERN **p**102; Getty Images/National Geographic **p**137

Every effort has been made to contact copyright holders of material reproduced in this book. Any omissions will be rectified in subsequent printings if notice is given to the publishers.

After completing this chapter you should be able to:

- write down the definitions of the hyperbolic functions $\sinh x$ and $\cosh x$
- write down the definitions of the hyperbolic functions $\tanh x$, $\operatorname{sech} x$, $\operatorname{cosech} x$ and $\coth x$ in terms of $\sinh x$ and $\cosh x$
- sketch the graphs of the six hyperbolic functions and know their properties
- establish identities for hyperbolic functions (similar to trigonometric identities)
- solve equations involving hyperbolic functions, using definitions or identities
- understand and use inverse hyperbolic functions, including their graphs and properties
- understand and use the logarithmic equivalents of the inverse hyperbolic functions.

1

Hyperbolic functions

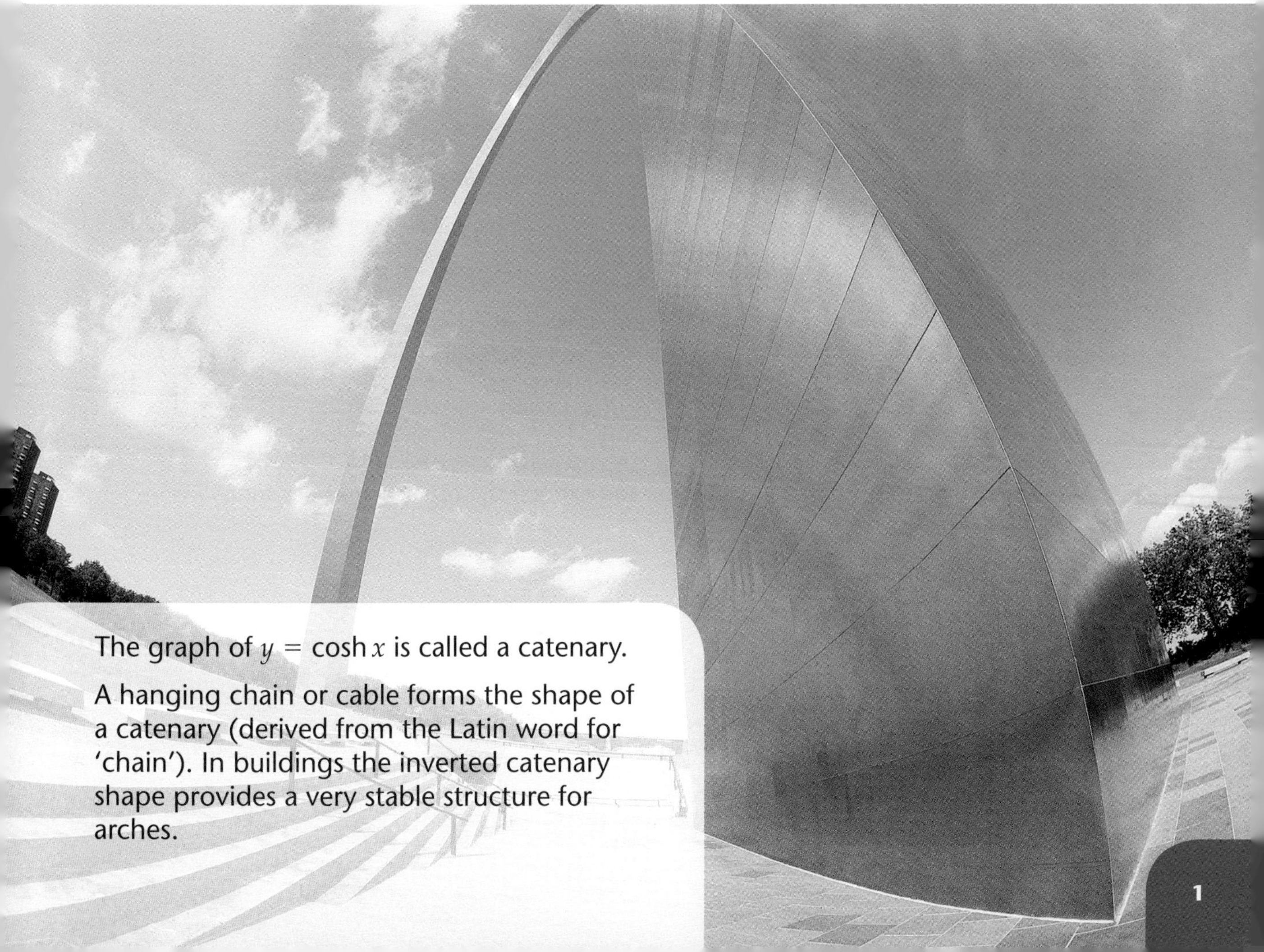

The graph of $y = \cosh x$ is called a catenary.

A hanging chain or cable forms the shape of a catenary (derived from the Latin word for 'chain'). In buildings the inverted catenary shape provides a very stable structure for arches.

1.1 You know the definitions of the hyperbolic functions.

Hyperbolic functions are similar to trigonometric functions in certain respects. Some of the similarities will become clear in this chapter.

The hyperbolic functions are defined in terms of exponential functions.

Hyperbolic sine, written as sinh

Often pronounced 'shine'.

■ $\sinh x = \dfrac{e^x - e^{-x}}{2} \qquad x \in \mathbb{R}$

Hyperbolic cosine, written as cosh

Often pronounced 'cosh'.

■ $\cosh x = \dfrac{e^x + e^{-x}}{2} \qquad x \in \mathbb{R}$

The other four hyperbolic functions are related to sinh and cosh in the same way that the corresponding trigonometric functions are related to sine and cosine.

Hyperbolic tangent, written as tanh

Often pronounced 'tanch' or 'than' (like 'thin').

■ $\tanh x = \dfrac{\sinh x}{\cosh x} \qquad x \in \mathbb{R}$

Hyperbolic secant, written as sech

Often pronounced 'setch' or 'sheck'.

■ $\operatorname{sech} x = \dfrac{1}{\cosh x} \qquad x \in \mathbb{R}$

Hyperbolic cosecant, written as cosech

Often pronounced 'cosetch' or 'cosheck'.

■ $\operatorname{cosech} x = \dfrac{1}{\sinh x} \qquad x \in \mathbb{R}, x \neq 0$

Hyperbolic cotangent, written as coth

Often pronounced 'coth'.

■ $\coth x = \dfrac{1}{\tanh x} \qquad x \in \mathbb{R}, x \neq 0$

■ **Using the definitions of sinh and cosh, you can express the other hyperbolic functions in terms of exponentials.**

$$\tanh x = \frac{\sinh x}{\cosh x} = \frac{e^x - e^{-x}}{2} \times \frac{2}{e^x + e^{-x}} = \frac{e^x - e^{-x}}{e^x + e^{-x}} = \frac{e^{2x} - 1}{e^{2x} + 1} \qquad x \in \mathbb{R}$$

$$\operatorname{sech} x = \frac{1}{\cosh x} = \frac{2}{e^x + e^{-x}} \qquad x \in \mathbb{R}$$

$$\operatorname{cosech} x = \frac{1}{\sinh x} = \frac{2}{e^x - e^{-x}} \qquad x \in \mathbb{R}, x \neq 0$$

$$\coth x = \frac{1}{\tanh x} = \frac{e^{2x} + 1}{e^{2x} - 1} \qquad x \in \mathbb{R}, x \neq 0$$

Example 1

Use your calculator to find, to 2 decimal places, the value of

a sinh 3

b cosh 1

c tanh 0.8.

a $\sinh 3 = 10.02$ (2 d.p.)

Use the hyperbolic function on your calculator. You could also find sinh 3 as $\frac{e^3 - e^{-3}}{2}$.

b $\cosh 1 = 1.54$ (2 d.p.)

Use the hyperbolic function on your calculator. You could also find cosh 1 as $\frac{e^1 + e^{-1}}{2}$.

c $\tanh 0.8 = 0.66$ (2 d.p.)

Use the hyperbolic function on your calculator. You could also find tanh 0.8 as $\frac{e^{1.6} - 1}{e^{1.6} + 1}$.

Example 2

Write in terms of e

a cosh 2

b cosech 3.

a $\cosh 2 = \frac{e^2 + e^{-2}}{2}$

b $\operatorname{cosech} 3 = \frac{1}{\sinh 3} = \frac{2}{e^3 - e^{-3}}$

Example 3

Find the exact value of tanh (ln 4).

$$\tanh(\ln 4) = \frac{e^{2\ln 4} - 1}{e^{2\ln 4} + 1} = \frac{e^{\ln 4^2} - 1}{e^{\ln 4^2} + 1} = \frac{e^{\ln 16} - 1}{e^{\ln 16} + 1}$$

$$\tanh(\ln 4) = \frac{16 - 1}{16 + 1} = \frac{15}{17}$$

Use $e^{\ln k} = k$.

Example 4

Use the definition of $\sinh x$ to find, to 2 decimal places, the value of x for which $\sinh x = 5$.

$\dfrac{e^x - e^{-x}}{2} = 5 \Rightarrow e^x - e^{-x} = 10$

$e^{2x} - 1 = 10e^x$ — Multiply throughout by e^x.

$e^{2x} - 10e^x - 1 = 0$

$e^x = \dfrac{10 \pm \sqrt{100 + 4}}{2}$ — Solve as a quadratic in e^x.

$e^x = 10.099$ or $e^x = -0.099$

$e^x = 10.099$ — e^x cannot be negative.

$x = \ln 10.099 = 2.31$ (2 d.p.) — Use an inverse hyperbolic function on your calculator to check this answer.

Exercise 1A

1 Use your calculator to find, to 2 decimal places, the value of

a $\sinh 4$ **b** $\cosh\left(\frac{1}{2}\right)$

c $\tanh(-2)$ **d** $\operatorname{sech} 5$.

2 Write in terms of e

a $\sinh 1$ **b** $\cosh 4$

c $\tanh 0.5$ **d** $\operatorname{sech}(-1)$.

3 Find the exact value of

a $\sinh(\ln 2)$ **b** $\cosh(\ln 3)$

c $\tanh(\ln 2)$ **d** $\operatorname{cosech}(\ln \pi)$.

In questions 4 to 8, use definitions of the hyperbolic functions (in terms of exponentials) to find each answer, then check your answers using an inverse hyperbolic function on your calculator.

4 Find, to 2 decimal places, the values of x for which $\cosh x = 2$.

5 Find, to 2 decimal places, the value of x for which $\sinh x = 1$.

6 Find, to 2 decimal places, the value of x for which $\tanh x = -\frac{1}{2}$.

7 Find, to 2 decimal places, the value of x for which $\coth x = 10$.

8 Find, to 2 decimal places, the values of x for which $\operatorname{sech} x = \frac{1}{8}$.

1.2 You can sketch the graphs of hyperbolic functions.

Consider the graphs of $y = e^x$ and $y = e^{-x}$.

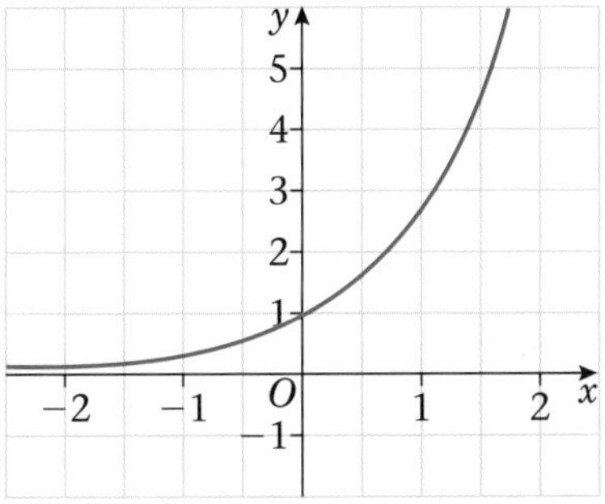

$y = e^x$

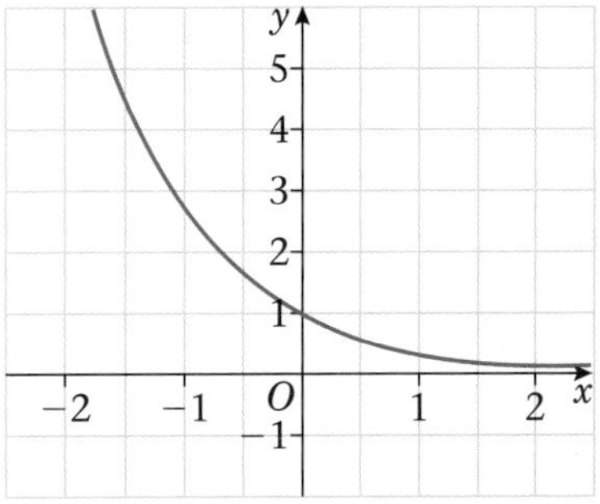

$y = e^{-x}$

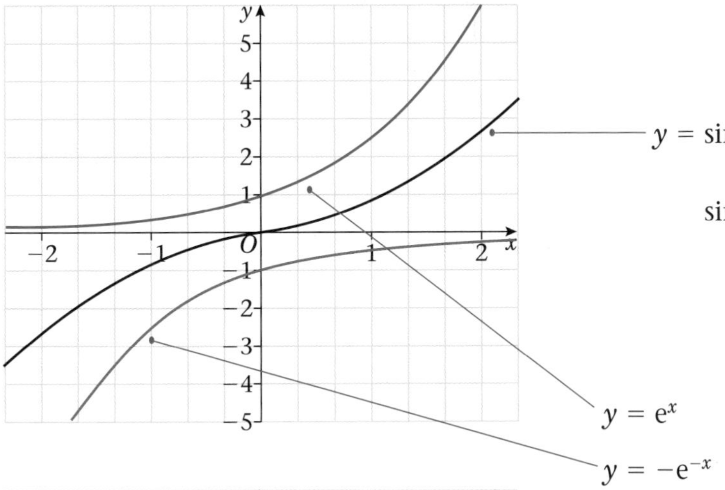

$\sinh x$ is the 'average' of e^x and $-e^{-x}$

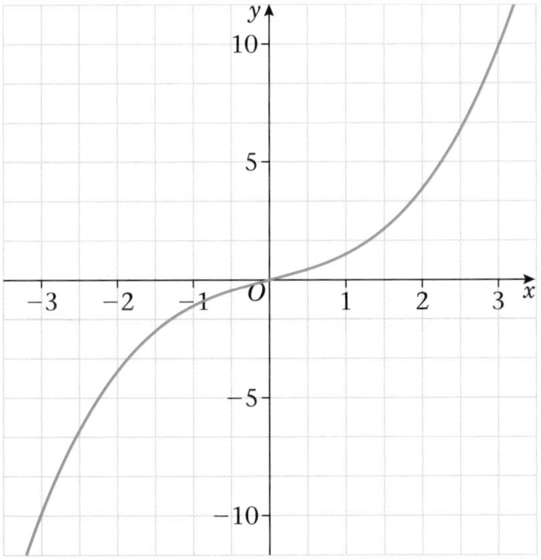

$y = \sinh x$

Features of the $\sinh x$ graph:

When x is large and positive, e^{-x} is small, so $\sinh x \approx \frac{1}{2}e^x$

When x is large and negative, e^x is small, so $\sinh x \approx -\frac{1}{2}e^{-x}$

- **For any value a, $\sinh(-a) = -\sinh a$** **(Similarly $\sin(-a) = -\sin a$)**

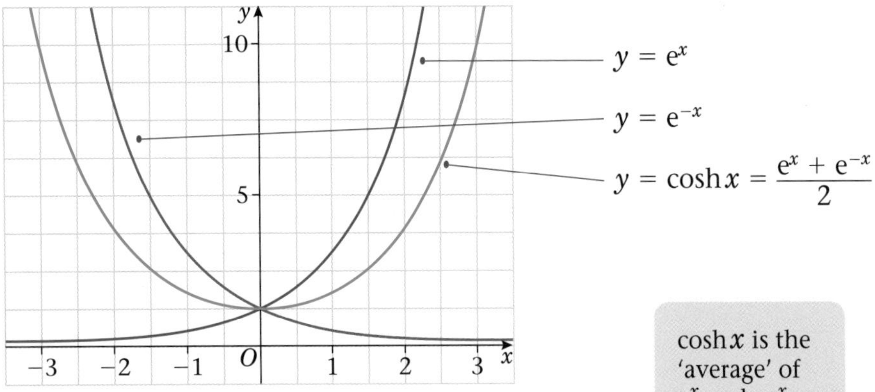

$\cosh x$ is the 'average' of e^x and e^{-x}

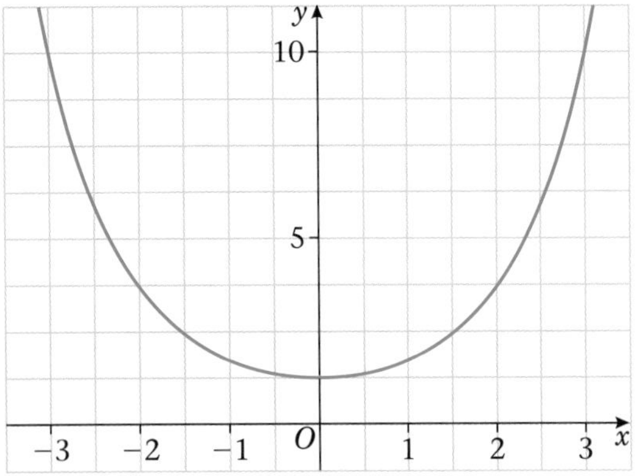

$y = \cosh x$

Features of the $\cosh x$ graph:

When x is large and positive, e^{-x} is small, so $\cosh x \approx \frac{1}{2}e^x$

When x is large and negative, e^x is small, so $\cosh x \approx \frac{1}{2}e^{-x}$

- **For any value a, $\cosh(-a) = \cosh a$** **(Similarly $\cos(-a) = \cos a$)**

Example 5

Sketch the graph of $y = \tanh x$.

Using $\tanh x = \dfrac{\sinh x}{\cosh x}$

When $x = 0$, $\tanh x = \frac{0}{1} = 0$

When x is large and positive, $\sinh x \approx \frac{1}{2}e^x$ and $\cosh x \approx \frac{1}{2}e^x$, so $\tanh x \approx 1$

When x is large and negative, $\sinh x \approx -\frac{1}{2}e^{-x}$ and $\cosh x \approx \frac{1}{2}e^{-x}$, so $\tanh x \approx -1$

As $x \to \infty$, $\tanh x \to 1$ and as $x \to -\infty$, $\tanh x \to -1$

For $f(x) = \tanh x$, $x \in \mathbb{R}$, the range of f is $-1 < f(x) < 1$

$y = -1$ and $y = 1$ are asymptotes to the curve.

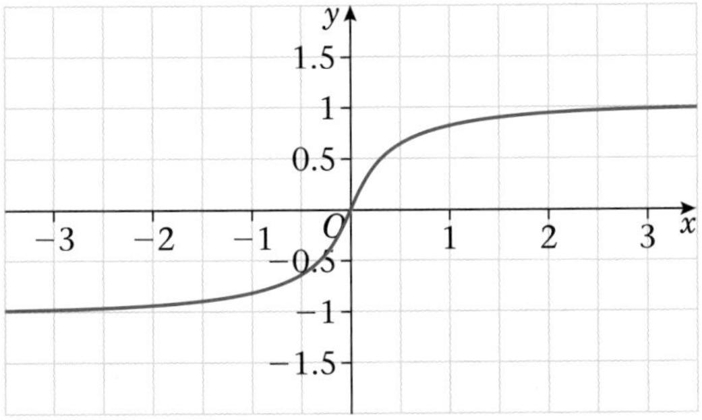

$y = \tanh x$

Check this sketch using the graphic function on your calculator.

Example 6

Sketch the graph of $y = \operatorname{sech} x$.

Using $\operatorname{sech} x = \dfrac{1}{\cosh x}$

When $x = 0$, $\operatorname{sech} x = \dfrac{1}{1} = 1$

As $x \to \infty$, $\cosh x \to \infty$, so $\operatorname{sech} x \to 0$

As $x \to -\infty$, $\cosh x \to \infty$, so $\operatorname{sech} x \to 0$

The x-axis is an asymptote to the curve.

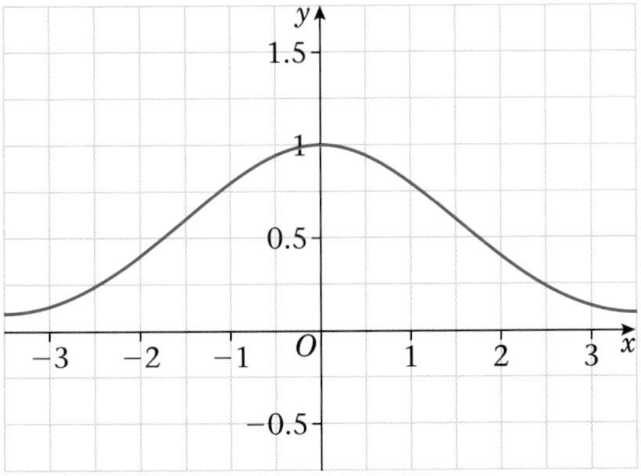

$y = \operatorname{sech} x$

Check this sketch using the graphic function on your calculator.

Example 7

Sketch the graph of $y = \text{cosech}\,x$, $x \neq 0$.

Using $\text{cosech}\,x = \dfrac{1}{\sinh x}$

For positive x, as $x \to 0$, $\text{cosech}\,x \to \infty$

For negative x, as $x \to 0$, $\text{cosech}\,x \to -\infty$

As $x \to \infty$, $\sinh x \to \infty$, so $\text{cosech}\,x \to 0$

As $x \to -\infty$, $\sinh x \to -\infty$, so $\text{cosech}\,x \to 0$

The x- and y-axes are asymptotes to the curve.

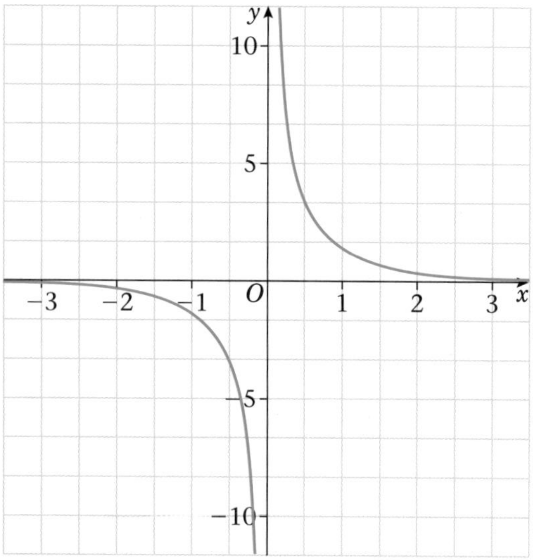

$y = \text{cosech}\,x$

Check this sketch using the graphic function on your calculator.

Example 8

Sketch the graph of $y = \coth x$, $x \neq 0$.

Using $\coth x = \dfrac{1}{\tanh x}$

For positive x, as $x \to 0$, $\coth x \to \infty$

For negative x, as $x \to 0$, $\coth x \to -\infty$

As $x \to \infty$, $\tanh x \to 1$, so $\coth x \to 1$

As $x \to -\infty$, $\tanh x \to -1$, so $\coth x \to -1$

The y-axis is an asymptote to the curve.

$y = -1$ and $y = 1$ are asymptotes to the curve.

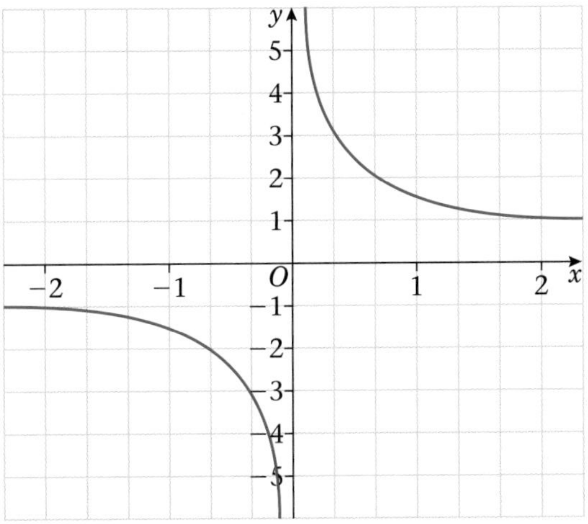

Check this sketch using the graphic function on your calculator.

Exercise 1B

1 On the same diagram, sketch the graphs of $y = \cosh 2x$ and $y = 2\cosh x$.

2 **a** On the same diagram, sketch the graphs of $y = \operatorname{sech} x$ and $y = \sinh x$.

b Show that, at the point of intersection of the graphs, $x = \frac{1}{2}\ln(2 + \sqrt{5})$.

3 Find the range of each hyperbolic function.

a $f(x) = \sinh x, x \in \mathbb{R}$

b $f(x) = \cosh x, x \in \mathbb{R}$

c $f(x) = \tanh x, x \in \mathbb{R}$

d $f(x) = \operatorname{sech} x, x \in \mathbb{R}$

e $f(x) = \operatorname{cosech} x, x \in \mathbb{R}, x \neq 0$

f $f(x) = \coth x, x \in \mathbb{R}, x \neq 0$

4 **a** Sketch the graph of $y = 1 + \coth x, x \in \mathbb{R}, x \neq 0$.

b Write down the equations of the asymptotes to this curve.

5 **a** Sketch the graph of $y = 3\tanh x, x \in \mathbb{R}$.

b Write down the equations of the asymptotes to this curve.

1.3 For the hyperbolic functions, you can find and use identities that are very similar to trigonometric identities.

Example 9

Show that $\cosh^2 A - \sinh^2 A = 1$

$$\text{L.H.S.} = \cosh^2 A - \sinh^2 A = \left(\frac{e^A + e^{-A}}{2}\right)^2 - \left(\frac{e^A - e^{-A}}{2}\right)^2$$

Use the definitions of cosh and sinh.

$$= \left(\frac{e^{2A} + 2 + e^{-2A}}{4}\right) - \left(\frac{e^{2A} - 2 + e^{-2A}}{4}\right)$$

Note that $e^A \times e^{-A} = \frac{e^A}{e^A} = 1.$

$$= \frac{4}{4} = 1 = \text{R.H.S.}$$

■ $\boldsymbol{\cosh^2 A - \sinh^2 A = 1}$

Dividing $\cosh^2 A - \sinh^2 A = 1$ by $\cosh^2 A$ gives

$$\frac{\cosh^2 A}{\cosh^2 A} - \frac{\sinh^2 A}{\cosh^2 A} = \frac{1}{\cosh^2 A} \Rightarrow 1 - \tanh^2 A = \operatorname{sech}^2 A$$

■ $\boldsymbol{\operatorname{sech}^2 A = 1 - \tanh^2 A}$

Dividing $\cosh^2 A - \sinh^2 A = 1$ by $\sinh^2 A$ gives

$$\frac{\cosh^2 A}{\sinh^2 A} - \frac{\sinh^2 A}{\sinh^2 A} = \frac{1}{\sinh^2 A} \Rightarrow \coth^2 A - 1 = \operatorname{cosech}^2 A,\ A \neq 0$$

■ $\boldsymbol{\operatorname{cosech}^2 A = \coth^2 A - 1}$

Example 10

Show that $\sinh(A + B) = \sinh A \cosh B + \cosh A \sinh B$

$$\text{R.H.S.} = \sinh A \cosh B + \cosh A \sinh B$$

$$= \left(\frac{e^A - e^{-A}}{2}\right)\left(\frac{e^B + e^{-B}}{2}\right) + \left(\frac{e^A + e^{-A}}{2}\right)\left(\frac{e^B - e^{-B}}{2}\right)$$

$$= \left(\frac{e^{A+B} + e^{A-B} - e^{-A+B} - e^{-A-B}}{4}\right) + \left(\frac{e^{A+B} - e^{A-B} + e^{-A+B} - e^{-A-B}}{4}\right)$$

$$= \frac{2e^{A+B} - 2e^{-A-B}}{4} = \frac{e^{A+B} - e^{-(A+B)}}{2} = \sinh(A + B) = \text{L.H.S.}$$

You can prove other sinh and cosh addition formulae similarly, giving:

■ $\boldsymbol{\sinh(A + B) = \sinh A \cosh B + \cosh A \sinh B}$

- $\sinh(A - B) = \sinh A \cosh B - \cosh A \sinh B$
- $\cosh(A + B) = \cosh A \cosh B + \sinh A \sinh B$
- $\cosh(A - B) = \cosh A \cosh B - \sinh A \sinh B$

Example 11

Using $\tanh(A + B) = \dfrac{\sinh(A + B)}{\cosh(A + B)}$, show that $\tanh(A + B) = \dfrac{\tanh A + \tanh B}{1 + \tanh A \tanh B}$.

$$\tanh(A + B) = \frac{\sinh(A + B)}{\cosh(A + B)} = \frac{\sinh A \cosh B + \cosh A \sinh B}{\cosh A \cosh B + \sinh A \sinh B}$$

$$= \frac{\dfrac{\sinh A \cosh B}{\cosh A \cosh B} + \dfrac{\cosh A \sinh B}{\cosh A \cosh B}}{\dfrac{\cosh A \cosh B}{\cosh A \cosh B} + \dfrac{\sinh A \sinh B}{\cosh A \cosh B}} = \frac{\tanh A + \tanh B}{1 + \tanh A \tanh B}$$

Divide top and bottom by $\cosh A \cosh B$.

Example 12

Show that $\cosh 2A = 1 + 2\sinh^2 A$

$$\text{R.H.S.} = 1 + 2\sinh^2 A$$

$$= 1 + 2\left(\frac{e^A - e^{-A}}{2}\right)\left(\frac{e^A - e^{-A}}{2}\right)$$

Use the definition of sinh.

$$= 1 + 2\left(\frac{e^{2A} - 2 + e^{-2A}}{4}\right) = 1 - 1 + \left(\frac{e^{2A} + e^{-2A}}{2}\right)$$

$$= \cosh 2A = \text{L.H.S.}$$

- **Given a trigonometric identity, it is generally possible to write down the corresponding hyperbolic identity using what is known as Osborn's Rule:**

  Replace cos by cosh: $\cos A \rightarrow \cosh A$

  Replace sin by sinh: $\sin A \rightarrow \sinh A$

  However …

  replace any product (or implied product) of 2 sine terms by minus the product of 2 sinh terms:

  e.g. $\sin A \sin B \rightarrow -\sinh A \sinh B$

  $\tan^2 A \rightarrow -\tanh^2 A$

Implied product of 2 sine terms because $\tan^2 A = \dfrac{\sin^2 A}{\cos^2 A}$.

Example 13

Write down the hyperbolic identity corresponding to

a $\cos 2A = 2\cos^2 A - 1$

b $\tan(A - B) = \dfrac{\tan A - \tan B}{1 + \tan A \tan B}$.

a $\cosh 2A = 2\cosh^2 A - 1$

b $\tanh(A - B) = \dfrac{\tanh A - \tanh B}{1 - \tanh A \tanh B}$

Implied product of 2 sine terms because $\tan A \tan B = \dfrac{\sin A \sin B}{\cos A \cos B}$.

Example 14

Given that $\sinh x = \frac{3}{4}$, find the exact value of

a $\cosh x$

b $\tanh x$

c $\sinh 2x$.

a Using $\cosh^2 x - \sinh^2 x = 1$,

$\cosh^2 x - \frac{9}{16} = 1 \Rightarrow \cosh^2 x = \frac{25}{16}$

$\cosh x = \frac{5}{4}$

$\cosh x \geqslant 1$, so $\cosh x = -\frac{5}{4}$ is not possible.

b Using $\tanh x = \dfrac{\sinh x}{\cosh x}$,

$\tanh x = \frac{3}{4} \div \frac{5}{4} = \frac{3}{5}$

c Using $\sinh 2x = 2\sinh x \cosh x$,

$\sinh 2x = 2 \times \frac{3}{4} \times \frac{5}{4} = \frac{15}{8}$

Exercise 1C

Prove the following identities, using the definitions of $\sinh x$ and $\cosh x$.

1 $\sinh 2A = 2\sinh A \cosh A$

2 $\cosh(A - B) = \cosh A \cosh B - \sinh A \sinh B$

3 $\cosh 3A = 4\cosh^3 A - 3\cosh A$

4 $\sinh A - \sinh B = 2\sinh\left(\dfrac{A - B}{2}\right)\cosh\left(\dfrac{A + B}{2}\right)$

5 $\coth A - \tanh A = 2\,\text{cosech}\, 2A$

Use Osborn's Rule to write down the hyperbolic identities corresponding to the following trigonometric identities.

6 $\sin(A - B) = \sin A \cos B - \cos A \sin B$

7 $\sin 3A = 3 \sin A - 4 \sin^3 A$

8 $\cos A + \cos B = 2 \cos\left(\frac{A + B}{2}\right) \cos\left(\frac{A - B}{2}\right)$

9 $\cos 2A = \frac{1 - \tan^2 A}{1 + \tan^2 A}$

10 $\cos 2A = \cos^4 A - \sin^4 A$

11 Given that $\cosh x = 2$, find the exact value of

a $\sinh x$

b $\tanh x$

c $\cosh 2x$.

12 Given that $\sinh x = -1$, find the exact value of

a $\cosh x$

b $\sinh 2x$

c $\tanh 2x$.

1.4 You can define and use the inverses of the hyperbolic functions, similar to those of the trigonometric functions.

- **If $f(x) = \sinh x$, the inverse function f^{-1} is called $\text{arsinh}\, x$ (sometimes written as $\sinh^{-1} x$).**
- **Note that if $y = \text{arsinh}\, x$, then $x = \sinh y$.**
- **As for other inverse functions, the graph of $y = \text{arsinh}\, x$ is the reflection of the graph of $y = \sinh x$ in the line $y = x$.**

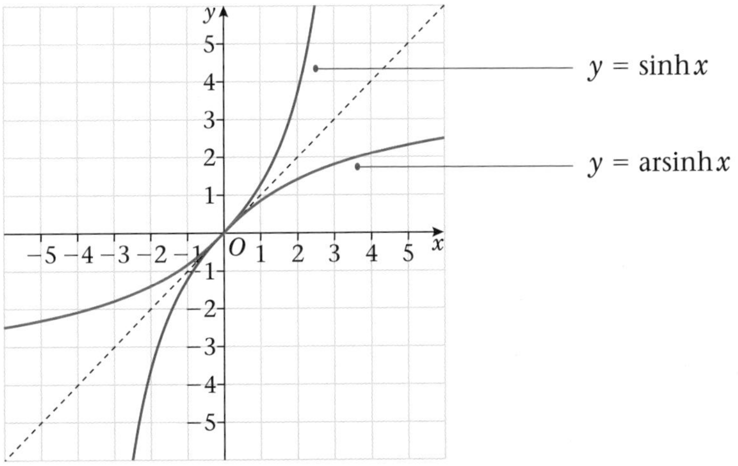

■ **The inverse of a function is defined only if the function is one-to-one, so for $\cosh x$ the domain must be restricted in order to define an inverse.**

For $f(x) = \cosh x, x \geq 0$,

$f^{-1}(x) = \text{arcosh}\, x, (x \geq 1)$

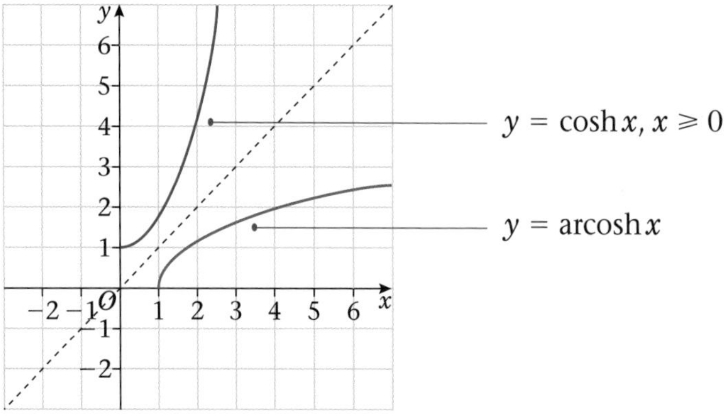

The following table shows all the inverse hyperbolic functions, with domains restricted where necessary.

Hyperbolic function	Inverse hyperbolic function
$y = \sinh x$	$y = \text{arsinh}\, x$
$y = \cosh x, x \geq 0$	$y = \text{arcosh}\, x, x \geq 1$
$y = \tanh x$	$y = \text{artanh}\, x, \lvert x \rvert < 1$
$y = \text{sech}\, x, x \geq 0$	$y = \text{arsech}\, x, 0 < x \leq 1$
$y = \text{cosech}\, x, x \neq 0$	$y = \text{arcosech}\, x, x \neq 0$
$y = \coth x, x \neq 0$	$y = \text{arcoth}\, x, \lvert x \rvert > 1$

Example 15

Sketch the graph of $y = \text{arcoth}\, x, \lvert x \rvert > 1$.

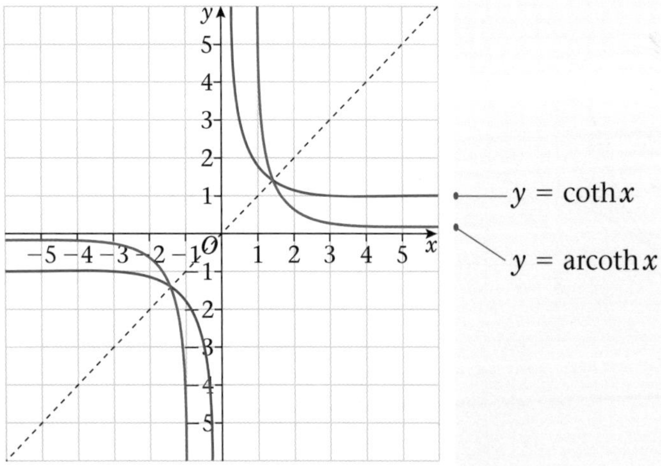

Reflect the graph of $y = \coth x$ in the line $y = x$.

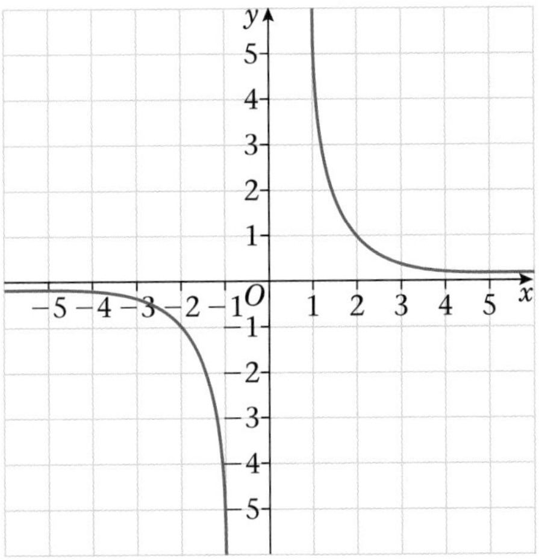

$y = \text{arcoth}\,x$

Note that $\text{arcoth}\,x$ is **not** defined for $|x| \leqslant 1$.

■ **You can express inverse hyperbolic functions in terms of natural logarithms.**

Example 16

Show that $\text{arsinh}\,x = \ln(x + \sqrt{x^2 + 1})$.

Let $y = \text{arsinh}\,x$

$x = \sinh y$

$x = \dfrac{e^y - e^{-y}}{2}$ — Use the definition of sinh.

$e^y - e^{-y} = 2x$ — Multiply by e^y.

$e^{2y} - 1 = 2xe^y$

$e^{2y} - 2xe^y - 1 = 0$ — Form a quadratic in e^y.

$a = 1$, $b = -2x$, $c = -1$

$e^y = \dfrac{2x \pm \sqrt{4x^2 + 4}}{2} = x \pm \sqrt{x^2 + 1}$ — Use the quadratic formula.

$e^y = x - \sqrt{x^2 + 1}$ can be ignored since $\sqrt{x^2 + 1} > x$, which would give a negative value of e^y, which is not possible.

So $e^y = x + \sqrt{x^2 + 1}$

$y = \ln(x + \sqrt{x^2 + 1})$

$\text{arsinh}\,x = \ln(x + \sqrt{x^2 + 1})$

Example 17

Show that $\text{arcosh}\, x = \ln(x + \sqrt{x^2 - 1}),\ x \geqslant 1$.

Let $y = \text{arcosh}\, x$

$x = \cosh y$

$x = \dfrac{e^y + e^{-y}}{2}$ — Use the definition of sinh.

$e^y + e^{-y} = 2x$ — Multiply by e^y.

$e^{2y} + 1 = 2xe^y$

$e^{2y} - 2xe^y + 1 = 0$ — Form a quadratic in e^y.

$a = 1,\ b = -2x,\ c = 1$

$e^y = \dfrac{2x \pm \sqrt{4x^2 - 4}}{2} = x \pm \sqrt{x^2 - 1}$ — Use the quadratic formula.

So $e^y = x \pm \sqrt{x^2 - 1}$

$y = \ln(x \pm \sqrt{x^2 - 1})$ — Note that both $y = \ln(x + \sqrt{x^2 - 1})$ and $y = \ln(x - \sqrt{x^2 - 1})$ are possible ... (see Example 21). See below.

$\text{arcosh}\, x = \ln(x + \sqrt{x^2 - 1})$ — ... but $\text{arcosh}\, x$ is 'single-valued'.

$(x + \sqrt{x^2 - 1})(x - \sqrt{x^2 - 1}) = x^2 - (x^2 - 1) = 1$

so $x - \sqrt{x^2 - 1} = \dfrac{1}{x + \sqrt{x^2 - 1}}$ and so

$\ln(x - \sqrt{x^2 - 1}) = -\ln(x + \sqrt{x^2 - 1})$

Thus $\ln(x + \sqrt{x^2 + 1})$ gives the positive value of $\text{arcosh}\, x$

and $\ln(x - \sqrt{x^2 - 1})$ the (excluded) negative value (see graph on page 14).

You can use a similar method (using the definition of tanh in terms of exponentials) to express $\text{artanh}\, x$ in terms of natural logarithms.

The following formulae can be used directly (unless you are asked to prove them).

- $\textbf{arsinh}\, x = \ln(x + \sqrt{x^2 + 1})$
- $\textbf{arcosh}\, x = \ln(x + \sqrt{x^2 - 1}),\ x \geqslant 1$
- $\textbf{artanh}\, x = \frac{1}{2}\ln\left(\dfrac{1 + x}{1 - x}\right),\ |x| < 1$

Example 18

Express as natural logarithms.

a arsinh 1 **b** arcosh 2 **c** $\text{artanh}\, \frac{1}{3}$

a $\text{arsinh}\, 1 = \ln(1 + \sqrt{1^2 + 1}) = \ln(1 + \sqrt{2})$

b $\text{arcosh}\, 2 = \ln(2 + \sqrt{2^2 - 1}) = \ln(2 + \sqrt{3})$

c $\text{artanh}\frac{1}{3} = \frac{1}{2}\ln\left(\frac{1+\frac{1}{3}}{1-\frac{1}{3}}\right) = \frac{1}{2}\ln 2 = \ln\sqrt{2}$ — You can use $a\ln x = \ln x^a$.

Exercise 1D

1 Sketch the graph of $y = \text{artanh}\,x$, $|x| < 1$.

2 Sketch the graph of $y = \text{arsech}\,x$, $0 < x \leqslant 1$.

3 Sketch the graph of $y = \text{arcosech}\,x$, $x \neq 0$.

4 Sketch the graph of $y = (\text{arsinh}\,x)^2$.

5 Show that $\text{artanh}\,x = \frac{1}{2}\ln\left(\frac{1+x}{1-x}\right)$, $|x| < 1$.

6 Show that $\text{arsech}\,x = \ln\left(\frac{1+\sqrt{1-x^2}}{x}\right)$, $0 < x \leqslant 1$.

7 Express as natural logarithms.

a $\text{arsinh}\,2$ **b** $\text{arcosh}\,3$ **c** $\text{artanh}\,\frac{1}{2}$

8 Express as natural logarithms.

a $\text{arsinh}\,\sqrt{2}$ **b** $\text{arcosh}\,\sqrt{5}$ **c** $\text{artanh}\,0.1$

9 Express as natural logarithms.

a $\text{arsinh}\,(-3)$ **b** $\text{arcosh}\,\frac{3}{2}$ **c** $\text{artanh}\,\frac{1}{\sqrt{3}}$

10 Given that $\text{artanh}\,x + \text{artanh}\,y = \ln\sqrt{3}$, show that $y = \frac{2x-1}{x-2}$.

1.5 You can solve equations involving hyperbolic functions.

Sometimes you can use a hyperbolic identity, but sometimes you will need to use basic definitions.

Example 19

Solve, for real values of x,

$$6\sinh x - 2\cosh x = 7$$

$$6\left(\frac{e^x - e^{-x}}{2}\right) - 2\left(\frac{e^x + e^{-x}}{2}\right) = 7$$

There is no hyperbolic identity that will easily transform the equation into an equation in just one hyperbolic function, so use the basic definitions.

$$3e^x - 3e^{-x} - e^x - e^{-x} = 7$$

$$2e^x - 7 - 4e^{-x} = 0$$

$$2e^{2x} - 7e^x - 4 = 0$$

$$(2e^x + 1)(e^x - 4) = 0$$

$$e^x = -\tfrac{1}{2},\ e^x = 4$$

$$e^x = 4$$

There are no real values of x for which $e^x = -\frac{1}{2}$.

$$x = \ln 4\ (\approx 1.386)$$

Example 20

Solve $2\cosh^2 x - 5\sinh x = 5$, giving your answers as natural logarithms.

Using $\cosh^2 x - \sinh^2 x = 1$,

$2(1 + \sinh^2 x) - 5\sinh x = 5$

$2\sinh^2 x - 5\sinh x - 3 = 0$

$(2\sinh x + 1)(\sinh x - 3) = 0$

$\sinh x = -\frac{1}{2}$, $\sinh x = 3$

$x = \text{arsinh}\left(-\frac{1}{2}\right)$, $x = \text{arsinh}\,3$

$x = \ln\left(-\frac{1}{2} + \sqrt{\frac{1}{4} + 1}\right)$, $x = \ln(3 + \sqrt{9 + 1})$

$x = \ln\left(-\frac{1}{2} + \frac{\sqrt{5}}{2}\right)$, $x = \ln(3 + \sqrt{10})$

Using this identity will transform the equation into an equation in just one hyperbolic function.

Use $\text{arsinh}\,x = \ln(x + \sqrt{x^2 + 1})$.

Example 21

Solve $\cosh 2x - 5\cosh x + 4 = 0$, giving your answers as natural logarithms where appropriate.

Using $\cosh 2x = 2\cosh^2 x - 1$,

$2\cosh^2 x - 1 - 5\cosh x + 4 = 0$

$2\cosh^2 x - 5\cosh x + 3 = 0$

$(2\cosh x - 3)(\cosh x - 1) = 0$

$\cosh x = \frac{3}{2}$, $\cosh x = 1$

$x = \ln\left(\frac{3}{2} \pm \sqrt{\frac{9}{4} - 1}\right)$, $x = 0$

$x = \ln\left(\frac{3}{2} \pm \frac{\sqrt{5}}{2}\right)$, $x = 0$

Using this identity will transform the equation into an equation in just one hyperbolic function.

You can use $\text{arcosh}\,x = \ln(x + \sqrt{x^2 - 1})$, but remember that both $\ln(x + \sqrt{x^2 - 1})$ and $\ln(x - \sqrt{x^2 - 1})$ are possible.
For any value of k greater than 1, $\cosh x = k$ will have two values (positive and negative).

Exercise 1E

Solve the following equations, giving your answers as natural logarithms.

1 $3\sinh x + 4\cosh x = 4$

2 $7\sinh x - 5\cosh x = 1$

3 $30\cosh x = 15 + 26\sinh x$

4 $13\sinh x - 7\cosh x + 1 = 0$

5 $\cosh 2x - 5\sinh x = 13$

6 $2\tanh^2 x + 5\operatorname{sech} x - 4 = 0$

7 $3\sinh^2 x - 13\cosh x + 7 = 0$

8 $\sinh 2x - 7\sinh x = 0$

9 $4\cosh x + 13e^{-x} = 11$

10 $2\tanh x = \cosh x$

Mixed exercise 1F

1 Find the exact value of **a** $\sinh(\ln 3)$ **b** $\cosh(\ln 5)$ **c** $\tanh(\ln \frac{1}{4})$.

2 **a** Sketch on the same diagram the graphs of $y = 2\operatorname{sech} x$ and $y = e^x$.

b Find the exact coordinates of the point of intersection of the graphs.

3 Using the definitions of $\sinh x$ and $\cosh x$, prove that

$$\sinh(A - B) = \sinh A\cosh B - \cosh A\sinh B.$$

4 Using definitions in terms of exponentials, prove that

$$\sinh x = \frac{2\tanh\frac{1}{2}x}{1 - \tanh^2\frac{1}{2}x}.$$

5 **a** Given that $13\cosh x + 5\sinh x = R\cosh(x + \alpha)$, $R > 0$, use the identity $\cosh(A + B) = \cosh A\cosh B + \sinh A\sinh B$ to find the values of R and α, giving the value of α to 3 decimal places.

b Write down the minimum value of $13\cosh x + 5\sinh x$.

6 **a** Show that, for $x > 0$, $\operatorname{arcosech} x = \ln\left(\frac{1 + \sqrt{1 + x^2}}{x}\right)$.

b Use the answer to part **a** to write down the value of arcosech 3.

c Use the logarithmic form of arsinh x to verify that your answer to part **b** is the same as the value for $\operatorname{arsinh}(\frac{1}{3})$.

7 Solve, giving your answers as natural logarithms

$$9\cosh x - 5\sinh x = 15$$

8 Solve, giving your answers as natural logarithms

$$23\sinh x - 17\cosh x + 7 = 0$$

9 Solve, giving your answers as natural logarithms

$$3\cosh^2 x + 11\sinh x = 17$$

10 Solve, giving your answers as natural logarithms

$$6\tanh x - 7\operatorname{sech} x = 2$$

11 Show that $\sinh[\ln(\sin x)] = -\frac{1}{2}\cos x \cot x$.

12 **a** On the same diagram, sketch the graphs of $y = 6 + \sinh x$ and $y = \sinh 3x$.

b Using the identity $\sinh 3x = 3\sinh x + 4\sinh^3 x$, show that the graphs intersect where $\sinh x = 1$ and hence find the exact coordinates of the point of intersection.

13 Given that $\operatorname{artanh} x - \operatorname{artanh} y = \ln 5$, find y in terms of x.

14 **a** Express $3\cosh x + 5\sinh x$ in the form $R\sinh(x + \alpha)$, where $R > 0$. Give α to 3 decimal places.

b Use the answer to part **a** to solve the equation $3\cosh x + 5\sinh x = 8$, giving your answer to 2 decimal places.

c Solve $3\cosh x + 5\sinh x = 8$ by using the definitions of $\cosh x$ and $\sinh x$.

Summary of key points

1
- $\sinh x = \dfrac{e^x - e^{-x}}{2}$ $\quad x \in \mathbb{R}$
- $\cosh x = \dfrac{e^x + e^{-x}}{2}$ $\quad x \in \mathbb{R}$
- $\tanh x = \dfrac{\sinh x}{\cosh x} = \dfrac{e^{2x} - 1}{e^{2x} + 1}$ $\quad x \in \mathbb{R}$
- $\operatorname{sech} x = \dfrac{1}{\cosh x}$ $\quad x \in \mathbb{R}$
- $\operatorname{cosech} x = \dfrac{1}{\sinh x}$ $\quad x \in \mathbb{R}, x \neq 0$
- $\coth x = \dfrac{1}{\tanh x}$ $\quad x \in \mathbb{R}, x \neq 0$

2 The graph of $y = \sinh x$

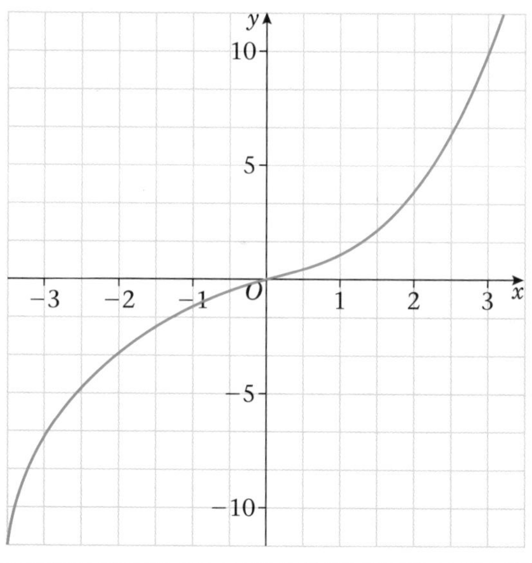

For any value a, $\sinh(-a) = -\sinh a$.

3 The graph of $y = \cosh x$

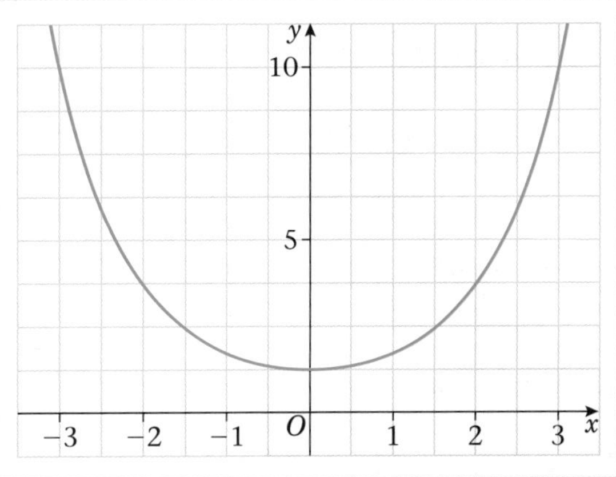

For any value a, $\cosh(-a) = \cosh a$.

4 $\cosh^2 A - \sinh^2 A = 1$

5 $\text{sech}^2 A = 1 - \tanh^2 A$

6 $\text{cosech}^2 A = \coth^2 A - 1$

7 $\sinh(A \pm B) = \sinh A \cosh B \pm \cosh A \sinh B$

8 $\cosh(A \pm B) = \cosh A \cosh B \pm \sinh A \sinh B$

9 Osborn's Rule for finding a hyperbolic identity from the corresponding trigonometric identity:
Replace cos by cosh and replace sin by sinh, but...
replace any product (or implied product) of 2 sine terms by **minus** the product of 2 sinh terms.

10 If $f(x) = \sinh x$, the inverse function f^{-1} is called $\text{arsinh}\, x$ (sometimes written as $\sinh^{-1} x$).

11 If $y = \text{arsinh}\, x$, then $x = \sinh y$.

12 The graph of $y = \text{arsinh}\, x$ is the reflection of the graph of $y = \sinh x$ in the line $y = x$.

13 The inverse of a function is defined only if the function is one-to-one, so for $\cosh x$ the domain must be restricted in order to define an inverse.

For $f(x) = \cosh x \quad x \geqslant 0, \qquad f^{-1}(x) = \text{arcosh}\, x \quad (x \geqslant 1)$

14 $\text{arsinh}\, x = \ln(x + \sqrt{x^2 + 1})$

15 $\text{arcosh}\, x = \ln(x + \sqrt{x^2 - 1}) \qquad x \geqslant 1$

16 $\text{artanh}\, x = \frac{1}{2}\ln\left(\frac{1 + x}{1 - x}\right) \qquad |x| < 1$

2

Further coordinate systems

After completing this chapter you should be able to:

- identify an ellipse or a hyperbola from its Cartesian or parametric equations
- find tangents and normals to these curves
- find the focus and directrix for an ellipse or a hyperbola
- solve simple loci questions.

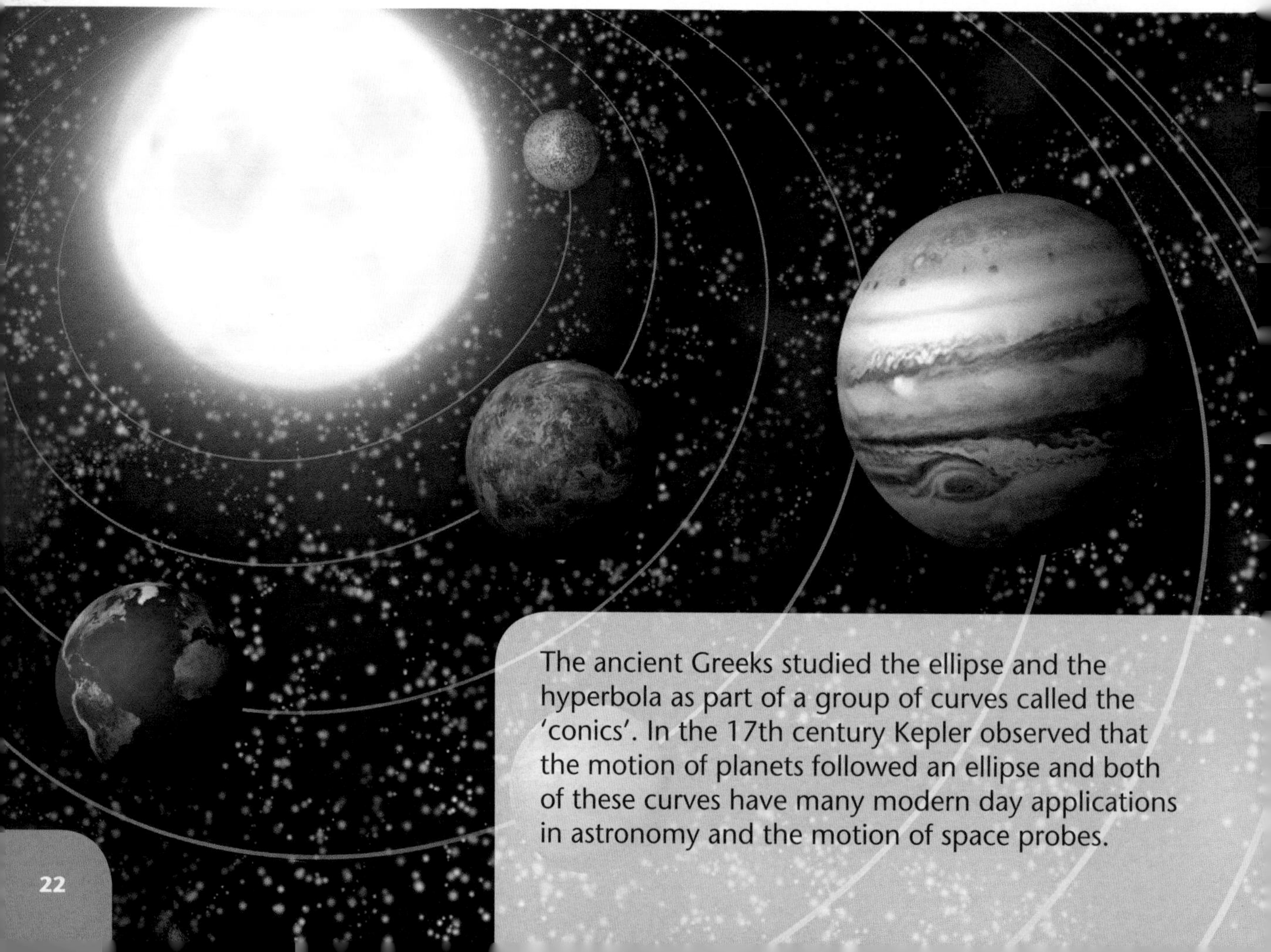

The ancient Greeks studied the ellipse and the hyperbola as part of a group of curves called the 'conics'. In the 17th century Kepler observed that the motion of planets followed an ellipse and both of these curves have many modern day applications in astronomy and the motion of space probes.

2.1 You can find Cartesian and parametric equations for an ellipse.

■ **A standard ellipse has the Cartesian equation**

$$\frac{x^2}{a^2} + \frac{y^2}{b^2} = 1$$

and a sketch looks like this.

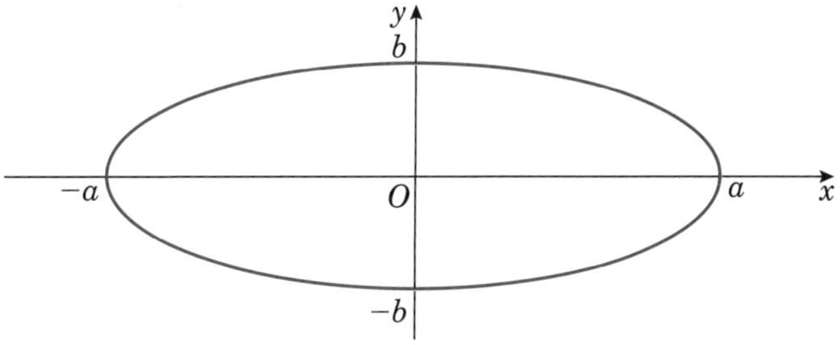

When $x = 0$ then $\frac{y^2}{b^2} = 1$ and so $y = \pm b$

When $y = 0$ then $\frac{x^2}{a^2} = 1$ and so $x = \pm a$

In FP1 you met the idea of a general point on a curve using a **parameter** t.

A general point P on the ellipse can be given by $(a\cos t, b\sin t)$.

If $x = a\cos t$ and $y = b\sin t$ are substituted in $\frac{x^2}{a^2} + \frac{y^2}{b^2}$, you get $\cos^2 t + \sin^2 t$. You know, from C2, that this equals 1.

■ **We sometimes use the parametric equations for an ellipse**

$$x = a\cos t$$
$$y = b\sin t$$

Example 1

The ellipse E has equation $4x^2 + 9y^2 = 36$.

a Sketch E.

b Write down the parametric equations for E.

a $4x^2 + 9y^2 = 36$

$$\frac{4x^2}{36} + \frac{9y^2}{36} = 1$$

First put the equation for E into standard form.

$$\frac{x^2}{9} + \frac{y^2}{4} = 1$$

So $a = 3$ and $b = 2$

Identify the value of a and the value of b.

So sketch is

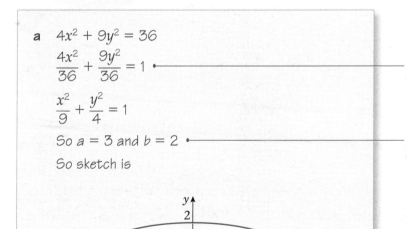

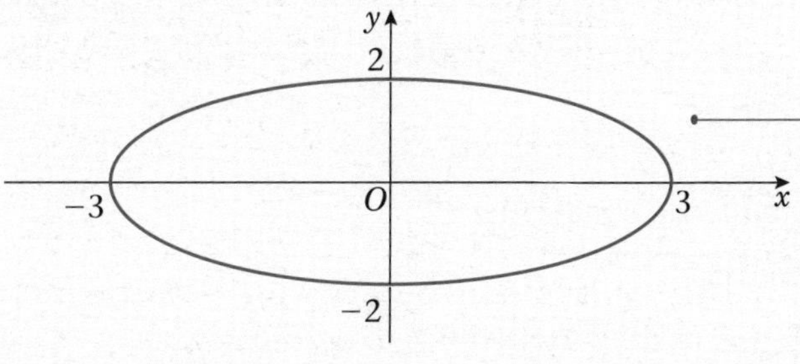

Draw the sketch – mark on intersections with the axes.

b Parametric equations are

$x = 3\cos\theta$

$y = 2\sin\theta$

Example 2

The ellipse E has parametric equations

$$x = 3\cos\theta$$
$$y = 5\sin\theta$$

a Sketch E.

b Find a Cartesian equation of E.

a $-5 \leqslant y \leqslant 5$

$-3 \leqslant x \leqslant 3$

Since $\sin\theta$ and $\cos\theta$ are both between -1 and 1.

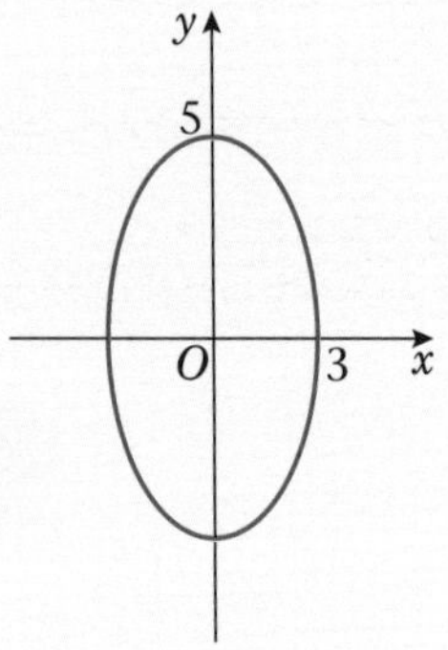

b $a = 3$ and $b = 5$

So the equation is

$$\frac{x^2}{9} + \frac{y^2}{25} = 1$$

Compare with the standard formulae.

Exercise 2A

1 **a** Sketch the following ellipses showing clearly where the curve crosses the coordinate axes.

i $x^2 + 4y^2 = 16$ **ii** $4x^2 + y^2 = 36$ **iii** $x^2 + 9y^2 = 25$

b Find parametric equations for these curves.

2 **a** Sketch ellipses with the following parametric equations.

b Find a Cartesian equation for each ellipse.

i $x = 2\cos\theta, y = 3\sin\theta$ **ii** $x = 4\cos\theta, y = 5\sin\theta$

iii $x = \cos\theta$, $y = 5\sin\theta$ **iv** $x = 4\cos\theta, y = 3\sin\theta$

2.2 You can find the equations of tangents and normals to an ellipse using the parametric equations.

Equations of tangents and normals are often easier to deal with using parametric equations. In a specific equation it is usually simpler to derive the equation rather than memorising formulae.

Example 3

Find the equation of the tangent to the ellipse with equation $\frac{x^2}{9} + \frac{y^2}{4} = 1$ at the point $P(3\cos\theta, 2\sin\theta)$.

$$\frac{dy}{dx} = \frac{\frac{dy}{d\theta}}{\frac{dx}{d\theta}} = \frac{2\cos\theta}{-3\sin\theta}$$

First, find the gradient.

$$y - 2\sin\theta = \frac{2\cos\theta}{-3\sin\theta}(x - 3\cos\theta)$$

Second, write down the equation of the tangent using $y - b = m(x - a)$.

$$3y\sin\theta - 6\sin^2\theta = -2x\cos\theta + 6\cos^2\theta$$

Simplify.

$$3y\sin\theta + 2x\cos\theta = 6(\cos^2\theta + \sin^2\theta)$$

Use $\cos^2\theta + \sin^2\theta = 1$.

$$3y\sin\theta + 2x\cos\theta = 6$$

Example 4

Show that the equation of the normal to the ellipse with equation $\frac{x^2}{a^2} + \frac{y^2}{b^2} = 1$ at the point $P(a\cos\theta, b\sin\theta)$ is $by\cos\theta = ax\sin\theta + (b^2 - a^2)\cos\theta\sin\theta$.

$$\frac{dy}{dx} = \frac{b\cos\theta}{-a\sin\theta}$$

First, find the gradient.

Gradient of normal is $\frac{a\sin\theta}{b\cos\theta}$

Use the perpendicular gradient rule.

Equation is $y - b\sin\theta = \frac{a\sin\theta}{b\cos\theta}(x - a\cos\theta)$

i.e. $by\cos\theta - b^2\cos\theta\sin\theta = ax\sin\theta - a^2\cos\theta\sin\theta$

or $by\cos\theta = ax\sin\theta + (b^2 - a^2)\cos\theta\sin\theta$

Use $y - b = m(x - a)$ and simplify.

Example 5

The point $P\left(2, 3\frac{\sqrt{3}}{2}\right)$ lies on the ellipse E with parametric equations $x = 4\cos\theta$, $y = 3\sin\theta$.

a Find the value of θ at the point P.

The normal to the ellipse at P cuts the x-axis at the point A.

b Find the coordinates of the point A.

a $4\cos\theta = 2 \quad \Rightarrow \cos\theta = \frac{1}{2}$ so $\theta = \frac{\pi}{3}, \ldots$

$3\sin\theta = 3\frac{\sqrt{3}}{2} \quad \Rightarrow \sin\theta = \frac{\sqrt{3}}{2}$ so $\theta = \frac{\pi}{3}, \ldots$

So $\theta = \frac{\pi}{3}$

Set $a\cos\theta$ = the x-coordinate and $b\sin\theta$ = the y-coordinate and solve to find θ. Choose the value of θ that satisfies both equations.

b $\frac{dy}{dx} = \frac{3\cos\theta}{-4\sin\theta}$

Use the general point to find the gradient.

So gradient of normal is $\frac{4\sin\theta}{3\cos\theta}$

Use perpendicular gradient rule then substitute the value of θ.

At P the gradient of the normal is

$$\frac{4 \times \frac{\sqrt{3}}{2}}{3 \times \frac{1}{2}} = 4\frac{\sqrt{3}}{3}$$

This can be found by implicit differentiation on the Cartesian equation $\frac{x^2}{16} + \frac{y^2}{9} = 1$. Differentiating: $\frac{2}{16}x + \frac{2}{9}y\frac{dy}{dx} = 0$ so $\frac{dy}{dx} = -\frac{9x}{16y}$ and using the coordinates of P, $\frac{dy}{dx} = \frac{-18}{16 \times 3\frac{\sqrt{3}}{2}} = \frac{-3}{4\sqrt{3}}$ so normal gradient is $\frac{4\sqrt{3}}{3}$.

Equation of normal at P is

$$y - 3\frac{\sqrt{3}}{2} = 4\frac{\sqrt{3}}{3}(x - 2)$$

Cuts x-axis at $-9\sqrt{3} = 8\sqrt{3}(x - 2)$

Let $y = 0$.

So A is $(\frac{7}{8}, 0)$

Example 6

Show that the condition for $y = mx + c$ to be a tangent to the ellipse $\frac{x^2}{a^2} + \frac{y^2}{b^2} = 1$ is $a^2m^2 + b^2 = c^2$.

The line meets the ellipse when

$$\frac{x^2}{a^2} + \frac{(mx + c)^2}{b^2} = 1$$

Substitute $mx + c$ for y.

So $b^2x^2 + a^2m^2x^2 + 2a^2mxc + a^2c^2 = a^2b^2$

$x^2(b^2 + a^2m^2) + 2a^2mcx + a^2(c^2 - b^2) = 0$

Multiply out and rearrange as a quadratic equation in x.

To be a tangent there must be only one real root.
Therefore the discriminant of this quadratic = 0.

> Use the properties of the discriminant from C1.

$$(2a^2mc)^2 = 4(b^2 + a^2m^2)a^2(c^2 - b^2)$$

$$\text{So } \cancel{4}a^{\cancel{4}2}m^2c^2 = \cancel{4}\cancel{a^2}(b^2c^2 - b^4 + a^2m^2c^2 - a^2b^2m^2)$$

> Multiply out and simplify.

$$\cancel{a^2m^2c^2} = b^2c^2 - b^4 + \cancel{a^2m^2c^2} - a^2b^2m^2$$

$$b^4 + a^2b^2m^2 = b^2c^2$$

> Cancel b^2.

$$b^2 + a^2m^2 = c^2$$

> This is a general result which can be quoted.

Exercise 2B

1 Find the equations of tangents and normals to the following ellipses at the points given.

a $\dfrac{x^2}{4} + y^2 = 1$ at $(2\cos\theta, \sin\theta)$

b $\dfrac{x^2}{25} + \dfrac{y^2}{9} = 1$ at $(5\cos\theta, 3\sin\theta)$

2 Find equations of tangents and normals to the following ellipses at the points given.

a $\dfrac{x^2}{9} + \dfrac{y^2}{1} = 1$ at $(\sqrt{5}, \frac{2}{3})$

b $\dfrac{x^2}{16} + \dfrac{y^2}{4} = 1$ at $(-2, \sqrt{3})$

3 Show that the equation of the tangent to the ellipse $\dfrac{x^2}{a^2} + \dfrac{y^2}{b^2} = 1$ at the point $(a\cos t, b\sin t)$ is $xb\cos t + ya\sin t = ab$

4 **a** Show that the line $y = x + \sqrt{5}$ is a tangent to the ellipse with equation $\dfrac{x^2}{4} + \dfrac{y^2}{1} = 1$.

b Find the point of contact of this tangent.

5 **a** Find an equation of the normal to the ellipse with equation $\dfrac{x^2}{9} + \dfrac{y^2}{4} = 1$ at the point $P(3\cos\theta, 2\sin\theta)$.

This normal crosses the x-axis at the point $(-\frac{5}{6}, 0)$.

b Find the value of θ and the exact coordinates of the possible positions of P.

6 The line $y = 2x + c$ is a tangent to $x^2 + \dfrac{y^2}{4} = 1$.
Find the possible values of c.

7 The line with equation $y = mx + 3$ is a tangent to $x^2 + \dfrac{y^2}{5} = 1$.
Find the possible values of m.

8 The line $y = mx + 4$ ($m > 0$) is a tangent to the ellipse E with equation $\frac{x^2}{3} + \frac{y^2}{4} = 1$ at the point P.

a Find the value of m.

b Find the coordinates of the point P.

The normal to E at P crosses the y-axis at the point A.

c Find the coordinates of A.

The tangent to E at P crosses the y-axis at the point B.

d Find the area of triangle APB.

9 The ellipse E has equation $\frac{x^2}{9} + \frac{y^2}{4} = 1$.

a Show that the gradient of the tangent to E at the point $P(3\cos\theta, 2\sin\theta)$ is $-\frac{2}{3}\cot\theta$.

b Show that the point $Q(\frac{9}{5}, -\frac{8}{5})$ lies on E.

c Find the gradient of the tangent to E at Q.

The tangents to E at the points P and Q are perpendicular.

d Find the value of $\tan\theta$ and hence the exact coordinates of P.

10 The line $y = mx + c$ is a tangent to both the ellipses $\frac{x^2}{9} + \frac{y^2}{46} = 1$ and $\frac{x^2}{25} + \frac{y^2}{14} = 1$.

Find the possible values of m and c.

2.3 You can find Cartesian and parametric equations for a hyperbola.

A standard hyperbola has the Cartesian equation

$$\frac{x^2}{a^2} - \frac{y^2}{b^2} = 1$$

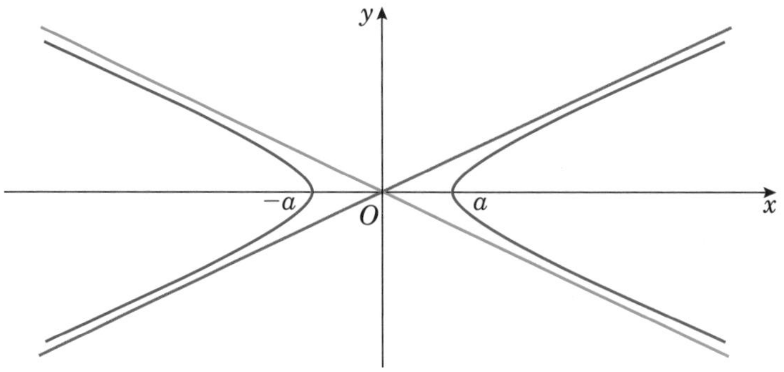

When $y = 0$, $x^2 = a^2$ and so the curve crosses the x-axis at $(\pm a, 0)$.
As x and y tend to infinity then

$\frac{x^2}{a^2} \approx \frac{y^2}{b^2}$ and so the equations of the asymptotes are $y = \pm\frac{b}{a}x$.

The equations of the asymptotes are given in the formula booklet.

In Section 2.1 you saw that the parametric equations of the ellipse were connected to the trigonometric relationship $\cos^2\theta + \sin^2\theta = 1$.

In Chapter 1 you met a similar relationship for **hyperbolic functions**: $\cosh^2 t - \sinh^2 t = 1$ and this can be used to find parametric equations for the hyperbola.

This is one reason hyperbolic functions have that name.

■ **Parametric equations for the hyperbola with equation**

$$\frac{x^2}{a^2} - \frac{y^2}{b^2} = 1$$
$$x = a\cosh t$$
$$y = b\sinh t$$

There is also a trigonometric relationship which has a similar pattern, namely $\sec^2\theta - \tan^2\theta = 1$, and this can also be used to provide parametric equations for a hyperbola.

■ **Alternative parametric equations for the hyperbola with equation**

$$\frac{x^2}{a^2} - \frac{y^2}{b^2} = 1$$
$$x = a\sec\theta$$
$$y = b\tan\theta$$

Example 7

The hyperbola H has equation $9x^2 - 4y^2 = 36$.

a Sketch H.

b Write down the equations of the asymptotes of H.

c Find parametric equations for H.

a Rearrange equation to get

$$\frac{x^2}{4} - \frac{y^2}{9} = 1$$

So $a = 2$ and $b = 3$

Write the equation in the $\frac{x^2}{a^2} - \frac{y^2}{b^2} = 1$ form and identify values for a and b.

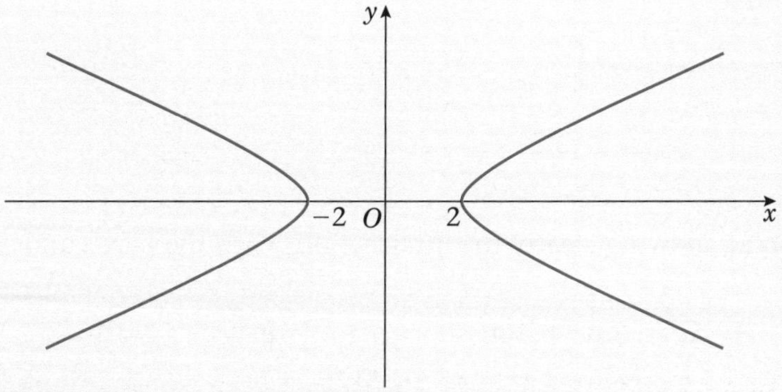

b Equations of the asymptotes are

$y = \frac{3}{2}x$ and $y = -\frac{3}{2}x$

Use the $y = \pm\frac{b}{a}x$ formula.

c Parametric equations

$x = 2\cosh t$ and $y = 3\sinh t$

Use $x = a\cosh t$ and $y = b\sinh t$.

Example 8

A hyperbola H has parametric equations

$$x = 4\sec t$$
$$y = \tan t$$

a Find a Cartesian equation for H.

b Sketch H.

c Write down the equations of the asymptotes of H.

a Using $\sec^2 t - \tan^2 t = 1$

$$\left(\frac{x}{4}\right)^2 - y^2 = 1$$

Cartesian equation is

$$\frac{x^2}{16} - y^2 = 1$$

Alternatively, compare with $x = a\sec\theta$ and $y = b\tan\theta$ and use the values of a and b in the standard formula.

b $a = 4$ and $b = 1$

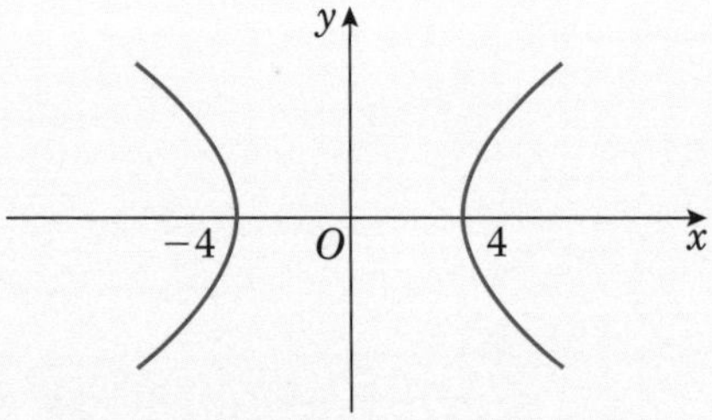

By comparing with $\frac{x^2}{a^2} - \frac{y^2}{b^2} = 1$ and using $a = 4$ and $b = 1$.

c Equations of asymptotes are

$$y = \pm\tfrac{1}{4}x$$

Use the $y = \pm\frac{b}{a}x$ formula.

Exercise 2C

1 Sketch the following hyperbolae showing clearly the intersections with the x-axis and the equations of the asymptotes.

a $x^2 - 4y^2 = 16$ **b** $4x^2 - 25y^2 = 100$ **c** $\frac{x^2}{8} - \frac{y^2}{2} = 1$

2 **a** Sketch the hyperbolae with the following parametric equations. Give the equations of the asymptotes and show points of intersection with the x-axis.

b Find the Cartesian equation for each hyperbola.

i $x = 2\sec\theta$, $y = 3\tan\theta$ **ii** $x = 4\cosh t$, $y = 3\sinh t$ **iii** $x = \cosh t$, $y = 2\sinh t$ **iv** $x = 5\sec\theta$, $y = 7\tan\theta$

2.4 You can find equations of tangents and normals to a hyperbola.

Example 9

Find the equation of the tangent to the hyperbola with equation $\frac{x^2}{9} - \frac{y^2}{4} = 1$ at the point $(6, 2\sqrt{3})$.

Differentiating:

$$\frac{2}{9}x - \frac{2}{4}y\frac{dy}{dx} = 0$$

Use implicit differentiation.

At $(6, 2\sqrt{3})$ $\frac{12}{9} - \frac{4\sqrt{3}}{4}\frac{dy}{dx} = 0 \Rightarrow \frac{dy}{dx} = \frac{4\sqrt{3}}{9}$

Equation of tangent is

Use $y - b = m(x - a)$.

$$y - 2\sqrt{3} = \frac{4\sqrt{3}}{9}(x - 6)$$

or $$y = \frac{4\sqrt{3}}{9}x - \frac{2\sqrt{3}}{3}$$

Example 10

Show that the equation of the tangent to the hyperbola with equation $\frac{x^2}{a^2} - \frac{y^2}{b^2} = 1$ at the point $(a\cosh t, b\sinh t)$ can be written $ay\sinh t + ab = bx\cosh t$.

$x = a\cosh t$, $y = b\sinh t$

See Chapter 3 for differentiation of $\sinh t$ and $\cosh t$.

$$\frac{dy}{dx} = \frac{\frac{dy}{dt}}{\frac{dx}{dt}} = \frac{b\cosh t}{a\sinh t}$$

Use the chain rule to find $\frac{dy}{dx}$.

Equation of tangent is

$$y - b\sinh t = \frac{b\cosh t}{a\sinh t}(x - a\cosh t)$$

Use $y - b = m(x - a)$.

$$ya\sinh t - ab\sinh^2 t = bx\cosh t - ab\cosh^2 t$$

$$ya\sinh t + ab(\cosh^2 t - \sinh^2 t) = bx\cosh t$$

Use $\cosh^2 t - \sinh^2 t = 1$.

$$ay\sinh t + ab = bx\cosh t$$

■ **An equation of a tangent to the hyperbola $\frac{x^2}{a^2} - \frac{y^2}{b^2} = 1$ at the point $(a\cosh t, b\sinh t)$ is $ay\sinh t + ab = bx\cosh t$.**

Example 11

Show that an equation of the normal to the hyperbola with equation $\frac{x^2}{a^2} - \frac{y^2}{b^2} = 1$ at $(a\sec t, b\tan t)$ is $by + ax\sin t = (a^2 + b^2)\tan t$.

$$\frac{dy}{dx} = \frac{\frac{dy}{dt}}{\frac{dx}{dt}} = \frac{b\sec^2 t}{a\sec t\tan t} = \frac{b}{a\sin t}$$

Use the chain rule to find $\frac{dy}{dx}$.

So gradient of normal is $\frac{-a\sin t}{b}$

Use the perpendicular gradient rule.

Equation of the normal is

$$y - b\tan t = \frac{-a\sin t}{b}(x - a\sec t)$$

Use $y - b = m(x - a)$.

$$by - b^2\tan t = -ax\sin t + a^2\tan t$$

So $by + ax\sin t = (a^2 + b^2)\tan t$

- **An equation of a normal to the hyperbola $\frac{x^2}{a^2} - \frac{y^2}{b^2} = 1$ at the point $(a\sec t, b\tan t)$ is $by + a\sin t\,x = (a^2 + b^2)\tan t$**

Example 12

Show that the condition for the line $y = mx + c$ to be a tangent to the hyperbola $\frac{x^2}{a^2} - \frac{y^2}{b^2} = 1$ is that m and c satisfy $b^2 + c^2 = a^2m^2$.

$$\frac{x^2}{a^2} - \frac{(mx + c)^2}{b^2} = 1$$

Substitute $mx + c$ for y into the equation of the hyperbola.

$$b^2x^2 - a^2(m^2x^2 + 2mxc + c^2) = a^2b^2$$

Multiply out and collect terms as a 3 term quadratic in x.

$$(b^2 - a^2m^2)x^2 - 2mca^2x - a^2(c^2 + b^2) = 0$$

Use discriminant properties from C1.

Since the line is a tangent the discriminant must be zero.

$$4m^2c^2a^4 = -4(b^2 - a^2m^2)a^2(c^2 + b^2)$$

Cancel $4a^2$.

$$m^2c^2a^2 = -b^4 - b^2c^2 + a^2m^2c^2 + a^2m^2b^2$$

Cancel b^2.

$$b^2 + c^2 = a^2m^2$$

This condition is a general result and may be quoted.

Example 13

The tangent to the hyperbola with equation $\frac{x^2}{9} - \frac{y^2}{4} = 1$ at the point $(3\cosh t, 2\sinh t)$ crosses the y-axis at the point $(0, -1)$. Find the value of t.

Tangent equation is

$$3y\sinh t + 6 = 2x\cosh t$$

Passes through $(0, -1)$

$$-3\sinh t + 6 = 0$$

So $\sinh t = 2$

i.e. $t = \text{arsinh}(2)$

But $\text{arsinh}\, x = \ln(x + \sqrt{x^2 + 1})$

So $t = \ln(2 + \sqrt{5})$

Identify $a = 3$ and $b = 2$ and use the formula for a tangent from page 31.

Substitute $x = 0$ and $y = -1$.

Use formula for arsinh (x) from the formula booklet.

Exercise 2D

1 Find the equations of the tangents and normals to the hyperbolae with the following equations at the points indicated.

a $\frac{x^2}{16} - \frac{y^2}{2} = 1$ at the point $(12, 4)$

b $\frac{x^2}{36} - \frac{y^2}{12} = 1$ at the point $(12, 6)$

c $\frac{x^2}{25} - \frac{y^2}{3} = 1$ at the point $(10, 3)$

2 Find the equations of the tangents and normals to the hyperbolae with the following equations at the points indicated.

a $\frac{x^2}{25} - \frac{y^2}{4} = 1$ at the point $(5\cosh t, 2\sinh t)$

b $\frac{x^2}{1} - \frac{y^2}{9} = 1$ at the point $(\sec t, 3\tan t)$

3 Show that an equation of the tangent to the hyperbola with equation $\frac{x^2}{a^2} - \frac{y^2}{b^2} = 1$ at the point $(a\sec t, b\tan t)$ is $bx\sec t - ay\tan t = ab$.

4 Show that an equation of the normal to the hyperbola with equation $\frac{x^2}{a^2} - \frac{y^2}{b^2} = 1$ at the point $(a\cosh t, b\sinh t)$ is $b\cosh t y + a\sinh t x = (a^2 + b^2)\sinh t\cosh t$.

5 The point $P(4\cosh t, 3\sinh t)$ lies on the hyperbola with equation $\frac{x^2}{16} - \frac{y^2}{9} = 1$.

The tangent at P crosses the y-axis at the point A.

a Find, in terms of t, the coordinates of A.

The normal to the hyperbola at P crosses the y-axis at B.

b Find, in terms of t, the coordinates of B.

c Find , in terms of t, the area of triangle APB.

6 The tangents from the points P and Q on the hyperbola with equation $\frac{x^2}{4} - \frac{y^2}{9} = 1$ meet at the point (1, 0).

Find the exact coordinates of P and Q.

7 The line $y = 2x + c$ is a tangent to the hyperbola $\frac{x^2}{10} - \frac{y^2}{4} = 1$.

Find the possible values of c.

8 The line $y = mx + 12$ is a tangent to the hyperbola $\frac{x^2}{49} - \frac{y^2}{25} = 1$ at the point P.

Find the possible values of m.

9 The line $y = -x + c$, $c > 0$, touches the hyerbola $\frac{x^2}{25} - \frac{y^2}{16} = 1$ at the point P.

a Find the value of c.

b Find the exact coordinates of P.

10 The line with equation $y = mx + c$ is a tangent to both hyperbolae

$\frac{x^2}{4} - \frac{y^2}{15} = 1$ and $\frac{x^2}{9} - \frac{y^2}{95} = 1$.

Find the possible values of m and c.

2.5 You can define an ellipse and a hyperbola in terms of the focus and directrix.

In FP1 you saw that the parabola with equation $y^2 = 4ax$ can be thought of as **locus** of all the points $P(x, y)$ that are equidistant from a fixed point S (the **focus**) and a fixed line (the **directrix**).

In this section we shall extend this idea

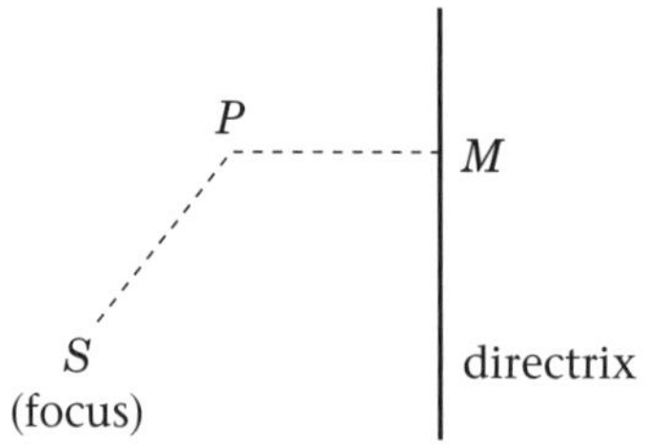

so that the ratio $\frac{PS}{PM} = e$, where e is a constant called the **eccentricity**.

The following examples will show that

- **If $0 < e < 1$ the point P describes an ellipse.**
- **If $e = 1$ the point P describes a parabola.**
- **If $e > 1$ the point P describes a hyperbola.**

Example 14

Show that for $0 < e < 1$ the ellipse with focus $(ae, 0)$ and directrix $x = \frac{a}{e}$ has equation $\frac{x^2}{a^2} + \frac{y^2}{b^2} = 1$.

Let $P(x, y)$

$$\frac{PS}{PM} = e \Rightarrow PS^2 = e^2PM^2$$

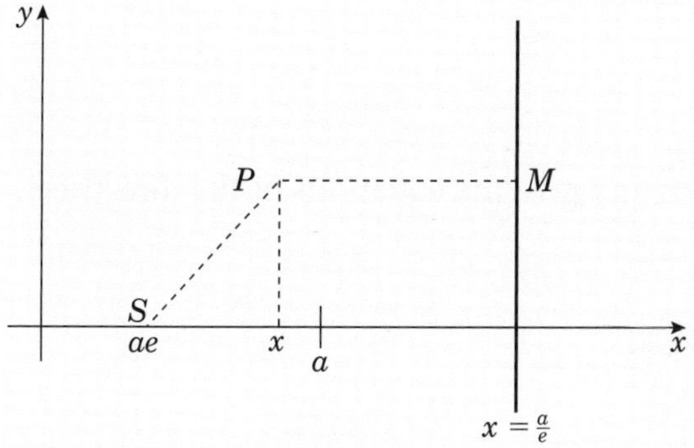

Draw a diagram.

$PS^2 = (x - ae)^2 + y^2$

$PM^2 = \left(\frac{a}{e} - x\right)^2 = \frac{(a - ex)^2}{e^2}$

Find expressions for PS^2 and PM^2 in terms of a, e and x, y.

So $PS^2 = e^2PM^2$ gives

$x^2 - \cancel{2aex} + a^2e^2 + y^2 = a^2 - \cancel{2aex} + e^2x^2$

Simplify.

$x^2(1 - e^2) + y^2 = a^2(1 - e^2)$

$$\frac{x^2}{a^2} + \frac{y^2}{a^2(1 - e^2)} = 1$$

So if $b^2 = a^2(1 - e^2)$ then you have the standard equation of the ellipse.

Because the ellipse is symmetrical about the y-axis the above derivation will also work for a focus $(-ae, 0)$ with a directrix $x = -\frac{a}{e}$.

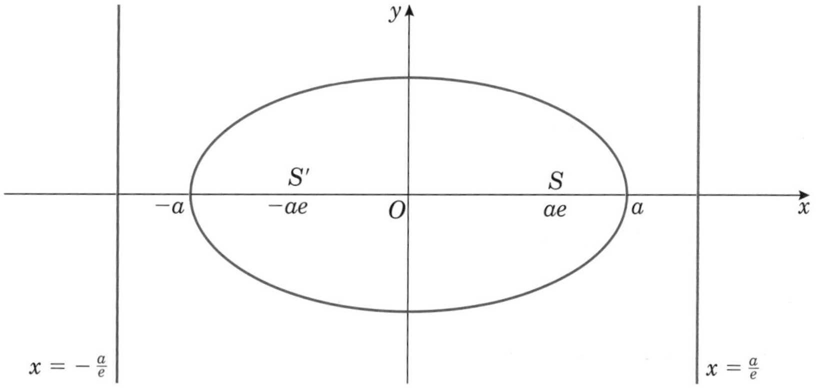

- **For an ellipse with equation $\frac{x^2}{a^2} + \frac{y^2}{b^2} = 1$, and $a > b$,**
  the eccentricity $0 < e < 1$ is given by $b^2 = a^2(1 - e^2)$
  the foci are at $(\pm ae, 0)$
  the directrices are $x = \pm\frac{a}{e}$

Directrices is the plural of directrix.

Notice that the foci are on the **major axis** which in this case is the x-axis because $a > b$.

If the major axis is along the y-axis ($b > a$) then the foci will be on the y-axis at $(0, \pm be)$ and the directrices will have equations $y = \pm\frac{b}{e}$. The eccentricity will be given by $a^2 = b^2(1 - e^2)$.

Example 15

Find foci of the ellipses with the following equations and give the equations of the directrices.

a $\frac{x^2}{9} + \frac{y^2}{4} = 1$ **b** $\frac{x^2}{16} + \frac{y^2}{25} = 1$

In each case sketch the ellipse and show the directrices.

a $b^2 = a^2(1 - e^2)$ gives $4 = 9(1 - e^2)$ so $e^2 = \frac{5}{9}$

Note that $a = 3$ and $b = 2$ so since $a > b$ use $b^2 = a^2(1 - e^2)$.

So $e = \frac{\sqrt{5}}{3}$

So foci are at $(\pm\sqrt{5}, 0)$

Use $(\pm ae, 0)$.

Directrices are $x = \pm\frac{9}{\sqrt{5}}$

Use $x = \pm\frac{a}{e}$.

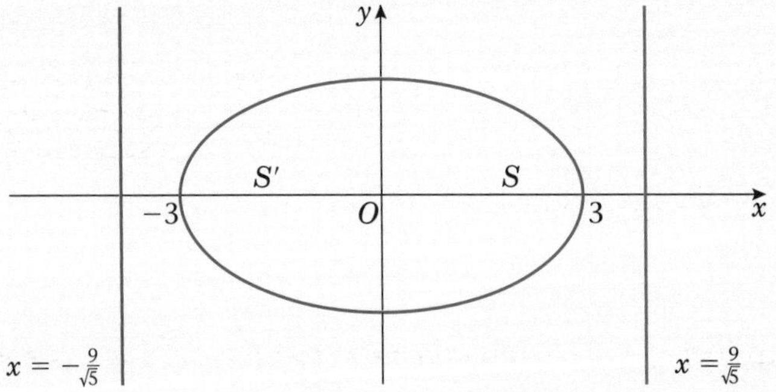

b $\frac{x^2}{16} + \frac{y^2}{25} = 1$

Note that $a = 4$ and $b = 5$. Since $b > a$ use $a^2 = b^2(1 - e^2)$.

$a^2 = b^2(1 - e^2)$ gives $16 = 25(1 - e^2)$

So $e^2 = \frac{9}{25}$ and $e = \frac{3}{5}$

Foci are at $(0, \pm3)$

Use $(0, \pm be)$.

Directrices are $y = \pm\frac{25}{3}$

Use $y = \pm\frac{b}{e}$.

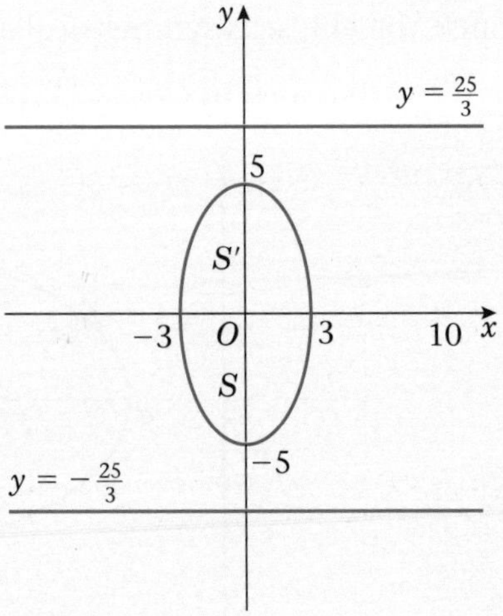

Example 16

The ellipse with equation $\frac{x^2}{a^2} + \frac{y^2}{b^2} = 1$ has foci at $S(ae, 0)$ and $S'(-ae, 0)$. Show that if P is any point on the ellipse then $PS + PS' = 2a$.

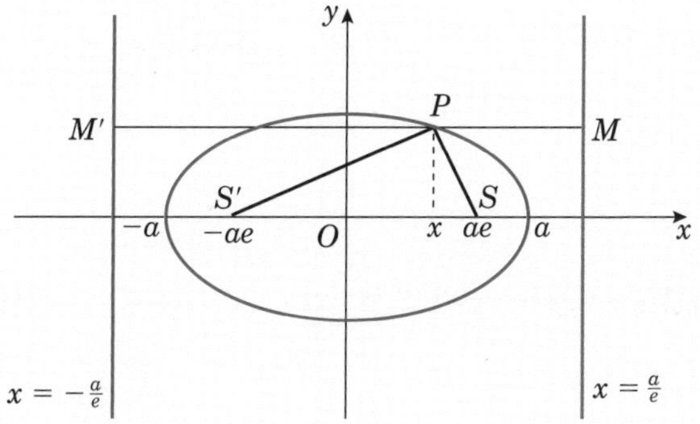

Let M' be the point on the directrix $x = -\frac{a}{e}$ where $PS' = ePM'$

Let M be the point on the directrix $x = \frac{a}{e}$ where $PS = ePM$

Let P be (x, y)

$PM' = x + \frac{a}{e}$

$PM = \frac{a}{e} - x$

So $PS + PS' = ePM + ePM'$

$= e\left(\frac{a}{e} - x\right) + e\left(\frac{a}{e} + x\right)$

$= a - ex + a + ex$

$= 2a$

Use the focus and directrix definitions of an ellipse from Section 2.5.

PM' and PM are parallel to the x-axis.

This is an important property of an ellipse.

Example 17

Show that for $e > 1$ the hyperbola with foci at $(\pm ae, 0)$ and directrices at $x = \pm\frac{a}{e}$ has equation $\frac{x^2}{a^2} - \frac{y^2}{b^2} = 1$.

Let $P(x, y)$ be a point on the hyperbola.

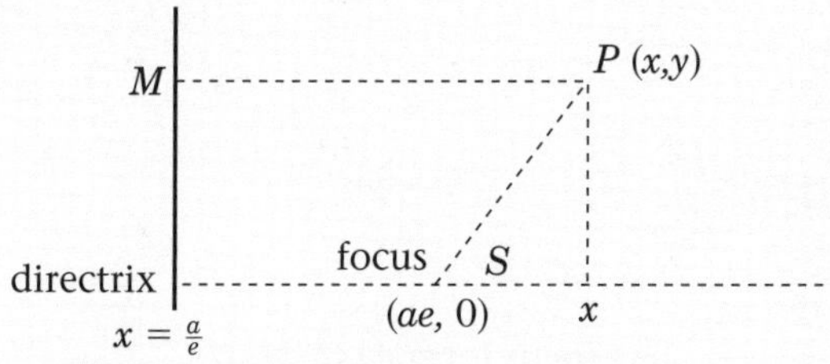

Draw a diagram.

$\frac{PS}{PM} = e \Rightarrow PS^2 = e^2PM^2$

$PS^2 = (x - ae)^2 + y^2$

$PM^2 = \left(x - \frac{a}{e}\right)^2 = \frac{(ex - a)^2}{e^2}$

Find expressions for PS^2 and PM^2 in terms of a, e and x, y.

So $PS^2 = e^2PM^2$ gives

$x^2 - 2aex + a^2e^2 + y^2 = e^2x^2 - 2aex + a^2$

Simplify.

$a^2(e^2 - 1) = x^2(e^2 - 1) - y^2$

i.e. $1 = \frac{x^2}{a^2} - \frac{y^2}{a^2(e^2 - 1)}$

So if $b^2 = a^2(e^2 - 1)$ you have the standard equation of a hyperbola.

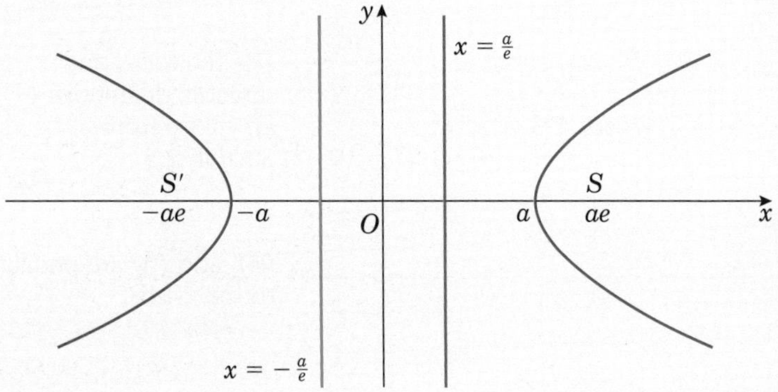

Example 18

Find foci of the following hyperbolae.
In each case sketch the hyperbola showing clearly its asymptotes.

a $\frac{x^2}{9} - \frac{y^2}{4} = 1$ **b** $\frac{x^2}{16} - \frac{y^2}{25} = 1$

a $\frac{x^2}{9} - \frac{y^2}{4} = 1$ so $a = 3$ and $b = 2$

Compare the equation with $1 = \frac{x^2}{a^2} - \frac{y^2}{b^2}$ and identify a and b.

Eccentricity is given by $b^2 = a^2(e^2 - 1)$.

$4 = 9(e^2 - 1)$

Use $b^2 = a^2(e^2 - 1)$.

So $\frac{4}{9} + 1 = e^2$

i.e. $e = \sqrt{\frac{13}{9}} = \frac{\sqrt{13}}{3}$

So foci at $(\pm\sqrt{13}, 0)$.

Use focus formula $(\pm ae, 0)$.

Asymptotes are $y = \pm\frac{2}{3}x$

> Use formula for asymptotes $y = \pm\frac{b}{a}x$ from Section 2.3.

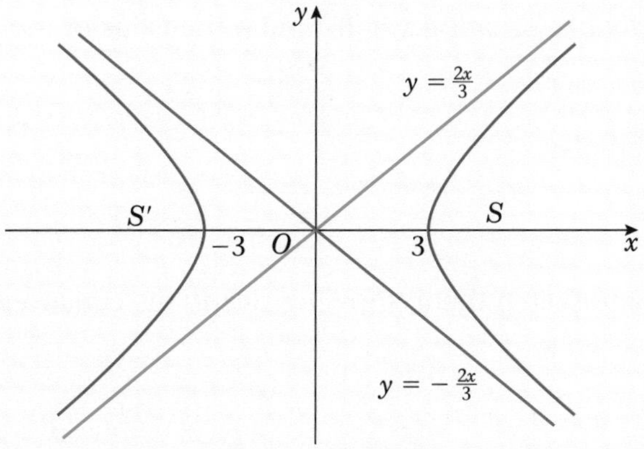

b $\frac{x^2}{16} - \frac{y^2}{25} = 1$ so $a = 4$ and $b = 5$

> Compare the equation with $1 = \frac{x^2}{a^2} - \frac{y^2}{b^2}$ and identify a and b.

Eccentricity is given by $b^2 = a^2(e^2 - 1)$

> Notice that with the ellipse, when $b > a$ the foci were on the y-axis. For the hyperbola this cannot happen since $x = 0$ is not possible.

$25 = 16(e^2 - 1)$

> Use $b^2 = a^2(e^2 - 1)$.

$\frac{25}{16} + 1 = e^2$ so $e = \sqrt{\frac{41}{16}} = \frac{\sqrt{41}}{4}$

Foci at $(\pm\sqrt{41}, 0)$

> Foci at $(\pm ae, 0)$.

Asymptotes are $y = \pm 1.25x$.

> Use formula for asymptotes $y = \pm\frac{b}{a}x$ from Section 2.3.

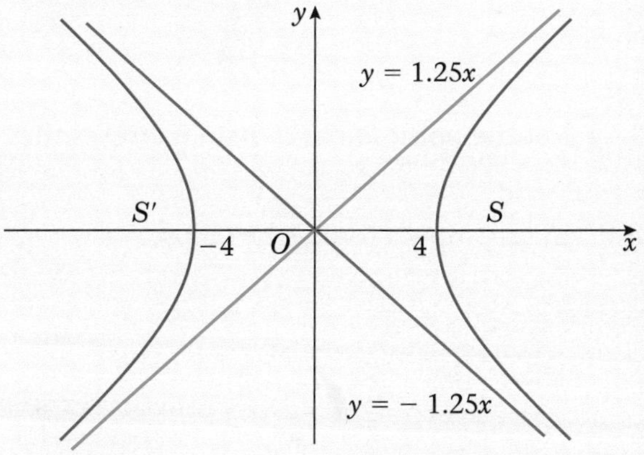

Exercise 2E

1 Find the eccentricity of the following ellipses.

a $\frac{x^2}{9} + \frac{y^2}{5} = 1$ **b** $\frac{x^2}{16} + \frac{y^2}{9} = 1$ **c** $\frac{x^2}{4} + \frac{y^2}{8} = 1$

2 Find the foci and directrices of the following ellipses.

a $\frac{x^2}{4} + \frac{y^2}{3} = 1$ **b** $\frac{x^2}{16} + \frac{y^2}{7} = 1$ **c** $\frac{x^2}{5} + \frac{y^2}{9} = 1$

3 An ellipse E has focus (3, 0) and the equation of the directrix is $x = 12$. Find **a** the value of the eccentricity **b** the equation of the ellipse.

4 An ellipse E has focus (2, 0) and the directrix has equation $x = 8$. Find **a** the value of the eccentricity **b** the equation of the ellipse.

5 Find the eccentricity of the following hyperbolae.

a $\frac{x^2}{5} - \frac{y^2}{3} = 1$ **b** $\frac{x^2}{9} - \frac{y^2}{7} = 1$ **c** $\frac{x^2}{9} - \frac{y^2}{16} = 1$

6 Find the foci of the following hyperbolae and sketch them, showing clearly the equations of the asymptotes.

a $\frac{x^2}{4} - \frac{y^2}{8} = 1$ **b** $\frac{x^2}{16} - \frac{y^2}{9} = 1$ **c** $\frac{x^2}{4} - \frac{y^2}{5} = 1$

7 Ellipse E has equation $\frac{x^2}{a^2} + \frac{y^2}{b^2} = 1$. The foci are at S and S' and the point P is $(0, b)$. Show that $\cos(PSS') = e$, the eccentricity of E.

8 The ellipse E has foci at S and S'. The point P on E is such that angle PSS' is a right angle and angle $PS'S = 30°$.

Show that the eccentricity of the ellipse, e, is $\frac{1}{\sqrt{3}}$.

2.6 You can find the equations of simple loci connected with these curves.

A **locus** is the equation of a curve and it is usually associated with the position of a variable point.

Example 19

The tangent to the ellipse with equation $\frac{x^2}{a^2} + \frac{y^2}{b^2} = 1$ at the point $P(a\cos t, b\sin t)$ crosses the x-axis at A and the y-axis at B.

Find an equation for the locus of the mid-point of AB as P moves round the ellipse.

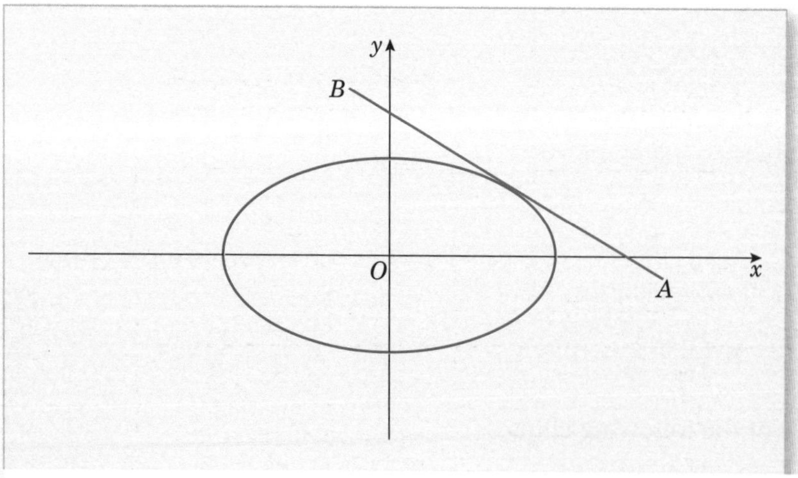

A diagram might help and it is always worth drawing a rough sketch.

Parametric equations $x = a\cos t, y = b\sin t$

Gradient: $\frac{dy}{dx} = \frac{\dot{y}}{\dot{x}} = \frac{b\cos t}{-a\sin t}$

Equation of tangent:

$y - b\sin t = \frac{b\cos t}{-a\sin t}(x - a\cos t)$

or $ay\sin t + bx\cos t = ab$

A is $(a\sec t, 0)$

B is $(0, b\operatorname{cosec} t)$

The mid-point of AB has coordinates (X, Y) where

$X = \frac{a\sec t}{2}$

$Y = \frac{b\operatorname{cosec} t}{2}$

Rearranging:

$\cos t = \frac{a}{2X}$ and $\sin t = \frac{b}{2Y}$

So locus is:

$\left(\frac{a}{2X}\right)^2 + \left(\frac{b}{2Y}\right)^2 = 1$

First find the equation of the tangent at P.

This result was found in Exercise 2B question 3.

Use $x = 0$ to find B and $y = 0$ to find A.

To find the locus of the mid-point, let the coordinates of the mid-point be (X, Y) and then form parametric equations for X and Y.

To find the locus simply eliminate the parameter (t in this case) to find an equation in X and Y.

Use $\sin^2 t + \cos^2 t = 1$ to eliminate t.

Sometimes in the examination you will be asked to show the locus has a particular form, but if you are simply asked to find *an* equation then this form is sufficient.

In FP3 you might be asked simple loci questions based on the parabola or the rectangular hyperbola you met in FP1.

The following table summarises some of the results about these two curves which you may find useful.

	Parabola	**Rectangular hyperbola**
Standard Cartesian equation	$y^2 = 4ax$	$xy = c^2$
Parametric equations	$x = at^2$ $y = 2at$	$x = ct$ $y = \frac{c}{t}$
General point, P	$(at^2, 2at)$	$\left(ct, \frac{c}{t}\right)$
Equation of tangent at P	$ty = x + at^2$	$x + t^2y = 2ct$
Equation of normal at P	$y + tx = 2at + at^3$	$t^3x - ty = c(t^4 - 1)$

Example 20

The normal at $P(ap^2, 2ap)$ and the normal at $Q(aq^2, 2aq)$ to the parabola with equation $y^2 = 4ax$ meet at R.

a Find the coordinates of R.

The chord PQ passes through the focus $(a, 0)$ of the parabola.

b Show that $pq = -1$.

c Show that the locus of R is a parabola with equation $y^2 = a(x - 3a)$.

a To find R, find the intersections of the normals.

Normal at P is $y + px = 2ap + ap^3$

Normal at Q is $y + qx = 2aq + aq^3$

Use results from the table on page 41.

Subtracting:

$$(p - q)x = 2a(p - q) + a(p^3 - q^3)$$

i.e. $\cancel{(p - q)}x = 2a\cancel{(p - q)} + a\cancel{(p - q)}(p^2 + pq + q^2)$

The factorisations of $(p^3 \pm q^3) = (p \pm q)(p^2 \mp pq + q^2)$ are particularly useful in this type of problem and should be learnt.

i.e. $x = 2a + a(p^2 + pq + q^2)$

so $y = \cancel{2ap} + \cancel{ap^3} - \cancel{2ap} - \cancel{ap^3} - ap^2q - apq^2$

i.e. $y = -apq(p + q)$

Substitute for x to find y.

So R is $(2a + a(p^2 + pq + q^2), -apq(p + q))$

b Chord PQ has gradient

$$\frac{2a(p - q)}{a(p^2 - q^2)} = \frac{2\cancel{(p - q)}}{\cancel{(p - q)}(p + q)} = \frac{2}{p + q}$$

Use $\dfrac{y_1 - y_2}{x_1 - x_2}$.

Equation of chord is

$$y - 2ap = \frac{2}{p + q}(x - ap^2)$$

i.e. $y(p + q) = 2x + 2apq$

Notice that if you let $p = q$ in this equation you get the equation of the tangent at Q. This is sometimes a useful technique in this work.

Since the chord passes through (a, 0)

$$0 = 2a + 2apq$$

i.e. $pq = -1$

c Using $pq = -1$ the coordinates of R become

$(a + a[p^2 + q^2], a[p + q])$

Let R be (X, Y) then

$$X = a + a[p^2 + q^2]$$

$$Y = a[p + q]$$

So $X = a + a[(p + q)^2 - 2pq]$

The following technique is particularly useful when tackling questions of this sort.

Since $(p + q)^2 = p^2 + q^2 + 2pq$

then $p^2 + q^2 = (p + q)^2 - 2pq$.

Using $pq = -1$ gives $p^2 + q^2 = (p + q)^2 + 2$.

and using $pq = -1$

$$X = 3a + a(p + q)^2$$

But $p + q = \dfrac{Y}{a}$

Now use Y to eliminate p and q.

So $X = 3a + a\left(\dfrac{Y}{a}\right)^2$

i.e. $Y^2 = a(X - 3a)$

Rearrange to the specified form.

Exercise 2F

1 The tangent at $P(ap^2, 2ap)$ and the tangent at $Q(aq^2, 2aq)$ to the parabola with equation $y^2 = 4ax$ meet at R.

a Find the coordinates of R.

The chord PQ passes through the focus $(a, 0)$ of the parabola.

b Show that the locus of R is the line $x = -a$.

Given instead that the chord PQ has gradient 2,

c find the locus of R.

2 The tangent at $P(a\sec t, b\tan t)$ to the hyperbola with equation $\frac{x^2}{a^2} - \frac{y^2}{b^2} = 1$ cuts the x-axis at A and the y-axis at B.

Find the locus of the mid-point of AB.

3 The normal at $P(a\sec t, b\tan t)$ to the hyperbola with equation $\frac{x^2}{a^2} - \frac{y^2}{b^2} = 1$ cuts the x-axis at A and the y-axis at B.

Find the locus of the mid-point of AB.

4 The normal at $P(a\cos t, b\sin t)$ to the ellipse with equation $\frac{x^2}{a^2} + \frac{y^2}{b^2} = 1$ cuts the x-axis at A and the y-axis at B.

Find the locus of the mid-point of AB.

5 The tangent from the point $P\left(cp, \frac{c}{p}\right)$ and the tangent from the point $Q\left(cq, \frac{c}{q}\right)$ to the rectangular hyperbola $xy = c^2$, intersect at the point R.

a Show that R is $\left(\frac{2cpq}{p+q}, \frac{2c}{p+q}\right)$

b Show that the chord PQ has equation $ypq + x = c(p + q)$

c Find the locus of R in the following cases

i when the chord PQ has gradient 2

ii when the chord PQ passes through the point $(1, 0)$

iii when the chord PQ passes through the point $(0, 1)$.

6 The chord PQ to the rectangular hyperbola $xy = c^2$ passes through the point $(0, 1)$.

Find the locus of the mid-point of PQ as P and Q vary.

Mixed exercise 2G

1 A hyperbola of the form $\frac{x^2}{\alpha^2} - \frac{y^2}{\beta^2} = 1$ has asymptotes with equations $y = \pm mx$ and passes through the point $(a, 0)$.

a Find an equation of the hyperbola in terms of x, y, a and m.

A point P on this hyperbola is equidistant from one of its asymptotes and the x-axis.

b Prove that, for all values of m, P lies on the curve with equation

$$(x^2 - y^2)^2 = 4x^2(x^2 - a^2)$$

E

2 **a** Prove that the gradient of the chord joining the point $P\left(cp, \frac{c}{p}\right)$ and the point $Q\left(cq, \frac{c}{q}\right)$ on the rectangular hyperbola with equation $xy = c^2$ is $-\frac{1}{pq}$.

The points P, Q and R lie on a rectangular hyperbola, the angle QPR being a right angle.

b Prove that the angle between QR and the tangent at P is also a right angle. **E**

3 **a** Show that an equation of the tangent to the rectangular hyperbola with equation $xy = c^2$ (with $c > 0$) at the point $\left(ct, \frac{c}{t}\right)$ is

$$t^2y + x = 2ct$$

Tangents are drawn from the point $(-3, 3)$ to the rectangular hyperbola with equation $xy = 16$.

b Find the coordinates of the points of contact of these tangents with the hyperbola. **E**

4 The point P lies on the ellipse with equation $9x^2 + 25y^2 = 225$, and A and B are the points $(-4, 0)$ and $(4, 0)$ respectively.

a Prove that $PA + PB = 10$

b Prove also that the normal at P bisects the angle APB. **E**

5 A curve is given parametrically by $x = ct$, $y = \frac{c}{t}$.

a Show that an equation of the tangent to the curve at the point $\left(ct, \frac{c}{t}\right)$ is

$$t^2y + x = 2ct$$

The point P is the foot of the perpendicular from the origin to this tangent.

b Show that the locus of P is the curve with equation

$$(x^2 + y^2)^2 = 4c^2xy$$

E

6 **a** Find the gradient of the parabola with equation $y^2 = 4ax$ at the point $P(at^2, 2at)$.

b Hence show that the equation of the tangent at this point is $x - ty + at^2 = 0$.

The tangent meets the y-axis at T, and O is the origin.

c Show that the coordinates of the centre of the circle through O, P and T are $\left(\frac{at^2}{2} + a, \frac{at}{2}\right)$.

d Deduce that, as t varies, the locus of the centre of this circle is another parabola. **E**

7 The points $P(ap^2, 2ap)$ and $Q(aq^2, 2aq)$ lie on the parabola with equation $y^2 = 4ax$. The angle $POQ = 90°$, where O is the origin.

a Prove that $pq = -4$

Given that the normal at P to the parabola has equation

$$y + xp = ap^3 + 2ap$$

b write down an equation of the normal to the parabola at Q.

c Show that these two normals meet at the point R, with coordinates

$$(ap^2 + aq^2 - 2a, 4a[p + q])$$

d Show that, as p and q vary, the locus of R has equation $y^2 = 16ax - 96a^2$. **E**

8 Show that for all values of m, the straight lines with equations $y = mx \pm \sqrt{b^2 + a^2m^2}$ are tangents to the ellipse with equation $\frac{x^2}{a^2} + \frac{y^2}{b^2} = 1$. **E**

9 The chord PQ, where P and Q are points on $xy = c^2$, has gradient 1.
Show that the locus of the point of intersection of the tangents from P and Q is the line $y = -x$.

10 **a** Show that the asymptotes of the hyperbola H with equation $x^2 - y^2 = 1$ are perpendicular.

Using $(\sec t, \tan t)$ as a general point on H and the rotation matrix $\begin{pmatrix} \frac{1}{\sqrt{2}} & -\frac{1}{\sqrt{2}} \\ \frac{1}{\sqrt{2}} & \frac{1}{\sqrt{2}} \end{pmatrix}$

b show that a rotation of 45° will transform H into a rectangular hyperbola with equation $xy = c^2$ and find the positive value of c.

Summary of key points

1 The ellipse with equation $\frac{x^2}{a^2} + \frac{y^2}{b^2} = 1$ $(a > b)$ has eccentricity e $(0 < e < 1)$ and
- $b^2 = a^2(1 - e^2)$
- foci at $(\pm ae, 0)$
- directrices at $x = \pm\frac{a}{e}$

2 The parametric equations of the ellipse $\frac{x^2}{a^2} + \frac{y^2}{b^2} = 1$ are

$x = a\cos t$

$y = b\sin t$

3 Equation of tangent and normal to the ellipse $\frac{x^2}{a^2} + \frac{y^2}{b^2} = 1$ at $(a\cos t, b\sin t)$

tangent: $bx\cos t + ay\sin t = ab$

normal: $ax\sin t - by\cos t = (a^2 - b^2)\cos t\sin t$

4 The hyperbola with equation $\frac{x^2}{a^2} - \frac{y^2}{b^2} = 1$ has eccentricity e $(e > 1)$ and
- $b^2 = a^2(e^2 - 1)$
- foci at $(\pm ae, 0)$
- directrices at $x = \pm\frac{a}{e}$

5 The parametric equations of the hyperbola $\frac{x^2}{a^2} - \frac{y^2}{b^2} = 1$ are

$x = a\sec t$ or $y = a\cosh t$

$y = b\tan t$ $\quad y = b\sinh t$

6 Equation of tangent and normal to the hyperbola $\frac{x^2}{a^2} - \frac{y^2}{b^2} = 1$ at $(a\sec t, b\tan t)$

tangent: $bx\sec t - ay\tan t = ab$

normal: $ax\sin t + by = (a^2 + b^2)\tan t$

3 Differentiation

After completing this chapter you should be able to:

- find the derivatives of hyperbolic functions and expressions involving them
- find the derivatives of inverse trigonometric functions
- find the derivatives of inverse hyperbolic functions.

Hyperbolic functions arise in many problems in mathematics and physics which involve circular functions. For example, the hyperbolic sine function arises in the gravitational potential of a cylinder and the hyperbolic cosine function arises in the shape of a hanging cable.

In this chapter you will be introduced to the derivatives of the hyperbolic functions. You will also learn how to differentiate inverse functions, including trigonometric and hyperbolic functions.

This chapter builds on what you learned in C1, C2, C3 and C4.

3.1 You can differentiate hyperbolic functions.

- $\frac{d}{dx}(\sinh x) = \cosh x$
- $\frac{d}{dx}(\cosh x) = \sinh x$
- $\frac{d}{dx}(\tanh x) = \text{sech}^2 x$
- $\frac{d}{dx}(\coth x) = -\text{cosech}^2 x$

Example 1

Show that $\frac{d}{dx}(\cosh x) = \sinh x$.

$$\cosh x = \frac{e^x + e^{-x}}{2}$$

You need to remember hyperbolic functions in terms of e^x.

$$\text{So } \frac{d}{dx}(\cosh x) = \frac{d}{dx}\left(\frac{e^x + e^{-x}}{2}\right) = \frac{e^x - e^{-x}}{2}$$

Differentiate with respect to x. $\frac{d}{dx}(e^{-x}) = -e^{-x}$

$$\frac{e^x - e^{-x}}{2} = \sinh x$$

By definition (see page 2).

$$\text{So } \frac{d}{dx}(\cosh x) = \sinh x$$

Example 2

Differentiate $\cosh 3x$ with respect to x.

$$\frac{d}{dx}(\cosh 3x) = 3\sinh 3x$$

Use the chain rule. $\frac{d}{dx}(\cosh 3x) = \frac{d}{dx}(3x) \times \sinh 3x$.

Example 3

Differentiate $x^2 \cosh 4x$ with respect to x.

$$\frac{d}{dx}(x^2\cosh 4x) = \frac{d}{dx}(x^2)\cosh 4x + x^2\frac{d}{dx}(\cosh 4x)$$

Use the product rule.

$$= 2x\cosh 4x + x^2 \times 4\sinh 4x$$

$$= 2x\cosh 4x + 4x^2\sinh 4x$$

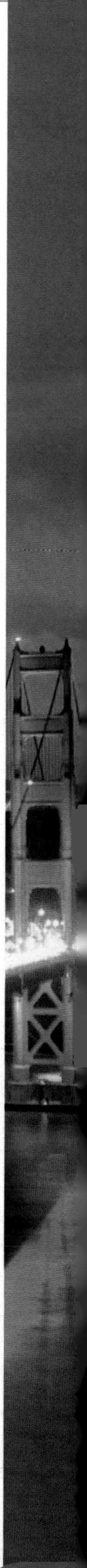

Example 4

Given that $y = A\cosh 3x + B\sinh 3x$, where A and B are constants, prove that $\frac{d^2y}{dx^2} = 9y$.

$$\frac{dy}{dx} = 3A\sinh 3x + 3B\cosh 3x$$ — Differentiate.

$$\frac{d^2y}{dx^2} = 9A\cosh 3x + 9B\sinh 3x$$ — Differentiate again.

$$\frac{d^2y}{dx^2} = 9(A\cosh 3x + B\sinh 3x)$$ — Factorise.

$$\frac{d^2y}{dx^2} = 9y$$ — Set $y = A\cosh 3x + B\sinh 3x$.

Exercise 3A

In questions 1–16, differentiate with respect to x.

1 $\sinh 2x$ **2** $\cosh 5x$ **3** $\tanh 2x$

4 $\sinh 3x$ **5** $\coth 4x$ **6** $\text{sech}\, 2x$

Hint: $\text{sech}\, 2x = \frac{1}{\cosh 2x}$.

7 $e^{-x}\sinh x$ **8** $x\cosh 3x$ **9** $\frac{\sinh x}{3x}$

10 $x^2\cosh 3x$ **11** $\sinh 2x\cosh 3x$ **12** $\ln(\cosh x)$

13 $\sinh x^3$ **14** $\cosh^2 2x$ **15** $e^{\cosh x}$

16 $\text{cosech}\, x$

Hint: $\text{cosech}\, x = \frac{1}{\sinh x}$.

17 If $y = a\cosh nx + b\sinh nx$, where a and b are constants, prove that $\frac{d^2y}{dx^2} = n^2y$.

18 Find the stationary values of the curve with equation $y = 12\cosh x - \sinh x$.

19 Given that $y = \cosh 3x\sinh x$, find $\frac{d^2y}{dx^2}$.

20 Find the equation of the tangent and normal to the hyperbola $\frac{x^2}{256} - \frac{y^2}{16} = 1$ at the point $(16\cosh q, 4\sinh q)$.

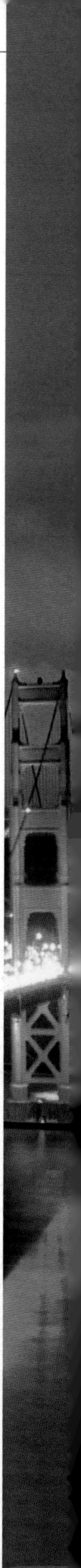

3.2 You can differentiate inverse hyperbolic functions.

- $\frac{d}{dx}(\text{arsinh}\,x) = \frac{1}{\sqrt{x^2 + 1}}$
- $\frac{d}{dx}(\text{arcosh}\,x) = \frac{1}{\sqrt{x^2 - 1}}$
- $\frac{d}{dx}(\text{artanh}\,x) = \frac{1}{1 - x^2}$

arsinh x may also be written as $\sinh^{-1} x$.

Example 5

Show that $\frac{d}{dx}(\text{arsinh}\,x) = \frac{1}{\sqrt{1 + x^2}}$

Let $y = \text{arsinh}\,x$

then $\sinh y = x$

$\Rightarrow \frac{dx}{dy} = \cosh y$ — Differentiate.

$\frac{dx}{dy} = \sqrt{\sinh^2 y + 1}$ — Use $\cosh^2 x - \sinh^2 x = 1$.

but $\sinh y = x$

so $\frac{dx}{dy} = \sqrt{x^2 + 1}$

therefore $\frac{dy}{dx} = \frac{1}{\sqrt{x^2 + 1}}$ — Invert both sides.

Example 6

Given $y = x \,\text{arcosh}\, x$, find $\frac{dy}{dx}$.

$\frac{dy}{dx} = \text{arcosh}\,x + x \times \frac{1}{\sqrt{x^2 - 1}}$ — Use the product rule.

$= \text{arcosh}\,x + \frac{x}{\sqrt{x^2 - 1}}$

Example 7

Given $y = (\text{arcosh}\, x)^2$ prove that $(x^2 - 1)\left(\frac{dy}{dx}\right)^2 = 4y$.

E

$$\frac{dy}{dx} = 2(\text{arcosh}\, x) \times \frac{1}{\sqrt{x^2 - 1}}$$

Use the chain rule.

$$\sqrt{x^2 - 1}\frac{dy}{dx} = 2(\text{arcosh}\, x)$$

Multiply by $\sqrt{x^2 - 1}$.

$$(x^2 - 1)\left(\frac{dy}{dx}\right)^2 = 4(\text{arcosh}\, x)^2$$

Square all terms.

but $y = (\text{arcosh}\, x)^2$

so $(x^2 - 1)\left(\frac{dy}{dx}\right)^2 = 4y$

Exercise 3B

1 Differentiate

a $\text{arcosh}\, 2x$ **b** $\text{arsinh}\,(x + 1)$ **c** $\text{artanh}\, 3x$

d $\text{arsech}\, x$ **e** $\text{arcosh}\, x^2$ **f** $\text{arcosh}\, 3x$

g $x^2\, \text{arcosh}\, x$ **h** $\text{arsinh}\,\frac{x}{2}$ **i** $e^{x^3}\, \text{arsinh}\, x$

j $\text{arsinh}\, x\, \text{arcosh}\, x$ **k** $\text{arcosh}\, x\, \text{sech}\, x$ **l** $x\, \text{arcosh}\, 3x$

2 Prove that

a $\frac{d}{dx}(\text{arcosh}\, x) = \frac{1}{\sqrt{x^2 - 1}}$ **b** $\frac{d}{dx}(\text{artanh}\, x) = \frac{1}{1 - x^2}$

3 Given that $y = \text{artanh}\left(\frac{e^x}{2}\right)$, prove that

$(4 - e^{2x})\frac{dy}{dx} = 2e^x$.

4 Given that $y = \text{arsinh}\, x$, show that

$$(1 + x^2)\frac{d^3y}{dx^3} + 3x\frac{d^2y}{dx^2} + \frac{dy}{dx} = 0$$

5 If $y = (\text{arcosh}\, x)^2$, find $\frac{d^2y}{dx^2}$.

6 Find the equation of the tangent at the point where $x = \frac{12}{13}$ on the curve with equation $y = \text{artanh}\, x$.

3.3 You can differentiate inverse trigonometric functions.

- $\frac{d}{dx}(\arcsin x) = \frac{1}{\sqrt{1 - x^2}}$
- $\frac{d}{dx}(\arccos x) = -\frac{1}{\sqrt{1 - x^2}}$
- $\frac{d}{dx}(\arctan x) = \frac{1}{1 + x^2}$

Example 8

Show that $\frac{d}{dx}(\arcsin x) = \frac{1}{\sqrt{1 - x^2}}$.

Let $y = \arcsin x$

then $\sin y = x$

$\cos y \frac{dy}{dx} = 1$ — Differentiate.

$\frac{dy}{dx} = \frac{1}{\cos y}$ — Divide by $\cos y$.

$= \frac{1}{\sqrt{1 - \sin^2 y}}$ — Use $\cos^2 y = 1 - \sin^2 y$.

but $\sin y = x$

so $\frac{dy}{dx} = \frac{1}{\sqrt{1 - x^2}}$

Example 9

Given $y = \arcsin x^2$ find $\frac{dy}{dx}$.

Method I

$\sin y = x^2$

$\cos y \frac{dy}{dx} = 2x$ — Differentiate.

$\frac{dy}{dx} = \frac{2x}{\cos y}$ — Divide by $\cos y$.

$\frac{dy}{dx} = \frac{2x}{\sqrt{1 - \sin^2 y}}$ — Use $\cos^2 y = 1 - \sin^2 y$.

but $\sin y = x^2$

so $\frac{dy}{dx} = \frac{2x}{\sqrt{1 - x^4}}$

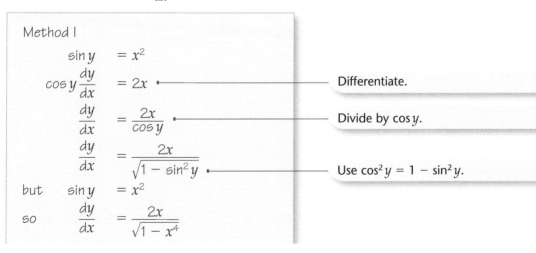

Method II

Let $t = x^2$, then $y = \arcsin t$

Substitute $t = x^2$ to get $\arcsin x^2$ in the form $\arcsin x$.

Then $\frac{dt}{dx} = 2x \qquad \frac{dy}{dt} = \frac{1}{\sqrt{1 - t^2}}$

Differentiate t and y.

$$\frac{dy}{dx} = \frac{dy}{dt} \cdot \frac{dt}{dx}$$

Use chain rule.

$$= \frac{2x}{\sqrt{1 - x^4}}$$

Example 10

Given $y = \tan^{-1}\left(\frac{1 - x}{1 + x}\right)$, find $\frac{dy}{dx}$.

$$\tan y = \left(\frac{1 - x}{1 + x}\right)$$

$$\sec^2 y \frac{dy}{dx} = \frac{-(1 + x) - 1(1 - x)}{(1 + x)^2}$$

Differentiate using quotient rule on $\left(\frac{1 - x}{1 + x}\right)$.

$$\frac{dy}{dx} = \frac{1}{\sec^2 y} \times -\left[\frac{1 + x + 1 - x}{(1 + x)^2}\right]$$

Divide by $\sec^2 y$.

$$= \frac{1}{1 + \tan^2 y} \times -\left[\frac{2}{(1 + x)^2}\right]$$

Use $1 + \tan^2 y = \sec^2 y$ and simplify brackets.

but $\tan y = \left(\frac{1 - x}{1 + x}\right)$

$$\frac{dy}{dx} = \frac{1}{1 + \left(\frac{1 - x}{1 + x}\right)^2} \times -\left[\frac{2}{(1 + x)^2}\right]$$

$$= \frac{(1 + x)^2}{(1 + x)^2 + (1 - x)^2} \times -\frac{2}{(1 + x)^2}$$

Cancel $(1 + x)^2$.

$$= \frac{-2}{2 + 2x^2}$$

$$= -\frac{1}{1 + x^2}$$

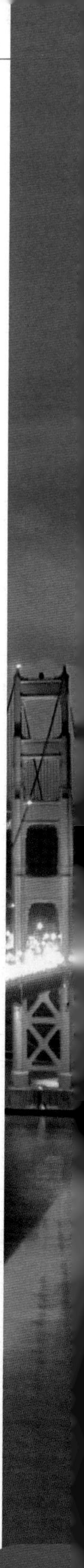

Exercise 3C

1 Given that $y = \arccos x$ prove that

$$\frac{dy}{dx} = -\frac{1}{\sqrt{1 - x^2}}$$

2 Differentiate with respect to x

a $\arccos 2x$ **b** $\arctan \frac{x}{2}$ **c** $\arcsin 3x$

d $\text{arccot}\, x$ **e** $\text{arcsec}\, x$ **f** $\text{arccosec}\, x$

g $\arcsin\left(\frac{x}{x - 1}\right)$ **h** $\arccos x^2$ **i** $e^x \arccos x$

j $\arcsin x \cos x$ **k** $x^2 \arccos x$ **l** $e^{\arctan x}$

3 If $\tan y = x \arctan x$, find $\frac{dy}{dx}$.

4 Given that $y = \arcsin x$ prove that

$$(1 - x^2)\frac{d^2y}{dx^2} - x\frac{dy}{dx} = 0$$

E

5 Find an equation of the tangent to the curve with equation $y = \arcsin 2x$ at the point where $x = \frac{1}{4}$.

Mixed exercise 3D

1 Given $y = \cosh 2x$, find $\frac{dy}{dx}$.

2 Differentiate with respect to x.

a $\text{arsinh}\, 3x$ **b** $\text{arsinh}\, x^2$ **c** $\text{arcosh}\, \frac{x}{2}$ **d** $x^2\, \text{arcosh}\, 2x$

3 Given that $y = \arctan x$ prove that

$$\frac{dy}{dx} = \frac{1}{1 + x^2}$$

4 Given that $y = (\text{arsinh}\, x)^2$ prove that

$$(1 + x^2)\frac{d^2y}{dx^2} + x\frac{dy}{dx} - 2 = 0$$

5 Given $y = 5\cosh x - 3\sinh x$

a find $\frac{dy}{dx}$ **b** find the minimum turning points.

6 Given that $y = (\arcsin x)^2$ show that

$$(1 - x^2)\frac{d^2y}{dx^2} - x\frac{dy}{dx} - 2 = 0$$

7 Differentiate $\text{arcosh}\, (\sinh 2x)$.

8 Given that $y = x - \arctan x$ prove that

$$\frac{d^2y}{dx^2} = 2x\left(1 - \frac{dy}{dx}\right)^2$$

9 Differentiate $\arcsin \dfrac{x}{\sqrt{1+x^2}}$.

10 Show that the curve with equation $y = \operatorname{sech} x$ has $\dfrac{d^2y}{dx^2} = 0$ at the point where $x = \pm \ln p$ and state a value of p.

E

11 Find the equation of the tangent and normal to the hyperbola $\dfrac{x^2}{a^2} - \dfrac{y^2}{b^2} = 1$ at the point $(a \cosh q, b \sinh q)$.

Summary of key points

$$\frac{d}{dx}(\sinh x) = \cosh x$$

$$\frac{d}{dx}(\cosh x) = \sinh x$$

$$\frac{d}{dx}(\tanh x) = \operatorname{sech}^2 x$$

$$\frac{d}{dx}(\coth x) = -\operatorname{cosech}^2 x$$

$$\frac{d}{dx}(\operatorname{cosech} x) = -\coth x \operatorname{cosech} x$$

$$\frac{d}{dx}(\operatorname{sech} x) = -\tanh x \operatorname{sech} x$$

$$\frac{d}{dx}(\operatorname{arsinh} x) = \frac{1}{\sqrt{x^2+1}}$$

$$\frac{d}{dx}(\operatorname{arcosh} x) = \frac{1}{\sqrt{x^2-1}}$$

$$\frac{d}{dx}(\operatorname{artanh} x) = \frac{1}{1-x^2}$$

$$\frac{d}{dx}(\arcsin x) = \frac{1}{\sqrt{1-x^2}}$$

$$\frac{d}{dx}(\arccos x) = -\frac{1}{\sqrt{1-x^2}}$$

$$\frac{d}{dx}(\arctan x) = \frac{1}{1+x^2}$$

After completing this chapter you should be able to:

- integrate
  hyperbolic functions,
  functions requiring trigonometric or hyperbolic substitutions,
  functions involving quadratic surds,
  inverse trigonometric and inverse hyperbolic functions
- derive and use reduction formulae
- use integration to calculate
  the length of an arc of a curve,
  the area of a surface of revolution.

4

Integration

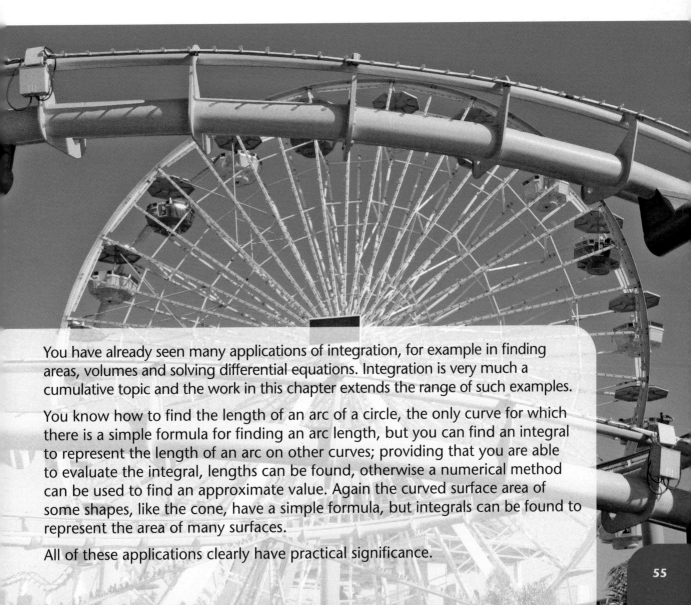

You have already seen many applications of integration, for example in finding areas, volumes and solving differential equations. Integration is very much a cumulative topic and the work in this chapter extends the range of such examples.

You know how to find the length of an arc of a circle, the only curve for which there is a simple formula for finding an arc length, but you can find an integral to represent the length of an arc on other curves; providing that you are able to evaluate the integral, lengths can be found, otherwise a numerical method can be used to find an approximate value. Again the curved surface area of some shapes, like the cone, have a simple formula, but integrals can be found to represent the area of many surfaces.

All of these applications clearly have practical significance.

4.1 You need to be able to recognise standard integrals.

As integration is the reverse process to differentiation, the results found in Chapter 3 mean that you can add the following to your list of standard integrals.
You should know which results are given in your formula booklet; those included in the Edexcel booklet are denoted by (*) throughout the chapter.

■ **You should be familiar with the following integrals:**

1 $\int \sinh x \, dx = \cosh x + C$ (*) since $\frac{d}{dx}(\cosh x) = \sinh x$

2 $\int \cosh x \, dx = \sinh x + C$ (*) since $\frac{d}{dx}(\sinh x) = \cosh x$

3 $\int \text{sech}^2 x \, dx = \tanh x + C$ since $\frac{d}{dx}(\tanh x) = \text{sech}^2 x$

4 $\int \text{cosech}^2 x \, dx = -\coth x + C$ since $\frac{d}{dx}(\coth x) = -\text{cosech}^2 x$

5 $\int \text{sech}\, x \tanh x dx = -\text{sech}\, x + C$ since $\frac{d}{dx}(\text{sech}\, x) = -\text{sech}\, x \tanh x$

6 $\int \text{cosech}\, x \coth x dx = -\text{cosech}\, x + C$ since $\frac{d}{dx}(\text{cosech}\, x) = -\text{cosech}\, x \coth x$

7 $\int \frac{1}{\sqrt{(1 - x^2)}} dx = \arcsin x + C, |x| < 1$ since $\frac{d}{dx}(\arcsin x) = \frac{1}{\sqrt{(1 - x^2)}}$

8 $\int \frac{1}{1 + x^2} dx = \arctan x + C$ since $\frac{d}{dx}(\arctan x) = \frac{1}{1 + x^2}$

9 $\int \frac{1}{\sqrt{(1 + x^2)}} dx = \text{arsinh}\, x + C$ since $\frac{d}{dx}(\text{arsinh}\, x) = \frac{1}{\sqrt{(1 + x^2)}}$

10 $\int \frac{1}{\sqrt{(x^2 - 1)}} dx = \text{arcosh}\, x + C, x > 1$ since $\frac{d}{dx}(\text{arcosh}\, x) = \frac{1}{\sqrt{(x^2 - 1)}}$

If x is replaced by a linear function of x in the results **1** to **6**, they can be generalised using $\int f'(ax + b) dx = \frac{1}{a} f(ax + b) + C$.

Example 1

Find **a** $\int \cosh(4x - 1) dx$ **b** $\int \text{cosech}\, 3x \coth 3x dx$

a $\int \cosh(4x - 1) dx = \frac{1}{4}\sinh(4x - 1) + C$

b $\int \text{cosech}\, 3x \coth 3x dx = -\frac{1}{3}\text{cosech}\, 3x + C$

Results **7** to **10** will be generalised in Sections 4.3 and 4.4, but at this stage it is important to recognise their structure. There are many integrals that have the same denominators as those in results **7** to **10**, that you found in C4, for example $\int \frac{x}{1+x^2}\,dx$ and $\int \frac{x}{\sqrt{1+x^2}}\,dx$.

The results of these integrals were found using one of the two general results:

$$\int f'(x)[f(x)]^n dx = \frac{[f(x)]^{n+1}}{n+1} + C,\ n \neq -1 \qquad ①$$

$$\int \frac{f'(x)}{f(x)}dx = \ln|f(x)| + C \qquad ②$$

You should be confident in recognising these forms (they will occur frequently in this chapter); the next Example is included as revision.

Example 2

Integrate with respect to x.

a $\frac{4x}{1+x^2}$ **b** $\frac{5x}{\sqrt{(1+x^2)}}$

a $\int \frac{4x}{1+x^2}dx = 2\int \frac{2x}{1+x^2}dx$

$= 2\ln|(1+x^2)| + C$

$= 2\ln(1+x^2) + C$

This is of the form $k\int \frac{f'(x)}{f(x)}dx$, so use ②.

An integral with a denominator of $1 + x^2$ does not automatically imply $\arctan x$.

b $\int \frac{5x}{\sqrt{(1+x^2)}}dx = 5\int x(1+x^2)^{-\frac{1}{2}}dx$

$= \frac{5}{2}\int (2x)(1+x^2)^{-\frac{1}{2}}dx$

This is of the form $k\int f'(x)[f(x)]^n dx$, so use ①.

$= \frac{5}{2}\left\{\frac{(1+x)^{\frac{1}{2}}}{\left(\frac{1}{2}\right)}\right\} + C$

Result is $k\frac{[f(x)]^{n+1}}{n+1} + C$, with $f(x) = 1 + x^2$, $n = -\frac{1}{2}$

$= 5\sqrt{1+x^2} + C$

An integral with a denominator of $\sqrt{(1+x^2)}$ does not automatically imply $\operatorname{arsinh} x$.

It may be possible to reduce more complicated looking integrals into two parts, one of which is one of those listed in **7** to **10** and one of which you already know how to integrate.

Example 3

Find $\int \frac{2+5x}{\sqrt{(x^2+1)}}dx$.

$\int \frac{2+5x}{\sqrt{(x^2+1)}}dx = \int \frac{2}{\sqrt{(x^2+1)}}dx + \int \frac{5x}{\sqrt{(x^2+1)}}dx$

Splitting the numerator gives two recognisable integrals.

$= 2\int \frac{1}{\sqrt{(x^2+1)}}dx + 5\int x(1+x^2)^{-\frac{1}{2}}dx$

Standard form **9**.

$= 2\operatorname{arsinh} x + 5\sqrt{(1+x^2)} + C$

See Example 2**b**.

Exercise 4A

1 Integrate the following with respect to x.

a $\sinh x + 3\cosh x$ **b** $5\,\text{sech}^2 x$ **c** $\dfrac{1}{\sinh^2 x}$

d $\cosh x - \dfrac{1}{\cosh^2 x}$ **e** $\dfrac{\sinh x}{\cosh^2 x}$ **f** $\dfrac{3}{\sinh x \tanh x}$

g $\text{sech}\, x(\text{sech}\, x + \tanh x)$ **h** $(\text{sech}\, x + \text{cosech}\, x)(\text{sech}\, x - \text{cosech}\, x)$

2 Find

a $\int \sinh 2x\,dx$ **b** $\int \cosh\left(\frac{x}{3}\right)dx$ **c** $\int \text{sech}^2(2x - 1)dx$

d $\int \text{cosech}^2\, 5x\,dx$ **e** $\int \text{cosech}\, 2x \coth 2x\,dx$ **f** $\int \text{sech}\left(\frac{x}{\sqrt{2}}\right)\tanh\left(\frac{x}{\sqrt{2}}\right)dx$

g $\int\left\{5\sinh 5x - 4\cosh 4x + 3\,\text{sech}^2\left(\frac{x}{2}\right)\right\}dx$

3 Write down the results of the following. (This is a recognition exercise and involves some integrals from C4.)

a $\int \frac{1}{1 + x^2}dx$ **b** $\int \frac{1}{\sqrt{1 + x^2}}dx$ **c** $\int \frac{1}{1 + x}dx$ **d** $\int \frac{2x}{1 + x^2}dx$

e $\int \frac{1}{\sqrt{1 - x^2}}dx,\ |x| < 1$ **f** $\int \frac{1}{\sqrt{x^2 - 1}}dx$ **g** $\int \frac{3x}{\sqrt{x^2 - 1}}dx$ **h** $\int \frac{3}{(1 + x)^2}dx$

4 Find

a $\int \frac{2x + 1}{\sqrt{1 - x^2}}dx$ **b** $\int \frac{1 + x}{\sqrt{x^2 - 1}}dx$ **c** $\int \frac{x - 3}{\sqrt{1 + x^2}}dx$

5 **a** Show that $\dfrac{x^2}{1 + x^2} = 1 - \dfrac{1}{1 + x^2}$

b Hence find $\int \frac{x^2}{1 + x^2}dx$

4.2 You need to be able to integrate expressions involving hyperbolic functions.

- **The method for integrating hyperbolic expressions is usually the same as that applied to the corresponding trigonometric expressions.**

Many hyperbolic functions can be integrated by recognising that they are of the form

$$\int f'(x)[f(x)]^n dx \text{ or } \int \frac{f'(x)}{f(x)}dx.$$

Example 4

Find

a $\int \text{sech}^6 x \tanh x\,dx$ **b** $\int \cosh^5 2x \sinh 2x\,dx$ **c** $\int \tanh x\,dx$ **d** $\int \frac{\text{sech}^2 x}{2 + 5\tanh x}dx$

a $\int \text{sech}^6 x \tanh x \, dx = -\int \text{sech}^5 x(-\text{sech}\, x \tanh x) dx$

$= -\frac{1}{6}\text{sech}^6 x + C$

Use $\int [f(x)]^n f'(x) dx = \frac{[f(x)]^{n+1}}{n+1} + C$, with $f(x) = \text{sech}\, x$ and $n = 5$.

b $\int \cosh^5 2x \sinh 2x \, dx = \frac{1}{2}\int (\cosh 2x)^5 (2 \sinh 2x) dx$

$= \frac{1}{12}\cosh^6 2x + C$

Use $\int [f(x)]^n f'(x) dx = \frac{[f(x)]^{n+1}}{n+1} + C$, with $f(x) = \cosh 2x$ and $n = 5$.

c $\int \tanh x \, dx = \int \frac{\sinh x}{\cosh x} dx$

$= \ln \cosh x + C \; (*)$

Use $\int \frac{f'(x)}{f(x)} dx = \ln|f(x)| + C$, with $f(x) = \cosh x$ (modulus signs are not necessary because $\cosh x > 0$, for all x).

d $\int \frac{\text{sech}^2 x}{2 + 5\tanh x} dx = \frac{1}{5}\int \frac{5\,\text{sech}^2 x}{2 + 5\tanh x} dx$

$= \frac{1}{5}\ln|(2 + 5\tanh x)| + C$

You can arrange so that it is of the form $k\int \frac{f'(x)}{f(x)} dx$

Remember that you can always check your result; differentiating it should give the integrand (the expression to be integrated).

In C4, you saw how using trigonometric identities often transformed a trigonometric expression that you could not integrate directly into one that you could. The same technique can be used with hyperbolic functions.

Example 5

Find **a** $\int \tanh^2 x \, dx$ **b** $\int \cosh^2 3x \, dx$ **c** $\int \sinh^3 x \, dx$

a $\int \tanh^2 x \, dx = \int (1 - \text{sech}^2 x) dx$

$= x - \tanh x + C$

Using $1 - \tanh^2 x = \text{sech}^2 x$ gives two standard integrals.

b $\int \cosh^2 3x \, dx = \int \frac{(1 + \cosh 6x)}{2} dx$

$= \frac{1}{2}\left(x + \frac{\sinh 6x}{6}\right) + C$

$= \frac{1}{2}x + \frac{1}{12}\sinh 6x + C$

Using $\cosh 2A = 2\cosh^2 A - 1$ with $A = 3x$.

c $\int \sinh^3 x \, dx = \int \sinh^2 x \sinh x \, dx$

$= \int (\cosh^2 x - 1)\sinh x \, dx$

$= \int \cosh^2 x \sinh x \, dx - \int \sinh x \, dx$

$= \frac{1}{3}\cosh^3 x - \cosh x + C$

For small odd values of n, you can use $\int \sinh^n x \, dx = \int \sinh^{n-1} x \sinh x \, dx$. ($\int \cosh^n x \, dx$, n odd, can be found similarly.)

■ **Sometimes however, the method used for trigonometric functions may break down, or may not be the simplest.**

In such cases you can use the exponential definition of the hyperbolic functions.

Example 6

Find $\int e^{2x}\sinh x\,dx$.

$\int e^{2x}\sinh x\,dx$ can be found using integration by parts twice.
However using integration by parts on $\int e^{ax}\sinh ax\,dx$ breaks down.

$$\int e^{2x}\sinh x\,dx = \int e^{2x}\left(\frac{e^x - e^{-x}}{2}\right)dx$$

Using the definition of $\sinh x$.

$$= \frac{1}{2}\int (e^{3x} - e^x)\,dx$$

$$= \frac{1}{2}\left(\frac{e^{3x}}{3} - e^x\right) + C$$

$$= \frac{1}{6}(e^{3x} - 3e^x) + C$$

Example 7

Find $\int \operatorname{sech} x\,dx$.

$\int \sec x\,dx$ can be found by noting that

$$\frac{d}{dx}\{\ln(\sec x + \tan x)\}$$
$$= \frac{1}{\sec x + \tan x} \times (\sec x\tan x + \sec^2 x)$$
$$= \sec x$$

so that $\int \sec x\,dx = \ln(\sec x + \tan x) + C$,
but $\int \operatorname{sech} x\,dx$ needs a different approach.

Writing $\operatorname{sech} x$ as $\frac{1}{\cosh x}$ and using the exponential form of $\cosh x$, gives

$$\int \operatorname{sech} x\,dx = \int \frac{2}{e^x + e^{-x}}\,dx$$

$$= \int \frac{2e^x}{e^{2x} + 1}\,dx$$

Multiply numerator and denominator by e^x.

Use the substitution $u = e^x$, then $\frac{du}{dx} = e^x$

so '$e^x\,dx$' can be replaced by 'du',

so $\int \operatorname{sech} x\,dx = \int \frac{2}{u^2 + 1}\,du = 2\int \frac{1}{u^2 + 1}\,du$

This is now standard form **8** with variable u.

$$= 2\arctan u + C$$

$$= 2\arctan(e^x) + C$$

Exercise 4B

1 Find

a $\int \sinh^3 x \cosh x \, dx$ **b** $\int \tanh 4x \, dx$ **c** $\int \tanh^5 x \operatorname{sech}^2 x \, dx$

d $\int \operatorname{cosech}^7 x \coth x \, dx$ **e** $\int \sqrt{\cosh 2x} \sinh 2x \, dx$ **f** $\int \operatorname{sech}^{10} 3x \tanh 3x \, dx$.

2 Find

a $\int \frac{\sinh x}{2 + 3\cosh x} dx$ **b** $\int \frac{1 + \tanh x}{\cosh^2 x} dx$ **c** $\int \frac{5\cosh x + 2\sinh x}{\cosh x} dx$.

3 **a** Show that $\int \coth x \, dx = \ln \sinh x + C$.

b Show that $\int_1^2 \coth 2x \, dx = \ln\sqrt{\left(e^2 + \frac{1}{e^2}\right)}$.

4 Use integration by parts to find

a $\int x \sinh 3x \, dx$ **b** $\int x \operatorname{sech}^2 x \, dx$.

5 Find

a $\int e^x \cosh x \, dx$ **b** $\int e^{-2x} \sinh 3x \, dx$ **c** $\int \cosh x \cosh 3x \, dx$.

6 By writing $\cosh 3x$ in exponential form, find $\int \cosh^2 3x \, dx$ and show that it is equivalent to the result found in Example 5**b**.

7 Evaluate $\int_0^1 \frac{1}{\sinh x + \cosh x} dx$, giving your answer in terms of e.

8 Use appropriate identities to find

a $\int \sinh^2 x \, dx$ **b** $\int (\operatorname{sech} x - \tanh x)^2 dx$ **c** $\int \frac{\cosh^2 3x}{\sinh^2 3x} dx$

d $\int \sinh^2 x \cosh^2 x \, dx$ **e** $\int \cosh^5 x \, dx$ **f** $\int \tanh^3 2x \, dx$.

9 Show that $\int_0^{\ln 2} \cosh^2\left(\frac{x}{2}\right) dx = \frac{1}{8}(3 + \ln 16)$.

10 The region bounded by the curve $y = \sinh x$, the line $x = 1$ and the positive x-axis is rotated through 360° about the x-axis. Show that the volume of the solid of revolution formed is

$$\frac{\pi}{8e^2}(e^4 - 4e^2 - 1).$$

11 Using the result for $\int \operatorname{sech} x \, dx$ given in Example 7, find

a $\int \frac{2}{\cosh x} dx$ **b** $\int \operatorname{sech} 2x \, dx$ **c** $\int \sqrt{1 - \tanh^2\left(\frac{x}{2}\right)} dx$.

12 Using the substitution $u = x^2$,or otherwise, find

a $\int x \cosh^2(x^2) dx$ **b** $\int \frac{x}{\cosh^2(x^2)} dx$.

4.3 You need to be able to use trigonometric and hyperbolic substitutions in integration.

The standard results below, which you met in Section 4.1, can be derived directly by using a substitution.

7 $\displaystyle\int \frac{1}{\sqrt{(1-x^2)}}\,dx = \arcsin x + C,\ |x| < 1$

8 $\displaystyle\int \frac{1}{1+x^2}\,dx = \arctan x + C$

9 $\displaystyle\int \frac{1}{\sqrt{(1+x^2)}}\,dx = \operatorname{arsinh} x + C$

10 $\displaystyle\int \frac{1}{\sqrt{(x^2-1)}}\,dx = \operatorname{arcosh} x + C,\ x > 1$

In these cases algebraic substitutions, such as $u = 1 - x^2$ for result **7**, do not help, but an appropriate trigonometric or hyperbolic substitution can be used. The suggested substitutions below are made so that the two termed expressions in the denominator are transformed into one, by use of a relevant identity.

- **For an integral involving $\sqrt{(1-x^2)}$ try $x = \sin\theta$ or $x = \tanh u$**
- **For an integral involving $1 + x^2$ try $x = \tan\theta$ or $x = \sinh u$**
- **For an integral involving $\sqrt{(1+x^2)}$ try $x = \sinh u$ or $x = \tan\theta$**
- **For an integral involving $\sqrt{(x^2-1)}$ try $x = \cosh u$ or $x = \sec\theta$**

As $1 - \sin^2\theta = \cos^2\theta$
$1 - \tanh^2 u = \operatorname{sech}^2 u$

As $1 + \tan^2\theta = \sec^2\theta$
$1 + \sinh^2 u = \cosh^2 u$

As $\cosh^2 u - 1 = \sinh^2 u$
$\sec^2\theta - 1 = \tan^2\theta$

The first substitution in each suggested pair is the one more likely to prove the better choice.

Example 8

By the use of an appropriate substitution, show that $\displaystyle\int \frac{1}{1+x^2}\,dx = \arctan x + C$.

Using the substitution $x = \tan\theta$, then $\dfrac{dx}{d\theta} = \sec^2\theta$
so 'dx' can be replaced by '$\sec^2\theta\, d\theta$',

and then $\displaystyle\int \frac{1}{1+x^2}\,dx = \int \frac{1}{1+\tan^2\theta}\sec^2\theta\, d\theta$

$\displaystyle = \int 1\, d\theta$

$= \theta + C$

$= \arctan x + C$

Use $1 + \tan^2\theta = \sec^2\theta$.

If the substitution $x = \sinh u$ is used, the resulting integral reduces to $\int \operatorname{sech} u\, du$.

■ **For integrals of the form**

$$\int \frac{1}{\sqrt{(a^2 - x^2)}}\,dx,\ |x| < a,\ \int \frac{1}{a^2 + x^2}\,dx,\ \int \frac{1}{\sqrt{(a^2 + x^2)}}\,dx \text{ and } \int \frac{1}{\sqrt{(x^2 - a^2)}}\,dx, \text{ the substitutions}$$

$x = a\sin\theta$, $x = a\tan\theta$, $x = a\sinh u$, and $x = a\cosh u$ **respectively are suggested.**

Example 9

By using an appropriate substitution in each case,

a find $\int \frac{1}{\sqrt{(x^2 - a^2)}}\,dx$, $x > a$ **b** show that $\int \frac{1}{4 + x^2}\,dx = \frac{1}{2}\arctan\left(\frac{x}{2}\right) + C$.

a As $\cosh^2 u - 1 = \sinh^2 u$, it follows that

$a^2\cosh^2 u - a^2 = a^2\sinh^2 u$.

So, using the substitution $x = a\cosh u$,

$\frac{dx}{du} = a\sinh u$ so 'dx' can be replaced by '$a\sinh u\,du$', and

$$\int \frac{1}{\sqrt{(x^2 - a^2)}}\,dx = \int \frac{1}{\sqrt{(a^2\cosh^2 u - a^2)}}\,a\sinh u\,du$$

$$= \int \frac{1}{\cancel{a\sinh u}}\,\cancel{a\sinh u}\,du$$

$$= u + C$$

$$= \operatorname{arcosh}\left(\frac{x}{a}\right) + C$$

As $x = a\cosh u$, $\cosh u = \frac{x}{a}$ so $u = \operatorname{arcosh}\left(\frac{x}{a}\right)$.

b Let $x = 2\tan\theta$,

then $4 + x^2 = 4 + 4\tan^2\theta = 4(1 + \tan^2\theta) = 4\sec^2\theta$

and $\frac{dx}{d\theta} = 2\sec^2\theta$ so 'dx' can be replaced by '$2\sec^2\theta\,d\theta$',

$$\text{so } \int \frac{1}{4 + x^2}\,dx = \int \frac{1}{4\sec^2\theta}\,2\sec^2\theta\,d\theta$$

$$= \frac{1}{2}\int 1\,d\theta$$

$$= \frac{1}{2}\theta + C$$

$$= \frac{1}{2}\arctan\left(\frac{x}{2}\right) + C$$

As $x = 2\tan\theta$, $\tan\theta = \frac{x}{2}$ so $\theta = \arctan\left(\frac{x}{2}\right)$.

The following results are given in the Edexcel formula booklet.

11 $\int \frac{1}{\sqrt{(a^2 - x^2)}}\,dx = \arcsin\left(\frac{x}{a}\right)$, $|x| < a$ **(*)**

12 $\int \frac{1}{a^2 + x^2}\,dx = \frac{1}{a}\arctan\left(\frac{x}{a}\right)$ **(*)**

13 $\int \frac{1}{\sqrt{(a^2 + x^2)}}\,dx = \operatorname{arsinh}\left(\frac{x}{a}\right)$ **(*)**

14 $\int \frac{1}{\sqrt{(x^2 - a^2)}}\,dx = \operatorname{arcosh}\left(\frac{x}{a}\right)$, $x > a$ **(*)**

When $a = 1$, these become the results **7** to **10**. Only **12** has the factor $\frac{1}{a}$ in the result.

You may still be asked to find a result by using a suitable substitution, but usually you will be able to use the results **11** to **14** for integrals of this type.

Example 10

a Find $\int \frac{4}{5 + x^2}\,dx$

b Show that $\int_5^8 \frac{1}{\sqrt{x^2 - 16}}\,dx = \ln\left(\frac{2 + \sqrt{3}}{2}\right)$

a $\int \frac{4}{5 + x^2}\,dx = 4\int \frac{1}{5 + x^2}\,dx$

$= 4\left\{\frac{1}{\sqrt{5}}\arctan\left(\frac{x}{\sqrt{5}}\right)\right\} + C$ — Using **12** with $a = \sqrt{5}$.

$= \frac{4}{\sqrt{5}}\arctan\left(\frac{x}{\sqrt{5}}\right) + C$

b $\int_5^8 \frac{1}{\sqrt{x^2 - 16}}\,dx = \left[\text{arcosh}\left(\frac{x}{4}\right)\right]_5^8$ — Using **14** with $a = 4$.

$= \text{arcosh}\,2 - \text{arcosh}\left(\frac{5}{4}\right)$

$= \ln(2 + \sqrt{3}) - \ln\left(\frac{5}{4} + \sqrt{\frac{9}{16}}\right)$ — Using $\text{arcosh}\,x = \ln(x + \sqrt{x^2 - 1})$ (*).

$= \ln(2 + \sqrt{3}) - \ln 2$

$= \ln\left(\frac{2 + \sqrt{3}}{2}\right)$ — Using $\ln a - \ln b = \ln\left(\frac{a}{b}\right)$.

■ **Integrals of the form**

$$\int \frac{1}{\sqrt{(a^2 - b^2x^2)}}\,dx,\ \int \frac{1}{a^2 + b^2x^2}\,dx,\ \int \frac{1}{\sqrt{(a^2 + b^2x^2)}}\,dx \text{ and } \int \frac{1}{\sqrt{(b^2x^2 - a^2)}}\,dx$$

can be easily manipulated to use the results 11 to 14.

Example 11

a Find $\int \frac{1}{25 + 9x^2}\,dx$.

b Evaluate $\int_{-\frac{\sqrt{3}}{4}}^{\frac{\sqrt{3}}{4}} \frac{1}{\sqrt{3 - 4x^2}}$, leaving your answer in terms of π.

a $\int \frac{1}{25 + 9x^2}\,dx = \int \frac{1}{9(\frac{25}{9} + x^2)}\,dx$ — You need to write $25 + 9x^2$ in the form $k(a^2 + x^2)$.

$= \frac{1}{9}\left\{\left(\frac{1}{(\frac{5}{3})}\right)\arctan\left(\frac{x}{(\frac{5}{3})}\right)\right\} + C$ — Using **12** with $a = \frac{5}{3}$.

$= \frac{1}{15}\arctan\left(\frac{3x}{5}\right) + C$

b $\displaystyle\int_{-\frac{\sqrt{3}}{4}}^{\frac{\sqrt{3}}{4}} \frac{1}{\sqrt{3 - 4x^2}}\,dx = \int_{-\frac{\sqrt{3}}{4}}^{\frac{\sqrt{3}}{4}} \frac{1}{\sqrt{4\left(\frac{3}{4} - x^2\right)}}\,dx$

$\displaystyle = \frac{1}{2}\int_{-\frac{\sqrt{3}}{4}}^{\frac{\sqrt{3}}{4}} \frac{1}{\sqrt{\left(\frac{3}{4} - x^2\right)}}\,dx$

$\displaystyle = \frac{1}{2}\left[\arcsin\left(\frac{2x}{\sqrt{3}}\right)\right]_{-\frac{\sqrt{3}}{4}}^{\frac{\sqrt{3}}{4}}$

$\displaystyle = \frac{1}{2}\left[\arcsin\left(\frac{1}{2}\right)\right] - \frac{1}{2}\left[\arcsin\left(-\frac{1}{2}\right)\right]$

$\displaystyle = \left[\frac{\pi}{12}\right] - \left[-\frac{\pi}{12}\right]$

$\displaystyle = \frac{\pi}{6}$

You need to write $3 - 4x^2$ in the form $k(a^2 - x^2)$.

Using **11** with $a = \frac{\sqrt{3}}{2}$.

$\frac{-\pi}{2} \leqslant \arcsin x \leqslant \frac{\pi}{2}$

so $\arcsin\left(\frac{1}{2}\right) = \left(\frac{\pi}{6}\right)$;
$\arcsin\left(-\frac{1}{2}\right) = -\frac{\pi}{6}$

The substitutions suggested in the previous pages can be used in a wide range of integrals.

Example 12

Show that $\int \sqrt{1 + x^2}\,dx = \frac{1}{2}\text{arsinh}\,x + \frac{1}{2}x\sqrt{1 + x^2} + C$.

Using $x = \sinh u$, then $\frac{dx}{du} = \cosh u$ so 'dx' can be replaced by '$\cosh u\,du$'

So $\displaystyle\int \sqrt{1 + x^2}\,dx = \int \sqrt{1 + \sinh^2 u}\cosh u\,du$

$\displaystyle = \int \cosh^2 u\,du$

$\displaystyle = \frac{1}{2}\int (1 + \cosh 2u)\,du$ — Using $\cosh 2u = 2\cosh^2 u - 1$.

$\displaystyle = \frac{1}{2}\left(u + \frac{\sinh 2u}{2}\right) + C$

$\displaystyle = \frac{1}{2}(u + \sinh u \cosh u) + C$ — You need to be able to use $x = \sinh u$, so use $\sinh 2u = 2\sinh u \cosh u$.

$\displaystyle = \frac{1}{2}\text{arsinh}\,x + \frac{1}{2}x\sqrt{1 + x^2} + C$ — As $u = \text{arsinh}\,x$ and $\cosh u = \sqrt{1 + \sinh^2 u}$.

Example 13

By using a hyperbolic substitution, evaluate $\displaystyle\int_0^6 \frac{x^3}{\sqrt{x^2 + 9}}\,dx$.

You could use integration by parts.

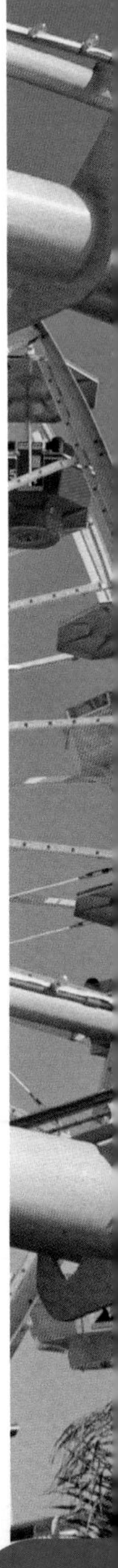

Use the substitution $x = 3\sinh u$ then $\frac{dx}{du} = 3\cosh u$, and 'dx' can be replaced by '$3\cosh u\,du$',

so $\int_0^6 \frac{x^3}{\sqrt{x^2+9}}\,dx = \int_0^{\text{arsinh}2} \frac{27\sinh^3 u}{3\cosh u} 3\cosh u\,du$

$= 27\int_0^{\text{arsinh}2} \sinh^3 u\,du$

$= 27\left[\frac{1}{3}\cosh^3 u - \cosh u\right]_0^{\text{arsinh}2}$

$= 27\left[\frac{5\sqrt{5}}{3} - \sqrt{5}\right] - 27\left[\frac{1}{3} - 1\right]$

$= 18\sqrt{5} + 18$

$= 18(\sqrt{5} + 1)$ or 58.2 (3 s.f.)

You need to reduce $x^2 + 9$ to a single term; using $x = 3\sinh u$ gives $9\sinh^2 u + 9 = 9(\sinh^2 u + 1) = 9\cosh^2 u$.

Limits: When $x = 6$, $\sinh u = 2 \Rightarrow u = \text{arsinh}\,2$.

When $x = 0$, $\sinh u = 0 \Rightarrow u = 0$.

See Example 5**c**.

As $\sinh u = 2$, $\cosh u = \sqrt{\{1 + (2)^2\}} = \sqrt{5}$.

Exercise 4C

Unless a substitution is given or asked for, use the standard results **7** to **14.** Give numerical answers to 3 significant figures, unless otherwise stated.

1 Use the substitution $x = a\tan\theta$ to show that $\int \frac{1}{a^2 + x^2}\,dx = \frac{1}{a}\arctan\left(\frac{x}{a}\right) + C$.

2 Use the substitution $x = \cos\theta$ to show that $\int \frac{1}{\sqrt{1 - x^2}}\,dx = -\arccos x + C$.

3 Use suitable substitutions to find

a $\int \frac{3}{\sqrt{4 - x^2}}\,dx$ **b** $\int \frac{1}{\sqrt{x^2 - 9}}\,dx$ **c** $\int \frac{4}{5 + x^2}\,dx$ **d** $\int \frac{1}{\sqrt{4x^2 + 25}}\,dx$.

4 Write down the results for the following:

a $\int \frac{1}{\sqrt{25 - x^2}}\,dx$ **b** $\int \frac{3}{\sqrt{x^2 + 9}}\,dx$ **c** $\int \frac{1}{\sqrt{x^2 - 2}}\,dx$ **d** $\int \frac{2}{16 + x^2}\,dx$.

5 Find

a $\int \frac{1}{\sqrt{4x^2 - 12}}\,dx$ **b** $\int \frac{1}{4 + 3x^2}\,dx$ **c** $\int \frac{1}{\sqrt{9x^2 + 16}}\,dx$ **d** $\int \frac{1}{\sqrt{3 - 4x^2}}\,dx$.

6 Evaluate

a $\int_1^3 \frac{2}{1 + x^2}\,dx$ **b** $\int_1^2 \frac{3}{\sqrt{1 + 4x^2}}\,dx$ **c** $\int_{-1}^2 \frac{1}{\sqrt{21 - 3x^2}}\,dx$.

7 Evaluate, giving your answers in terms of π or as a single natural logarithm, whichever is appropriate.

a $\int_0^4 \frac{1}{\sqrt{x^2 + 16}}\,dx$ **b** $\int_{13}^{15} \frac{1}{\sqrt{x^2 - 144}}\,dx$ **c** $\int_{\sqrt{2}}^{\sqrt{3}} \frac{1}{\sqrt{4 - x^2}}\,dx$

8 The curve C has equation $y = \dfrac{2}{\sqrt{2x^2 + 9}}$. The region R is bounded by C, the coordinate axes and the lines $x = -1$ and $x = 3$.

a Find the area of R.

The region R is rotated through 360° about the x-axis.

b Find the volume of the solid generated.

9 A circle C has centre the origin and radius r.

a Show that the area of C can be written as $4\displaystyle\int_0^r \sqrt{r^2 - x^2}\,dx$.

b Hence show that the area of C is πr^2.

10 **a** Use the substitution $x = \frac{2}{3}\tan\theta$ to find $\displaystyle\int \frac{x^2}{9x^2 + 4}\,dx$.

b Use the substitution $x = \sinh^2 u$ to find $\displaystyle\int \sqrt{\frac{x}{x + 1}}\,dx$, $x > 0$.

11 By splitting up each integral into two separate integrals, or otherwise, find

a $\displaystyle\int \frac{x - 2}{\sqrt{x^2 - 4}}\,dx$ **b** $\displaystyle\int \frac{2x - 1}{\sqrt{2 - x^2}}\,dx$ **c** $\displaystyle\int \frac{2 + 3x}{1 + 3x^2}\,dx$.

12 Use the method of partial fractions to find $\displaystyle\int \frac{x^2 + 4x + 10}{x^3 + 5x}\,dx$, $x > 0$.

13 Show that $\displaystyle\int_0^1 \frac{2}{(x + 1)(x^2 + 1)}\,dx = \frac{1}{4}(\pi + 2\ln 2)$.

14 By using the substitution $u = x^2$, evaluate $\displaystyle\int_2^3 \frac{2x}{\sqrt{x^4 - 1}}\,dx$.

15 By using the substitution $x = \frac{1}{2}\sin\theta$, show that $\displaystyle\int_0^{\frac{1}{4}} \frac{x^2}{\sqrt{1 - 4x^2}}\,dx = \frac{1}{192}(2\pi - 3\sqrt{3})$.

16 **a** Use the substitution $x = 2\cosh u$ to show that $\displaystyle\int \sqrt{x^2 - 4}\,dx = \frac{1}{2}x\sqrt{x^2 - 4} - 2\,\text{arcosh}\left(\frac{x}{2}\right) + C$.

b Find the area enclosed between the hyperbola with equation $\dfrac{x^2}{4} - \dfrac{y^2}{9} = 1$ and the line $x = 4$.

17 **a** Show that $\displaystyle\int \frac{1}{2\cosh x - \sinh x}\,dx$ can be written as $\displaystyle\int \frac{2e^x}{e^{2x} + 3}\,dx$.

b Hence, by using the substitution $u = e^x$, find $\displaystyle\int \frac{1}{2\cosh x - \sinh x}\,dx$.

18 Using the substitution $u = \frac{2}{3}\sinh x$, evaluate $\displaystyle\int_0^1 \frac{\cosh x}{\sqrt{4\sinh^2 x + 9}}\,dx$.

19 **a** Find $\displaystyle\int \frac{dx}{a^2 - x^2}$, $|x| < a$, by using **i** partial fractions,

ii the substitution $x = a\tanh\theta$.

b Deduce the logarithmic form of $\text{artanh}\left(\dfrac{x}{a}\right)$.

20 Using the substitution $x = \sec\theta$, find

a $\displaystyle\int \frac{1}{x\sqrt{x^2 - 1}}\,dx$ **b** $\displaystyle\int \frac{\sqrt{x^2 - 1}}{x}\,dx$.

4.4 You need to be able to integrate expressions of the form $\int \frac{1}{px^2 + qx + r}\,dx$ and $\int \frac{1}{\sqrt{px^2 + qx + r}}\,dx$.

- You can use the method of **completing the square** to reduce integrals of the type $\int \frac{1}{px^2 + qx + r}\,dx$ and $\int \frac{1}{\sqrt{px^2 + qx + r}}$ to one of the forms in the results below.

11 $\int \frac{1}{\sqrt{(a^2 - x^2)}}\,dx = \arcsin\left(\frac{x}{a}\right),\ |x| < a$ (*)

12 $\int \frac{1}{a^2 + x^2}\,dx = \frac{1}{a}\arctan\left(\frac{x}{a}\right)$ (*)

13 $\int \frac{1}{\sqrt{(a^2 + x^2)}}\,dx = \text{arsinh}\left(\frac{x}{a}\right)$ (*)

14 $\int \frac{1}{\sqrt{(x^2 - a^2)}}\,dx = \text{arcosh}\left(\frac{x}{a}\right),\ x > a$ (*)

15 $\int \frac{1}{a^2 - x^2}\,dx = \frac{1}{2a}\ln\left|\frac{a + x}{a - x}\right|,\ |x| < a$ (*)

16 $\int \frac{1}{x^2 - a^2}\,dx = \frac{1}{2a}\ln\left|\frac{x - a}{x + a}\right|$ (*)

Results **15** and **16** are found using partial fractions.

If $px^2 + qx + r$ factorises, then integrals of the form $\int \frac{1}{px^2 + qx + r}\,dx$ are best obtained by using the method of partial fractions, which was covered in C4.

Example 14

Find **a** $\int \frac{1}{x^2 - 8x + 8}\,dx$ **b** $\int \frac{1}{2x^2 + 4x + 11}\,dx$

a $x^2 - 8x + 8 = (x - 4)^2 - 8$

First 'complete the square' to express in the form $(x + b)^2 + c$.

So $\int \frac{1}{x^2 - 8x + 8}\,dx = \int \frac{1}{(x - 4)^2 - 8}\,dx$

Put $u = x - 4$, then 'du' = 'dx'

Reduce to one of the forms **11** to **16**. Select the appropriate standard form.

So $\int \frac{1}{x^2 - 8x + 8}\,dx = \int \frac{1}{u^2 - 8}\,du$

$= \frac{1}{4\sqrt{2}}\ln\left|\frac{u - 2\sqrt{2}}{u + 2\sqrt{2}}\right| + C$

Using **16** with $a = \sqrt{8} = 2\sqrt{2}$.

$= \frac{\sqrt{2}}{8}\ln\left|\frac{x - 4 - 2\sqrt{2}}{x - 4 + 2\sqrt{2}}\right| + C$

Remember to write as f(x).

b $2x^2 + 4x + 11 \quad = 2\left(x^2 + 2x + \frac{11}{2}\right)$

$= 2\left\{(x+1)^2 + \frac{9}{2}\right\}$

So $\displaystyle\int \frac{1}{2x^2 + 4x + 11}\,dx = \int \frac{1}{2\left\{(x+1)^2 + \frac{9}{2}\right\}}\,dx$

Put $u = x + 1$, then 'du' = 'dx' so that

$$\int \frac{1}{2x^2 + 4x + 11}\,dx = \frac{1}{2}\int \frac{1}{u^2 + \frac{9}{2}}\,du$$

$$= \frac{1}{2}\,\frac{1}{\left(\frac{3}{\sqrt{2}}\right)}\arctan\frac{u}{\left(\frac{3}{\sqrt{2}}\right)} + C$$

$$= \frac{1}{3\sqrt{2}}\arctan\left(\frac{\sqrt{2}(x+1)}{3}\right) + C$$

First 'complete the square' to express in the form $a[(x + b)^2 + c]$.

Using **12** with $a = \sqrt{\frac{9}{2}} = \frac{3}{\sqrt{2}}$.

As $u = x + 1$.

Example 15

Find $\displaystyle\int \frac{1}{\sqrt{12x + 2x^2}}\,dx$.

$$12x + 2x^2 = 2(x^2 - 6x)$$

$$= 2\{(x+3)^2 - 9\}$$

So $\displaystyle\int \frac{1}{\sqrt{12x + 2x^2}}\,dx = \int \frac{1}{\sqrt{2\{(x+3)^2 - 9\}}}\,dx$

Put $u = x + 3$, then $du = dx$ and

$$\int \frac{1}{\sqrt{12x + 2x^2}}\,dx = \frac{1}{\sqrt{2}}\int \frac{1}{\sqrt{u^2 - 9}}\,du$$

$$= \frac{1}{\sqrt{2}}\text{arcosh}\left(\frac{u}{3}\right) + C$$

$$= \frac{1}{\sqrt{2}}\text{arcosh}\left(\frac{x+3}{3}\right) + C$$

Complete the square.

Choose the substitution.

Select the standard form.

Using **14** with $a = 3$.

As $u = x + 3$.

You may be asked to find any of these integrals by using a trigonometric or hyperbolic substitution, so you should be prepared for that situation.

Example 16

Use a suitable trigonometric substitution to find $\int \frac{1}{\sqrt{4 - 2x - x^2}} \, dx$.

$$4 - 2x - x^2 = -(x^2 + 2x - 4)$$
$$= -\{(x + 1)^2 - 5\}$$
$$= 5 - (x + 1)^2$$

You still need to complete the square.

So $\int \frac{1}{\sqrt{4 - 2x - x^2}} dx = \int \frac{1}{\sqrt{5 - (x + 1)^2}} dx$

Use the substitution $x + 1 = \sqrt{5} \sin \theta$

For $\sqrt{a^2 - X^2}$ you use $X = a \sin \theta$.

Then as $\frac{dx}{d\theta} = \sqrt{5} \cos \theta$, dx can be replaced by $\sqrt{5} \cos \theta d\theta$

so $\int \frac{1}{\sqrt{4 - 2x - x^2}} dx = \int \frac{1}{\sqrt{5 - 5 \sin^2 \theta}} \sqrt{5} \cos \theta d\theta$

$$= \int \frac{1}{\cancel{\sqrt{5} \cos \theta}} \cancel{\sqrt{5} \cos \theta} d\theta$$
$$= \int 1 d\theta$$
$$= \theta + C$$
$$= \arcsin\left(\frac{x + 1}{\sqrt{5}}\right) + C$$

As $x + 1 = \sqrt{5} \sin \theta$.

You may also be directed to use a particular substitution.

Example 17

Use the substitution $x = \frac{1}{2}(3 + 4 \cosh u)$ to find $\int \frac{1}{\sqrt{4x^2 - 12x - 7}} \, dx$.

For $x = \frac{1}{2}(3 + 4 \cosh u)$, $\frac{dx}{du} = \frac{1}{2}(4 \sinh u) = 2 \sinh u$ so dx can be replaced by $2 \sinh u \, du$,

and $4x^2 - 12x - 7 = 4\left\{\frac{1}{4}(9 + 24 \cosh u + 16 \cosh^2 u)\right\} - 6(3 + 4 \cosh u) - 7$

$$= 9 + 24 \cosh u + 16 \cosh^2 u - 18 - 24 \cosh u - 7$$
$$= 16 \cosh^2 u - 16$$
$$= 16 \sinh^2 u$$

Using $\cosh^2 u - \sinh^2 u = 1$.

So $\int \frac{1}{\sqrt{4x^2 - 12x - 7}} dx = \int \frac{1}{4 \sinh u} 2 \sinh u \, du$

$$= \frac{1}{2} \int 1 du$$
$$= \frac{1}{2} u + C$$
$$= \frac{1}{2} \text{arcosh}\left(\frac{2x - 3}{4}\right) + C$$

As $x = \frac{1}{2}(3 + 4 \cosh u)$, $\cosh u = \left(\frac{2x - 3}{4}\right)$.

Exercise 4D

1 Find the following.

a $\int \frac{1}{\sqrt{5 - 4x - x^2}}\,dx$ **b** $\int \frac{1}{\sqrt{x^2 - 4x - 12}}\,dx$ **c** $\int \frac{1}{\sqrt{x^2 + 6x + 10}}\,dx$

d $\int \frac{1}{\sqrt{x(x - 2)}}\,dx$ **e** $\int \frac{1}{2x^2 + 4x + 7}\,dx$ **f** $\int \frac{1}{\sqrt{-4x^2 - 12x}}\,dx$

g $\int \frac{1}{\sqrt{14 - 12x - 2x^2}}\,dx$ **h** $\int \frac{1}{\sqrt{9x^2 - 8x + 1}}\,dx$

2 Find

a $\int \frac{1}{\sqrt{4x^2 - 12x + 10}}\,dx$ **b** $\int \frac{1}{\sqrt{4x^2 - 12x + 4}}\,dx$.

3 Evaluate the following, giving answers to 3 significant figures.

a $\int_1^2 \frac{1}{\sqrt{x^2 + 2x + 5}}\,dx$ **b** $\int_1^3 \frac{1}{x^2 + x + 1}\,dx$ **c** $\int_0^1 \frac{1}{\sqrt{2 + 3x - 2x^2}}\,dx$

4 Evaluate

a $\int_1^3 \frac{1}{\sqrt{x^2 - 2x + 2}}\,dx$, giving your answer as a single natural logarithm,

b $\int_1^2 \frac{1}{\sqrt{1 + 6x - 3x^2}}\,dx$, giving your answer in the form $k\pi$.

5 Show that $\int_1^3 \frac{1}{\sqrt{3x^2 - 6x + 7}}\,dx = \frac{1}{\sqrt{3}}\ln(2 + \sqrt{3})$.

6 Using a suitable hyperbolic or trigonometric substitution find

a $\int \frac{1}{\sqrt{x^2 + 4x + 5}}\,dx$ **b** $\int \frac{1}{\sqrt{-x^2 + 4x + 5}}\,dx$.

7 Using the substitution $x = \frac{1}{5}(\sqrt{3}\tan\theta - 1)$, obtain $\int_{-0.2}^{0} \frac{1}{25x^2 + 10x + 4}\,dx$, giving your answer in terms of π.

8 Evaluate $\int_3^4 \frac{1}{\sqrt{(x - 2)(x + 4)}}\,dx$, giving your answer in the form $\ln(a + b\sqrt{c})$, where a, b and c are integers to be found.

9 Using the substitution $x = 1 + \sinh\theta$, show that $\int \frac{1}{(x^2 - 2x + 2)^{\frac{3}{2}}}\,dx = \frac{x - 1}{\sqrt{x^2 - 2x + 2}} + C$.

10 Use the substitution $x = 2\sin\theta - 1$ to find $\int \frac{x}{\sqrt{3 - 2x - x^2}}\,dx$.

4.5 You can integrate inverse trigonometric and hyperbolic functions using integration by parts.

In Chapter 6 of C4 you integrated the single function $\ln x$ by writing $\int \ln x \, dx = \int (\ln x \times 1) dx$ and then using integration by parts with $u = \ln x$ and $\frac{dv}{dx} = 1$. You can use the same technique to integrate inverse trigonometric and hyperbolic functions.

Example 18

Find $\int \text{artanh}\, x \, dx$.

Let $I = \int \text{artanh}\, x \, dx = \int \text{artanh}\, x \times 1 \, dx$

Using $u = \text{artanh}\, x$ and $\frac{dv}{dx} = 1$

$\frac{du}{dx} = \frac{1}{1 - x^2}$ and $v = x$

So $I = x\,\text{artanh}\, x - \int \frac{x}{1 - x^2} dx$

$= x\,\text{artanh}\, x - \left(-\frac{1}{2}\right)\int \frac{(-2x)}{1 - x^2} dx$

$= x\,\text{artanh}\, x + \frac{1}{2}\ln|1 - x^2| + C$

Using $\int u\frac{dv}{dx}dx = uv - \int v\frac{du}{dx}dx$.

This is of the form $\int \frac{f'(x)}{f(x)}dx$, where $f(x) = 1 - x^2$.

This could be written in terms of ln by using $\text{artanh}\, x = \frac{1}{2}\ln\left(\frac{1 + x}{1 - x}\right)$ (*).

Example 19

Evaluate $\int_{-\frac{1}{2}}^{\frac{\sqrt{3}}{2}} \arcsin x \, dx$.

Let $I = \int \arcsin x \, dx = \int \arcsin x \times 1 \, dx$

Using $u = \arcsin x$ and $\frac{dv}{dx} = 1$

$\frac{du}{dx} = \frac{1}{\sqrt{1 - x^2}}$ and $v = x$

So $I = x \arcsin x - \int \frac{x}{\sqrt{1 - x^2}} dx$

$= x \arcsin x - \left(-\frac{1}{2}\right)\int (-2x)(1 - x^2)^{-\frac{1}{2}} dx$

$= x \arcsin x + \frac{1}{2}\frac{(1 - x^2)^{\frac{1}{2}}}{\left(\frac{1}{2}\right)} + C$

$= x \arcsin x + \sqrt{1 - x^2} + C$

So $\int_{-\frac{1}{2}}^{\frac{\sqrt{3}}{2}} \arcsin x \, dx = \left[x \arcsin x + \sqrt{1 - x^2}\right]_{-\frac{1}{2}}^{\frac{\sqrt{3}}{2}}$

$= \left[\frac{\sqrt{3}}{2}\arcsin\left(\frac{\sqrt{3}}{2}\right) + \frac{1}{2}\right] - \left[-\frac{1}{2}\arcsin\left(-\frac{1}{2}\right) + \sqrt{\frac{3}{4}}\right]$

$= \frac{\sqrt{3}\pi}{6} + \frac{1}{2} - \frac{\pi}{12} - \frac{\sqrt{3}}{2}$

$= 0.279$ (3 s.f.)

Using $\int u\frac{dv}{dx}dx = uv - \int v\frac{du}{dx}dx$.

This is of the form $\int f'(x)[f(x)]^n dx$.

This is $\frac{[f(x)]^{n+1}}{n + 1}$, with $n = -\frac{1}{2}$.

Remember that $-\frac{\pi}{2} \leqslant \arcsin x \leqslant \frac{\pi}{2}$.

Exercise 4E

1 **a** Show that $\int \text{arsinh}\, x \, dx = x \, \text{arsinh}\, x - \sqrt{1 + x^2} + C$.

b Evaluate $\int_0^1 \text{arsinh}\, x \, dx$, giving your answer to 3 significant figures.

c Using the substitution $u = 2x + 1$ and the result in **a**, or otherwise, find

$\int \text{arcsinh}(2x + 1) \, dx$.

2 Show that $\int \arctan 3x \, dx = x \arctan 3x - \frac{1}{6}\ln(1 + 9x^2) + C$.

3 **a** Show that $\int \text{arcosh}\, x \, dx = x \, \text{arcosh}\, x - \sqrt{x^2 - 1} + C$.

b Hence show that $\int_1^2 \text{arcosh}\, x = \ln(7 + 4\sqrt{3}) - \sqrt{3}$.

4 **a** Show that $\int \arctan x \, dx = x \arctan x - \frac{1}{2}\ln(1 + x^2) + C$.

b Hence show that $\int_{-1}^{\sqrt{3}} \arctan x \, dx = \dfrac{(4\sqrt{3} - 3)\pi}{12} - \frac{1}{2}\ln 2$.

The curve C has equation $y = 2 \arctan x$. The region R is enclosed by C, the y-axis, the line $y = \pi$ and the line $x = 3$.

c Find the area of R, giving your answer to 3 significant figures.

5 Evaluate **a** $\int_0^{\frac{\sqrt{2}}{2}} \arcsin x \, dx$ **b** $\int_0^1 x \arctan x \, dx$

giving your answers in terms of π.

6 Using the result that if $y = \text{arcsec}\, x$, then $\dfrac{dy}{dx} = \dfrac{1}{x\sqrt{x^2 - 1}}$, show that

$$\int \text{arcsec}\, x \, dx = x \, \text{arcsec}\, x - \ln\{x + \sqrt{x^2 - 1}\} + C.$$

4.6 You need to be able to derive and use reduction formulae.

Often a method used to integrate a function involving n, usually a power, where n is small, is not viable as n becomes large. For example, the methods used to find $\int \sin^2 x \, dx$, using the double angle formula for $\cos 2x$ to give $\int \sin^2 x \, dx = \frac{1}{2}\int (1 - \cos 2x) dx$, to find $\int \sin^3 x \, dx$ by writing as $\int \sin x(1 - \cos^2 x) dx$, and to find $\int x^2 e^x dx$, by using integration by parts, become increasingly unwieldy when applied to $\int \sin^n x \, dx$ and $\int x^n e^x dx$, as n increases. In such cases it may be possible, usually by using integration by parts, to relate the given integral in n to a similar integral in $n - 1$ (or $n - 2$, or lower); this relation is called a **reduction formula**. By repeated application of the reduction formula the given integral may be reduced to a form where only simple integration is required.

Example 20

Given that $I_n = \int x^n e^x dx$, where n is a positive integer,

a show that $I_n = x^n e^x - nI_{n-1}$, $n \geqslant 1$.

b Find $\int x^4 e^x dx$.

> The symbol I_n is introduced to avoid the repeated use of integral signs.

a Let
$$u = x^n \qquad \frac{dv}{dx} = e^x$$

so that
$$\frac{du}{dx} = nx^{n-1} \qquad v = e^x$$

Then $I_n = \int x^n e^x dx = x^n e^x - \int nx^{n-1}e^x dx$

$$= x^n e^x - n\int x^{n-1}e^x dx$$

so $\qquad I_n = x^n e^x - nI_{n-1}$

> Using the integration by parts formula
> $$\int u\frac{dv}{dx}dx = uv - \int v\frac{du}{dx}dx.$$

> Replacing n by $n-1$ in $I_n = \int x^n e^x dx$, gives $I_{n-1} = \int x^{n-1}e^x dx$.
> This is the reduction formula for I_n.

b $\int x^4 e^x dx = I_4$

Using the reduction formula

$$I_4 = x^4 e^x - 4I_3$$

$$= x^4 e^x - 4(x^3 e^x - 3I_2)$$

$$= x^4 e^x - 4x^3 e^x + 12(x^2 e^x - 2I_1)$$

$$= x^4 e^x - 4x^3 e^x + 12x^2 e^x - 24(xe^x - I_0)$$

$$= x^4 e^x - 4x^3 e^x + 12x^2 e^x - 24xe^x + 24\int e^x dx$$

$$= x^4 e^x - 4x^3 e^x + 12x^2 e^x - 24xe^x + 24e^x + C$$

> As the formula reduces n by 1 each time it is applied, I_n can be written, after sufficient steps, in terms of I_0, i.e. $\int e^x dx$, a standard integral.

> Using $I_n = x^n e^x - nI_{n-1}$ with $n = 3$.

> Using $I_n = x^n e^x - nI_{n-1}$ with $n = 2$.

> Using $I_n = x^n e^x - nI_{n-1}$ with $n = 1$.

> As $I_0 = \int e^x dx$.

Sometimes, after using integration by parts, you may need to use an algebraic or trigonometric identity to produce the reduction formula.

Example 21

Show that, if $I_n = \int_0^1 x^n\sqrt{1-x}\,dx$, then $I_n = \dfrac{2n}{2n+3}I_{n-1}$, $n \geqslant 1$.

Let $\qquad u = x^n \qquad \dfrac{dv}{dx} = \sqrt{1-x}$

So $\qquad \dfrac{du}{dx} = nx^{n-1} \qquad v = -\frac{2}{3}(1-x)^{\frac{3}{2}}$

Then integrating by parts

$$I_n = \left[-\frac{2}{3}x^n(1-x)^{\frac{3}{2}}\right]_0^1 + \int_0^1 \frac{2}{3}nx^{n-1}(1-x)^{\frac{3}{2}}dx$$

$$= [0 - 0] + \int_0^1 \frac{2}{3}nx^{n-1}(1-x)^{\frac{3}{2}}dx$$

Using the identity $(1-x)^{\frac{3}{2}} \equiv (1-x)\sqrt{1-x}$

> If $n \geqslant 1$, $[\ldots\ldots]_0^1 = 0$.

> You need to write this so that the term $\sqrt{1-x}$ appears.

$$I_n = \frac{2n}{3}\int_0^1 x^{n-1}(1-x)\sqrt{1-x}\,dx$$

$$= \frac{2n}{3}\int_0^1 x^{n-1}\sqrt{1-x}\,dx - \frac{2n}{3}\int_0^1 x^n\sqrt{1-x}\,dx$$

$$= \frac{2n}{3}I_{n-1} - \frac{2n}{3}I_n$$

So $(3 + 2n)I_n = 2nI_{n-1}$

$$I_n = \frac{2n}{2n+3}I_{n-1}$$

Collecting up terms in I_n.

Example 22

Given that $I_n = \int_0^{\frac{\pi}{2}} \sin^n x\,dx$, $n \geqslant 0$,

a derive the reduction formula $nI_n = (n-1)I_{n-2}$, $n \geqslant 2$.

b Deduce the values of **i** $\int_0^{\frac{\pi}{2}} \sin^5 x\,dx$ **ii** $\int_0^{\frac{\pi}{2}} \sin^6 x\,dx$.

a First write $\sin^n x$ as $\sin^{n-1}x \sin x$

To find $\int \cos^n x\,dx$ you would write $\cos^n x$ as $\cos^{n-1}x\cos x$.

Using integration by parts on $\int \sin^{n-1}x \sin x\,dx$

Let $u = \sin^{n-1}x$ $\qquad \frac{dv}{dx} = \sin x$

$\Rightarrow \frac{du}{dx} = (n-1)\sin^{n-2}x\cos x$ $\qquad v = -\cos x$

Take care with signs.

$$\text{So } I_n = \int_0^{\frac{\pi}{2}} \sin^n x\,dx = \left[-\sin^{n-1}x\cos x\right]_0^{\frac{\pi}{2}} + \int_0^{\frac{\pi}{2}}(n-1)\sin^{n-2}x\cos^2 x\,dx$$

$$= [0 - 0] + (n-1)\int_0^{\frac{\pi}{2}} \sin^{n-2}x(1-\sin^2 x)dx$$

$$= (n-1)\int_0^{\frac{\pi}{2}} \sin^{n-2}x\,dx - (n-1)\int_0^{\frac{\pi}{2}} \sin^n x\,dx$$

This is not in a convenient form but you can use $\sin^2 x + \cos^2 x = 1$ to express as powers of $\sin x$ only.

$$I_n = (n-1)I_{n-2} - (n-1)I_n$$

$\Rightarrow \quad I_n + (n-1)I_n = (n-1)I_{n-2}$

Collect up terms in I_n and I_{n-2}.

So $\qquad nI_n = (n-1)I_{n-2}$, $n \geqslant 2$ **is the reduction formula.**

As $I_{n-2} = \left(\frac{n-3}{n-2}\right)I_{n-4}$, $n \geqslant 4$, $I_n = \left(\frac{n-1}{n}\right)\left(\frac{n-3}{n-2}\right)I_{n-4}$, $= \left(\frac{n-1}{n}\right)\left(\frac{n-3}{n-2}\right)\left(\frac{n-5}{n-4}\right)I_{n-6}$

and so on.

i **If n is odd,**

$$I_n = \left(\frac{n-1}{n}\right)\left(\frac{n-3}{n-2}\right)\cdots\left(\frac{2}{3}\right)I_1$$

$$= \left(\frac{n-1}{n}\right)\left(\frac{n-3}{n-2}\right)\cdots\left(\frac{2}{3}\right)\int_0^{\frac{\pi}{2}} \sin x\,dx$$

$$= \left(\frac{n-1}{n}\right)\left(\frac{n-3}{n-2}\right)\cdots\left(\frac{2}{3}\right)(1) \quad ①$$

ii **If n is even,**

$$I_n = \left(\frac{n-1}{n}\right)\left(\frac{n-3}{n-2}\right)\cdots\left(\frac{3}{4}\right)\left(\frac{1}{2}\right)I_0$$

$$= \left(\frac{n-1}{n}\right)\left(\frac{n-3}{n-2}\right)\cdots\left(\frac{3}{4}\right)\left(\frac{1}{2}\right)\int_0^{\frac{\pi}{2}} 1\,dx$$

$$= \left(\frac{n-1}{n}\right)\left(\frac{n-3}{n-2}\right)\cdots\left(\frac{3}{4}\right)\left(\frac{1}{2}\right)\left(\frac{\pi}{2}\right) \quad ②$$

b **i** $\int_0^{\frac{\pi}{2}} \sin^5 x \, dx = I_5.$

$= \left(\frac{4}{5}\right)\left(\frac{2}{3}\right)(1) = \frac{8}{15}$ — Using ① with $n = 5$.

ii $\int_0^{\frac{\pi}{2}} \sin^6 x \, dx = I_6.$

$= \left(\frac{5}{6}\right)\left(\frac{3}{4}\right)\left(\frac{1}{2}\right)\left(\frac{\pi}{2}\right) = \frac{5\pi}{32}$ — Using ② with $n = 6$.

It is not always necessary to use integration by parts to produce a reduction formula.

Example 23

$I_n = \int \tan^n x \, dx$, where n is a positive integer.

By writing $\tan^n x$ as $\tan^{n-2} x \tan^2 x$, and using $1 + \tan^2 x \equiv \sec^2 x$, establish the reduction formula

$$I_n = \frac{1}{n-1}\tan^{n-1} x - I_{n-2}, \; n \geqslant 2.$$

$$I_n = \int \tan^{n-2} x \tan^2 x \, dx = \int \tan^{n-2} x(\sec^2 x - 1)dx$$

$$= \int \tan^{n-2} x \sec^2 x \, dx - \int \tan^{n-2} x \, dx$$

So $I_n = \frac{1}{n-1}\tan^{n-1} x - I_{n-2}$

Use $\int [f(x)]^n f'(x) dx = \frac{[f(x)]^{n+1}}{n+1} + C.$

Exercise 4F

1 Given that $I_n = \int x^n e^{\frac{x}{2}} dx$,

a show that $I_n = 2x^n e^{\frac{x}{2}} - 2nI_{n-1}, \; n \geqslant 1.$

b Hence find $\int x^3 e^{\frac{x}{2}} dx$.

2 Given that $I_n = \int_1^e x(\ln x)^n dx, \; n \in N,$

a show that $I_n = \frac{e^2}{2} - \frac{n}{2}I_{n-1}, \; n \in N.$

b Hence show that $\int_1^e x(\ln x)^4 dx = \frac{e^2 - 3}{4}.$

3 In Example 21, you saw that, if $I_n = \int_0^1 x^n \sqrt{1-x} \, dx$, then $I_n = \frac{2n}{2n+3}I_{n-1}, \; n \geqslant 1.$

Use this reduction formula to evaluate $\int_0^1 (x+1)(x+2)\sqrt{1-x} \, dx.$

4 Given that $I_n = \int x^n e^{-x}\,dx$, where n is a positive integer,

a show that $I_n = -x^n e^{-x} + nI_{n-1}$, $n \geqslant 1$.

b Find $\int x^3 e^{-x} dx$.

c Evaluate $\int_0^1 x^4 e^{-x} dx$, giving your answer in terms of e.

5 $I_n = \int \tanh^n x\,dx$,

a By writing $\tanh^n x = \tanh^{n-2} x \tanh^2 x$ show that for $n \geqslant 2$,

$$I_n = I_{n-2} - \frac{1}{n-1}\tanh^{n-1} x.$$

b Find $\int \tanh^5 x\,dx$.

c Show that $\int_0^{\ln 2} \tanh^4 x\,dx = \ln 2 - \frac{84}{125}$.

6 Given that $\int \tan^n x\,dx = \frac{1}{n-1}\tan^{n-1} x - \int \tan^{n-2} x\,dx$ (derived in Example 23)

a find $\int \tan^4 x\,dx$.

b Evaluate $\int_0^{\frac{\pi}{4}} \tan^5 x\,dx$.

c Show that $\int_0^{\frac{\pi}{3}} \tan^6 x\,dx = \frac{9\sqrt{3}}{5} - \frac{\pi}{3}$.

7 Given that $I_n = \int_1^a (\ln x)^n dx$, where $a > 1$ is a constant,

a show that, for $n \geqslant 1$, $I_n = a(\ln a)^n - nI_{n-1}$.

b Find the exact value of $\int_1^2 (\ln x)^3 dx$.

c Show that $\int_1^e (\ln x)^6 dx = 5(53e - 144)$.

8 Using the results given in Example 22, evaluate

a $\int_0^{\frac{\pi}{2}} \sin^7 x\,dx$

b $\int_0^{\frac{\pi}{2}} \sin^2 x \cos^4 x\,dx$

c $\int_0^1 x^5\sqrt{1 - x^2}\,dx$, using the substitution $x = \sin\theta$

d $\int_0^{\frac{\pi}{6}} \sin^8 3t\,dt$, using a suitable substitution.

9 Given that $I_n = \int \frac{\sin^{2n} x}{\cos x}\,dx$,

a write down a similar expression for I_{n+1} and hence show that $I_n - I_{n+1} = \frac{\sin^{2n+1} x}{2n+1}$.

b Find $\int \frac{\sin^4 x}{\cos x}\,dx$ and hence show that $\int_0^{\frac{\pi}{4}} \frac{\sin^4 x}{\cos x}\,dx = \ln(1 + \sqrt{2}) - \frac{7\sqrt{2}}{12}$.

10 **a** Given that $I_n = \int_0^1 x(1 - x^3)^n dx$, show that $I_n = \frac{3n}{3n+2} I_{n-1}$.

b Use your reduction formula to evaluate I_4.

Hint: After integrating by parts, write x^4 as $x\{1 - (1 - x^3)\}$.

11 Given that $I_n = \int_0^a (a^2 - x^2)^n \, dx$, where a is a positive constant,

a show that, for $n > 0$, $I_n = \dfrac{2na^2}{2n+1} I_{n-1}$.

b Use the reduction formula to evaluate

i $\int_0^1 (1 - x^2)^4 \, dx$ **ii** $\int_0^3 (9 - x^2)^3 \, dx$ **iii** $\int_0^2 \sqrt{4 - x^2} \, dx$.

c Check your answer to part **b iii** by using another method.

12 Given that $I_n = \int_0^4 x^n \sqrt{4 - x} \, dx$,

a establish the reduction formula $I_n = \dfrac{8n}{2n+3} I_{n-1}$, $n \geqslant 1$.

b Evaluate $\int_0^4 x^3 \sqrt{4 - x}$, giving your answer correct to 3 significant figures.

13 Given that $I_n = \int \cos^n x \, dx$,

a establish, for $n \geqslant 2$, the reduction formula $nI_n = \cos^{n-1} x \sin x + (n - 1)I_{n-2}$.

Defining $J_n = \int_0^{2\pi} \cos^n x \, dx$,

b write down a reduction formula relating J_n and J_{n-2}, for $n \geqslant 2$.

c Hence evaluate **i** J_4 **ii** J_8.

d Show that if n is odd, J_n is always equal to zero.

14 Given $I_n = \int_0^1 x^n \sqrt{(1 - x^2)} \, dx$, $n \geqslant 0$,

a show that $(n + 2)I_n = (n - 1)I_{n-2}$, $n \geqslant 2$.

b Hence evaluate $\int_0^1 x^7 \sqrt{(1 - x^2)} \, dx$.

Hint: Write $x^n\sqrt{1 - x^2}$ as $x^{n-1}\{x\sqrt{1 - x^2}\}$ before integrating by parts.

15 Given $I_n = \int x^n \cosh x \, dx$

a show that for $n \geqslant 2$, $I_n = x^n \sinh x - nx^{n-1} \cosh x + n(n - 1)I_{n-2}$

b Find $\int x^4 \cosh x \, dx$.

c Evaluate $\int_0^1 x^3 \cosh x \, dx$, giving your answer in terms of e.

16 Given that $I_n = \int \dfrac{\sin nx}{\sin x} \, dx$, $n > 0$,

a write down a similar expression for I_{n-2}, and hence show that

$$I_n - I_{n-2} = \frac{2\sin(n-1)x}{n-1}.$$

b Find **i** $\int \dfrac{\sin 4x}{\sin x} \, dx$ **ii** the exact value of $\int_{\frac{\pi}{6}}^{\frac{\pi}{3}} \dfrac{\sin 5x}{\sin x} \, dx$.

17 Given that $I_n = \int \sinh^n x \, dx$, $n \in N$,

a derive the reduction formula $nI_n = \sinh^{n-1} x \cosh x - (n - 1)I_{n-2}$, $n \geqslant 2$.

b Hence **i** evaluate $\int_0^{\ln 3} \sinh^5 x \, dx$,

ii show that $\int_0^{\text{arsinh} 1} \sinh^4 x \, dx = \frac{1}{8}\{3\ln(1 + \sqrt{2}) - \sqrt{2}\}$.

4.7 You can use integration to find the length of an arc of a curve.

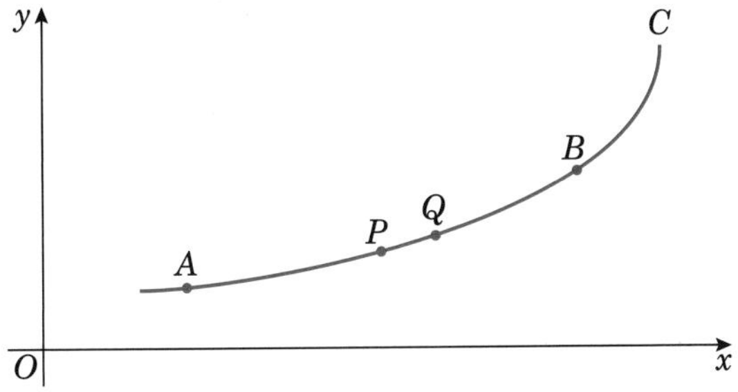

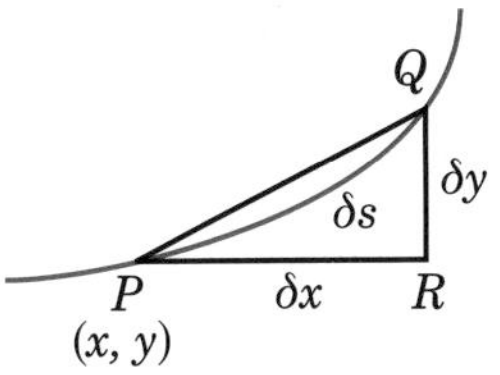

Suppose that $P(x, y)$ is any point on the curve C, whose equation is $y = \mathrm{f}(x)$, and that the length of the arc from a fixed point on C to P is denoted by s. Let $Q(x + \delta x, y + \delta y)$ be a neighbouring point on C, and the length of the arc PQ be δs.

As P and Q are close together, $\delta s \approx$ the length of the chord PQ

See triangle PQR.

$$\text{so } (\delta s)^2 \approx (\delta x)^2 + (\delta y)^2 \quad ①$$

Remember this; it is the key to deriving all the formulae.

$$\Rightarrow \left(\frac{\delta s}{\delta x}\right)^2 \approx 1 + \left(\frac{\delta y}{\delta x}\right)^2$$

As $\delta x \to 0$ (Q approaches P), $\dfrac{\delta s}{\delta x} \to \dfrac{\mathrm{d}s}{\mathrm{d}x}$ and $\dfrac{\delta y}{\delta x} \to \dfrac{\mathrm{d}y}{\mathrm{d}x}$

so, in the limit $\quad \left(\dfrac{\mathrm{d}s}{\mathrm{d}x}\right)^2 = 1 + \left(\dfrac{\mathrm{d}y}{\mathrm{d}x}\right)^2$

and $\quad \dfrac{\mathrm{d}s}{\mathrm{d}x} = \sqrt{1 + \left(\dfrac{\mathrm{d}y}{\mathrm{d}x}\right)^2}$

The positive square root is taken so that s increases as x increases.

Integrating this with respect to x gives an expression for s, the arc length.
So, if s is the length of the arc joining $A(x_A, y_A)$ and $B(x_B, y_B)$,

■ $$s = \int_{x_A}^{x_B} \sqrt{1 + \left(\frac{\mathrm{d}y}{\mathrm{d}x}\right)^2}\,\mathrm{d}x \qquad (*)$$

The curve must be continuous between the end points of the arc. Then, providing the integration is possible, the arc length can be evaluated.

Alternatively, dividing ① throughout by $(\delta y)^2$ and proceeding to the limit, gives

$$\left(\frac{\mathrm{d}s}{\mathrm{d}y}\right)^2 = 1 + \left(\frac{\mathrm{d}x}{\mathrm{d}y}\right)^2.$$

Integrating with respect to y gives

■ $$s = \int_{y_A}^{y_B} \sqrt{1 + \left(\frac{\mathrm{d}x}{\mathrm{d}y}\right)^2}\,\mathrm{d}y$$

Use whichever formula is convenient.

If the equation of the curve is given parametrically, i.e. in the form $x = \mathrm{f}(t)$, $y = g(t)$, then dividing ① by $(\delta t)^2$ and proceeding to the limit, gives

$$\left(\frac{\mathrm{d}s}{\mathrm{d}t}\right)^2 = \left(\frac{\mathrm{d}x}{\mathrm{d}t}\right)^2 + \left(\frac{\mathrm{d}y}{\mathrm{d}t}\right)^2.$$

Given that the parameters at A and B are t_A and t_B respectively, then integrating with respect to t,

■ $$s = \int_{t_A}^{t_B} \sqrt{\left(\frac{\mathrm{d}x}{\mathrm{d}t}\right)^2 + \left(\frac{\mathrm{d}y}{\mathrm{d}t}\right)^2}\,\mathrm{d}t \qquad (*)$$

Example 24

Find the exact length of the arc on the parabola with equation $y = \frac{1}{2}x^2$, from the origin to the point $P(4, 8)$.

$y = \frac{1}{2}x^2 \Rightarrow \frac{dy}{dx} = x$

First find $\frac{dy}{dx}$.

Using $s = \int_{x_A}^{x_B} \sqrt{1 + \left(\frac{dy}{dx}\right)^2}\, dx$,

Choose the appropriate formula.

length of arc $OP = \int_0^4 \sqrt{1 + x^2}\, dx$

$x_A = 0$, $x_B = 4$.

Using the substitution $x = \sinh u$,
so that $dx = \cosh u\, du$,

Choose the appropriate method of integration.

$$\begin{aligned}
\text{arc length} &= \int_0^{\text{arsinh}\,4} \sqrt{1 + \sinh^2 u}\, \cosh u\, du \\
&= \int_0^{\text{arsinh}\,4} \cosh^2 u\, du \\
&= \int_0^{\text{arsinh}\,4} \frac{(1 + \cosh 2u)}{2}\, du \\
&= \frac{1}{2}\left[u + \frac{1}{2}\sinh 2u\right]_0^{\text{arsinh}\,4} \\
&= \frac{1}{2}\left[u + \sinh u \cosh u\right]_0^{\text{arsinh}\,4} \\
&= \frac{1}{2}\text{arsinh}\,4 + \frac{1}{2}(4\sqrt{1 + 16}) \\
&= \frac{1}{2}\text{arsinh}\,4 + 2\sqrt{17} \\
&= \frac{1}{2}\ln(4 + \sqrt{17}) + 2\sqrt{17}
\end{aligned}$$

Use $\cosh u = \sqrt{1 + \sinh^2 u}$ and $\sinh u = 4$.

Use $\text{arsinh}\, x = \ln\{x + \sqrt{(1 + x^2)}\}$.

Example 25

The curve C has parametric equations

$x = t + \frac{1}{t}$, $y = 2\ln t$, $t > 0$

Find the length of the arc between points A and B with $t = 1$ and $t = 2$ respectively.

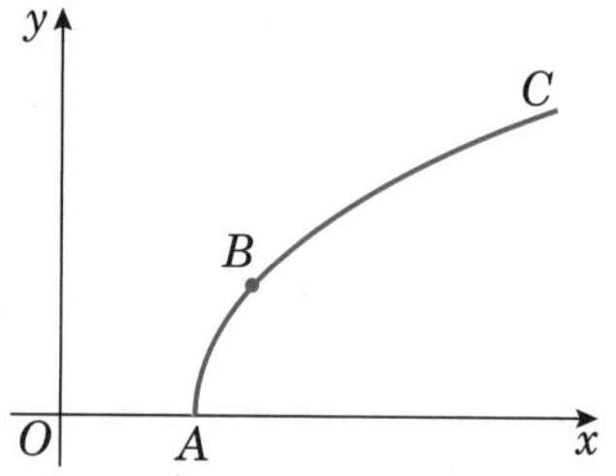

$x = t + \frac{1}{t}$, $y = 2\ln t$, $t > 0$.

$\frac{dx}{dt} = 1 - \frac{1}{t^2}$, $\frac{dy}{dt} = \frac{2}{t}$

So $\left(\frac{dx}{dt}\right)^2 + \left(\frac{dy}{dt}\right)^2 = \left\{\left(1 - \frac{2}{t^2} + \frac{1}{t^4}\right) + \left(\frac{4}{t^2}\right)\right\} = 1 + \frac{2}{t^2} + \frac{1}{t^4} = \left(1 + \frac{1}{t^2}\right)^2$

$$\text{Arc length} = \int_1^2 \sqrt{\left(1 + \frac{1}{t^2}\right)^2}\, dt$$
$$= \int_1^2 \left(1 + \frac{1}{t^2}\right) dt$$
$$= \left[t - \frac{1}{t}\right]_1^2$$
$$= 1.5$$

Use $s = \int_{t_A}^{t_B} \left\{\left(\frac{dx}{dt}\right)^2 + \left(\frac{dy}{dt}\right)^2\right\} dt$.

Exercise 4G

1 Find the length of the arc of the curve with equation $y = \frac{1}{3}x^{\frac{3}{2}}$, from the origin to the point with x-coordinate 12.

2 The curve C has equation $y = \ln\cos x$. Find the length of the arc of C between the points with x-coordinates 0 and $\frac{\pi}{3}$.

3 Find the length of the arc on the catenary, with equation $y = 2\cosh\left(\frac{x}{2}\right)$, between the points with x-coordinates 0 and $\ln 4$.

4 Find the length of the arc of the curve with equation $y^2 = \frac{4}{9}x^3$, from the origin to the point $(3, 2\sqrt{3})$.

5 The curve C has equation $y = \frac{1}{2}\sinh^2 2x$. Find the length of the arc on C from the origin to the point whose x-coordinate is 1, giving your answer to 3 significant figures.

6 The curve C has equation $y = \frac{1}{4}(2x^2 - \ln x)$, $x > 0$. The points A and B on C have x-coordinates 1 and 2 respectively. Show that the length of the arc from A to B is $\frac{1}{4}(6 + \ln 2)$.

7 Find the length of the arc on the curve $y = 2\text{arcosh}\left(\frac{x}{2}\right)$, from the point at which the curve crosses the x-axis to the point with x-coordinate $\frac{5}{2}$. Compare your answer with that in Example 25 and explain the relationship.

8 The line $y = 4$ intersects the parabola with equation $y = x^2$ at the points A and B. Find the length of the arc of the parabola from A to B.

9 The circle C has parametric equations $x = r\cos\theta$, $y = r\sin\theta$. Use the formula for arc length on page 79 to show that the length of the circumference is $2\pi r$.

10 The diagram shows the astroid, with parametric equations $x = 2a\cos^3 t$, $y = 2a\sin^3 t$, $0 \leqslant t < 2\pi$.

Find the length of the arc of the curve AB, and hence find the total length of the curve.

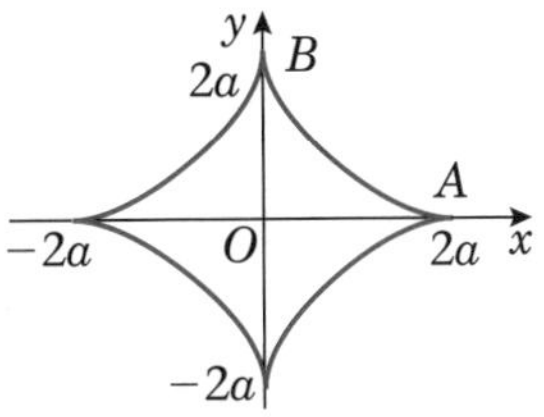

11 Calculate the length of the arc on the curve with parametric equations $x = \tanh u$, $y = \operatorname{sech} u$, between the points with parameters $u = 0$ and $u = 1$.

12 The cycloid has parametric equations $x = a(\theta + \sin\theta)$, $y = a(1 - \cos\theta)$. Find the length of the arc from $\theta = 0$ to $\theta = \pi$.

13 Show that the length of the arc, between the points with parameters $t = 0$ and $t = \frac{\pi}{3}$ on the curve defined by the equations $x = t + \sin t$, $y = 1 - \cos t$, is 2.

14 Find the length of the arc of the curve given by the equations $x = e^t \cos t$, $y = e^t \sin t$, between the points with parameters $t = 0$ and $t = \frac{\pi}{4}$.

15 **a** Denoting the length of one complete wave of the sine curve with equation $y = \sqrt{3}\sin x$ by L, show that $L = 4\int_0^{\frac{\pi}{2}} \sqrt{1 + 3\cos^2 x}\, dx$.

b An ellipse has parametric equations $x = \cos t$, $y = 2\sin t$. Show that the length of its circumference is equal to that of the wave in **a**.

4.8 You can use integration to find the area of a surface of revolution.

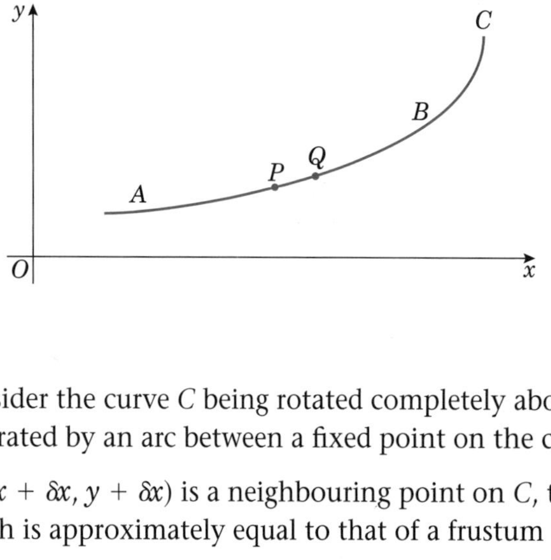

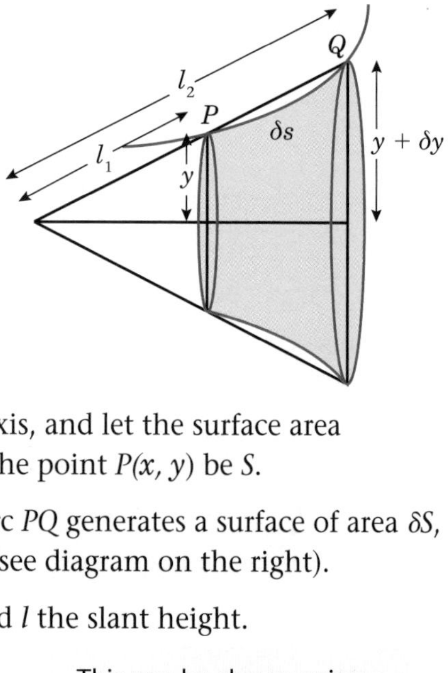

Consider the curve C being rotated completely about the x-axis, and let the surface area generated by an arc between a fixed point on the curve and the point $P(x, y)$ be S.

If $Q(x + \delta x, y + \delta x)$ is a neighbouring point on C, then the arc PQ generates a surface of area δS, which is approximately equal to that of a frustum of a cone (see diagram on the right).

The surface area of a cone is $\pi r l$, where r is the base radius and l the slant height.

So the area of the frustum $= \pi(y + \delta y)l_2 - \pi y l_1$ (see diagram)

$= \pi(2y + \delta y)(l_2 - l_1)$

This can be shown using $\frac{l_2}{l_1} = \frac{y + \delta y}{y}$, (similar triangles) $\Rightarrow \frac{l_2 + l_1}{l_1} = \frac{2y + \delta y}{y}$.

As P and Q are close together, $\delta s \approx$ chord $PQ = l_2 - l_1$

so $\delta S \approx \pi(2y + \delta y)\delta s$

and $\frac{\delta S}{\delta x} \approx \pi(2y + \delta y)\frac{\delta s}{\delta x}$

Dividing by δx.

As Q approaches P, $\delta x \to 0$, $\delta y \to 0$, $\frac{\delta s}{\delta x} \to \frac{ds}{dx}$ and $\frac{\delta S}{\delta x} \to \frac{dS}{dx}$

so in the limit $\frac{dS}{dx} = 2\pi y \frac{ds}{dx}$

S can be found by integrating w.r.t. x.

■ **The surface area S, generated when an arc is rotated about the x-axis, is**

$S = \int 2\pi y \frac{ds}{dx} dx = \int 2\pi y \, ds.$ (*)

Similarly if the curve is rotated about the y-axis, then $S = \int 2\pi x \, ds.$

Using results derived in Section 4.7, these formulae for S can be rewritten to apply to the appropriate coordinate system.

For rotation of a curve about the x-axis:

In Cartesian form $\quad S = 2\pi \int_{x_A}^{x_B} y\sqrt{1 + \left(\frac{dy}{dx}\right)^2} dx \quad$ since $S = \int 2\pi y \, ds = \int 2\pi y \frac{ds}{dx} dx$

In parametric form $\quad S = 2\pi \int_{t_A}^{t_B} y\sqrt{\left(\frac{dx}{dt}\right)^2 + \left(\frac{dy}{dt}\right)^2} dt \quad$ (*) since $S = \int 2\pi y \, ds = \int 2\pi y \frac{ds}{dt} dt$

For rotation of a curve about the y-axis:

In Cartesian form $\quad S = 2\pi \int_{y_A}^{y_B} x\sqrt{1 + \left(\frac{dx}{dy}\right)^2} dy \quad$ $S = \int 2\pi x \, ds = \int 2\pi x \frac{ds}{dy} dy$

or $\quad S = 2\pi \int_{x_A}^{x_B} x\sqrt{1 + \left(\frac{dy}{dx}\right)^2} dx \quad$ $S = \int 2\pi x \, ds = \int 2\pi x \frac{ds}{dx} dx$

In parametric form $\quad S = 2\pi \int_{t_A}^{t_B} x\sqrt{\left(\frac{dx}{dt}\right)^2 + \left(\frac{dy}{dt}\right)^2} dt$

This form is often the more convenient.

Example 26

The curve C has equation $y = \frac{1}{3}\sqrt{x}(3 - x)$. The arc of the curve between the points with x-coordinates 1 and 3 is completely rotated about the x-axis. Find the area of the surface generated.

$y = x^{\frac{1}{2}} - \frac{1}{3}x^{\frac{3}{2}} \Rightarrow \frac{dy}{dx} = \frac{1}{2}(x^{-\frac{1}{2}} - x^{\frac{1}{2}})$

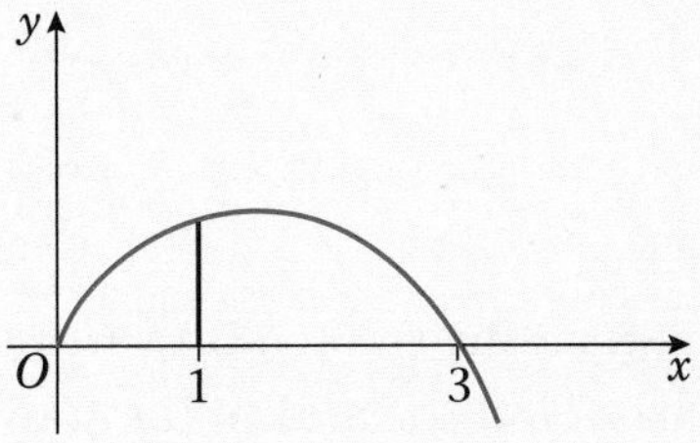

So $1 + \left(\frac{dy}{dx}\right)^2 = 1 + \frac{1}{4}x^{-1} - \frac{1}{2} + \frac{1}{4}x$

$= \frac{1}{4}x^{-1} + \frac{1}{2} + \frac{1}{4}x$

$= \frac{1}{4}(x^{-\frac{1}{2}} + x^{\frac{1}{2}})^2$

Area of the surface generated $= \int_1^3 2\pi y\sqrt{1 + \left(\frac{dy}{dx}\right)^2} dx$

$= 2\pi \int_1^3 \left(x^{\frac{1}{2}} - \frac{1}{3}x^{\frac{3}{2}}\right)\frac{1}{2}\left(x^{-\frac{1}{2}} + x^{\frac{1}{2}}\right)dx$

$= \pi \int_1^3 \left(1 + \frac{2}{3}x - \frac{1}{3}x^2\right)dx$

$= \pi\left[x + \frac{1}{3}x^2 - \frac{1}{9}x^3\right]_1^3$

$= 3\pi - \frac{11}{9}\pi$

$= \frac{16}{9}\pi$

Example 27

The arc of the curve with equation $y = \cosh x$, from the point (0, 1) to $(\ln 2, \frac{5}{4})$ is rotated completely about the y-axis. Find the area of the surface generated.

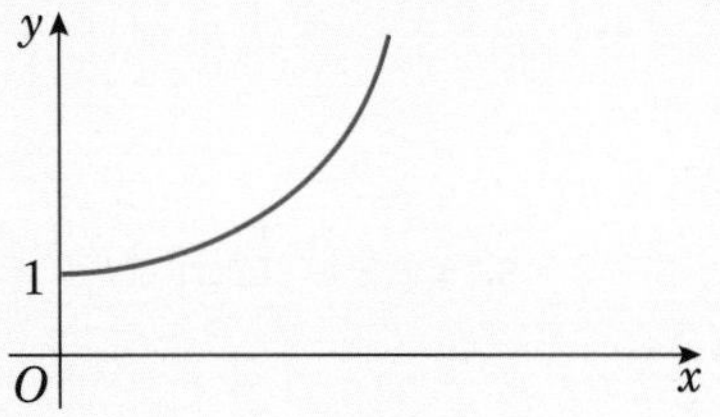

$$y = \cosh x \Rightarrow \frac{dy}{dx} = \sinh x$$

Using $\int 2\pi x \, ds$ in the form $\int 2\pi x \frac{ds}{dx} dx = \int_{x_1}^{x_2} 2\pi x \sqrt{1 + \left(\frac{dy}{dx}\right)^2} \, dx$

$$\text{area of the surface generated} = 2\pi \int_0^{\ln 2} x\sqrt{1 + \sinh^2 x} \, dx$$

$$= 2\pi \int_0^{\ln 2} x \cosh x \, dx$$

$$= 2\pi \left[x \sinh x - \int \sinh x \, dx \right]_0^{\ln 2}$$

Use integration by parts with $u = x$ and $\frac{dv}{dx} = \cosh x$.

$$= 2\pi [x \sinh x - \cosh x]_0^{\ln 2}$$

$$= 2\pi [\ln 2 \sinh(\ln 2) - \cosh(\ln 2) + 1]$$

$$= 2\pi [\ln 2(\tfrac{3}{4}) - (\tfrac{5}{4}) + 1]$$

$$= \frac{\pi}{2}(3 \ln 2 - 1)$$

Example 28

The curve with parametric equations $x = t - \sin t$, $y = 1 - \cos t$, from $t = 0$ to $t = 2\pi$, is rotated through 360° about the x-axis. Find the area of the surface generated.

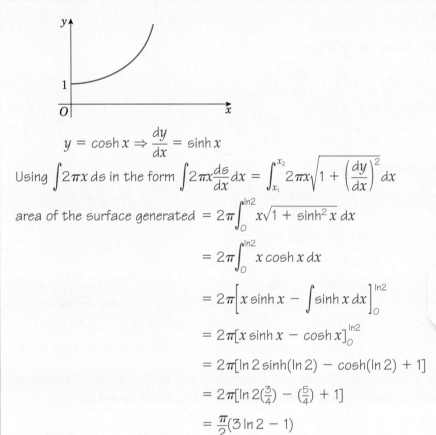

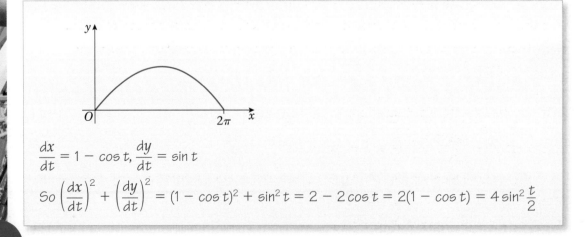

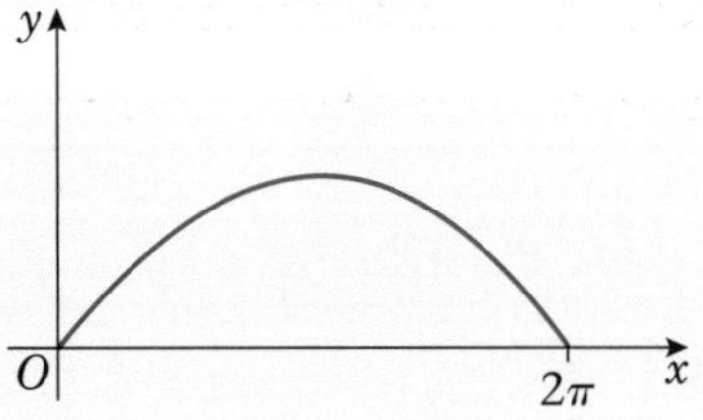

$$\frac{dx}{dt} = 1 - \cos t, \quad \frac{dy}{dt} = \sin t$$

So $\left(\frac{dx}{dt}\right)^2 + \left(\frac{dy}{dt}\right)^2 = (1 - \cos t)^2 + \sin^2 t = 2 - 2\cos t = 2(1 - \cos t) = 4 \sin^2 \frac{t}{2}$

$$\text{Area of the surface generated} = \int_0^{2\pi} 2\pi y\sqrt{\left(\frac{dx}{dt}\right)^2 + \left(\frac{dy}{dt}\right)^2}\,dt$$

$$= 2\pi\int_0^{2\pi} (1 - \cos t)2\sin\frac{t}{2}\,dt$$

$$= 2\pi\int_0^{2\pi} 4\sin^3\frac{t}{2}\,dt$$

$$= 8\pi\int_0^{2\pi} \sin^2\frac{t}{2}\sin\frac{t}{2}\,dt$$

$$= 8\pi\int_0^{2\pi} \left(1 - \cos^2\frac{t}{2}\right)\sin\frac{t}{2}\,dt$$

$$= 8\pi\left[-2\cos\frac{t}{2} + \tfrac{2}{3}\cos^3\frac{t}{2}\right]_0^{2\pi}$$

$$= 8\pi\left[\left(2 - \tfrac{2}{3}\right) - \left(-2 + \tfrac{2}{3}\right)\right]$$

$$= \frac{64}{3}\pi$$

Exercise 4H

1 **a** The section of the line $y = \frac{3}{4}x$ between points with x-coordinates 4 and 8 is rotated completely about the x-axis. Use integration to find the area of the surface generated.

b The same section of line is rotated completely about the y-axis. Show that the area of the surface generated is 60π.

2 The arc of the curve $y = x^3$, between the origin and the point (1, 1), is rotated through 4 right-angles about the x-axis. Find the area of the surface generated.

3 The arc of the curve $y = \frac{1}{2}x^2$, between the origin and the point (2, 2), is rotated through 4 right-angles about the y-axis. Find the area of the surface generated.

4 The points A and B, in the first quadrant, on the curve $y^2 = 16x$ have x-coordinates 5 and 12 respectively. Find, in terms π, the area of the surface generated when the arc AB is rotated completely about the x-axis.

5 The curve C has equation $y = \cosh x$. The arc s on C, has end points (0, 1) and (1, cosh 1).

a Find the area of the surface generated when s is rotated completely about the x-axis.

b Show that the area of the surface generated when s is rotated completely about the y-axis is $2\pi\left(\frac{e - 1}{e}\right)$.

6 The curve C has equation $y = \dfrac{1}{2x} + \dfrac{x^3}{6}$.

a Show that $\sqrt{1 + \left(\dfrac{dy}{dx}\right)^2} = \frac{1}{2}\left(x^2 + \dfrac{1}{x^2}\right)$.

The arc of the curve between points with x-coordinates 1 and 3 is rotated completely about the x-axis.

b Find the area of the surface generated.

7 The diagram shows part of the curve with equation $x^{\frac{2}{3}} + y^{\frac{2}{3}} = 4$. Find the area of the surface generated when this arc is rotated completely about the y-axis.

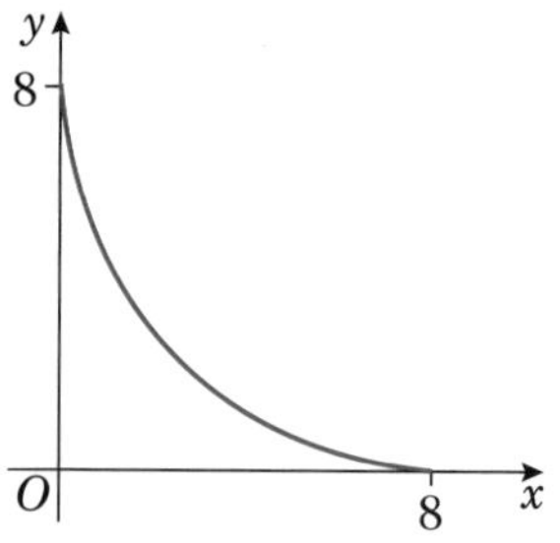

8 **a** The arc of the circle with equation $x^2 + y^2 = R^2$, between the points $(-R, 0)$ and $(R, 0)$, is rotated through 2π radians about the x-axis. Use integration to find the surface area of the sphere S formed.

b The axis of a cylinder C of radius R is the x-axis. Show that the areas of the surfaces of S and C, contained between planes with equations $x = a$ and $x = b$, where $a < b < R$, are equal.

9 The finite arc of the parabola with parametric equations $x = at^2$, $y = 2at$, where a is a positive constant, cut off by the line $x = 4a$, is rotated through 180° about the x-axis. Show that the area of the surface generated is $\frac{8}{3}\pi a^2(5\sqrt{5} - 1)$.

10 The arc, in the first quadrant, of the curve with parametric equations $x = \operatorname{sech} t$, $y = \tanh t$, between the points where $t = 0$ and $t = \ln 2$, is rotated completely about the x-axis. Show that the area of the surface generated is $\frac{2\pi}{5}$.

11 The arc of the curve given by $x = 3t^2$, $y = 2t^3$, from $t = 0$ and $t = 2$, is completely rotated about the y-axis.

a Show that the area of the surface generated can be expressed as $36\pi\int_0^2 t^3\sqrt{1 + t^2}\,dt$.

b Using integration by parts, find the exact value of this area.

12 The arc of the curve with parametric equations $x = t^2$, $y = t - \frac{1}{3}t^3$, between the points where $t = 0$ and $t = 1$, is rotated through 360° about the x-axis. Calculate the area of the surface generated.

13 The astroid C has parametric equations $x = a\cos^3 t$, $y = a\sin^3 t$, where a is a positive constant. The arc of C, between $t = \frac{\pi}{6}$ and $t = \frac{\pi}{2}$, is rotated through 2π radians about the x-axis. Find the area of the surface of revolution formed.

14 The part of the curve $y = e^x$, between $(0, 1)$ and $(\ln 2, 2)$, is rotated completely about the x-axis. Show that the area of the surface generated is $\pi(\operatorname{arsinh} 2 - \operatorname{arsinh} 1 + 2\sqrt{5} - \sqrt{2})$.

Mixed exercise 4I

1 Show that the volume of the solid generated when the finite region enclosed by the curve with equation $y = \tanh x$, the line $x = 1$ and the x-axis is rotated through 2π radians about the x-axis is $\frac{2\pi}{1 + e^2}$. E

2 $4x^2 + 4x + 17 \equiv (ax + b)^2 + c,\ a > 0.$

a Find the values of a, b and c.

b Find the exact value of $\displaystyle\int_{-0.5}^{1.5} \frac{1}{4x^2 + 4x + 17}\,dx$ **E**

3 Find the following.

a $\displaystyle\int \sinh 4x \cosh 6x\,dx$ **b** $\displaystyle\int \frac{\operatorname{sech} x \tanh x}{1 + 2\operatorname{sech} x}\,dx$ **c** $\displaystyle\int e^x \sinh x\,dx$

4

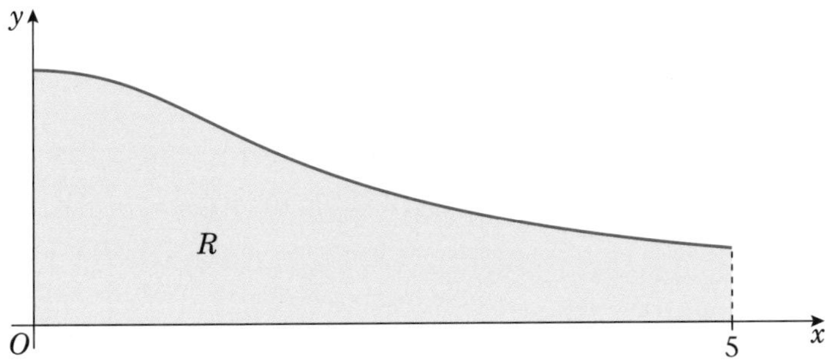

The diagram shows the cross-section R of an artificial ski slope. The slope is modelled by the curve with equation

$$y = \frac{10}{\sqrt{(4x^2 + 9)}},\quad 0 \leqslant x \leqslant 5.$$

Given that 1 unit on each axis represents 10 metres, use integration to calculate the area R. Show your method clearly and give your answer to 2 significant figures. **E**

5 **a** Find $\displaystyle\int \frac{1 + 2x}{1 + 4x^2}\,dx.$

b Find the exact value of

$$\int_0^{0.5} \frac{1 + 2x}{1 + 4x^2}\,dx.$$

6 A rope is hung from points two points on the same horizontal level. The curve formed by the rope is modelled by the equation

$$y = 4\cosh\left(\frac{x}{4}\right),\quad -20 \leqslant x \leqslant 20,$$

Find the length of the rope, giving your answer to 3 significant figures.

7 Show that $\displaystyle\int_0^{\frac{1}{2}} \operatorname{artanh} x\,dx = \tfrac{1}{4}\ln\left(\frac{a}{b}\right)$, where a and b are positive integers to be found.

8 Given that $I_n = \displaystyle\int_0^{\frac{\pi}{2}} x^n \cos x\,dx$,

a find the values of **i** I_0 and **ii** I_1,

b show, by using integration by parts twice, that $I_n = \left(\frac{\pi}{2}\right)^n - n(n-1)I_{n-2},\ n \geqslant 2.$

c Hence show that $\displaystyle\int_0^{\frac{\pi}{2}} x^3 \cos x\,dx = \tfrac{1}{8}(\pi^3 - 24\pi + 48).$

d Evaluate $\displaystyle\int_0^{\frac{\pi}{2}} x^4 \cos x\,dx$, leaving your answer in terms of π.

9 **a** Find $\int \frac{dx}{\sqrt{x^2 - 2x + 10}}$.

b Find $\int \frac{dx}{x^2 - 2x + 10}$.

c By using the substitution $x = \sin\theta$, show that $\int_0^{\frac{1}{2}} \frac{x^4}{\sqrt{(1 - x^2)}} = \frac{(4\pi - 7\sqrt{3})}{64}$

10 Given that $I_n = \int_0^1 x^n(1 - x)^{\frac{1}{3}}dx, \quad n \geqslant 0,$

a show that $I_n = \frac{3n}{3n + 4}I_{n-1}, \quad n \geqslant 1$

b Hence find the exact value of $\int_0^1 (1 + x)(1 - x)^{\frac{4}{3}}dx$.

11

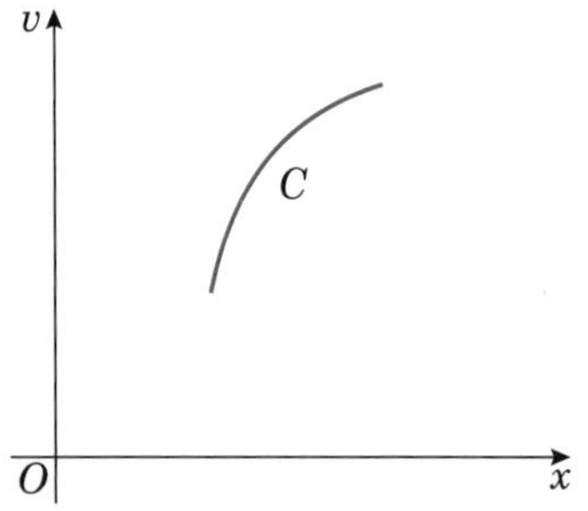

The curve C has parametric equations

$x = t - \ln t,$

$y = 4\sqrt{t}, \quad 1 \leqslant t \leqslant 4.$

a Show that the length of C is $3 + \ln 4$.

The curve is rotated through 2π radians about the x-axis.

b Find the exact area of the curved surface generated.

12

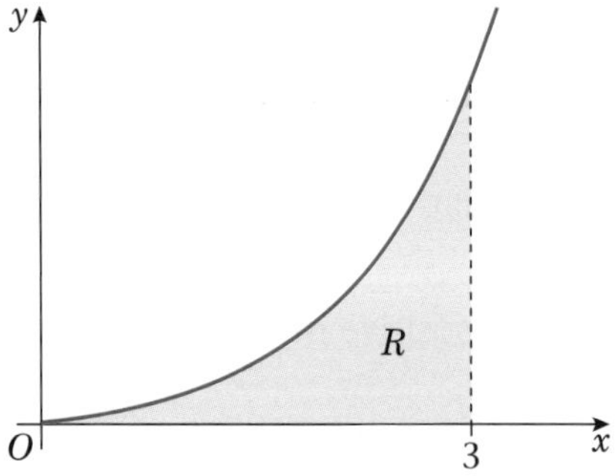

Above is a sketch of part of the curve with equation

$y = x^2 \operatorname{arsinh} x.$

The region R, shown shaded, is bounded by the curve, the x-axis and the line $x = 3$.

Show that the area of R is

$9\ln(3 + \sqrt{10}) - \frac{1}{9}(2 + 7\sqrt{10}).$

13 **a** Use the substitution $u = x^2$ to find $\int_0^1 \frac{x}{1 + x^4} dx$

b Find

i $\int \frac{1}{\sqrt{4x - x^2}} dx$ **ii** $\int \frac{4 - 2x}{\sqrt{4x - x^2}} dx.$

Hence, or otherwise, evaluate

iii $\int_3^4 \frac{5 - 2x}{\sqrt{4x - x^2}} dx.$

14 The curve C shown in the diagram has equation $y^2 = 4x$, $0 \leqslant x \leqslant 1$.

The part of the curve in the first quadrant is rotated through 2π radians about the x-axis.

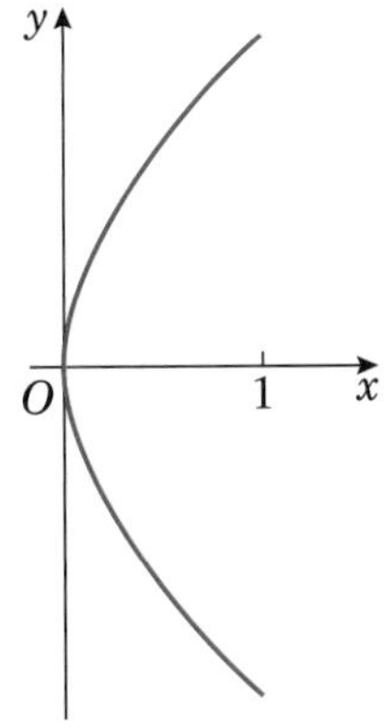

a Show that the surface area of the solid generated is given by

$$4\pi \int_0^1 \sqrt{(1 + x)}\, dx.$$

b Find the exact value of this surface area.

c Show also that the length of the curve C, between the points $(1, -2)$ and $(1, 2)$, is given by

$$2\int_0^1 \sqrt{\left(\frac{x + 1}{x}\right)} dx.$$

d Use the substitution $x = \sinh^2\theta$ to show that the exact value of this length is

$$2[\sqrt{2} + \ln(1 + \sqrt{2})].$$

E

15 **a** Show that $\int x \operatorname{arcosh} x\, dx = \frac{1}{4}(2x^2 - 1)\operatorname{arcosh} x - \frac{1}{4}x\sqrt{x^2 - 1} + C$

b Hence, using the substitution $x = u^2$, find $\int \operatorname{arcosh}(\sqrt{x})\, dx$.

16 Given that $I_n = \int \frac{\sin(2n + 1)x}{\sin x} dx$,

a show that $I_n - I_{n-1} = \frac{\sin 2nx}{n}$.

b Hence find I_5.

c Show that, for all positive integers n, $\int_0^{\frac{\pi}{2}} \frac{\sin(2n + 1)x}{\sin x} dx$ always has the same value, which should be found.

17 The diagram shows part of the graph of the curve with equation $y^2 = \frac{1}{3}x(x - 1)^2$.

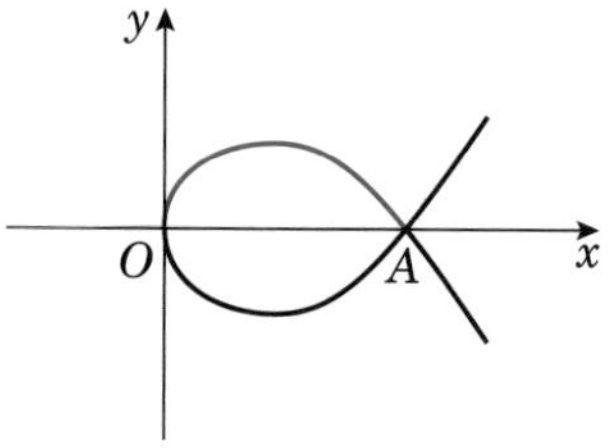

a Show that the length of the loop is $\frac{4\sqrt{3}}{3}$.

The arc OA (in red) is rotated completely about the x-axis.

b Find the area of the surface generated.

18 **a** Find $\int \frac{1}{\sinh x + 2\cosh x}\,dx$.

b Show that $\int_1^4 \frac{3x - 1}{\sqrt{x^2 - 2x + 10}}\,dx = 9(\sqrt{2} - 1) + 2\,\text{arsinh}\,1$. E

19 Given that $I_n = \int \sec^n x\,dx$,

a by writing $\sec^n x = \sec^{n-2} x \sec^2 x$, show that, for $n \geqslant 2$,

$(n - 1)I_n = \sec^{n-2} x \tan x + (n - 2)I_{n-2}$.

b Find I_5.

c Hence show that $\int_0^{\frac{\pi}{4}} \sec^5 x\,dx = \frac{1}{8}\{7\sqrt{2} + 3\ln(1 + \sqrt{2})\}$

20 **a** Show, by using a suitable substitution for x, that

$$\int \sqrt{a^2 - x^2}\,dx = \frac{a^2}{2}\arcsin\left(\frac{x}{a}\right) + \frac{x}{2}\sqrt{a^2 - x^2} + C$$

b Hence show that the area of the region enclosed by the ellipse with equation

$\frac{x^2}{a^2} + \frac{y^2}{b^2} = 1$ is πab.

Summary of key points

1 You should be familiar with the following standard forms.

(Results marked (*) are in the Edexcel formula booklet)

$\int \sinh x \, dx = \cosh x + C$ (*)

$\int \cosh x \, dx = \sinh x + C$ (*)

$\int \text{sech}^2 x \, dx = \tanh x + C$

$\int \text{cosech}^2 x \, dx = -\coth x + C$

$\int \text{sech}\, x \tanh x dx = -\text{sech}\, x + C$

$\int \text{cosech}\, x \coth x dx = -\text{cosech}\, x + C$

$\int \frac{1}{\sqrt{(a^2 - x^2)}} dx = \arcsin\left(\frac{x}{a}\right), \ |x| < a$ (*) $\qquad \int \frac{1}{\sqrt{(1 - x^2)}} dx = \arcsin x + C, \ |x| < 1$

$\int \frac{1}{a^2 + x^2} dx = \frac{1}{a} \arctan\left(\frac{x}{a}\right)$ (*) $\qquad \int \frac{1}{1 + x^2} dx = \arctan x + C$

$\int \frac{1}{\sqrt{(a + x^2)}} dx = \text{arsinh}\left(\frac{x}{a}\right)$ (*) $\qquad \int \frac{1}{\sqrt{(1 + x^2)}} dx = \text{arsinh}\, x + C$

$\int \frac{1}{\sqrt{(x^2 - a^2)}} dx = \text{arcosh}\left(\frac{x}{a}\right), \ x > a$ (*) $\qquad \int \frac{1}{\sqrt{(x^2 - 1)}} dx = \text{arcosh}\, x + C$

$\int \frac{1}{a^2 - x^2} dx = \frac{1}{2a} \ln\left|\frac{a + x}{a - x}\right|, \ |x| < a$ (*)

$\int \frac{1}{x^2 - a^2} dx = \frac{1}{2a} \ln\left|\frac{x - a}{x + a}\right|$ (*)

2 Integration of hyperbolic functions

a Usually you can use the same method as for the corresponding trigonometric expressions.

For example: $\int \cosh^2 3x \, dx = \int \frac{(1 + \cosh 6x)}{2} dx = \frac{1}{2}x + \frac{1}{12}\sinh 6x + C$

$\int \tanh^2 x \, dx = \int (1 - \text{sech}^2 x) dx = x - \tanh x + C$

b Sometimes you may need to use, or it may be better to use, the exponential form of the functions.

For example: $\int e^x \sinh x \, dx = \int e^x \left(\frac{e^x - e^{-x}}{2}\right) dx = \frac{1}{2}\int (e^{2x} - 1) \, dx = \frac{1}{2}\left(\frac{e^{2x}}{2} - x\right) + C$

$\int \text{sech}\, x \, dx$ (See Example 7)

$\int \frac{1}{\sinh x + \cosh x} dx = \int \frac{1}{e^x} dx = -e^{-x} + C$

3 To integrate expressions of the form $\int \frac{1}{px^2 + qx + r} dx$ and $\int \frac{1}{\sqrt{px^2 + qx + r}} dx$, complete the square on $px^2 + qx + r$ and use the appropriate standard form in **1** above.

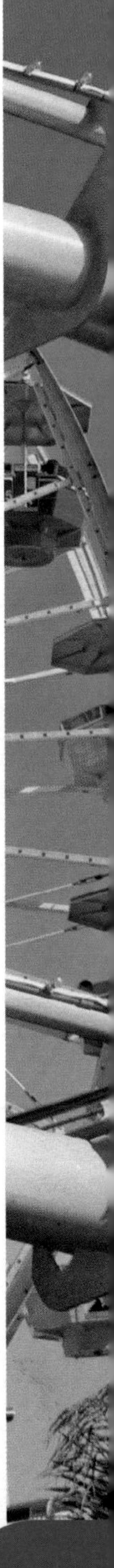

4 To integrate inverse trigonometric and hyperbolic functions you can use integration by parts in the same way as you integrate $\ln x$. For example, write $\int \arcsin x \, dx$ as $\int (\arcsin x \times 1) dx$ and use integration by parts with $u = \arcsin x$ and $\frac{dv}{dx} = 1$.

5 A reduction formula relates I_n, an integral of an expression involving an integer n, usually a power, to an integral of the same form involving a lower value of n.

- This is usually derived using integration by parts.
  For example: if $I_n = \int x^n e^x dx$, then $I_n = x^n e^x - nI_{n-1}$, $n \geqslant 1$, where $I_{n-1} = \int x^{n-1} e^x dx$.
  By repeated application of the formula, I_n can be reduced to a form in which it can be found directly.
- Some reduction formulae can be derived without using integration by parts.
  For example: if $I_n = \int \tan^n x \, dx$, then, by using $\tan^2 x \equiv \sec^2 x - 1$, it can be shown directly that $I_n = \frac{1}{n-1}\tan^{n-1} x - I_{n-2}$, $n \geqslant 2$.

6 The length of an arc on the curve C, between the points $A(x_A, y_B)$ and $B(x_B, y_B)$, is given by

$$\int_{x_A}^{x_B} \sqrt{1 + \left(\frac{dy}{dx}\right)^2} \, dx \quad (*) \quad \text{or} \quad \int_{y_A}^{y_B} \sqrt{1 + \left(\frac{dx}{dy}\right)^2} \, dy$$

If the equation of C is given parametrically, with the parameters at A and B being t_A and t_B respectively, then the arc length is given by

$$\int_{t_A}^{t_B} \sqrt{\left(\frac{dx}{dt}\right)^2 + \left(\frac{dy}{dt}\right)^2} \, dt \quad (*)$$

7 The area of the surface generated when the arc AB on the curve C, is rotated completely about the x-axis is $2\pi \int y \, ds$ (*) or about the y-axis is $2\pi \int x \, ds$.

These can be used to give the following results:

i about the x-axis $S = 2\pi \int_{x_A}^{x_B} y \sqrt{1 + \left(\frac{dy}{dx}\right)^2} \, dx$

ii about the y-axis $S = 2\pi \int_{y_A}^{y_B} x \sqrt{1 + \left(\frac{dx}{dy}\right)^2} \, dy$ or $S = 2\pi \int_{x_A}^{x_B} x \sqrt{1 + \left(\frac{dy}{dx}\right)^2} \, dx$

This is often the more convenient.

If C is given in parametric form, the results are

i about the x-axis $S = 2\pi \int_{t_A}^{t_B} y \sqrt{\left(\frac{dx}{dt}\right)^2 + \left(\frac{dy}{dt}\right)^2} \, dt$ (*)

ii about the y-axis $S = 2\pi \int_{t_A}^{t_B} x \sqrt{\left(\frac{dx}{dt}\right)^2 + \left(\frac{dy}{dt}\right)^2} \, dt$

Review Exercise 1

1 Find the value of x for which

$$2\tanh x - 1 = 0,$$

giving your answer in terms of a natural logarithm. **E**

2 Starting from the definition of $\cosh x$ in terms of exponentials, find, in terms of natural logarithms, the values of x for which

$$5 = 3\cosh x.$$

E

3 The curves with equations $y = 5\sinh x$ and $y = 4\cosh x$ meet at the point $A(\ln p, q)$. Find the exact values of p and q. **E**

4 Find the values of x for which

$$5\cosh x - 2\sinh x = 11,$$

giving your answers as natural logarithms. **E**

5 By expressing $\sinh 2x$ and $\cosh 2x$ in terms of exponentials, find the exact values of x for which

$$6\sinh 2x + 9\cosh 2x = 7,$$

giving each answer in the form $\frac{1}{2}\ln p$, where p is a rational number. **E**

6 Given that

$$\sinh x + 2\cosh x = k,$$

where k is a positive constant,

a find the set of values of k for which at least one real solution of this equation exists,

b solve the equation when $k = 2$. **E**

7 Using the definitions of $\cosh x$ and $\sinh x$ in terms of exponentials,

a prove that $\cosh^2 x - \sinh^2 x = 1$,

b solve the equation $\operatorname{cosech} x - 2\coth x = 2$, giving your answer in the form $k\ln a$, where k and a are integers. **E**

8 **a** From the definition of $\cosh x$ in terms of exponentials, show that

$$\cosh 2x = 2\cosh^2 x - 1.$$

b Solve the equation

$$\cosh 2x - 5\cosh x = 2,$$

giving the answers in terms of natural logarithms. **E**

9 **a** Using the definition of $\cosh x$ in terms of exponentials, prove that

$$4\cosh^3 x - 3\cosh x = \cosh 3x.$$

b Hence, or otherwise, solve the equation

$\cosh 3x = 5\cosh x$,

giving your answer as natural logarithms. **E**

10 **a** Starting from the definitions of $\cosh x$ and $\sinh x$ in terms of exponentials, prove that

$\cosh(A - B) = \cosh A \cosh B - \sinh A \sinh B$.

b Hence, or otherwise, given that $\cosh(x - 1) = \sinh x$, show that

$$\tanh x = \frac{e^2 + 1}{e^2 + 2e - 1}.$$ **E**

11 **a** Starting from the definition

$$\sinh y = \frac{e^y - e^{-y}}{2},$$

prove that, for all real values of x,

$\text{arsinh}\, x = \ln[x + \sqrt{(1 + x^2)}]$.

b Hence, or otherwise, prove that, for $0 < \theta < \pi$,

$$\text{arsinh}(\cot\theta) = \ln\left(\cot\frac{\theta}{2}\right).$$ **E**

12 Given that $n \in \mathbb{Z}^+$, $x \in \mathbb{R}$ and

$$\mathbf{M} = \begin{pmatrix} \cosh^2 x & \cosh^2 x \\ -\sinh^2 x & -\sinh^2 x \end{pmatrix},$$

prove that $\mathbf{M}^n = \mathbf{M}$. **E**

13 Solve for real x and y, the simultaneous equations

$\cosh x = 3\sinh y$

$2\sinh x = 5 - 6\cosh y$,

expressing your answers in terms of natural logarithms. **E**

14 **a** Starting from the definition of $\tanh x$ in terms of e^x, show that

$$\text{artanh}\, x = \tfrac{1}{2}\ln\left(\frac{1 + x}{1 - x}\right)$$

and sketch the graph of $y = \text{artanh}\, x$.

b Solve the equation $x = \tanh[\ln\sqrt{(6x)}]$ for $0 < x < 1$. **E**

15 **a** Show that, for $0 < x \leqslant 1$.

$$\ln\left(\frac{1 - \sqrt{(1 - x^2)}}{x}\right) = -\ln\left(\frac{1 + \sqrt{(1 - x^2)}}{x}\right).$$

b Using the definitions of $\cosh x$ and $\sinh x$ in terms of exponentials, show that, for $0 < x \leqslant 1$,

$$\text{arsech}\, x = \ln\left(\frac{1 + \sqrt{(1 - x^2)}}{x}\right).$$

c Solve the equation

$3\tanh^2 x - 4\,\text{sech}\, x + 1 = 0$,

giving exact answers in terms of natural logarithms. **E**

16 **a** Express $\cosh 3\theta$ and $\cosh 5\theta$ in terms of $\cosh\theta$.

b Hence determine the real roots of the equation

$2\cosh 5x + 10\cosh 3x + 20\cosh x = 243$,

giving your answers to 2 decimal places. **E**

17 An ellipse has equation $\frac{x^2}{16} + \frac{y^2}{9} = 1$.

a Sketch the ellipse.

b Find the value of the eccentricity e.

c State the coordinates of the foci of the ellipse. **E**

18 The hyperbola H has equation $\frac{x^2}{16} - \frac{y^2}{4} = 1$.

Find

a the value of the eccentricity of H,

b the distance between the foci of H.

The ellipse E has equation $\frac{x^2}{16} + \frac{y^2}{4} = 1$.

c Sketch H and E on the same diagram, showing the coordinates of the points where each curve crosses the axes. **E**

19 The ellipse D has equation $\frac{x^2}{25} + \frac{y^2}{9} = 1$

and the ellipse E has equation $\frac{x^2}{4} + \frac{y^2}{9} = 1$.

a Sketch D and E on the same diagram, showing the coordinates of the points where each curve crosses the axes.

The point S is a focus of D and the point T is a focus of E.

b Find the length of ST. **E**

20 An ellipse, with equation $\frac{x^2}{9} + \frac{y^2}{4} = 1$, has foci S and S'.

a Find the coordinates of the foci of the ellipse.

b Using the focus-directrix property of the ellipse, show that, for any point P on the ellipse,

$SP + S'P = 6.$ **E**

21 **a** Find the eccentricity of the ellipse with equation $3x^2 + 4y^2 = 12$.

b Find an equation of the tangent to the ellipse with equation $3x^2 + 4y^2 = 12$ at the point with coordinates $(1, \frac{3}{2})$.

This tangent meets the y-axis at G. Given that S and S' are the foci of the ellipse,

c find the area of $\triangle SS'G$. **E**

22 The point P lies on the hyperbola $\frac{x^2}{a^2} - \frac{y^2}{b^2} = 1$, and N is the foot of the perpendicular from P onto the x-axis. The tangent to the hyperbola at P meets the x-axis at T.

Show that $OT.ON = a^2$, where O is the origin. **E**

23 The hyperbola C has equation $\frac{x^2}{a^2} - \frac{y^2}{b^2} = 1$.

a Show that an equation of the normal to C at the point $P\ (a \sec t, b \tan t)$ is

$ax \sin t + by = (a^2 + b^2)\tan t.$

The normal to C at P cuts the x-axis at the point A and S is a focus of C. Given that the eccentricity of C is $\frac{3}{2}$, and that $OA = 3OS$, where O is the origin,

b determine the possible values of t, for $0 \leqslant t \leqslant 2\pi$. **E**

24 An ellipse has equation $\frac{x^2}{a^2} + \frac{y^2}{b^2} = 1$,

where a and b are constants and $a > b$.

a Find an equation of the tangent at the point $P(a \cos t, b \sin t)$.

b Find an equation of the normal at the point $P(a \cos t, b \sin t)$.

The normal at P meets the x-axis at the point Q. The tangent at P meets the y-axis at the point R.

c Find, in terms of a, b and t, the coordinates of M, the mid-point of QR.

Given that $0 < t < \frac{\pi}{2}$,

d show that, as t varies, the locus of M has equation $\left(\frac{2ax}{a^2 - b^2}\right)^2 + \left(\frac{b}{2y}\right)^2 = 1.$ **E**

25 The points S_1 and S_2 have Cartesian coordinates $\left(-\frac{a}{2}\sqrt{3}, 0\right)$ and $\left(\frac{a}{2}\sqrt{3}, 0\right)$ respectively.

a Find a Cartesian equation of the ellipse which has S_1 and S_2 as its two foci, and a semi-major axis of length a.

b Write down an equation of a directrix of this ellipse.

Given that parametric equations of this ellipse are

$x = a \cos \phi,\ y = b \sin \phi,$

c express b in terms of a.

The point P is given by $\phi = \frac{\pi}{4}$ and the point Q by $\phi = \frac{\pi}{2}$.

d Show that an equation of the chord PQ is

$(\sqrt{2} - 1)x + 2y - a = 0.$ **E**

26 Show that the equations of the tangents with gradient m to the hyperbola with equation

$x^2 - 4y^2 = 4$

are

$y = mx \pm \sqrt{(4m^2 - 1)}$, where $|m| > \frac{1}{2}$.

E

27 The line with equation $y = mx + c$ is a tangent to the ellipse with equation $\frac{x^2}{a^2} + \frac{y^2}{b^2} = 1$.

a Show that $c^2 = a^2m^2 + b^2$.

b Hence, or otherwise, find the equations of the tangents from the point (3, 4) to the ellipse with equation $\frac{x^2}{16} + \frac{y^2}{25} = 1$. **E**

28 The ellipse E has equation $\frac{x^2}{a^2} + \frac{y^2}{b^2} = 1$ and the line L has equation $y = mx + c$, where $m > 0$ and $c > 0$.

a Show that, if L and E have any points of intersection, the x-coordinates of these points are the roots of the equation

$$(b^2 + a^2m^2)x^2 + 2a^2mcx + a^2(c^2 - b^2) = 0.$$

Hence, given that L is a tangent to E,

b show that $c^2 = b^2 + a^2m^2$.

The tangent L meets the negative x-axis at the point A and the positive y-axis at the point B, and O is the origin.

c Find, in terms of m, a and b, the area of the triangle OAB.

d Prove that, as m varies, the minimum area of the triangle OAB is ab.

e Find, in terms of a, the x-coordinate of the point of contact of L and E when the area of the triangle is a minimum. **E**

29 **a** Find the eccentricity of the ellipse $\frac{x^2}{9} + \frac{y^2}{4} = 1$.

b Find also the coordinates of both foci and equations of both directrices of this ellipse.

c Show that an equation for the tangent to this ellipse at the point $P(3\cos\theta, 2\sin\theta)$ is

$$\frac{x\cos\theta}{3} + \frac{y\sin\theta}{2} = 1.$$

d Show that, as θ varies, the foot of the perpendicular from the origin to the tangent at P lies on the curve

$$(x^2 + y^2)^2 = 9x^2 + 4y^2.$$ **E**

30 **a** Show that the hyperbola $x^2 - y^2 = a^2$, $a > 0$, has eccentricity equal to $\sqrt{2}$.

b Hence state the coordinates of the focus S and an equation of the corresponding directrix L, where both S and L lie in the region $x > 0$.

The perpendicular from S to the line $y = x$ meets the line $y = x$ at P and the perpendicular from S to the line $y = -x$ meets the line $y = -x$ at Q.

c Show that both P and Q lie on the directrix L and give the coordinates of P and Q.

Given that the line SP meets the hyperbola at the point R,

d prove that the tangent at R passes through the point Q. **E**

31 **a** Show that an equation of the normal to the ellipse $\frac{x^2}{a^2} + \frac{y^2}{b^2} = 1$ at the point $P(a\cos\theta, b\sin\theta)$ is

$$ax\sec\theta - by\,\mathrm{cosec}\,\theta = a^2 - b^2.$$

The normal at P cuts the x-axis at G.

b Show that the coordinates of M, the mid-point of PG are

$$\left[\left(\frac{2a^2 - b^2}{2a}\right)\cos\theta, \left(\frac{b}{2}\right)\sin\theta\right].$$

c Show that, as θ varies, the locus of M is an ellipse and determine the equation of this locus.

Given that the normal at P meets the y-axis at H and that O is the origin,

d show that, if $a > b$,

area $\triangle OMG$:area $\triangle OGH = b^2{:}2(a^2 - b^2)$. **E**

32 **a** Find equations for the tangent and normal to the rectangular hyperbola

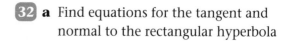

$x^2 - y^2 = 1$, at the point P with coordinates $(\cosh t, \sinh t)$, $t > 0$.

The tangent and normal intersect the x-axis at T and G respectively. The perpendicular from P to the x-axis meets an asymptote in the first quadrant at Q.

b Show that GQ is perpendicular to this asymptote.

The normal intercepts the y-axis at R.

c Show that R lies on the circle with centre at T and radius TG. **E**

33 **a** Find the equations for the tangent and normal to the hyperbola

$$\frac{x^2}{a^2} - \frac{y^2}{b^2} = 1$$

at the point $(a \sec \theta, b \tan \theta)$.

b If these lines meet the y-axis at P and Q respectively, show that the circle described on PQ as diameter passes through the foci of the hyperbola. **E**

34 Given that $r > a > 0$ and $0 < \arcsin\left(\frac{a}{r}\right) < \frac{\pi}{2}$, show that

$$\frac{d}{dr}\left[\arcsin\left(\frac{a}{r}\right)\right] = -\frac{a}{r\sqrt{(r^2 - a^2)}}$$ **E**

35 Given that $y = (\arcsin x)^2$,

a prove that $(1 - x^2)\left(\frac{dy}{dx}\right)^2 = 4y$,

b deduce that $(1 - x^2)\frac{d^2y}{dx^2} - x\frac{dy}{dx} = 2$. **E**

36 **a** Show that, for $x = \ln k$, where k is a positive constant,

$$\cosh 2x = \frac{k^4 + 1}{2k^2}.$$

b Given that $f(x) = px - \tanh 2x$, where p is a constant, find the value of p for which $f(x)$ has a stationary value at $x = \ln 2$, giving your answer as an exact fraction. **E**

37 The curve with equation

$$y = -x + \tanh 4x, \ x \geqslant 0,$$

has a maximum turning point A.

a Find, in exact logarithmic form, the x-coordinate of A.

b Show that the y-coordinate of A is $\frac{1}{4}\{2\sqrt{3} - \ln(2 + \sqrt{3})\}$. **E**

38 The curve C has equation

$$y = \operatorname{arcsec} e^x, \ x > 0, \ 0 \leqslant y < \tfrac{1}{2}\pi.$$

a Prove that $\frac{dy}{dx} = \frac{1}{\sqrt{(e^{2x} - 1)}}$.

b Sketch the graph of C

The point A on C has x-coordinate $\ln 2$. The tangent to C at A intersects the y-axis at the point B.

c Find the exact value of the y-coordinate of B. **E**

39 Evaluate $\int_1^4 \frac{1}{\sqrt{(x^2 - 2x + 17)}} dx$, giving your answer as an exact logarithm. **E**

40 Evaluate $\int_1^3 \frac{1}{\sqrt{(x^2 + 4x - 5)}} dx$, giving your answer as an exact logarithm. **E**

41 Use the substitution $x = \frac{a}{\sinh \theta}$, where a is a constant, to show that, for $x > 0$, $a > 0$,

$$\int \frac{1}{x\sqrt{(x^2 + a^2)}} dx = -\frac{1}{a}\operatorname{arsinh}\left(\frac{a}{x}\right) + \text{constant}.$$ **E**

42 **a** Prove that the derivative of $\operatorname{artanh} x$, $-1 < x < 1$, is $\frac{1}{1 - x^2}$.

b Find $\int \operatorname{artanh} x \, dx$. **E**

43 **a** Find $\int \frac{1 + x}{\sqrt{(1 - 4x^2)}} dx$.

b Find, to 3 decimal places, the value of

$$\int_0^{0.3} \frac{1 + x}{\sqrt{(1 - 4x^2)}} dx.$$ **E**

44 **a** Given that $y = \arctan 3x$, and assuming the derivative of $\tan x$, prove that

$$\frac{dy}{dx} = \frac{3}{1 + 9x^2}.$$

b Show that

$$\int_0^{\frac{\sqrt{3}}{3}} 6x \arctan 3x = \tfrac{1}{9}(4\pi - 3\sqrt{3}).$$ **E**

45 **a** Starting from the definition of $\sinh x$ in terms of e^x, prove that

$$\text{arsinh}\, x = \ln[x + \sqrt{(x^2 + 1)}].$$

b Prove that the derivative of $\text{arsinh}\, x$ is $(1 + x^2)^{-\frac{1}{2}}$.

c Show that the equation

$$(1 + x^2)\frac{d^2y}{dx^2} + x\frac{dy}{dx} - 2 = 0$$

is satisfied when $y = (\text{arsinh}\, x)^2$.

d Use integration by parts to find $\int_0^1 \text{arsinh}\, x\, dx$, giving your answer in terms of a natural logarithm. **E**

46 **a** Using the substitution $u = e^x$, find

$$\int \text{sech}\, x\, dx.$$

b Sketch the curve with equation $y = \text{sech}\, x$.

The finite region R is bounded by the curve with equation $y = \text{sech}\, x$, the lines $x = 2$, $x = -2$ and the x-axis.

c Using your result from **a**, find the area of R, giving your answer to 3 decimal places. **E**

47 **a** Prove that $\text{arsinh}\, x = \ln[x + \sqrt{(x^2 + 1)}]$.

b **i** Find, to 3 decimal places, the coordinates of the stationary points on the curve with equation $y = x - 2\,\text{arsinh}\, x$.

ii Determine the nature of each stationary point.

iii Hence, sketch the curve with equation $y = x - 2\,\text{arsinh}\, x$.

c Evaluate $\int_{-2}^{0} (x - 2\,\text{arsinh}\, x)dx$. **E**

48 Use the substitution $e^x = t - \frac{3}{5}$, or otherwise, to find

$$\int \frac{1}{3 + 5\cosh x} dx.$$ **E**

49

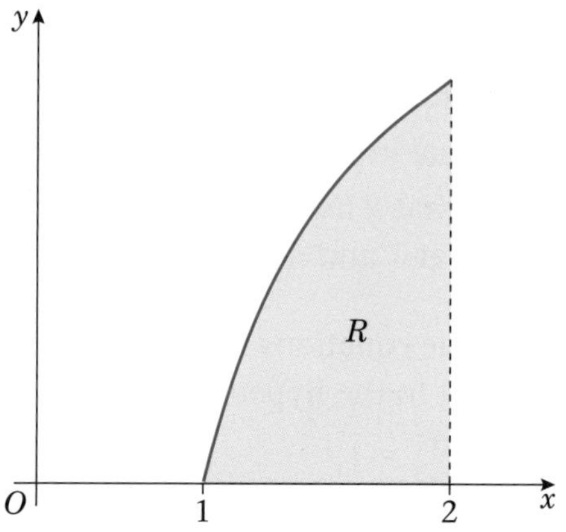

The figure above shows a sketch of the curve with equation

$$y = x\,\text{arcosh}\, x,\ 1 \leqslant x \leqslant 2.$$

The region R, shaded in the figure, is bounded by the curve, the x-axis and the line $x = 2$.

Show that the area of R is

$$\frac{7}{4}\ln(2 + \sqrt{3}) - \frac{\sqrt{3}}{2}.$$ **E**

50 $4x^2 + 4x + 5 \equiv (px + q)^2 + r$

a Find the values of the constants p, q and r.

b Hence, or otherwise, find

$$\int \frac{1}{4x^2 + 4x + 5} dx.$$

c Show that

$$\int \frac{2}{\sqrt{(4x^2 + 4x + 5)}} dx = \ln[(2x + 1) + \sqrt{(4x^2 + 4x + 5)}] + k,$$

where k is an arbitrary constant. **E**

51 Using the substitution $x = 2\cosh^2 t - \sinh^2 t$, evaluate

$$\int_2^3 (x-1)^{\frac{1}{2}}(x-2)^{\frac{1}{2}}\,dx.$$

E

52 $f(x) = \arcsin x$

a Show that $f'(x) = \dfrac{1}{\sqrt{(1-x^2)}}$.

b Given that $y = \arcsin 2x$, obtain $\dfrac{dy}{dx}$ as an algebraic fraction.

c Using the substitution $x = \frac{1}{2}\sin\theta$, show that

$$\int_0^{\frac{1}{4}} \frac{x \arcsin 2x}{\sqrt{(1-4x^2)}}\,dx = \tfrac{1}{48}(6 - \pi\sqrt{3}).$$

E

53 **a** Show that $\operatorname{artanh}\left(\sin\frac{\pi}{4}\right) = \ln(1+\sqrt{2})$.

b Given that $y = \operatorname{artanh}(\sin x)$, show that $\dfrac{dy}{dx} = \sec x$.

c Find the exact value of

$$\int_0^{\frac{\pi}{4}} \sin x \operatorname{artanh}(\sin x)\,dx.$$

E

54

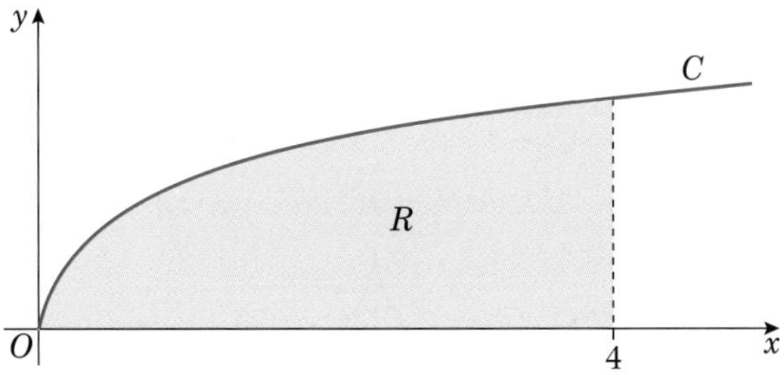

The figure shows part of the curve C with equation $y = \operatorname{arsinh}(\sqrt{x})$, $x \geqslant 0$.

a Find the gradient of C at the point where $x = 4$.

The region R, shown shaded in the figure, is bounded by C, the x-axis and the line $x = 4$.

b Using the substitution $x = \sinh^2\theta$, or otherwise, show that the area of R is

$$k\ln(2+\sqrt{5}) - \sqrt{5},$$

where k is a constant.

E

55 $I_n = \displaystyle\int_0^{\frac{\pi}{2}} x^n \cos x\,dx$, $n \geqslant 0$.

a Prove that $I_n = \left(\dfrac{\pi}{2}\right)^n - n(n-1)I_{n-2}$, $n \geqslant 2$.

b Find an exact expression for I_6.

E

56 Given that

$$I_n = \int_0^4 x^n\sqrt{(4-x)}\,dx,\ n \geqslant 0.$$

a show that $I_n = \dfrac{8n}{2n+3}I_{n-1}$, $n \geqslant 1$.

Given that $\displaystyle\int_0^4 \sqrt{(4-x)}\,dx = \frac{16}{3}$,

b use the result in part **a** to find the exact value of $\displaystyle\int_0^4 x^2\sqrt{(4-x)}\,dx$.

E

57 Given that $y = \sinh^{n-1}x\cosh x$,

a show that $\dfrac{dy}{dx} = (n-1)\sinh^{n-2}x + n\sinh^n x$.

The integral I_n is defined by

$$I_n = \int_0^{\operatorname{arsinh} 1} \sinh^n x\,dx,\ n \geqslant 0.$$

b Using the result in part **a**, or otherwise, show that

$$nI_n = \sqrt{2} - (n-1)I_{n-2},\ n \geqslant 2.$$

c Hence find the value of I_4.

E

58 Given that $I_n = \displaystyle\int_0^8 x^n(8-x)^{\frac{1}{3}}\,dx$, $n \geqslant 0$,

a show that $I_n = \dfrac{24n}{3n+4}I_{n-1}$, $n \geqslant 1$.

b Hence find the exact value of

$$\int_0^8 x(x+5)(8-x)^{\frac{1}{3}}\,dx.$$

E

59 $I_n = \int \frac{\sin nx}{\sin x} \mathrm{d}x \; n > 0, n \in \mathbb{Z}.$

a By considering $I_{n+2} - I_n$, or otherwise, show that

$$I_{n+2} = \frac{2\sin(n+1)x}{n+1} + I_n.$$

b Hence evaluate $\int_{\frac{\pi}{4}}^{\frac{\pi}{3}} \frac{\sin 6x}{\sin x} \mathrm{d}x$, giving your answer in the form $p\sqrt{2} + q\sqrt{3}$, where p and q are rational numbers to be found. **E**

60 $I_n = \int_0^1 x^n \mathrm{e}^x \, \mathrm{d}x$ and $J_n = \int_0^1 x^n \mathrm{e}^{-x} \, \mathrm{d}x$, $n \geqslant 0$.

a Show that, for $n \geqslant 1$,

$$I_n = \mathrm{e} - nI_{n-1}.$$

b Find a similar formula for J_n.

c Show that $J_2 = 2 - \frac{5}{\mathrm{e}}$.

d Show that $\int_0^1 x^n \cosh x \, \mathrm{d}x = \frac{1}{2}(I_n + J_n)$.

e Hence, or otherwise, evaluate $\int_0^1 x^2 \cosh x \, \mathrm{d}x$, giving your answer in terms of e. **E**

61 Given that $I_n = \int \sec^n x \, \mathrm{d}x$,

a show that

$(n-1)I_n = \tan x \sec^{n-2} x + (n-2)I_{n-2}$, $n \geqslant 2$.

b Hence find the exact value of $\int_0^{\frac{\pi}{3}} \sec^3 x \, \mathrm{d}x$, giving your answer in terms of natural logarithms and surds. **E**

62 $I_n = \int_0^1 (1 - x^2)^n \mathrm{d}x$, $n \geqslant 0$.

a Prove that $(2n+1)I_n = 2nI_{n-1}$, $n \geqslant 1$.

b Prove by induction that

$$I_n \leqslant \left(\frac{2n}{2n+1}\right)^n \text{ for } n \in \mathbb{Z}^+.$$ **E**

63 A curve is defined by

$$x = t + \sin t, \; y = 1 - \cos t,$$

where t is a parameter.

Find the length of the curve from $t = 0$ to $t = \frac{\pi}{2}$, giving your answer in surd form. **E**

64 Parametric equations for the curve C are

$$x = \cosh t + t, \; y = \cosh t - t, \; t \geqslant 0.$$

Show that the length of the arc of the curve C between points at which $t = 0$ and $t = a$, where a is a positive constant, is $(\sqrt{2})\sinh a$. **E**

65

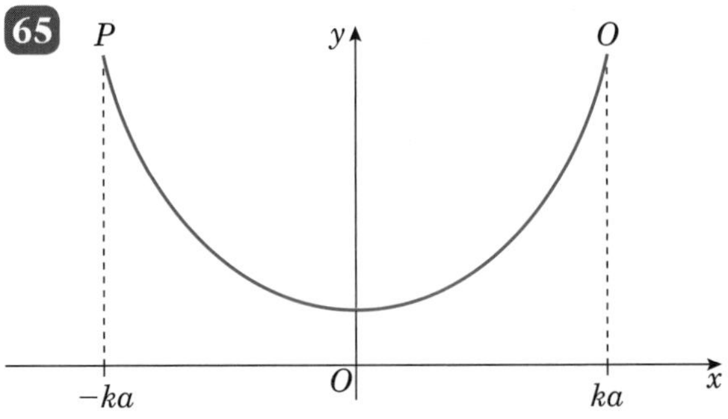

A rope is hung from points P and Q on the same horizontal line, as shown in the figure. The curve formed is modelled by the equation

$$y = a\cosh\left(\frac{x}{a}\right), \; -ka \leqslant x \leqslant ka.$$

where a and k are constants.

a Prove that the length of the rope is $2a \sinh k$.

Given that the length of the rope is $8a$,

b find the coordinates of Q, leaving your answer in terms of natural logarithms and surds, where appropriate. **E**

66

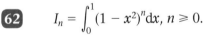

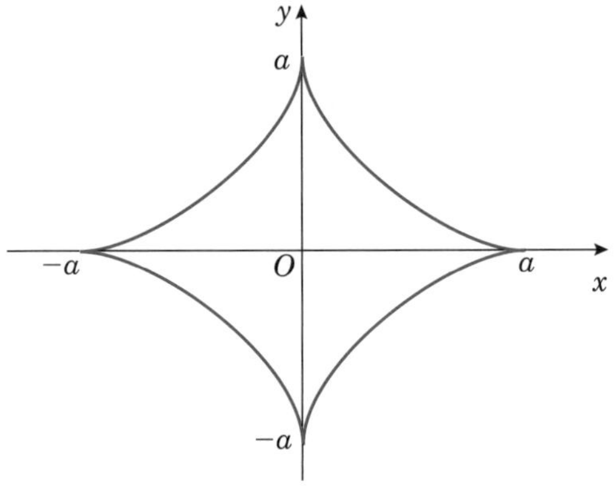

The figure shows the curve with parametric equations

$$x = a\cos^3\theta, \; y = a\sin^3\theta, \; 0 \leqslant \theta < 2\pi.$$

a Find the total length of the curve.

The curve is rotated through π radians about the x-axis.

b Find the area of the surface generated. *E*

67 **a** By using the definition of $\cosh x$ in terms of exponentials, show that

$\cosh^2 x = \frac{1}{2}(\cosh 2x + 1)$.

b The arc of the curve with equation $y = \cosh x$ from $x = 0$ to $x = \ln 2$ is rotated through 2π radians about the x-axis. Determine the area of the curved surface generated, leaving your answer in terms of π. *E*

5

After completing this chapter you should be able to:

- find the vector product $\mathbf{a} \times \mathbf{b}$ of two vectors $\mathbf{a}$ and $\mathbf{b}$
- find the triple scalar product $\mathbf{a}.\mathbf{b} \times \mathbf{c}$ of three vectors $\mathbf{a}$, $\mathbf{b}$ and $\mathbf{c}$
- interpret $|\mathbf{a} \times \mathbf{b}|$ as an area and $\mathbf{a}.\mathbf{b} \times \mathbf{c}$ as a volume
- write the vector equation of a line in the form $(\mathbf{r} - \mathbf{a}) \times \mathbf{b} = 0$
- write the equation of a plane in the form $\mathbf{r}.\mathbf{n} = p$, or in the form $\mathbf{r} = \mathbf{a} + s\mathbf{b} + t\mathbf{c}$
- use vectors in problems involving points, lines and planes and use the equivalent Cartesian forms for the equations of lines and planes.

Vectors

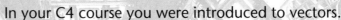

In your C4 course you were introduced to vectors.

You also learned how to find the vector equation of a line and the scalar product of two vectors.

In this chapter you will extend this work to find another kind of product of vectors, the vector product. You will use this in a variety of contexts.

You will also find an alternative form of the equation of a straight line and will find Cartesian and vector forms of the equation of a plane.

The vector product has applications in Physics, to calculate the turning effect or torque or moment of a force and in Electromagnetic theory to find the effect of magnetic fields on charged particles.

For example, the Lorentz Force, which is basic to the study of the motion of charged particles, is given by the equation

$$\mathbf{F} = q\mathbf{E} + q\mathbf{v} \times \mathbf{B},$$

where $\mathbf{F}$ is the force exerted, q is the charge on the particle, $\mathbf{E}$ is the electric field strength, $\mathbf{v}$ is the velocity of the particle and $\mathbf{B}$ is the magnetic field. This equation includes a vector product. The study of particle physics has resulted in the development of large experiments such as the CERN large hadron collider.

5.1 You need to know the definition of the vector product of two vectors.

■ **The scalar (or dot) product of two vectors a and b is written as a.b, and defined by**

$$\mathbf{a.b} = |\mathbf{a}||\mathbf{b}|\cos\theta,$$

where θ is the angle between **a** and **b**. (See book C4 Section 5.7.)

■ **The vector (or cross) product of the vectors a and b is defined as**

$$\mathbf{a} \times \mathbf{b} = |\mathbf{a}||\mathbf{b}|\sin\theta\,\hat{\mathbf{n}},$$

This is a key fact which you should learn.

where again θ is the angle between **a** and **b**, and where $\hat{\mathbf{n}}$ is a unit vector perpendicular to both **a** and **b**. The direction of $\hat{\mathbf{n}}$ is that in which a right-handed screw would move when turned from **a** to **b**.

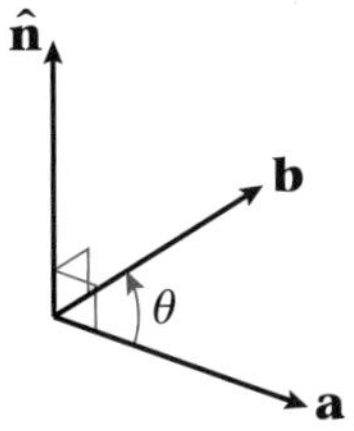

If the turn is in the opposite sense, i.e. from **b** to **a** then the movement of the screw is in the opposite direction to $\hat{\mathbf{n}}$, i.e. in the direction of $-\hat{\mathbf{n}}$.

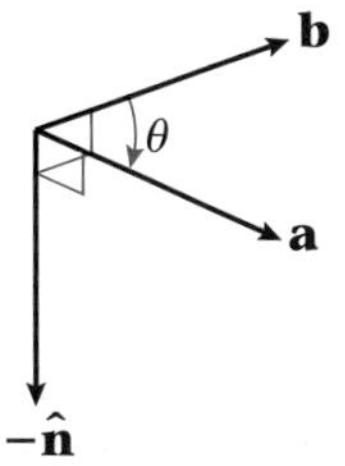

So $\mathbf{b} \times \mathbf{a} = |\mathbf{b}||\mathbf{a}|\sin\theta(-\hat{\mathbf{n}})$
$= -|\mathbf{a}||\mathbf{b}|\sin\theta\,\hat{\mathbf{n}}$
$= -\mathbf{a} \times \mathbf{b}$

■ **So $\mathbf{b} \times \mathbf{a} = -\mathbf{a} \times \mathbf{b}$**

The vector product is not commutative. The order matters.

Example 1

Find the value of

a $\mathbf{i} \times \mathbf{i}$ **b** $\mathbf{j} \times \mathbf{k}$ **c** $\mathbf{i} \times \mathbf{k}$.

a $\mathbf{i} \times \mathbf{i} = 0$

sin $\theta = 0$, as the angle between **i** and itself is zero.

b $\mathbf{j} \times \mathbf{k} = 1 \times 1 \times \sin 90\,\mathbf{i} = \mathbf{i}$

The angle between **j** and **k** is 90° and, as **j** and **k** are unit vectors, each has magnitude 1 unit.

c $\mathbf{i} \times \mathbf{k} = -\mathbf{k} \times \mathbf{i} = -1 \times 1 \times \sin 90\,\mathbf{j} = -\mathbf{j}$

i, **j** and **k** form a right-handed set. If you turn a screw from **k** to **i** it moves in the direction **j**.

- From Example 1 you can deduce that
  - $\mathbf{i} \times \mathbf{i} = 0$
  - $\mathbf{j} \times \mathbf{j} = 0$
  - $\mathbf{k} \times \mathbf{k} = 0$

  and that
  - $\mathbf{i} \times \mathbf{j} = \mathbf{k}$ and $\mathbf{j} \times \mathbf{i} = -\mathbf{k}$
  - $\mathbf{j} \times \mathbf{k} = \mathbf{i}$ and $\mathbf{k} \times \mathbf{j} = -\mathbf{i}$
  - $\mathbf{k} \times \mathbf{i} = \mathbf{j}$ and $\mathbf{i} \times \mathbf{k} = -\mathbf{j}$
  - Also if $\mathbf{a} \times \mathbf{b} = 0$, then either $\mathbf{a} = 0$ or $\mathbf{b} = 0$ or $\mathbf{a}$ and $\mathbf{b}$ are parallel

i, **j** and **k**, the unit vectors in the x, y, and z directions, form a right-handed set.

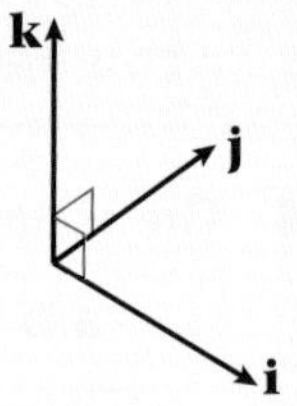

As $\mathbf{a} \times \mathbf{b} = |\mathbf{a}||\mathbf{b}|\sin\theta\hat{\mathbf{n}}$, $\mathbf{a} \times \mathbf{b} = 0$ implies $\mathbf{a} = 0$ or $\mathbf{b} = 0$ or $\sin\theta = 0$.

Solving $\sin\theta = 0$ **gives** $\theta = 0$ or $180°$ **and so a** and **b** are parallel.

Example 2

Given that $\mathbf{a} = \begin{pmatrix} a_1 \\ a_2 \\ a_3 \end{pmatrix}$ and $\mathbf{b} = \begin{pmatrix} b_1 \\ b_2 \\ b_3 \end{pmatrix}$ find $\mathbf{a} \times \mathbf{b}$.

$$\mathbf{a} \times \mathbf{b} = (a_1\mathbf{i} + a_2\mathbf{j} + a_3\mathbf{k}) \times (b_1\mathbf{i} + b_2\mathbf{j} + b_3\mathbf{k})$$

You may assume that vector product is distributive over vector addition.

$$= a_1b_1(\mathbf{i} \times \mathbf{i}) + a_1b_2(\mathbf{i} \times \mathbf{j}) + a_1b_3(\mathbf{i} \times \mathbf{k})$$
$$+ a_2b_1(\mathbf{j} \times \mathbf{i}) + a_2b_2(\mathbf{j} \times \mathbf{j}) + a_2b_3(\mathbf{j} \times \mathbf{k})$$
$$+ a_3b_1(\mathbf{k} \times \mathbf{i}) + a_3b_2(\mathbf{k} \times \mathbf{j}) + a_3b_3(\mathbf{k} \times \mathbf{k})$$
$$= a_1b_2\mathbf{k} + a_1b_3(-\mathbf{j}) + a_2b_1(-\mathbf{k}) + a_2b_3(\mathbf{i}) + a_3b_1(\mathbf{j}) + a_3b_2(-\mathbf{i})$$
$$= (a_2b_3 - a_3b_2)\mathbf{i} + (a_3b_1 - a_1b_3)\mathbf{j} + (a_1b_2 - a_2b_1)\mathbf{k}$$

Use the key point connecting the unit vectors, e.g. $\mathbf{i} \times \mathbf{j} = \mathbf{k}$ to simplify your answer then collect terms.

In determinant form

$$\mathbf{a} \times \mathbf{b} = \begin{vmatrix} \mathbf{i} & \mathbf{j} & \mathbf{k} \\ a_1 & a_2 & a_3 \\ b_1 & b_2 & b_3 \end{vmatrix} = \mathbf{i}\begin{vmatrix} a_2 & a_3 \\ b_2 & b_3 \end{vmatrix} - \mathbf{j}\begin{vmatrix} a_1 & a_3 \\ b_1 & b_3 \end{vmatrix} + \mathbf{k}\begin{vmatrix} a_1 & a_2 \\ b_1 & b_2 \end{vmatrix}$$
$$= (a_2b_3 - a_3b_2)\mathbf{i} + (a_3b_1 - a_1b_3)\mathbf{j} + (a_1b_2 - a_2b_1)\mathbf{k}$$

You evaluated 2×2 determinants in book FP1, and will do further work on 3×3 determinants in Section 6.2 of this book.

- $\mathbf{a} \times \mathbf{b} = (a_2b_3 - a_3b_2)\mathbf{i} + (a_3b_1 - a_1b_3)\mathbf{j} + (a_1b_2 - a_2b_1)\mathbf{k}$

- $\mathbf{a} \times \mathbf{b} = \begin{vmatrix} \mathbf{i} & \mathbf{j} & \mathbf{k} \\ a_1 & a_2 & a_3 \\ b_1 & b_2 & b_3 \end{vmatrix} = \mathbf{i}\begin{vmatrix} a_2 & a_3 \\ b_2 & b_3 \end{vmatrix} - \mathbf{j}\begin{vmatrix} a_1 & a_3 \\ b_1 & b_3 \end{vmatrix} + \mathbf{k}\begin{vmatrix} a_1 & a_2 \\ b_1 & b_2 \end{vmatrix}$

Example 3

Given that $\mathbf{a} = 2\mathbf{i} - 3\mathbf{j}$ and $\mathbf{b} = 4\mathbf{i} + \mathbf{j} - \mathbf{k}$, find $\mathbf{a} \times \mathbf{b}$

a directly **b** by a method involving a determinant.

a $(2\mathbf{i} - 3\mathbf{j}) \times (4\mathbf{i} + \mathbf{j} - \mathbf{k})$

$= 8(\mathbf{i} \times \mathbf{i}) + 2(\mathbf{i} \times \mathbf{j}) - 2(\mathbf{i} \times \mathbf{k}) - 12(\mathbf{j} \times \mathbf{i}) - 3(\mathbf{j} \times \mathbf{j}) + 3(\mathbf{j} \times \mathbf{k})$

Use the distributive property to multiply out the brackets.

$= 0 + 2\mathbf{k} + 2\mathbf{j} + 12\mathbf{k} - 0 + 3\mathbf{i}$

$= 3\mathbf{i} + 2\mathbf{j} + 14\mathbf{k}$

Use the key point connecting the unit vectors, e.g. $\mathbf{i} \times \mathbf{j} = \mathbf{k}$ to simplify your answer then collect terms.

b $\begin{vmatrix} \mathbf{i} & \mathbf{j} & \mathbf{k} \\ 2 & -3 & 0 \\ 4 & 1 & -1 \end{vmatrix} = \mathbf{i}\begin{vmatrix} -3 & 0 \\ 1 & -1 \end{vmatrix} - \mathbf{j}\begin{vmatrix} 2 & 0 \\ 4 & -1 \end{vmatrix} + \mathbf{k}\begin{vmatrix} 2 & -3 \\ 4 & 1 \end{vmatrix}$

$= \mathbf{i}(3 - 0) - \mathbf{j}(-2 - 0) + \mathbf{k}(2 + 12)$

$= 3\mathbf{i} + 2\mathbf{j} + 14\mathbf{k}$

You can see that the determinant method is clear and simple.

- **You can check your answer by taking the scalar products $(3\mathbf{i} + 2\mathbf{j} + 14\mathbf{k}).(2\mathbf{i} - 3\mathbf{j})$ and $(3\mathbf{i} + 2\mathbf{j} + 14\mathbf{k}).(4\mathbf{i} + \mathbf{j} - \mathbf{k})$.**

You should always check your answer after calculating a vector product.

- **Both answers should be zero as $\mathbf{a} \times \mathbf{b}$ is perpendicular to each of $\mathbf{a}$ and $\mathbf{b}$.**

Example 4

Find a unit vector perpendicular to both $(4\mathbf{i} + 3\mathbf{j} + 2\mathbf{k})$ and $(8\mathbf{i} + 3\mathbf{j} + 3\mathbf{k})$.

The vector product will give a perpendicular vector.

$\begin{vmatrix} \mathbf{i} & \mathbf{j} & \mathbf{k} \\ 4 & 3 & 2 \\ 8 & 3 & 3 \end{vmatrix} = \mathbf{i}\begin{vmatrix} 3 & 2 \\ 3 & 3 \end{vmatrix} - \mathbf{j}\begin{vmatrix} 4 & 2 \\ 8 & 3 \end{vmatrix} + \mathbf{k}\begin{vmatrix} 4 & 3 \\ 8 & 3 \end{vmatrix}$

Decide whether to use the determinant method or to calculate directly and find the vector product.

$= \mathbf{i}(9 - 6) - \mathbf{j}(12 - 16) + \mathbf{k}(12 - 24)$

$= 3\mathbf{i} + 4\mathbf{j} - 12\mathbf{k}$

Since $|3\mathbf{i} + 4\mathbf{j} - 12\mathbf{k}| = \sqrt{3^2 + 4^2 + (-12)^2} = 13$

Find the magnitude of your product vector.

A suitable unit vector is $\frac{1}{13}(3\mathbf{i} + 4\mathbf{j} - 12\mathbf{k})$.

If you divide a vector by its magnitude you obtain a unit vector.

Example 5

Find the sine of the acute angle between the vectors $\mathbf{a} = 2\mathbf{i} + \mathbf{j} + 2\mathbf{k}$ and $\mathbf{b} = -3\mathbf{j} + 4\mathbf{k}$.

As $\mathbf{a} \times \mathbf{b} = |\mathbf{a}||\mathbf{b}|\sin\theta\hat{\mathbf{n}}$

So $\dfrac{|\mathbf{a} \times \mathbf{b}|}{|\mathbf{a}||\mathbf{b}|} = \sin\theta$

Rearrange the formula to make $\sin\theta$ the subject.

$\mathbf{a} \times \mathbf{b} = \begin{vmatrix} \mathbf{i} & \mathbf{j} & \mathbf{k} \\ 2 & 1 & 2 \\ 0 & -3 & 4 \end{vmatrix}$

Calculate the vector product.

$= \mathbf{i}(4 + 6) - \mathbf{j}(8 - 0) + \mathbf{k}(-6 - 0)$

$= 10\mathbf{i} - 8\mathbf{j} - 6\mathbf{k}$

and $|10\mathbf{i} - 8\mathbf{j} - 6\mathbf{k}| = \sqrt{100 + 64 + 36}$ — Find the magnitude of **a** × **b**.

$$\text{So } \sin\theta = \frac{\sqrt{200}}{\sqrt{2^2 + 1^2 + 2^2}\sqrt{3^2 + (-4)^2}}$$

Also find the magnitude of **a** and of **b** and substitute the three surds into the formula for sin θ.

$$= \frac{\sqrt{200}}{\sqrt{9}\sqrt{25}}$$

$$= \frac{10\sqrt{2}}{3 \times 5}$$

$$= \frac{2\sqrt{2}}{3}$$

Simplify your answer.

In general, if you are asked to find the angle between two vectors, it is preferable to use the scalar product to find the cosine of the angle as the cosine of an angle indicates whether the angle is acute or obtuse. In the solution to Example 5 it is not clear whether the angle θ is acute or obtuse. This is similar to the ambiguous case when using the sine rule.

Exercise 5A

1 Simplify

a $5\mathbf{j} \times \mathbf{k}$

b $3\mathbf{i} \times \mathbf{k}$

c $\mathbf{k} \times 3\mathbf{i}$

d $3\mathbf{i} \times (9\mathbf{i} - \mathbf{j} + \mathbf{k})$

e $2\mathbf{j} \times (3\mathbf{i} + \mathbf{j} - \mathbf{k})$

f $(3\mathbf{i} + \mathbf{j} - \mathbf{k}) \times 2\mathbf{j}$

g $(5\mathbf{i} + 2\mathbf{j} - \mathbf{k}) \times (\mathbf{i} - \mathbf{j} + 3\mathbf{k})$

h $(2\mathbf{i} - \mathbf{j} + 6\mathbf{k}) \times (\mathbf{i} - 2\mathbf{j} + 3\mathbf{k})$

i $(\mathbf{i} + 5\mathbf{j} - 4\mathbf{k}) \times (2\mathbf{i} - \mathbf{j} - \mathbf{k})$

j $(3\mathbf{i} + \mathbf{k}) \times (\mathbf{i} - \mathbf{j} + 2\mathbf{k})$

2 Find the vector product of the vectors **a** and **b**, leaving your answers in terms of λ in each case.

a $\mathbf{a} = (\lambda\mathbf{i} + 2\mathbf{j} + \mathbf{k})$ $\quad \mathbf{b} = (\mathbf{i} - 3\mathbf{k})$

b $\mathbf{a} = (2\mathbf{i} - \mathbf{j} + 7\mathbf{k})$ $\quad \mathbf{b} = (\mathbf{i} - \lambda\mathbf{j} + 3\mathbf{k})$

3 Find a unit vector that is perpendicular to both $2\mathbf{i} - \mathbf{j}$ and to $4\mathbf{i} + \mathbf{j} + 3\mathbf{k}$.

4 Find a unit vector that is perpendicular to both of $4\mathbf{i} + \mathbf{k}$ and $\mathbf{j} - \sqrt{2}\mathbf{k}$.

5 Find a unit vector that is perpendicular to both $\mathbf{i} - \mathbf{j}$ and $3\mathbf{i} + 4\mathbf{j} - 6\mathbf{k}$.

6 Find a unit vector that is perpendicular to both $\mathbf{i} + 6\mathbf{j} + 4\mathbf{k}$ and to $5\mathbf{i} + 9\mathbf{j} + 8\mathbf{k}$.

7 Find a vector of magnitude 5 which is perpendicular to both $4\mathbf{i} + \mathbf{k}$ and $\sqrt{2}\mathbf{j} + \mathbf{k}$.

8 Find the magnitude of $(\mathbf{i} + \mathbf{j} - \mathbf{k}) \times (\mathbf{i} - \mathbf{j} + \mathbf{k})$. *E*

9 Given that $\mathbf{a} = -\mathbf{i} + 2\mathbf{j} - 5\mathbf{k}$, $\mathbf{b} = 5\mathbf{i} - 2\mathbf{j} + \mathbf{k}$ find

a $\mathbf{a}.\mathbf{b}$

b $\mathbf{a} \times \mathbf{b}$

c the unit vector in the direction $\mathbf{a} \times \mathbf{b}$. *E*

10 Find the sine of the angle between **a** and **b** in each of the following. You may leave your answers as surds, in their simplest form.

a $\mathbf{a} = 3\mathbf{i} - 4\mathbf{j}$, $\mathbf{b} = 2\mathbf{i} + 2\mathbf{j} + \mathbf{k}$

b $\mathbf{a} = \mathbf{j} + 2\mathbf{k}$, $\mathbf{b} = 5\mathbf{i} + 4\mathbf{j} - 2\mathbf{k}$

c $\mathbf{a} = 5\mathbf{i} + 2\mathbf{j} + 2\mathbf{k}$, $\mathbf{b} = 4\mathbf{i} + 4\mathbf{j} + \mathbf{k}$

11 The line l_1 has equation $\mathbf{r} = (\mathbf{i} - \mathbf{j}) + \lambda(\mathbf{i} + 2\mathbf{j} + 3\mathbf{k})$ and the line l_2 has equation $\mathbf{r} = (2\mathbf{i} + \mathbf{j} + \mathbf{k}) + \mu(2\mathbf{i} - \mathbf{j} + \mathbf{k})$. Find a vector that is perpendicular to both l_1 and l_2.

12 It is given that $\mathbf{a} = \mathbf{i} + 3\mathbf{j} - \mathbf{k}$ and $\mathbf{b} = 2\mathbf{i} + u\mathbf{j} + v\mathbf{k}$ and that $\mathbf{a} \times \mathbf{b} = w\mathbf{i} - 6\mathbf{j} - 7\mathbf{k}$, where u, v and w are scalar constants. Find the values of u, v and w.

13 Given that $\mathbf{p} = a\mathbf{i} - \mathbf{j} + 4\mathbf{k}$, that $\mathbf{q} = \mathbf{j} - \mathbf{k}$ and that their vector product $\mathbf{q} \times \mathbf{p} = 3\mathbf{i} - \mathbf{j} + b\mathbf{k}$ where a and b are scalar constants,

a find the values of a and b,

b find the value of the cosine of the angle between **p** and **q**.

14 If $\mathbf{a} \times \mathbf{b} = 0$, and $\mathbf{a} = 2\mathbf{i} + \mathbf{j} - \mathbf{k}$, and $\mathbf{b} = 3\mathbf{i} + \lambda\mathbf{j} + \mu\mathbf{k}$, where λ and μ are scalar constants, find the values of λ and μ.

15 If three vectors **a**, **b** and **c** satisfy $\mathbf{a} + \mathbf{b} + \mathbf{c} = 0$, show that

$$\mathbf{a} \times \mathbf{b} = \mathbf{b} \times \mathbf{c} = \mathbf{c} \times \mathbf{a}$$

5.2 You can interpret $|\mathbf{a} \times \mathbf{b}|$ as an area.

The vector product has a number of applications. For example, if you study the M5 specification you will use it to find moments of forces. Later in this chapter you will use it to give an alternative form of the equation of a straight line in vector form and to find the shortest distance between skew lines (i.e. lines which do not meet and are not parallel).

In this section you will find areas of triangles and parallelograms using vector products.

Example 6

Find the area of triangle OAB, where O is the origin, A is the point with position vector **a** and B is the point with position vector **b**.

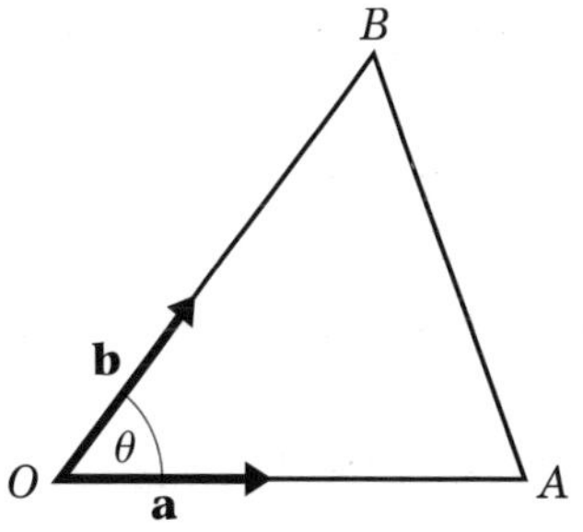

Area of triangle $OAB = \frac{1}{2}OA.OB\sin\theta$

$= \frac{1}{2}|\mathbf{a}||\mathbf{b}|\sin\theta$

$= \frac{1}{2}|\mathbf{a} \times \mathbf{b}|$

Use the trigonometric formula area of triangle $= \frac{1}{2}ab\sin C$, and let the angle $AOB = \theta$.

You use the definition of vector product to obtain this result.

■ **Area of triangle** $OAB = \frac{1}{2}|\mathbf{a} \times \mathbf{b}|$

Example 7

Find the area of triangle ABC, where the position vectors of A, B and C are $\mathbf{a}$, $\mathbf{b}$ and $\mathbf{c}$ respectively.

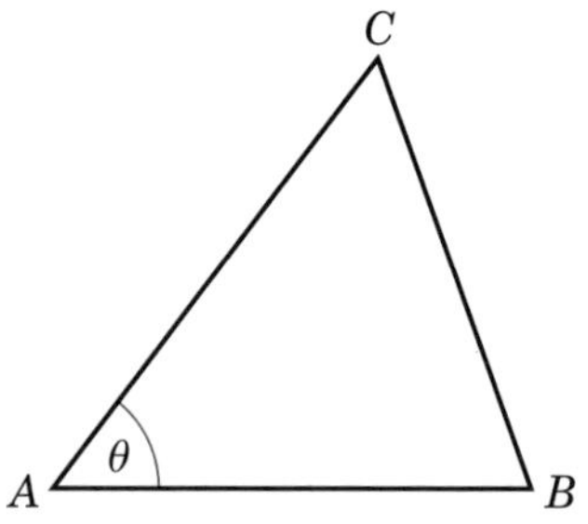

Area of triangle $ABC = \frac{1}{2}AB.AC\sin\theta$

$= \frac{1}{2}|\mathbf{b} - \mathbf{a}||\mathbf{c} - \mathbf{a}|\sin\theta$

$= \frac{1}{2}|(\mathbf{b} - \mathbf{a}) \times (\mathbf{c} - \mathbf{a})|$

$= \frac{1}{2}|(\mathbf{b} \times \mathbf{c}) - (\mathbf{b} \times \mathbf{a}) - (\mathbf{a} \times \mathbf{c}) + (\mathbf{a} \times \mathbf{a})|$

$= \frac{1}{2}|(\mathbf{b} \times \mathbf{c}) + (\mathbf{c} \times \mathbf{a}) + (\mathbf{a} \times \mathbf{b})|$

$= \frac{1}{2}|(\mathbf{a} \times \mathbf{b}) + (\mathbf{b} \times \mathbf{c}) + (\mathbf{c} \times \mathbf{a})|$

Let the angle $BAC = \theta$.

Use the definition of vector product.

Expand using the distributive law.

Use $\mathbf{a} \times \mathbf{a} = 0$, $\mathbf{a} \times \mathbf{b} = -\mathbf{b} \times \mathbf{a}$ and $\mathbf{c} \times \mathbf{a} = -\mathbf{a} \times \mathbf{c}$.

■ **Area of triangle $ABC = \frac{1}{2}|\overrightarrow{AB} \times \overrightarrow{AC}|$**

$$= \frac{1}{2}|(\mathbf{b} - \mathbf{a}) \times (\mathbf{c} - \mathbf{a})|$$

$$= \frac{1}{2}|(\mathbf{a} \times \mathbf{b}) + (\mathbf{b} \times \mathbf{c}) + (\mathbf{c} \times \mathbf{a})|$$

Example 8

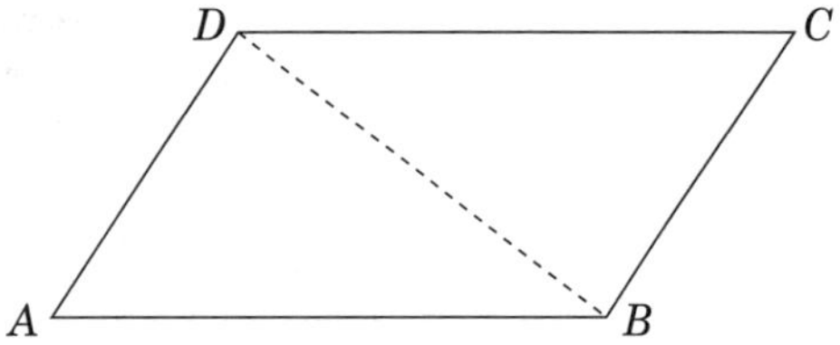

Find the area of the parallelogram $ABCD$, where the position vectors of A, B and D are $\mathbf{a}$, $\mathbf{b}$ and $\mathbf{d}$ respectively.

area of parallelogram $ABCD$

$=$ area of triangle ABD + area of triangle BCD

$= 2 \times$ area of triangle ABD

$= AB \cdot AD\sin\theta$

$= |\mathbf{b} - \mathbf{a}||\mathbf{d} - \mathbf{a}|\sin\theta$

$= |(\mathbf{b} - \mathbf{a}) \times (\mathbf{d} - \mathbf{a})|$

$= |(\mathbf{a} \times \mathbf{b}) + (\mathbf{b} \times \mathbf{d}) + (\mathbf{d} \times \mathbf{a})|$

As the two triangles are congruent and have equal area.

θ is the angle $B\hat{A}D$.

■ **Area of parallelogram $ABCD = |\overrightarrow{AB} \times \overrightarrow{AD}|$**

$$= |(\mathbf{b} - \mathbf{a}) \times (\mathbf{d} - \mathbf{a})|$$

$$= |(\mathbf{a} \times \mathbf{b}) + (\mathbf{b} \times \mathbf{d}) + (\mathbf{d} \times \mathbf{a})|$$

Example 9

Find the area of triangle *OAB*, where *O* is the origin, *A* is the point with position vector $\mathbf{i} - \mathbf{j}$ and *B* is the point with position vector $3\mathbf{i} + 4\mathbf{j} - 6\mathbf{k}$.

area of triangle $OAB = \frac{1}{2}|(\mathbf{i} - \mathbf{j}) \times (3\mathbf{i} + 4\mathbf{j} - 6\mathbf{k})|$

$$\tfrac{1}{2}(\mathbf{i} - \mathbf{j}) \times (3\mathbf{i} + 4\mathbf{j} - 6\mathbf{k}) = \frac{1}{2}\begin{vmatrix} \mathbf{i} & \mathbf{j} & \mathbf{k} \\ 1 & -1 & 0 \\ 3 & 4 & -6 \end{vmatrix}$$

First find the vector product using the determinant method.

$$= \tfrac{1}{2}(6\mathbf{i} + 6\mathbf{j} + 7\mathbf{k})$$

So area of triangle $= \frac{1}{2}|6\mathbf{i} + 6\mathbf{j} + 7\mathbf{k}| = \frac{1}{2}\sqrt{6^2 + 6^2 + 7^2}$

Then find its modulus.

$$= \frac{\sqrt{121}}{2} = 5.5$$

Example 10

Find the area of triangle *ABC*, where the position vectors of *A*, *B* and *C* are $4\mathbf{i} - 2\mathbf{j} + \mathbf{k}$, $-12\mathbf{i} + 14\mathbf{j} + \mathbf{k}$ and $-4\mathbf{i} - 2\mathbf{j} + \mathbf{k}$ respectively.

$$\overrightarrow{AB} = (-12\mathbf{i} + 14\mathbf{j} + \mathbf{k}) - (4\mathbf{i} - 2\mathbf{j} + \mathbf{k}) = -16\mathbf{i} + 16\mathbf{j}$$
$$\overrightarrow{AC} = (-4\mathbf{i} - 2\mathbf{j} + \mathbf{k}) - (4\mathbf{i} - 2\mathbf{j} + \mathbf{k}) = -8\mathbf{i}$$

Find vectors representing two of the sides of the triangle.

$$\tfrac{1}{2}|\overrightarrow{AB} \times \overrightarrow{AC}| = \frac{1}{2}\begin{vmatrix} \mathbf{i} & \mathbf{j} & \mathbf{k} \\ -16 & 16 & 0 \\ -8 & 0 & 0 \end{vmatrix}$$

So area of triangle $ABC = \frac{1}{2}|128\mathbf{k}| = 64$

Then find the vector product of the vectors you have found and find half the modulus of your answer.

Example 11

Find the area of the parallelogram *ABCD*, where the position vectors of *A*, *B* and *D* are $2\mathbf{i} + \mathbf{j} - \mathbf{k}$, $6\mathbf{i} + 4\mathbf{j} - 3\mathbf{k}$ and $14\mathbf{i} + 7\mathbf{j} - 6\mathbf{k}$ respectively.

Area of parallelogram $ABCD = |\overrightarrow{AB} \times \overrightarrow{AD}|$

$$\overrightarrow{AB} = (6\mathbf{i} + 4\mathbf{j} - 3\mathbf{k}) - (2\mathbf{i} + \mathbf{j} - \mathbf{k}) = 4\mathbf{i} + 3\mathbf{j} - 2\mathbf{k}$$
$$\overrightarrow{AD} = (14\mathbf{i} + 7\mathbf{j} - 6\mathbf{k}) - (2\mathbf{i} + \mathbf{j} - \mathbf{k}) = 12\mathbf{i} + 6\mathbf{j} - 5\mathbf{k}$$

Find vectors representing two adjacent sides of the parallelogram.

$$|\overrightarrow{AB} \times \overrightarrow{AD}| = \begin{vmatrix} \mathbf{i} & \mathbf{j} & \mathbf{k} \\ 4 & 3 & -2 \\ 12 & 6 & -5 \end{vmatrix}$$

So area of parallelogram $= |-3\mathbf{i} - 4\mathbf{j} - 12\mathbf{k}| = \mathbf{13}$

Then find the vector product of the vectors you have found and find the modulus of your answer.

Exercise 5B

Find the area of triangle OAB, where O is the origin, A is the point with position vector $\mathbf{a}$ and B is the point with position vector $\mathbf{b}$ in the following cases.

1 $\mathbf{a} = \mathbf{i} + \mathbf{j} - 4\mathbf{k}$ $\quad$ $\mathbf{b} = 2\mathbf{i} - \mathbf{j} - 2\mathbf{k}$

2 $\mathbf{a} = 3\mathbf{i} + 4\mathbf{j} - 5\mathbf{k}$ $\quad$ $\mathbf{b} = 2\mathbf{i} + \mathbf{j} - 2\mathbf{k}$

3 $\mathbf{a} = \begin{pmatrix} 2 \\ 3 \\ 0 \end{pmatrix}$ $\quad$ $\mathbf{b} = \begin{pmatrix} 2 \\ 6 \\ -9 \end{pmatrix}$

4 Find the area of the triangle with vertices $A(0, 0, 0)$, $B(1, -2, 1)$ and $C(2, -1, -1)$.

5 Find the area of triangle ABC, where the position vectors of A, B and C are $\mathbf{a}$, $\mathbf{b}$ and $\mathbf{c}$ respectively, in the following cases:

i $\mathbf{a} = \mathbf{i} - \mathbf{j} - \mathbf{k}$ $\quad$ $\mathbf{b} = 4\mathbf{i} + \mathbf{j} + \mathbf{k}$ $\quad$ $\mathbf{c} = 4\mathbf{i} - 3\mathbf{j} + \mathbf{k}$

ii $\mathbf{a} = \begin{pmatrix} 0 \\ 1 \\ 2 \end{pmatrix}$ $\quad$ $\mathbf{b} = \begin{pmatrix} 1 \\ 0 \\ 2 \end{pmatrix}$ $\quad$ $\mathbf{c} = \begin{pmatrix} 2 \\ 0 \\ -10 \end{pmatrix}$

6 Find the area of the triangle with vertices $A(1, 0, 2)$, $B(2, -2, 0)$ and $C(3, -1, 1)$.

7 Find the area of the triangle with vertices $A(-1, 1, 1)$, $B(1, 0, 2)$ and $C(0, 3, 4)$.

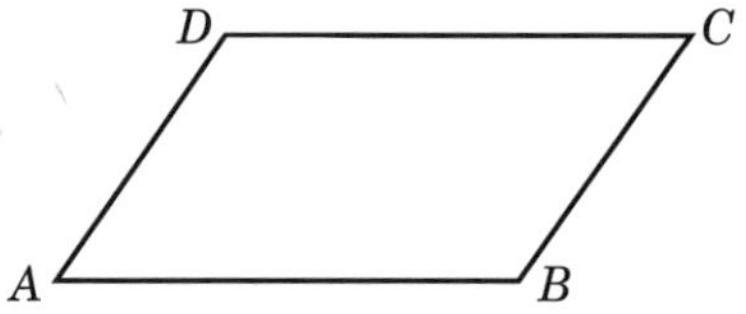

8 Find the area of the parallelogram $ABCD$, shown in the figure, where the position vectors of A, B and D are $\mathbf{i} + \mathbf{j} + \mathbf{k}$, $-3\mathbf{i} + 4\mathbf{j} + \mathbf{k}$ and $2\mathbf{i} - \mathbf{j}$ respectively.

9 Find the area of the parallelogram $ABCD$, shown in the figure, in which the vertices A, B and D have coordinates $(0, 5, 3)$, $(2, 1, -1)$ and $(1, 6, 6)$ respectively.

10 Find the area of the parallelogram $ABCD$, shown in the figure, where the position vectors of A, B and D are $\mathbf{j}$, $\mathbf{i} + 4\mathbf{j} + \mathbf{k}$ and $2\mathbf{i} + 6\mathbf{j} + 3\mathbf{k}$ respectively.

11 Relative to an origin O, the points P and Q have position vectors $\mathbf{p}$ and $\mathbf{q}$ respectively, where $\mathbf{p} = a(\mathbf{i} + \mathbf{j} + 2\mathbf{k})$ and $\mathbf{q} = a(2\mathbf{i} + \mathbf{j} + 3\mathbf{k})$ and $a > 0$.
Find the area of triangle OPQ. **E**

12 **a** Show that the area of the parallelogram $ABCD$ is also given by the formula $|(\mathbf{b} - \mathbf{a}) \times (\mathbf{c} - \mathbf{a})|$.

b Show that $(\mathbf{b} - \mathbf{a}) \times (\mathbf{c} - \mathbf{a}) = (\mathbf{b} - \mathbf{a}) \times (\mathbf{d} - \mathbf{a})$ implies that $(\mathbf{b} - \mathbf{a}) \times (\mathbf{c} - \mathbf{d}) = 0$ and explain the geometrical significance of this vector product.

5.3 You can find the triple scalar product **a**.(**b** × **c**) of three vectors **a**, **b** and **c**, and use it to find the volume of a parallelepiped and of a tetrahedron.

You know that $\mathbf{b} \times \mathbf{c} = (b_2c_3 - b_3c_2)\mathbf{i} + (b_3c_1 - b_1c_3)\mathbf{j} + (b_1c_2 - b_2c_1)\mathbf{k}$,
where $\mathbf{b} = (b_1\mathbf{i} + b_2\mathbf{j} + b_3\mathbf{k})$ and $c = (c_1\mathbf{i} + c_2\mathbf{j} + c_3\mathbf{k})$.

So if $\mathbf{a} = (a_1\mathbf{i} + a_2\mathbf{j} + a_3\mathbf{k})$ then

- $\mathbf{a}.(\mathbf{b} \times \mathbf{c}) = a_1(b_2c_3 - b_3c_2) + a_2(b_3c_1 - b_1c_3) + a_3(b_1c_2 - b_2c_1)$

This can also be written as

- $\mathbf{a}.(\mathbf{b} \times \mathbf{c}) = \begin{vmatrix} a_1 & a_2 & a_3 \\ b_1 & b_2 & b_3 \\ c_1 & c_2 & c_3 \end{vmatrix}$

a.(**b** × **c**) is known as a **triple scalar product**.

Example 12

Given that $\mathbf{a} = 3\mathbf{i} - \mathbf{j} + 4\mathbf{k}$, $\mathbf{b} = \mathbf{i} + \mathbf{j} - \mathbf{k}$ and $\mathbf{c} = 2\mathbf{i} + 3\mathbf{j} + 5\mathbf{k}$

Find

a **a**.(**b** × **c**) **b** **b**.(**c** × **a**) **c** **a**.(**a** × **c**).

a $\mathbf{b} \times \mathbf{c} = \begin{vmatrix} \mathbf{i} & \mathbf{j} & \mathbf{k} \\ 1 & 1 & -1 \\ 2 & 3 & 5 \end{vmatrix} = 8\mathbf{i} - 7\mathbf{j} + \mathbf{k}$

So $\mathbf{a}.(\mathbf{b} \times \mathbf{c}) = (3\mathbf{i} - \mathbf{j} + 4\mathbf{k}).(8\mathbf{i} - 7\mathbf{j} + \mathbf{k})$
$= 24 + 7 + 4$
$= 35$

You could also use the determinant $\begin{vmatrix} a_1 & a_2 & a_3 \\ b_1 & b_2 & b_3 \\ c_1 & c_2 & c_3 \end{vmatrix}$ in this example.

b $\mathbf{c} \times \mathbf{a} = \begin{vmatrix} \mathbf{i} & \mathbf{j} & \mathbf{k} \\ 2 & 3 & 5 \\ 3 & -1 & 4 \end{vmatrix} = 17\mathbf{i} + 7\mathbf{j} - 11\mathbf{k}$

So $\mathbf{b}.(\mathbf{c} \times \mathbf{a}) = (\mathbf{i} + \mathbf{j} - \mathbf{k}).(17\mathbf{i} + 7\mathbf{j} - 11\mathbf{k})$
$= 17 + 7 + 11$
$= 35$

Note that **a**.(**b** × **c**) = **b**.(**c** × **a**)

c $\mathbf{a} \times \mathbf{c} = -\mathbf{c} \times \mathbf{a} = -17\mathbf{i} - 7\mathbf{j} + 11\mathbf{k}$

Use the result that **a** × **c** = −**c** × **a**.

So $\mathbf{a}.(\mathbf{a} \times \mathbf{c}) = (3\mathbf{i} - \mathbf{j} + 4\mathbf{k}).(-17\mathbf{i} - 7\mathbf{j} + 11\mathbf{k})$
$= -51 + 7 + 44$
$= 0$

This scalar product is zero as **a** × **c** is perpendicular to **a**.

- **a**.(**b** × **c**) = **b**.(**c** × **a**) = **c**.(**a** × **b**).
- **a**.(**a** × x) = 0 for any vector x.

You can interpret $\mathbf{a}.(\mathbf{b} \times \mathbf{c})$ as a volume as you will see in the following example.

Example 13

Find the volume of the parallelepiped shown in the figure, given that O is the origin and A, B and C have position vectors $\mathbf{a}$, $\mathbf{b}$ and $\mathbf{c}$ respectively. The angle between $\mathbf{b}$ and $\mathbf{c}$ is θ and the angle between the perpendicular height and $\mathbf{a}$ is ϕ.

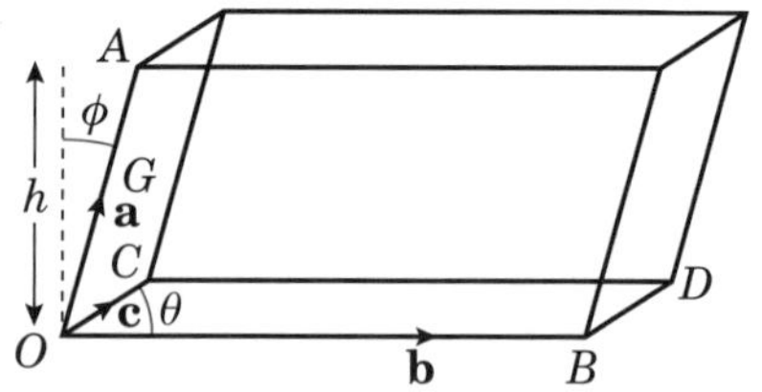

The volume of the parallelepiped is given by (area of base) $\times$ h where h is the perpendicular distance between the base and the top face.

The base, $OBDC$ is a parallelogram and its area is $|\mathbf{b} \times \mathbf{c}|$.

So the volume of the parallelepiped is $|\mathbf{b} \times \mathbf{c}|h$

But $h = OA \cos \phi$

As $\cos \phi = \frac{h}{OA}$.

So volume is $|\mathbf{b} \times \mathbf{c}| OA \cos \phi$

$= |\mathbf{b} \times \mathbf{c}||\mathbf{a}| \cos \phi$

$= \mathbf{a}.(\mathbf{b} \times \mathbf{c})$

From the definition of scalar product.

As $\mathbf{b} \times \mathbf{c}$ is in the direction of the perpendicular height, so ϕ is the angle between vector $\mathbf{a}$ and vector $\mathbf{b} \times \mathbf{c}$.

- **The volume of the parallelepiped is given by $|\mathbf{a}.(\mathbf{b} \times \mathbf{c})|$.**

Example 14

Find the volume of the tetrahedron shown in the figure, given that O is the origin and A, B and C have position vectors $\mathbf{a}$, $\mathbf{b}$ and $\mathbf{c}$ respectively. The angle between $\mathbf{b}$ and $\mathbf{c}$ is θ and the angle between the perpendicular height and $\mathbf{a}$ is ϕ.

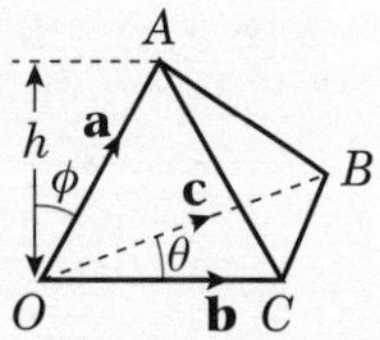

The volume of the tetrahedron is given by the formula $\frac{1}{3}$(area of base) $\times$ h

The volume of a pyramid is $\frac{1}{3}$(area of base) $\times$ h.

where h is the perpendicular height.

The triangular base, OBC has area $\frac{1}{2}|\mathbf{b} \times \mathbf{c}|$

And $h = OA \cos \phi = |\mathbf{a}| \cos \phi$

So volume of tetrahedron is $\frac{1}{3} \times \frac{1}{2}|\mathbf{b} \times \mathbf{c}||\mathbf{a}| \cos \phi$

$= \frac{1}{6}\mathbf{a}.(\mathbf{b} \times \mathbf{c})$

As in Example 13, $\mathbf{b} \times \mathbf{c}$ is in the direction of the perpendicular height, so ϕ is the angle between vector $\mathbf{a}$ and vector $\mathbf{b} \times \mathbf{c}$.

- **The volume of a tetrahedron is given by $\left|\frac{1}{6}\mathbf{a}.(\mathbf{b} \times \mathbf{c})\right|$.**

Example 15

A pyramid has a square base $ABCD$ and has vertices at $A(0, 0, 0)$, $B(4, -3, 0)$, $C(7, 1, 0)$, $D(3, 4, 0)$ and $E(3\frac{1}{2}, \frac{1}{2}, 6)$. Find the volume of this pyramid.

Area of base $ABCD = |\overrightarrow{AB} \times \overrightarrow{AD}|$

$= |(4\mathbf{i} - 3\mathbf{j}) \times (3\mathbf{i} + 4\mathbf{j})|$

$= |25\mathbf{k}|$

$= 25$

You could use $|\overrightarrow{AB} \times \overrightarrow{AC}|$ which gives the same answer.

Volume of pyramid $= \frac{1}{3}\overrightarrow{AE}.(\overrightarrow{AB} \times \overrightarrow{AD})$

$= \frac{1}{3}(3\frac{1}{2}\mathbf{i} + \frac{1}{2}\mathbf{j} + 6\mathbf{k}).25\mathbf{k}$

$= 50$

The volume of a pyramid is $\frac{1}{3}$ (area of base) $\times$ height.

or

$$\text{volume} = \frac{1}{3}\begin{vmatrix} 3\frac{1}{2} & \frac{1}{2} & 6 \\ 4 & -3 & 0 \\ 3 & 4 & 0 \end{vmatrix} = 50$$

You can use a determinant method directly. The first row should come from the vector $\overrightarrow{AE}$ and the next two rows from any two of the vectors $\overrightarrow{AB}$, $\overrightarrow{AC}$ and $\overrightarrow{AD}$.

Example 16

Find the volume of a tetrahedron which has vertices at $(1, 1, -1)$, $(2, 4, -1)$, $(3, 0, -2)$, and $(0, 4, 5)$.

If the vertices are labelled A, B, C and D in the order given above then they have position vectors $\mathbf{a}$, $\mathbf{b}$, $\mathbf{c}$ and $\mathbf{d}$.

$\overrightarrow{AB} = \mathbf{b} - \mathbf{a} = \mathbf{i} + 3\mathbf{j}$

$\overrightarrow{AC} = \mathbf{c} - \mathbf{a} = 2\mathbf{i} - \mathbf{j} - \mathbf{k}$

and $\overrightarrow{AD} = \mathbf{d} - \mathbf{a} = -\mathbf{i} + 3\mathbf{j} + 6\mathbf{k}$

Find expressions for the vectors describing the displacement from one of the vertices to the other three.

$$\text{Volume of tetrahedron} = \frac{1}{6}\begin{vmatrix} 1 & 3 & 0 \\ 2 & -1 & -1 \\ -1 & 3 & 6 \end{vmatrix} = \frac{1}{6} \times (-36) = -6$$

Use the determinant expression for the volume of a tetrahedron and note that the answer is negative.

So the volume is 6.

Ensure that you give a positive answer for the volume. If the vertices had been taken in a different order then a positive answer would have been obtained.

Exercise 5C

1 Given that $\mathbf{a} = 5\mathbf{i} + 2\mathbf{j} - \mathbf{k}$, $\mathbf{b} = \mathbf{i} + \mathbf{j} + \mathbf{k}$ and $\mathbf{c} = 3\mathbf{i} + 4\mathbf{k}$

find

a $\mathbf{a}.(\mathbf{b} \times \mathbf{c})$

b $\mathbf{b}.(\mathbf{c} \times \mathbf{a})$

c $\mathbf{c}.(\mathbf{a} \times \mathbf{b})$.

2 Given that $\mathbf{a} = \mathbf{i} - \mathbf{j} - 2\mathbf{k}$, $\mathbf{b} = 2\mathbf{i} + \mathbf{j} - \mathbf{k}$ and $\mathbf{c} = 2\mathbf{i} - 3\mathbf{j} - 5\mathbf{k}$

find $\mathbf{a}.(\mathbf{b} \times \mathbf{c})$. What can you deduce about the vectors $\mathbf{a}$, $\mathbf{b}$ and $\mathbf{c}$?

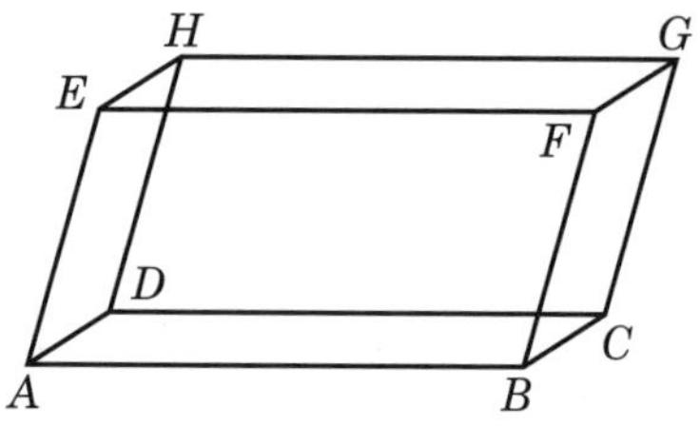

3 Find the volume of the parallelepiped *ABCDEFGH* where the vertices *A*, *B*, *D* and *E* have coordinates (0, 0, 0), (3, 0, 1), (1, 2, 0) and (1, 1, 3) respectively.

4 Find the volume of the parallelepiped *ABCDEFGH* where the vertices *A*, *B*, *D* and *E* have coordinates (−1, 0, 1), (3, 0, −1), (2, 2, 0) and (2, 1, 2) respectively.

5 A tetrahedron has vertices at *A*(1, 2, 3), *B*(4, 3, 4), *C*(1, 3, 1) and *D*(3, 1, 4).
Find the volume of the tetrahedron.

6 A tetrahedron has vertices at *A*(2, 2, 1), *B*(3, −1, 2), *C*(1, 1, 3) and *D*(3, 1, 4).

a Find the area of base *BCD*.

b Find a unit vector normal to the face *BCD*.

c Find the volume of the tetrahedron.

7 A tetrahedron has vertices at *A*(0, 0, 0), *B*(2, 0, 0), $C(1, \sqrt{3}, 0)$ and $D\left(1, \frac{\sqrt{3}}{3}, \frac{2\sqrt{6}}{3}\right)$.

a Show that the tetrahedron is regular.

b Find the volume of the tetrahedron.

8 A tetrahedron *OABC* has its vertices at the points
O(0, 0, 0), *A*(1, 2, −1), *B*(−1, 1, 2) and *C*(2, −1, 1).

a Write down expressions for $\overrightarrow{AB}$ and $\overrightarrow{AC}$ in terms of **i**, **j** and **k** and find $\overrightarrow{AB} \times \overrightarrow{AC}$.

b Deduce the area of triangle *ABC*.

c Find the volume of the tetrahedron. **E**

9 The points *A*, *B*, *C* and *D* have position vectors

$\mathbf{a} = (2\mathbf{i} + \mathbf{j})$ $\mathbf{b} = (3\mathbf{i} - \mathbf{j} + \mathbf{k})$ $\mathbf{c} = (-2\mathbf{j} - \mathbf{k})$ $\mathbf{d} = (2\mathbf{i} - \mathbf{j} + 3\mathbf{k})$

respectively.

a Find $\overrightarrow{AB} \times \overrightarrow{BC}$ and $\overrightarrow{BD} \times \overrightarrow{DC}$.

b Hence find

i the area of triangle *ABC*

ii the volume of the tetrahedron *ABCD*. **E**

10 The edges *OP*, *OQ*, *OR* of a tetrahedron *OPQR* are the vectors **a**, **b** and **c** respectively, where

$\mathbf{a} = 2\mathbf{i} + 4\mathbf{j}$
$\mathbf{b} = 2\mathbf{i} - \mathbf{j} + 3\mathbf{k}$
$\mathbf{c} = 4\mathbf{i} - 2\mathbf{j} + 5\mathbf{k}$

a Evaluate $(\mathbf{b} \times \mathbf{c})$ and deduce that *OP* is perpendicular to the plane *OQR*.

b Write down the length of *OP* and the area of triangle *OQR* and hence the volume of the tetrahedron.

c Verify your result by evaluating $\mathbf{a}.(\mathbf{b} \times \mathbf{c})$. **E**

5.4 You can write the vector equation of a line in the form $(\mathbf{r} - \mathbf{a}) \times \mathbf{b} = 0$.

In book C4 Section 5.8 you found that

- a vector equation of a straight line passing through a point A with position vector $\mathbf{a}$, and parallel to the vector $\mathbf{b}$, is $\mathbf{r} = \mathbf{a} + t\mathbf{b}$, where t is a scalar parameter.

You will now find an alternative equation for this straight line.

Example 17

Show that the equation of a straight line passing through a point A with position vector $\mathbf{a}$, and parallel to the vector $\mathbf{b}$, can be written in the form $(\mathbf{r} - \mathbf{a}) \times \mathbf{b} = 0$.

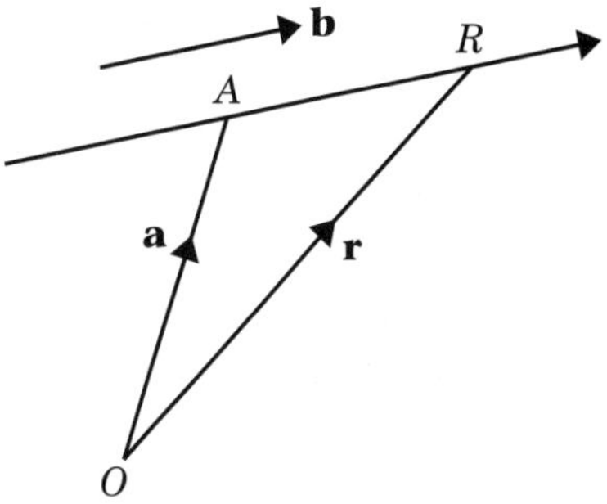

Let R be a point on the line, with position vector $\mathbf{r}$.

$\overrightarrow{AR} = \mathbf{r} - \mathbf{a}$

Use $\overrightarrow{AR} = \overrightarrow{OR} - \overrightarrow{OA}$

As $\overrightarrow{AR}$ is parallel to $\mathbf{b}$,

$(\mathbf{r} - \mathbf{a}) \times \mathbf{b} = 0$

The angle between parallel vectors is zero and so their cross product is zero.

- **$(\mathbf{r} - \mathbf{a}) \times \mathbf{b} = 0$ is an alternative form of the vector equation of a line passing through a point A with position vector $\mathbf{a}$, and parallel to the vector $\mathbf{b}$.**
- **This may also be written $\mathbf{r} \times \mathbf{b} = \mathbf{a} \times \mathbf{b}$**

Example 18

Find the vector equation of the line through the points $(1, 2, -1)$ and $(3, -2, 2)$ in the form $(\mathbf{r} - \mathbf{a}) \times \mathbf{b} = 0$.

The line is in the direction $\begin{pmatrix} 3 \\ -2 \\ 2 \end{pmatrix} - \begin{pmatrix} 1 \\ 2 \\ -1 \end{pmatrix} = \begin{pmatrix} 2 \\ -4 \\ 3 \end{pmatrix}$

Any multiple of this vector is also parallel to the direction of the line.

So the equation is $\left(\mathbf{r} - \begin{pmatrix} 3 \\ -2 \\ 2 \end{pmatrix}\right) \times \begin{pmatrix} 2 \\ -4 \\ 3 \end{pmatrix} = 0$

You could use the position vector $\begin{pmatrix} 1 \\ 2 \\ -1 \end{pmatrix}$ instead of $\begin{pmatrix} 3 \\ -2 \\ 2 \end{pmatrix}$ in this equation.

This may also be written $\mathbf{r} \times \begin{pmatrix} 2 \\ -4 \\ 3 \end{pmatrix} = \begin{vmatrix} \mathbf{i} & \mathbf{j} & \mathbf{k} \\ 3 & -2 & 2 \\ 2 & -4 & 3 \end{vmatrix}$

The right hand side is $\begin{pmatrix} 3 \\ -2 \\ 2 \end{pmatrix} \times \begin{pmatrix} 2 \\ -4 \\ 3 \end{pmatrix}$.

i.e. $\mathbf{r} \times \begin{pmatrix} 2 \\ -4 \\ 3 \end{pmatrix} = 2\mathbf{i} - 5\mathbf{j} - 8\mathbf{k}$

Example 19

Convert the straight line equation $(\mathbf{r} - \mathbf{a}) \times \mathbf{b} = 0$, into Cartesian form by replacing $\mathbf{r}$ by $x\mathbf{i} + y\mathbf{j} + z\mathbf{k}$, $\mathbf{a}$ by $x_1\mathbf{i} + y_1\mathbf{j} + z_1\mathbf{k}$, and $\mathbf{b}$ by $l\mathbf{i} + m\mathbf{j} + n\mathbf{k}$.

$((x - x_1)\mathbf{i} + (y - y_1)\mathbf{j} + (z - z_1)\mathbf{k}) \times (l\mathbf{i} + m\mathbf{j} + n\mathbf{k}) = 0$

So $(x - x_1)\mathbf{i} + (y - y_1)\mathbf{j} + (z - z_1)\mathbf{k} = \lambda(l\mathbf{i} + m\mathbf{j} + n\mathbf{k})$

$\Rightarrow (x - x_1) = \lambda l$, $(y - y_1) = \lambda m$ and $(z_1 - z_1) = \lambda n$

which may be written

$$\frac{(x - x_1)}{l} = \frac{(y - y_1)}{m} = \frac{(z - z_1)}{n} = \lambda$$

If the cross product of two non-zero vectors is zero, then one is a multiple of the other.

■ **The general Cartesian equation of a straight line is $\frac{(x - x_1)}{l} = \frac{(y - y_1)}{m} = \frac{(z - z_1)}{n} = \lambda$, where the line passes through the point (x_1, y_1, z_1), has direction ratios $l : m : n$, and where λ is a parameter.**

Exercise 5D

1 Find an equation of the straight line passing through the point with position vector $\mathbf{a}$ which is parallel to the vector $\mathbf{b}$, giving your answer in the form $\mathbf{r} \times \mathbf{b} = \mathbf{c}$, where $\mathbf{c}$ is evaluated:

a $\mathbf{a} = 2\mathbf{i} + \mathbf{j} + 2\mathbf{k}$ $\quad$ $\mathbf{b} = 3\mathbf{i} + \mathbf{j} - 2\mathbf{k}$

b $\mathbf{a} = 2\mathbf{i} - 3\mathbf{k}$ $\quad$ $\mathbf{b} = \mathbf{i} + \mathbf{j} + 5\mathbf{k}$

c $\mathbf{a} = 4\mathbf{i} - 2\mathbf{j} + \mathbf{k}$ $\quad$ $\mathbf{b} = -\mathbf{i} - 2\mathbf{j} + 3\mathbf{k}$

2 Find a Cartesian equation for each of the lines given in question 1.

3 Find, in the form $(\mathbf{r} - \mathbf{a}) \times \mathbf{b} = 0$, an equation of the straight line passing through the points with coordinates

a (1, 3, 5), (6, 4, 2) $\quad$ **b** (3, 4, 12), (4, 3, 5)

c (−2, 2, 6), (3, 7, 11) $\quad$ **d** (4, 2, −4), (1, 1, 1)

4 Find a Cartesian equation for each of the lines given in question 3.

5 Find, in the form $(\mathbf{r} - \mathbf{a}) \times \mathbf{b} = 0$, an equation of the straight line given by the equation, where λ is scalar

a $\mathbf{r} = \mathbf{i} + \mathbf{j} - 2\mathbf{k} + \lambda(2\mathbf{i} - \mathbf{k})$

b $\mathbf{r} = \mathbf{i} + 4\mathbf{j} + \lambda(3\mathbf{i} + \mathbf{j} - 5\mathbf{k})$

c $\mathbf{r} = 3\mathbf{i} + 4\mathbf{j} - 4\mathbf{k} + \lambda(2\mathbf{i} - 2\mathbf{j} - 3\mathbf{k})$

6 Find, in the form **i** $\mathbf{r} \times \mathbf{b} = \mathbf{c}$, and also in the form **ii** $\mathbf{r} = \mathbf{a} + t\mathbf{b}$, where t is a scalar parameter, the equation of the straight line with Cartesian equation

$$\frac{(x - 3)}{2} = \frac{(y + 1)}{5} = \frac{(2z - 3)}{3} = \lambda.$$

7 Given that the point with coordinates $(p, q, 1)$ lies on the line with equation

$$\mathbf{r} \times \begin{pmatrix} 2 \\ 1 \\ 3 \end{pmatrix} = \begin{pmatrix} 8 \\ -7 \\ -3 \end{pmatrix}$$, find the values of p and q.

8 Given that the equation of a straight line is

$$\mathbf{r} \times \begin{pmatrix} 1 \\ 1 \\ -1 \end{pmatrix} = \begin{pmatrix} -1 \\ 2 \\ 1 \end{pmatrix}$$

Hint: Let $\mathbf{a} = a_1\mathbf{i} + a_2\mathbf{j} + a_3\mathbf{k}$ and set up simultaneous equations.

find an equation for the line in the form $\mathbf{r} = \mathbf{a} + t\mathbf{b}$, where t is a scalar parameter.

5.5 You can write the equation of a plane in the scalar form r.n = p, or in the vector form r = a + sb + tc, or in the Cartesian form $ax + by + cz + d = 0$

Example 20

Given that the vector $\mathbf{n}$ is perpendicular to the plane Π and that Π passes through the point A with position vector $\mathbf{a}$, find an equation of the plane Π.

Let point R be a point in the plane with position vector $\mathbf{r}$,

then $\overrightarrow{AR} = \mathbf{r} - \mathbf{a}$

As $\overrightarrow{AR}$ is a vector which lies in the plane, $\overrightarrow{AR}.\mathbf{n} = 0$

So $(\mathbf{r} - \mathbf{a}).\mathbf{n} = 0$

i.e. $\mathbf{r}.\mathbf{n} = \mathbf{a}.\mathbf{n}$

So if $\mathbf{a}.\mathbf{n}. = p$, where p is a scalar, then the equation of the plane Π is $\mathbf{r}.\mathbf{n} = p$.

The normal to the plane is perpendicular to all lines which lie in the plane, and so **n** is perpendicular to $\overrightarrow{AR}$.

When two vectors are perpendicular their scalar product is zero.

- **The scalar product form of the equation of a plane is r.n = a.n = p where n is normal to the plane, a is the position vector of a point in the plane and r is the position vector of a general point on the plane. p is a scalar constant.**

Example 21

The point A with position vector $2\mathbf{i} + 3\mathbf{j} - 5\mathbf{k}$ lies in a plane. The vector $3\mathbf{i} + \mathbf{j} - \mathbf{k}$ is perpendicular to the plane. Find an equation of the plane

a in scalar product form

b in Cartesian form.

a $(\mathbf{r} - (2\mathbf{i} + 3\mathbf{j} - 5\mathbf{k})).(3\mathbf{i} + \mathbf{j} - \mathbf{k}) = 0$

So $\mathbf{r}.(3\mathbf{i} + \mathbf{j} - \mathbf{k}) = (2\mathbf{i} + 3\mathbf{j} - 5\mathbf{k}).(3\mathbf{i} + \mathbf{j} - \mathbf{k})$

$\mathbf{r}.(3\mathbf{i} + \mathbf{j} - \mathbf{k}) = 6 + 3 + 5$

So the equation of plane is $\mathbf{r}.(3\mathbf{i} + \mathbf{j} - \mathbf{k}) = 14$

b This may be written

$(x\mathbf{i} + y\mathbf{j} + z\mathbf{k}).(3\mathbf{i} + \mathbf{j} - \mathbf{k}) = 14$

i.e. $3x + y - z = 14$

which is a Cartesian equation of the plane.

Use $(\mathbf{r} - \mathbf{a}).\mathbf{n} = 0$.

Give your answer in the form $\mathbf{r}.\mathbf{n} = p$.

Replace $\mathbf{r}$ by $x\mathbf{i} + y\mathbf{j} + z\mathbf{k}$ to obtain the Cartesian equation.

Example 22

Convert the equation of a plane, $\mathbf{r}.\mathbf{n} = p$, into Cartesian form by replacing $\mathbf{r}$ by $x\mathbf{i} + y\mathbf{j} + z\mathbf{k}$ and $\mathbf{n}$ by $n_1\mathbf{i} + n_2\mathbf{j} + n_3\mathbf{k}$.

$(x\mathbf{i} + y\mathbf{j} + z\mathbf{k}).(n_1\mathbf{i} + n_2\mathbf{j} + n_3\mathbf{k}) = p$

So $xn_1 + yn_2 + zn_3 = p$ or $n_1x + n_2y + n_3z - p = 0$

which is of the form $ax + by + cz + d = 0$, where a, b, c and d are constants.

■ **The general Cartesian equation of a plane is $ax + by + cz + d = 0$**

Example 23

a Find, in the form $\mathbf{r}.\mathbf{n} = p$, an equation of the plane which contains the line l and the point with position vector $\mathbf{a}$ where l has equation

$\mathbf{r} = 3\mathbf{i} + 5\mathbf{j} - 2\mathbf{k} + \lambda(-\mathbf{i} + 2\mathbf{j} - \mathbf{k})$ and $\mathbf{a} = 4\mathbf{i} + 3\mathbf{j} + \mathbf{k}$.

b Give the equation of the plane in Cartesian form.

a The vector $(-\mathbf{i} + 2\mathbf{j} - \mathbf{k})$ is perpendicular to $\mathbf{n}$

The vector $4\mathbf{i} + 3\mathbf{j} + \mathbf{k} - (3\mathbf{i} + 5\mathbf{j} - 2\mathbf{k})$ also lies in the plane and is also perpendicular to $\mathbf{n}$

i.e. $\mathbf{i} - 2\mathbf{j} + 3\mathbf{k}$ is perpendicular to $\mathbf{n}$

$$\text{So } \mathbf{n} = \begin{vmatrix} \mathbf{i} & \mathbf{j} & \mathbf{k} \\ -1 & 2 & -1 \\ 1 & -2 & 3 \end{vmatrix}$$

$$= 4\mathbf{i} + 2\mathbf{j}$$

Line l lies in the plane. The direction of l is $-\mathbf{i} + 2\mathbf{j} - \mathbf{k}$, and so this vector is perpendicular to $\mathbf{n}$.

The point (4, 3, 1) lies on the plane, and the point (3, 5, −2) lies on the line and so also on the plane, so the vector joining these two points also lies on the plane. This vector $\mathbf{i} - 2\mathbf{j} + 3\mathbf{k}$ is also perpendicular to $\mathbf{n}$.

So $\mathbf{n}$ is in the direction of the vector product of $-\mathbf{i} + 2\mathbf{j} - \mathbf{k}$ and $\mathbf{i} - 2\mathbf{j} + 3\mathbf{k}$.

So the equation of the required plane is

$\mathbf{r}.(4\mathbf{i} + 2\mathbf{j}) = (4\mathbf{i} + 3\mathbf{j} + \mathbf{k}).(4\mathbf{i} + 2\mathbf{j})$

i.e. $\mathbf{r}.(4\mathbf{i} + 2\mathbf{j}) = 16 + 6$

An equation of the plane is $\mathbf{r}.(4\mathbf{i} + 2\mathbf{j}) = 22$

b In Cartesian form this may be written

$4x + 2y = 22$

i.e. $2x + y = 11$

Replace $\mathbf{r}$ with $x\mathbf{i} + y\mathbf{j} + z\mathbf{k}$ and perform the scalar product.

Example 24

Show that the vector equation of a plane passing through the point A, with position vector $\mathbf{a}$, may be written $\mathbf{r} = \mathbf{a} + \lambda\mathbf{b} + \mu\mathbf{c}$, where $\mathbf{b}$ and $\mathbf{c}$ are non parallel vectors in the plane and where λ and μ are scalars.

Let R be a general point on the plane.

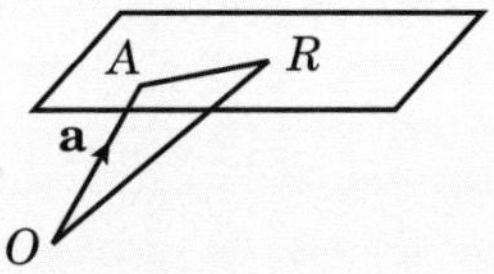

Then $\overrightarrow{OR} = \overrightarrow{OA} + \overrightarrow{AR}$.

This follows from the triangle law.

However, $\overrightarrow{AR}$ lies in the plane and so can be written as $\lambda\mathbf{b} + \mu\mathbf{c}$, where λ and μ are scalar parameters which depend on the position of R.

If a point lies on a plane its position is usually described as $x\mathbf{i} + y\mathbf{j}$, where $\mathbf{i}$ and $\mathbf{j}$ are unit vectors in the plane and x and y give the displacements in the $\mathbf{i}$ and $\mathbf{j}$ directions from an origin O.

The two independent vectors used to describe the position of a point on a plane do not need to be unit vectors and do not need to be perpendicular. $\mathbf{b}$ and $\mathbf{c}$ are non-parallel vectors, lying in the plane, and so multiples of them may be used to define $\overrightarrow{AR}$.

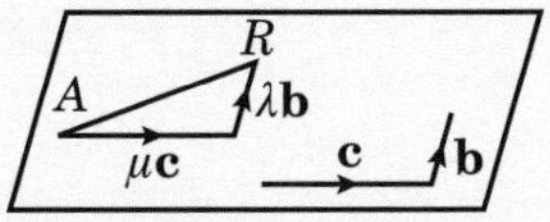

So $\mathbf{r} = \mathbf{a} + \lambda\mathbf{b} + \mu\mathbf{c}$ describes the position of R and is the vector equation of the plane.

- **The vector equation of a plane is $\mathbf{r} = \mathbf{a} + \lambda\mathbf{b} + \mu\mathbf{c}$ where a is the position vector of a point in the plane, b and c are non-parallel vectors in the plane and r is the position vector of a general point on the plane. λ and μ are scalars and b and c are non-zero.**

Example 25

Find, in the form $\mathbf{r} = \mathbf{a} + \lambda\mathbf{b} + \mu\mathbf{c}$ an equation of the plane that passes through the points $A(2, 2, -1)$, $B(3, 2, -1)$ and $C(4, 3, 5)$.

$\overrightarrow{AB}$ and $\overrightarrow{AC}$ are vectors which lie in the plane

$\overrightarrow{AB} = \overrightarrow{OB} - \overrightarrow{OA} = \mathbf{i}$

$\overrightarrow{AC} = \overrightarrow{OC} - \overrightarrow{OA} = 2\mathbf{i} + \mathbf{j} + 6\mathbf{k}$

So an equation of the plane is

$\mathbf{r} = 2\mathbf{i} + 2\mathbf{j} - \mathbf{k} + \lambda\mathbf{i} + \mu(2\mathbf{i} + \mathbf{j} + 6\mathbf{k})$

There are many other forms of this answer which are also correct. You could use $3\mathbf{i} + 2\mathbf{j} - \mathbf{k}$ or $4\mathbf{i} + 3\mathbf{j} + 5\mathbf{k}$ instead of $2\mathbf{i} + 2\mathbf{j} - \mathbf{k}$ in the equation.

You could also use $\overrightarrow{BC}$ as a direction in the plane, instead of $\overrightarrow{AB}$ or $\overrightarrow{AC}$.

Example 26

Find a Cartesian equation of the plane that passes through the points A (1, 0, −1), B(2, 1, 0) and C(2, 16, 6).

$\overrightarrow{AB} = \overrightarrow{OB} - \overrightarrow{OA} = \mathbf{i} + \mathbf{j} + \mathbf{k}$

$\overrightarrow{AC} = \overrightarrow{OC} - \overrightarrow{OA} = \mathbf{i} + 16\mathbf{j} + 7\mathbf{k}$

$$\overrightarrow{AB} \times \overrightarrow{AC} = \begin{vmatrix} \mathbf{i} & \mathbf{j} & \mathbf{k} \\ 1 & 1 & 1 \\ 1 & 16 & 7 \end{vmatrix}$$

$$= -9\mathbf{i} - 6\mathbf{j} + 15\mathbf{k}$$

This is the direction of the normal to the plane.

So $\mathbf{r}.(-9\mathbf{i} - 6\mathbf{j} + 15\mathbf{k}) = (\mathbf{i} - \mathbf{k}).(-9\mathbf{i} - 6\mathbf{j} + 15\mathbf{k})$

i.e. $\mathbf{r}.(-9\mathbf{i} - 6\mathbf{j} + 15\mathbf{k}) = -9 - 15 = -24$

Use $\mathbf{r.n} = \mathbf{a.n}$

So the equation of the plane may be written

$\mathbf{r}.(3\mathbf{i} + 2\mathbf{j} - 5\mathbf{k}) = 8$ or

$(x\mathbf{i} + y\mathbf{j} + z\mathbf{k}).(3\mathbf{i} + 2\mathbf{j} - 5\mathbf{k}) = 8$

Replace $\mathbf{r}$ by $x\mathbf{i} + y\mathbf{j} + z\mathbf{k}$ to obtain the Cartesian equation.

i.e. $3x + 2y - 5z = 8$, which is a Cartesian equation of the plane.

You may wish to check that each point lies on this plane.

Exercise 5E

1 Find, in the form $\mathbf{r.n} = p$, an equation of the plane that passes through the point with position vector $\mathbf{a}$ and is perpendicular to the vector $\mathbf{n}$ where

- **a** $\mathbf{a} = \mathbf{i} - \mathbf{j} - \mathbf{k}$ and $\mathbf{n} = 2\mathbf{i} + \mathbf{j} + \mathbf{k}$
- **b** $\mathbf{a} = \mathbf{i} + 2\mathbf{j} + \mathbf{k}$ and $\mathbf{n} = 5\mathbf{i} - \mathbf{j} - 3\mathbf{k}$
- **c** $\mathbf{a} = 2\mathbf{i} - 3\mathbf{k}$ and $\mathbf{n} = \mathbf{i} + 3\mathbf{j} + 4\mathbf{k}$
- **d** $\mathbf{a} = 4\mathbf{i} - 2\mathbf{j} + \mathbf{k}$ and $\mathbf{n} = 4\mathbf{i} + \mathbf{j} - 5\mathbf{k}$

2 Find a Cartesian equation for each of the planes in question 1.

3 Find, in the form $\mathbf{r} = \mathbf{a} + \lambda\mathbf{b} + \mu\mathbf{c}$ an equation of the plane that passes through the points

- **a** (1, 2, 0), (3, 1, −1) and (4, 3, 2)
- **b** (3, 4, 1), (−1, −2, 0) and (2, 1, 4)
- **c** (2, −1, −1), (3, 1, 2) and (4, 0, 1)
- **d** (−1, 1, 3), (−1, 2, 5) and (0, 4, 4).

4 Find a Cartesian equation for each of the planes in question 3.

5 Find a Cartesian equation of the plane that passes through the points

a (0, 4, 2), (1, 1, 2) and (−1, 5, 0)

b (1, 1, 0), (2, 3, −3) and (3, 7, −2)

c (3, 0, 0), (2, 0, −1) and (4, 1, 3)

d (1, −1, 6), (3, 1, −2) and (4, 1, 0).

6 Find, in the form $\mathbf{r.n} = p$, an equation of the plane which contains the line l and the point with position vector $\mathbf{a}$ where

a l has equation $\mathbf{r} = \mathbf{i} + \mathbf{j} - 2\mathbf{k} + \lambda(2\mathbf{i} - \mathbf{k})$ and $\mathbf{a} = 4\mathbf{i} + 3\mathbf{j} + \mathbf{k}$

b l has equation $\mathbf{r} = \mathbf{i} + 2\mathbf{j} + 2\mathbf{k} + \lambda(2\mathbf{i} + \mathbf{j} - 3\mathbf{k})$ and $\mathbf{a} = 3\mathbf{i} + 5\mathbf{j} + \mathbf{k}$

c l has equation $\mathbf{r} = 2\mathbf{i} - \mathbf{j} + \mathbf{k} + \lambda(\mathbf{i} + 2\mathbf{j} + 2\mathbf{k})$ and $\mathbf{a} = 7\mathbf{i} + 8\mathbf{j} + 6\mathbf{k}$

7 Find a Cartesian equation of the plane which passes through the point (1, 1, 1) and contains the line with equation $\frac{x-2}{3} = \frac{y+4}{1} = \frac{z-1}{2}$.

5.6 **You can use vectors in a variety of contexts including:**
- **the points of intersection of lines and planes which meet**
- **the angle between a line and a plane or between two planes**
- **the shortest distance between lines and planes which do not meet**
- **the shortest distance from a point to a line or to a plane.**

Example 27

Find the coordinates of the point of intersection of the lines l_1 and l_2 where

l_1 has equation $\mathbf{r} = 3\mathbf{i} + \mathbf{j} + \mathbf{k} + \lambda(\mathbf{i} - 2\mathbf{j} - \mathbf{k})$ and

l_2 has equation $\mathbf{r} = -2\mathbf{j} + 3\mathbf{k} + \mu(-5\mathbf{i} + \mathbf{j} + 4\mathbf{k})$

When the lines meet

$$\begin{pmatrix} 3+\lambda \\ 1-2\lambda \\ 1-\lambda \end{pmatrix} = \begin{pmatrix} -5\mu \\ -2+\mu \\ 3+4\mu \end{pmatrix}$$

Use column matrix notation for clarity, and to help to avoid errors.

Solve the simultaneous equations

$3 + \lambda = -5\mu$ ①

and $1 - \lambda = 3 + 4\mu$ ②

Choose two of the three equations obtained by equating x, y and z components and solve the resulting simultaneous equations.

Adding gives $4 = 3 - \mu$

and so $\mu = -1$

Substituting back into equation ① gives $\lambda = 2$

The point where the lines meet is (5, −3, −1)

Check that your values of λ and μ satisfy the third equation and that the point which you obtain after substitution lies on both straight lines.

Example 28

Find the coordinates of the point of intersection of the line l and the plane Π where l has equation $\mathbf{r} = -\mathbf{i} + \mathbf{j} - 5\mathbf{k} + \lambda(\mathbf{i} + \mathbf{j} + 2\mathbf{k})$ and Π has equation $\mathbf{r}.(\mathbf{i} + 2\mathbf{j} + 3\mathbf{k}) = 4$.

The line meets the plane when

$$\begin{pmatrix} -1 + \lambda \\ 1 + \lambda \\ -5 + 2\lambda \end{pmatrix} . \begin{pmatrix} 1 \\ 2 \\ 3 \end{pmatrix} = 4$$

i.e. $-1 + \lambda + 2(1 + \lambda) + 3(-5 + 2\lambda) = 4$

i.e. $9\lambda - 14 = 4$

So $9\lambda = 18$

i.e. $\lambda = 2$

and the line meets the plane at $(1, 3, -1)$

Write the equation of the line in column matrix form as $\begin{pmatrix} x \\ y \\ z \end{pmatrix} = \begin{pmatrix} -1 + \lambda \\ 1 + \lambda \\ -5 + 2\lambda \end{pmatrix}$ and substitute into the equation of the plane $\begin{pmatrix} x \\ y \\ z \end{pmatrix} . \begin{pmatrix} 1 \\ 2 \\ 3 \end{pmatrix} = 4$

Solve to find λ and substitute its value into the equation of the line.

Example 29

Find the equation of the line of intersection of the planes Π_1 and Π_2 where Π_1 has equation $\mathbf{r}.(2\mathbf{i} - 2\mathbf{j} - \mathbf{k}) = 2$ and Π_2 has equation $\mathbf{r}.(\mathbf{i} - 3\mathbf{j} + \mathbf{k}) = 5$.

In Cartesian form $\quad 2x - 2y - z = 2 \quad$ ①

and $\quad x - 3y + z = 5 \quad$ ②

Add equations ① and ②

Then $3x - 5y = 7$

So $x = \dfrac{7 + 5y}{3}$

Substituting into equation ② $z = 5 + 3y - \dfrac{7 + 5y}{3}$

i.e. $z = \dfrac{15 + 9y - (7 + 5y)}{3} = \dfrac{8 + 4y}{3}$

So $\dfrac{x - \frac{7}{3}}{\frac{5}{3}} = y = \dfrac{z - \frac{8}{3}}{\frac{4}{3}} = \lambda$

or $\mathbf{r} = \frac{7}{3}\mathbf{i} + \frac{8}{3}\mathbf{k} + \lambda(\frac{5}{3}\mathbf{i} + \mathbf{j} + \frac{4}{3}\mathbf{k})$

This is an equation for the line of intersection of the two planes.

Express the equations of the planes in Cartesian form.

Eliminate one of the variables from the two equations. (In this case z is the easiest to eliminate.)

By eliminating z, express x in terms of y. Then substitute to give z in terms of y.

Let $y = \lambda$ and make λ the subject of the formulae, to give the Cartesian equation of a straight line. This can also be written in vector form.

In book C4 you found that the acute angle, θ, between two straight lines was given by the formula

$$\cos \theta = \left| \frac{\mathbf{a}.\mathbf{b}}{|\mathbf{a}||\mathbf{b}|} \right|$$

where $\mathbf{a}$ and $\mathbf{b}$ are direction vectors of the lines. You will now extend this idea to find the angle between lines and planes, and between two planes.

Example 30

Find the acute angle between the line l with equation $\mathbf{r} = 2\mathbf{i} + \mathbf{j} - 5\mathbf{k} + \lambda(3\mathbf{i} + 4\mathbf{j} - 12\mathbf{k})$ and the plane with equation $\mathbf{r}.(2\mathbf{i} - 2\mathbf{j} - \mathbf{k}) = 2$.

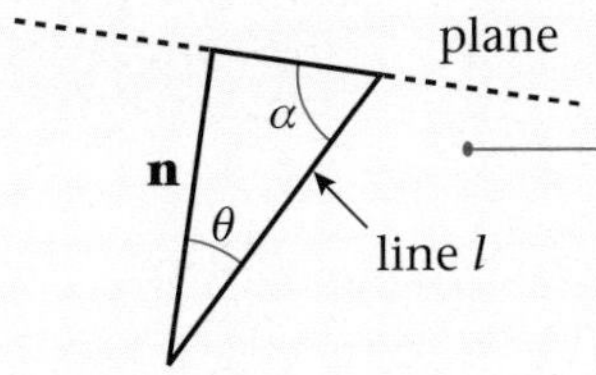

Draw a diagram showing the line, the plane and the normal to the plane. Let the required angle be α and show α and θ in your diagram.

The normal to the plane is in the direction $\mathbf{n} = 2\mathbf{i} - 2\mathbf{j} - \mathbf{k}$.

The angle between this normal and the line l is θ,

where $\cos\theta = \dfrac{(3\mathbf{i} + 4\mathbf{j} - 12\mathbf{k}).(2\mathbf{i} - 2\mathbf{j} - \mathbf{k})}{\sqrt{3^2 + 4^2 + (-12)^2}\sqrt{2^2 + (-2)^2 + (-1)^2}}$

First find the angle between the given line and the normal to the plane.

i.e. $\cos\theta = \dfrac{10}{13 \times 3} = \dfrac{10}{39}$

So the angle between the plane and the line l is α where $\alpha + \theta = 90°$.

Subtract the angle θ from 90°, to give angle α, or use the trigonometric connection that $\cos\theta = \sin\alpha$.

So $\sin\alpha = \dfrac{10}{39}$ and $\alpha = 14.9°$

You can use the method in Example 30 to show that, in general, the angle θ between the line with equation $\mathbf{r} = \mathbf{a} + \lambda\mathbf{b}$ and the plane with equation $\mathbf{r}.\mathbf{n} = p$ is given by the formula

■ $\sin\theta = \left|\dfrac{\mathbf{b}.\mathbf{n}}{|\mathbf{b}||\mathbf{n}|}\right|$

Example 31

Find the acute angle between the planes with equations $\mathbf{r}.(4\mathbf{i} + 4\mathbf{j} - 7\mathbf{k}) = 13$ and $\mathbf{r}.(7\mathbf{i} - 4\mathbf{j} + 4\mathbf{k}) = 6$ respectively.

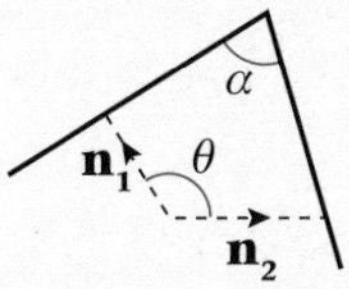

Draw a diagram showing the planes and the normals to the planes. Let the required angle be α and show α and θ in your diagram.

The normals to the planes are in the directions $\mathbf{n}_1 = 4\mathbf{i} + 4\mathbf{j} - 7\mathbf{k}$, and $\mathbf{n}_2 = 7\mathbf{i} - 4\mathbf{j} + 4\mathbf{k}$

The angle between these normals is θ, where

$$\cos\theta = \frac{(4\mathbf{i} + 4\mathbf{j} - 7\mathbf{k}).(7\mathbf{i} - 4\mathbf{j} + 4\mathbf{k})}{\sqrt{4^2 + 4^2 + (-7)^2}\sqrt{7^2 + (-4)^2 + (4)^2}}$$

$$= \frac{28 - 16 - 28}{\sqrt{16 + 16 + 49}\sqrt{49 + 16 + 16}}$$

$$= -\frac{16}{81}$$

So $\theta = 101.4°$

So the angle between the planes is

$180 - 101.4 = 78.6°$

First find the angle between the normals to the planes.

Subtract the angle θ from 180°, to give angle α.

You can use the method in Example 31 to show that, in general, the angle θ between the plane with equation $\mathbf{r}.\mathbf{n}_1 = p_1$ and the plane with equation $\mathbf{r}.\mathbf{n}_2 = p_2$ is given by the formula

■ $\cos\theta = \left|\frac{\mathbf{n}_1.\mathbf{n}_2}{|\mathbf{n}_1||\mathbf{n}_2|}\right|$

Example 32

Given that d is the length of the perpendicular from the origin to a plane Π, show that the equation of plane Π is $\mathbf{r}.\hat{\mathbf{n}} = d$, where $\hat{\mathbf{n}}$ is a unit vector perpendicular to Π.

In triangle OFR, R is a general point on the plane, F is the foot of the perpendicular from the origin O.

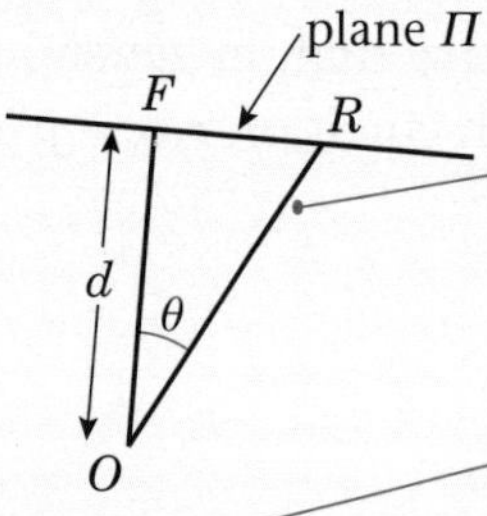

$\cos\theta = \frac{d}{OR}$

$d = OR\cos\theta = |\mathbf{r}| \times 1 \times \cos\theta$

So $d = \mathbf{r}.\hat{\mathbf{n}}$, as required

Draw a diagram showing the plane and the perpendicular from the origin to the plane.

Let R be a point on the plane and let the angle between OR and the perpendicular be θ.

As $\hat{\mathbf{n}}$ is a unit vector its modulus is 1.

■ **d is the length of the perpendicular from the origin to a plane Π, where the equation of plane Π is written in the form $\mathbf{r}.\hat{\mathbf{n}} = d$, where $\hat{\mathbf{n}}$ is a unit vector perpendicular to Π.**

Example 33

The plane Π has equation $\mathbf{r}.(\mathbf{i} + 2\mathbf{j} + 2\mathbf{k}) = 5$.

a Find the perpendicular distance from the origin to plane Π.

b Find the perpendicular distance from the point $(1, 3, -2)$ to the plane Π.

c Find the perpendicular distance from the point $(3, 1, -3)$ to the plane Π.

a The unit vector parallel to $\mathbf{i} + 2\mathbf{j} + 2\mathbf{k}$ is $\frac{1}{3}(\mathbf{i} + 2\mathbf{j} + 2\mathbf{k})$

The modulus of $\mathbf{i} + 2\mathbf{j} + 2\mathbf{k}$ is $\sqrt{1^2 + 2^2 + 2^2} = 3$.

So the equation of Π may be written as

$\mathbf{r}.\hat{\mathbf{n}} = \frac{5}{3}$, where $\hat{\mathbf{n}} = \frac{1}{3}(\mathbf{i} + 2\mathbf{j} + 2\mathbf{k})$

Divide both sides of the equation by 3 so that the equation is of the form $\mathbf{r}.\hat{\mathbf{n}} = d$, with the right hand side of the equation being the required distance.

This means the perpendicular distance from the origin to plane Π is $\frac{5}{3}$.

b

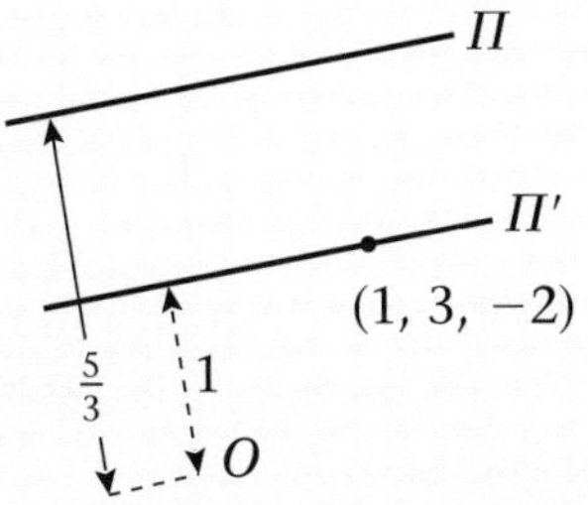

The plane Π' parallel to Π, passing through the point $(1, 3, -2)$ has equation

$\mathbf{r}.\frac{1}{3}(\mathbf{i} + 2\mathbf{j} + 2\mathbf{k}) = (\mathbf{i} + 3\mathbf{j} - 2\mathbf{k}).\,\frac{1}{3}(\mathbf{i} + 2\mathbf{j} + 2\mathbf{k})$

Construct a parallel plane Π' through the point $(1, 3, -2)$.

i.e. $\mathbf{r}.\hat{\mathbf{n}} = 1$, where $\hat{\mathbf{n}} = \frac{1}{3}(\mathbf{i} + 2\mathbf{j} + 2\mathbf{k})$

Find its equation and hence its distance from the origin.

So the perpendicular distance from the origin to plane Π' is 1.

The distance between the two planes Π and Π' is $\frac{5}{3} - 1 = \frac{2}{3}$.

Then subtract the distance 1 from Π' to O, from the distance $\frac{5}{3}$ from Π to O which was found in part **a**.

So the distance from the point $(1, 3, -2)$ to the plane Π is $\frac{2}{3}$.

c

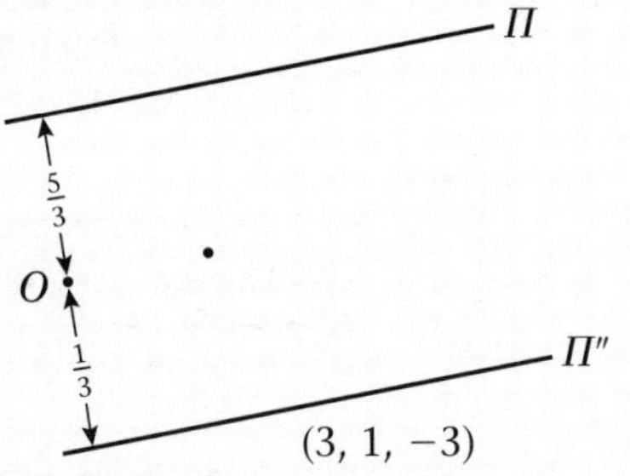

The plane Π'' parallel to Π, passing through the point $(3, 1, -3)$ has equation

Construct a parallel plane Π'' through the point $(3, 1, -3)$.

$\mathbf{r}.\frac{1}{3}(\mathbf{i} + 2\mathbf{j} + 2\mathbf{k}) = (3\mathbf{i} + \mathbf{j} - 3\mathbf{k}).\,\frac{1}{3}(\mathbf{i} + 2\mathbf{j} + 2\mathbf{k})$

i.e. $\mathbf{r}.\hat{\mathbf{n}} = -\frac{1}{3}$, where $\hat{\mathbf{n}} = \frac{1}{3}(\mathbf{i} + 2\mathbf{j} + 2\mathbf{k})$

The minus sign indicates that Π'' is on the other side of the origin from the previous two planes.

So the perpendicular distance from the origin to plane Π'' is $\frac{1}{3}$.

The distance between the two planes Π and Π'' is $\frac{5}{3} - (-\frac{1}{3}) = 2$ and the distance from the point $(3, 1, 3)$ to the plane Π is 2.

So as the planes are on opposite sides of O, the distance required is $\frac{5}{3} + \frac{1}{3}$.

Example 34

Show that the shortest distance between the parallel lines with equations $\mathbf{r} = \mathbf{i} + 2\mathbf{j} - \mathbf{k} + \lambda(5\mathbf{i} + 4\mathbf{j} + 3\mathbf{k})$ and $\mathbf{r} = 2\mathbf{i} + \mathbf{k} + \mu(5\mathbf{i} + 4\mathbf{j} + 3\mathbf{k})$, where λ and μ are scalars, is $\dfrac{21\sqrt{2}}{10}$.

Method I

Let A be a general point on the first line and B be a general point on the second line, then

$$\overrightarrow{AB} = \begin{pmatrix} 1 \\ -2 \\ 2 \end{pmatrix} + t\begin{pmatrix} 5 \\ 4 \\ 3 \end{pmatrix} \text{ where } t = \mu - \lambda$$

As $\begin{pmatrix} 1 \\ -2 \\ 2 \end{pmatrix} = \begin{pmatrix} 2 \\ 0 \\ 1 \end{pmatrix} - \begin{pmatrix} 1 \\ 2 \\ -1 \end{pmatrix}$

You can set $t = \mu - \lambda$ so that there is only one independent variable.

Let the distance $AB = x$ then

$$x^2 = (1 + 5t)^2 + (-2 + 4t)^2 + (2 + 3t)^2 = 50t^2 + 6t + 9$$

Use Pythagoras' Theorem to find an expression for the distance *AB*.

The minimum value of x^2 occurs when $t = -\frac{6}{100}$

and so $x^2 = \left(\frac{70}{100}\right)^2 + \left(-\frac{224}{100}\right)^2 + \left(\frac{182}{100}\right)^2$

So minimum value of $x = \left(\frac{14}{100}\right)\sqrt{5^2 + 16^2 + 13^2}$

Find the minimum value of the quadratic expression by using calculus or completion of the square.

i.e. $x = \left(\frac{7}{50}\right)\sqrt{450} = \left(\frac{7}{50}\right) \times 15\sqrt{2} = \dfrac{21\sqrt{2}}{10}$

Substitute and simplify to obtain the printed answer.

Method II

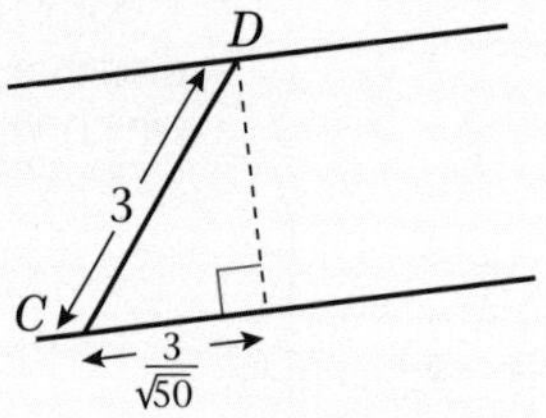

Draw a diagram and calculate the length *CD*.

Let C be point $(1, 2, -1)$ on the first line and D be point $(2, 0, 1)$ on the second line, then

$\overrightarrow{CD} = \mathbf{i} - 2\mathbf{j} + 2\mathbf{k}$, and $|\overrightarrow{CD}| = \sqrt{1^2 + (-2)^2 + 2^2} = 3$

The projection of CD onto one of the lines has

$$\text{length } \frac{(\mathbf{i} - 2\mathbf{j} + 2\mathbf{k}).(5\mathbf{i} + 4\mathbf{j} + 3\mathbf{k})}{\sqrt{5^2 + 4^2 + 3^2}} = \frac{3}{\sqrt{50}}$$

In this alternative method you project the length *CD* onto one of the lines (using scalar product).

Calculating the third side of the right angle triangle,

$$x^2 = 3^2 - \left(\frac{3}{\sqrt{50}}\right)^2 = \frac{441}{50}$$

and so $x = \dfrac{21\sqrt{2}}{10}$

i.e. the shortest distance is $\dfrac{21\sqrt{2}}{10}$.

Then you use Pythagoras' Theorem to calculate the required shortest distance.

Example 35

Show that the shortest distance between the two skew lines with equations $\mathbf{r} = \mathbf{a} + \lambda\mathbf{b}$ and $\mathbf{r} = \mathbf{c} + \mu\mathbf{d}$, where λ and μ are scalars, is given by the formula $\left|\dfrac{(\mathbf{a} - \mathbf{c}).(\mathbf{b} \times \mathbf{d})}{|\mathbf{b} \times \mathbf{d}|}\right|$.

The shortest distance between the lines is XY where XY is perpendicular to both lines.

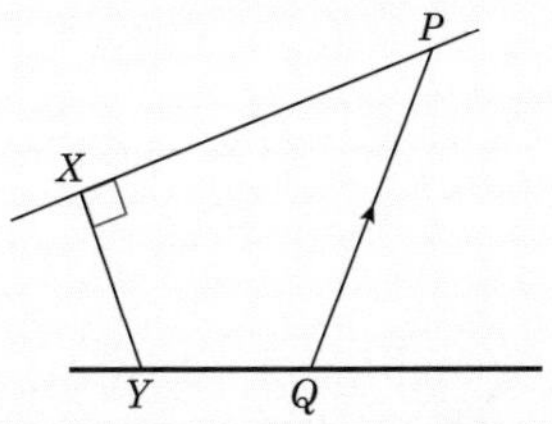

The common perpendicular to the two skew lines is in the direction $\mathbf{b} \times \mathbf{d}$ and a unit vector in that direction is $\dfrac{\mathbf{b} \times \mathbf{d}}{|\mathbf{b} \times \mathbf{d}|}$.

If P is a point on the line with equation $\mathbf{r} = \mathbf{a} + \lambda\mathbf{b}$ and Q is a point on the line with equation $\mathbf{r} = \mathbf{c} + \mu\mathbf{d}$ then

$$\overrightarrow{QP} = \mathbf{a} - \mathbf{c} + \lambda\mathbf{b} - \mu\mathbf{d}$$

The projection of PQ in the direction of the common perpendicular is

$$(\mathbf{a} - \mathbf{c} + \lambda\mathbf{b} - \mu\mathbf{d}).\frac{\mathbf{b} \times \mathbf{d}}{|\mathbf{b} \times \mathbf{d}|}.$$

This gives $PQ\cos\theta$, where θ is the angle between PQ and the common perpendicular.

i.e. $(\mathbf{a} - \mathbf{c}).\dfrac{\mathbf{b} \times \mathbf{d}}{|\mathbf{b} \times \mathbf{d}|} + \lambda\mathbf{b}.\dfrac{\mathbf{b} \times \mathbf{d}}{|\mathbf{b} \times \mathbf{d}|} - \mu\mathbf{d}.\dfrac{\mathbf{b} \times \mathbf{d}}{|\mathbf{b} \times \mathbf{d}|}$

Using the distributive property.

But $\mathbf{b}.(\mathbf{b} \times \mathbf{d}) = \mathbf{d}.(\mathbf{b} \times \mathbf{d}) = 0$ and the shortest distance must be a positive quantity.

So the shortest distance is given by $\left|\dfrac{(\mathbf{a} - \mathbf{c}).(\mathbf{b} \times \mathbf{d})}{|\mathbf{b} \times \mathbf{d}|}\right|$.

Use the modulus to ensure that the result is positive.

■ **The shortest distance between the two skew lines with equations $\mathbf{r} = \mathbf{a} + \lambda\mathbf{b}$ and $\mathbf{r} = \mathbf{c} + \mu\mathbf{d}$, where λ and μ are scalars, is given by the formula**

$$\left|\frac{(\mathbf{a} - \mathbf{c}).(\mathbf{b} \times \mathbf{d})}{|\mathbf{b} \times \mathbf{d}|}\right|.$$

Example 36

Find the shortest distance between the two skew lines with equations $\mathbf{r} = \mathbf{i} + \lambda(\mathbf{j} + \mathbf{k})$ and $\mathbf{r} = -\mathbf{i} + 3\mathbf{j} - \mathbf{k} + \mu(2\mathbf{i} - \mathbf{j} - \mathbf{k})$, where λ and μ are scalars.

$$\mathbf{a} - \mathbf{c} = 2\mathbf{i} - 3\mathbf{j} + \mathbf{k}$$

Using $\mathbf{a} = \mathbf{i}$ and $\mathbf{c} = -\mathbf{i} + 3\mathbf{j} - \mathbf{k}$.

$$\mathbf{b} \times \mathbf{d} = \begin{vmatrix} \mathbf{i} & \mathbf{j} & \mathbf{k} \\ 0 & 1 & 1 \\ 2 & -1 & -1 \end{vmatrix} = 2\mathbf{j} - 2\mathbf{k}$$

Take the vector product of the two direction vectors.

So the shortest distance is $\left|\dfrac{(2\mathbf{i} - 3\mathbf{j} + \mathbf{k}).(2\mathbf{j} - 2\mathbf{k})}{\sqrt{2^2 + (-2)^2}}\right| = \left|\dfrac{-8}{\sqrt{8}}\right| = \sqrt{8}$

$= 2\sqrt{2}$

Use the formula for shortest distance obtained in Example 35.

Example 37

Find the shortest distance between the point A with coordinates $(1, 2, -1)$ and the line with equation $\mathbf{r} = \mathbf{i} + \mathbf{j} - 3\mathbf{k} + \mu(2\mathbf{i} - 2\mathbf{j} - \mathbf{k})$, where μ is a scalar.

Let B be a general point on the given line,

then $\overrightarrow{AB} = \begin{pmatrix} 0 \\ -1 \\ -2 \end{pmatrix} + \mu \begin{pmatrix} 2 \\ -2 \\ -1 \end{pmatrix}$.

As in Example 34, at least two methods are possible. The method shown here is the most efficient.

Let the distance $AB = x$ then

$x^2 = (2\mu)^2 + (-1 - 2\mu)^2 + (-2 - \mu)^2 = 9\mu^2 + 8\mu + 5$

The minimum value of x^2 occurs when $\mu = -\frac{8}{18} = -\frac{4}{9}$

Find the minimum value of the quadratic expression by using calculus or completion of the square.

So $x^2 = (\frac{-8}{9})^2 + (-\frac{1}{9})^2 + (-\frac{14}{9})^2$

So minimum value of $x = (\frac{1}{9})\sqrt{8^2 + 1^2 + 14^2} = \frac{1}{9}\sqrt{261}$

The minimum value of x corresponds to the minimum value of x^2.

i.e. $x = (\frac{1}{9}) \times 3\sqrt{29} = \frac{\sqrt{29}}{3}$

i.e. the shortest distance is 1.80 (3 s.f.)

Give an exact answer and give your answer to 3 s.f.

Exercise 5F

1 In each case establish whether lines l_1 and l_2 meet and if they meet find the coordinates of their point of intersection:

a l_1 has equation $\mathbf{r} = \mathbf{i} + 3\mathbf{j} + \lambda(\mathbf{i} - \mathbf{j} + 5\mathbf{k})$ and
l_2 has equation $\mathbf{r} = -\mathbf{i} - 3\mathbf{j} + 2\mathbf{k} + \mu(\mathbf{i} + \mathbf{j} + 2\mathbf{k})$

b l_1 has equation $\mathbf{r} = 3\mathbf{i} + 2\mathbf{j} + \mathbf{k} + \lambda(\mathbf{i} + \mathbf{j} + 2\mathbf{k})$ and
l_2 has equation $\mathbf{r} = 4\mathbf{i} + 3\mathbf{j} + \mu(-\mathbf{i} + \mathbf{j} - \mathbf{k})$

c l_1 has equation $\mathbf{r} = \mathbf{i} + 3\mathbf{j} + 5\mathbf{k} + \lambda(2\mathbf{i} + 3\mathbf{j} + \mathbf{k})$ and
l_2 has equation $\mathbf{r} = \mathbf{i} + 2\frac{1}{2}\mathbf{j} + 2\frac{1}{2}\mathbf{k} + \mu(\mathbf{i} + \mathbf{j} - 2\mathbf{k})$

(In each of the above cases λ and μ are scalars.)

2 In each case establish whether the line l meets the plane Π and, if they meet, find the coordinates of their point of intersection.

a l: $\mathbf{r} = \mathbf{i} + \mathbf{j} + \mathbf{k} + \lambda(-2\mathbf{i} + \mathbf{j} - 4\mathbf{k})$
Π: $\mathbf{r}.(3\mathbf{i} - 4\mathbf{j} + 2\mathbf{k}) = 16$

b l: $\mathbf{r} = 2\mathbf{i} + 3\mathbf{j} - 2\mathbf{k} + \lambda(\mathbf{i} + \mathbf{j} + \mathbf{k})$
Π: $\mathbf{r}.(\mathbf{i} + \mathbf{j} - 2\mathbf{k}) = 1$

c l: $\mathbf{r} = \mathbf{i} + \mathbf{j} + \mathbf{k} + \lambda(2\mathbf{j} - 2\mathbf{k})$
Π: $\mathbf{r}.(3\mathbf{i} - \mathbf{j} - 6\mathbf{k}) = 1$

(In each of the above cases λ is a scalar.)

3 Find the equation of the line of intersection of the planes Π_1 and Π_2 where

a Π_1 has equation $\mathbf{r}.(3\mathbf{i} - 2\mathbf{j} - \mathbf{k}) = 5$ and Π_2 has equation $\mathbf{r}.(4\mathbf{i} - \mathbf{j} - 2\mathbf{k}) = 5$

b Π_1 has equation $\mathbf{r}.(5\mathbf{i} - \mathbf{j} - 2\mathbf{k}) = 16$ and Π_2 has equation $\mathbf{r}.(16\mathbf{i} - 5\mathbf{j} - 4\mathbf{k}) = 53$

c Π_1 has equation $\mathbf{r}.(\mathbf{i} - 3\mathbf{j} + \mathbf{k}) = 10$ and Π_2 has equation $\mathbf{r}.(4\mathbf{i} - 3\mathbf{j} - 2\mathbf{k}) = 1$.

4 Find the acute angle between the planes with equations $\mathbf{r}.(\mathbf{i} + 2\mathbf{j} - 2\mathbf{k}) = 1$ and $\mathbf{r}.(-4\mathbf{i} + 4\mathbf{j} + 7\mathbf{k}) = 7$ respectively.

5 Find the acute angle between the planes with equations $\mathbf{r}.(3\mathbf{i} - 4\mathbf{j} + 12\mathbf{k}) = 9$ and $\mathbf{r}.(5\mathbf{i} - 12\mathbf{k}) = 7$ respectively.

6 Find the acute angle between the line with equation $\mathbf{r} = 2\mathbf{i} + \mathbf{j} - 5\mathbf{k} + \lambda(4\mathbf{i} + 4\mathbf{j} + 7\mathbf{k})$ and the plane with equation $\mathbf{r}.(2\mathbf{i} + \mathbf{j} - 2\mathbf{k}) = 13$.

7 Find the acute angle between the line with equation $\mathbf{r} = -\mathbf{i} - 7\mathbf{j} + 13\mathbf{k} + \lambda(3\mathbf{i} + 4\mathbf{j} - 12\mathbf{k})$ and the plane with equation $\mathbf{r}.(4\mathbf{i} - 4\mathbf{j} - 7\mathbf{k}) = 9$.

8 Find the acute angle between the line with equation $(\mathbf{r} - 3\mathbf{j}) \times (-4\mathbf{i} - 7\mathbf{j} + 4\mathbf{k}) = 0$ and the plane with equation $\mathbf{r} = \lambda(4\mathbf{i} - \mathbf{j} - \mathbf{k}) + \mu(4\mathbf{i} - 5\mathbf{j} + 3\mathbf{k})$.

9 The plane Π has equation $\mathbf{r}.(10\mathbf{i} + 10\mathbf{j} + 23\mathbf{k}) = 81$.

a Find the perpendicular distance from the origin to plane Π.

b Find the perpendicular distance from the point $(-1, -1, 4)$ to the plane Π.

c Find the perpendicular distance from the point $(2, 1, 3)$ to the plane Π.

d Find the perpendicular distance from the point $(6, 12, -9)$ to the plane Π.

10 Find the shortest distance between the parallel planes.

a $\mathbf{r}.(6\mathbf{i} + 6\mathbf{j} - 7\mathbf{k}) = 55$ and $\mathbf{r}.(6\mathbf{i} + 6\mathbf{j} - 7\mathbf{k}) = 22$

b $\mathbf{r} = 3\mathbf{i} + 4\mathbf{j} + \mathbf{k} + \lambda(4\mathbf{i} + \mathbf{k}) + \mu(8\mathbf{i} + 3\mathbf{j} + 3\mathbf{k})$ and
$\mathbf{r} = 14\mathbf{i} + 2\mathbf{j} + 2\mathbf{k} + \lambda(3\mathbf{j} + \mathbf{k}) + \mu(8\mathbf{i} - 9\mathbf{j} - \mathbf{k})$

11 Find the shortest distance between the two skew lines with equations $\mathbf{r} = \mathbf{i} + \lambda(-3\mathbf{i} - 12\mathbf{j} + 11\mathbf{k})$ and $\mathbf{r} = 3\mathbf{i} - \mathbf{j} + \mathbf{k} + \mu(2\mathbf{i} + 6\mathbf{j} - 5\mathbf{k})$, where λ and μ are scalars.

12 Find the shortest distance between the parallel lines with equations $\mathbf{r} = 2\mathbf{i} - \mathbf{j} + \mathbf{k} + \lambda(-3\mathbf{i} - 4\mathbf{j} + 5\mathbf{k})$ and $\mathbf{r} = \mathbf{j} + \mathbf{k} + \mu(-3\mathbf{i} - 4\mathbf{j} + 5\mathbf{k})$, where λ and μ are scalars.

13 Determine whether the lines l_1 and l_2 meet. If they do, find their point of intersection. If they do not, find the shortest distance between them. (In each of the following cases λ and μ are scalars.)

a l_1 has equation $\mathbf{r} = \mathbf{i} + \mathbf{j} + \lambda(2\mathbf{i} - \mathbf{j} + 5\mathbf{k})$ and
l_2 has equation $\mathbf{r} = -\mathbf{i} + \mathbf{j} + 2\mathbf{k} + \mu(2\mathbf{i} - 5\mathbf{j} + \mathbf{k})$

b l_1 has equation $\mathbf{r} = 2\mathbf{i} + \mathbf{j} - 2\mathbf{k} + \lambda(2\mathbf{i} - 2\mathbf{j} + 2\mathbf{k})$ and
l_2 has equation $\mathbf{r} = \mathbf{i} - \mathbf{j} + 3\mathbf{k} + \mu(\mathbf{i} - \mathbf{j} + \mathbf{k})$

c l_1 has equation $\mathbf{r} = \mathbf{i} + \mathbf{j} + 5\mathbf{k} + \lambda(2\mathbf{i} + \mathbf{j} - 2\mathbf{k})$ and
l_2 has equation $\mathbf{r} = -\mathbf{i} - \mathbf{j} + 2\mathbf{k} + \mu(\mathbf{i} + \mathbf{j} + \mathbf{k})$

14 Find the shortest distance between the point with coordinates $(4, 1, -1)$ and the line with equation

$\mathbf{r} = 3\mathbf{i} - \mathbf{j} + 2\mathbf{k} + \mu(2\mathbf{i} - \mathbf{j} - \mathbf{k})$, where μ is a scalar.

15 The plane Π has equation $\mathbf{r}.(\mathbf{i} + \mathbf{j} - \mathbf{k}) = 4$.

a Show that the line with equation $\mathbf{r} = 2\mathbf{i} + 3\mathbf{j} + \mathbf{k} + \lambda(-\mathbf{i} + 2\mathbf{j} + \mathbf{k})$ lies in the plane Π.

b Show that the line with equation $\mathbf{r} = -\mathbf{i} + 2\mathbf{j} + 4\mathbf{k} + \lambda(-\mathbf{i} + 2\mathbf{j} + \mathbf{k})$ is parallel to the plane Π and find the shortest distance from the line to the plane.

Mixed exercise 5G

1 Find the shortest distance between the lines with vector equations

$\mathbf{r} = 3\mathbf{i} + s\mathbf{j} - \mathbf{k}$
and $\mathbf{r} = 9\mathbf{i} - 2\mathbf{j} - \mathbf{k} + t(\mathbf{i} - 2\mathbf{j} + \mathbf{k})$

where s, t are scalars. **E**

2 Obtain the shortest distance between the lines with equations

$\mathbf{r} = (3s - 3)\mathbf{i} - s\mathbf{j} + (s + 1)\mathbf{k}$
and $\mathbf{r} = (3 + t)\mathbf{i} + (2t - 2)\mathbf{j} + \mathbf{k}$

where s, t are parameters. **E**

3 The position vectors of the points A, B, C and D relative to a fixed origin O, are $(-\mathbf{j} + 2\mathbf{k})$, $(\mathbf{i} - 3\mathbf{j} + 5\mathbf{k})$, $(2\mathbf{i} - 2\mathbf{j} + 7\mathbf{k})$ and $(\mathbf{j} + 2\mathbf{k})$ respectively.

a Find $\mathbf{p} = \overrightarrow{AB} \times \overrightarrow{CD}$.

b Calculate $\overrightarrow{AC}.\mathbf{p}$.

Hence determine the shortest distance between the line containing AB and the line containing CD. **E**

4 Relative to a fixed origin O, the point M has position vector $-4\mathbf{i} + \mathbf{j} - 2\mathbf{k}$

The straight line l has equation $\mathbf{r} \times \overrightarrow{OM} = 5\mathbf{i} - 10\mathbf{k}$.

a Express the equation of the line l in the form $\mathbf{r} = \mathbf{a} + t\mathbf{b}$, where $\mathbf{a}$ and $\mathbf{b}$ are constant vectors and t is a parameter.

b Verify that the point N with coordinates $(2, -3, 1)$ lies on l and find the area of $\triangle OMN$. **E**

5 The line l_1 has equation $\mathbf{r} = \mathbf{i} - \mathbf{j} + \lambda(\mathbf{i} + 2\mathbf{j} + 3\mathbf{k})$ and the line l_2 has equation $\mathbf{r} = 2\mathbf{i} + \mathbf{j} + \mathbf{k} + \mu(2\mathbf{i} - \mathbf{j} + \mathbf{k})$.

a Find a vector which is perpendicular to both l_1 and l_2.

The point A lies on l_1 and the point B lies on l_2. Given that AB is also perpendicular to l_1 and l_2,

b find the coordinates of A and B. **E**

6 A plane passes through the three points A, B, C, whose position vectors, referred to an origin O, are $(\mathbf{i} + 3\mathbf{j} + 3\mathbf{k})$, $(3\mathbf{i} + \mathbf{j} + 4\mathbf{k})$, $(2\mathbf{i} + 4\mathbf{j} + \mathbf{k})$ respectively.

a Find, in the form $(l\mathbf{i} + m\mathbf{j} + n\mathbf{k})$, a unit vector normal to this plane.

b Find also a Cartesian equation of the plane.

c Find the perpendicular distance from the origin to this plane.

7 **a** Show that the vector $\mathbf{i} + \mathbf{k}$ is perpendicular to the plane with vector equation $\mathbf{r} = \mathbf{i} + s\mathbf{j} + t(\mathbf{i} - \mathbf{k})$.

b Find the perpendicular distance from the origin to this plane.

c Hence or otherwise obtain a Cartesian equation of the plane.

8 The points A, B and C have position vectors $\mathbf{i} + \mathbf{j} + \mathbf{k}$, $5\mathbf{i} - 2\mathbf{j} + \mathbf{k}$ and $3\mathbf{i} + 2\mathbf{j} + 6\mathbf{k}$ respectively, referred to an origin O.

a Find a vector perpendicular to the plane containing the points A, B and C.

b Hence, or otherwise, find an equation for the plane which contains the points A, B and C, in the form $ax + by + cz + d = 0$.

The point D has coordinates $(1, 5, 6)$.

c Find the volume of the tetrahedron $ABCD$.

9 The plane Π passes through $A(3, -5, -1)$, $B(-1, 5, 7)$ and $C(2, -3, 0)$.

a Find $\overrightarrow{AC} \times \overrightarrow{BC}$.

b Hence, or otherwise, find the equation, in the form $\mathbf{r.n} = p$, of the plane Π.

c The perpendicular from the point $(2, 3, -2)$ to Π meets the plane at P. Find the coordinates of P.

10 Given that P and Q are the points with position vectors $\mathbf{p}$ and $\mathbf{q}$ respectively, relative to an origin O, and that

$$\mathbf{p} = 3\mathbf{i} - \mathbf{j} + 2\mathbf{k}$$
$$\mathbf{q} = 2\mathbf{i} + \mathbf{j} - \mathbf{k},$$

a find $\mathbf{p} \times \mathbf{q}$.

b Hence, or otherwise, find an equation of the plane containing O, P and Q in the form $ax + by + cz = d$.

The line with equation $(\mathbf{r} - \mathbf{p}) \times \mathbf{q} = 0$ meets the plane with equation $\mathbf{r}.(\mathbf{i} + \mathbf{j} + \mathbf{k}) = 2$ at the point T.

c Find the coordinates of the point T.

11 The planes Π_1 and Π_2 are defined by the equations $2x + 2y - z = 9$ and $x - 2y = 7$ respectively.

a Find the acute angle between Π_1 and Π_2, giving your answer to the nearest degree.

b Find in the form $\mathbf{r} \times \mathbf{u} = \mathbf{v}$ an equation of the line of intersection of Π_1 and Π_2.

12 A pyramid has a square base $OPQR$ and vertex S. Referred to O, the points P, Q, R and S have position vectors $\overrightarrow{OP} = 2\mathbf{i}$, $\overrightarrow{OQ} = 2\mathbf{i} + 2\mathbf{j}$, $\overrightarrow{OR} = 2\mathbf{j}$, $\overrightarrow{OS} = \mathbf{i} + \mathbf{j} + 4\mathbf{k}$.

a Express PS in terms of $\mathbf{i}$, $\mathbf{j}$ and $\mathbf{k}$.

b Show that the vector $-4\mathbf{j} + \mathbf{k}$ is perpendicular to OS and PS.

c Find to the nearest degree the acute angle between the line SQ and the plane OSP.

13 The plane Π has vector equation

$$\mathbf{r} = \begin{pmatrix}1\\3\\4\end{pmatrix} + u\begin{pmatrix}4\\1\\2\end{pmatrix} + v\begin{pmatrix}3\\2\\-1\end{pmatrix},$$

where u and v are parameters.

The line L has vector equation

$$\mathbf{r} = \begin{pmatrix}2\\1\\-3\end{pmatrix} + t\begin{pmatrix}2\\3\\-4\end{pmatrix},$$

where t is a parameter.

a Show that L is parallel to Π.

b Find the shortest distance between L and Π. **E**

14 Planes Π_1 and Π_2 have equations given by

Π_1: $\mathbf{r}.(2\mathbf{i} - \mathbf{j} + \mathbf{k}) = 0$,

Π_2: $\mathbf{r}.(\mathbf{i} + 5\mathbf{j} + 3\mathbf{k}) = 1$.

a Show that the point $A(2, -2, 3)$ lies in Π_2.

b Show that Π_1 is perpendicular to Π_2.

c Find, in vector form, an equation of the straight line through A which is perpendicular to Π_1.

d Determine the coordinates of the point where this line meets Π_1.

e Find the perpendicular distance of A from Π_1.

f Find a vector equation of the plane through A parallel to Π_1. **E**

15 The plane Π has equation $2x + y + 3z = 21$ and the origin is O. The line l passes through the point $P(1, 2, 1)$ and is perpendicular to Π.

a Find a vector equation of l.

The line l meets the plane Π at the point M.

b Find the coordinates of M.

c Find $\overrightarrow{OP} \times \overrightarrow{OM}$.

d Hence, or otherwise, find the distance from P to the line OM, giving your answer in surd form.

The point Q is the reflection of P in Π.

e Find the coordinates of Q. **E**

16 With respect to a fixed origin O, the straight lines l_1 and l_2 are given by

l_1: $\mathbf{r} = \mathbf{i} - \mathbf{j} + \lambda(2\mathbf{i} + \mathbf{j} - 2\mathbf{k})$,

l_2: $\mathbf{r} = \mathbf{i} + 2\mathbf{j} + 2\mathbf{k} + \mu(-3\mathbf{i} + 4\mathbf{k})$,

where λ and μ are scalar parameters.

a Show that the lines intersect.

b Find the position vector of their point of intersection.

c Find the cosine of the acute angle contained between the lines.

d Find a vector equation of the plane containing the lines. *E*

17 Relative to an origin O, the points A and B have position vectors $\mathbf{a}$ metres and $\mathbf{b}$ metres respectively, where

$$\mathbf{a} = 5\mathbf{i} + 2\mathbf{j},\ \mathbf{b} = 2\mathbf{i} - \mathbf{j} - 3\mathbf{k}$$

The point C moves such that the volume of the tetrahedron $OABC$ is always $5\,\text{m}^3$.

Determine Cartesian equations of the locus of the point C. *E*

18 The lines L_1 and L_2 have equations $\mathbf{r} = \mathbf{a}_1 + s\mathbf{b}_1$ and $\mathbf{r} = \mathbf{a}_2 + t\mathbf{b}_2$ respectively, where

$$\mathbf{a}_1 = 3\mathbf{i} - 3\mathbf{j} - 2\mathbf{k}, \qquad \mathbf{b}_1 = \mathbf{j} + 2\mathbf{k},$$

$$\mathbf{a}_2 = 8\mathbf{i} + 3\mathbf{j}, \qquad \mathbf{b}_2 = 5\mathbf{i} + 4\mathbf{j} - 2\mathbf{k}.$$

a Verify that the point P with position vector $3\mathbf{i} - \mathbf{j} + 2\mathbf{k}$ lies on both L_1 and L_2.

b Find $\mathbf{b}_1 \times \mathbf{b}_2$.

c Find a Cartesian equation of the plane containing L_1 and L_2.

The points with position vectors $\mathbf{a}_1$ and $\mathbf{a}_2$ are A_1 and A_2 respectively.

d By expressing $\overrightarrow{A_1P}$ and $\overrightarrow{A_2P}$ as multiples of $\mathbf{b}_1$ and $\mathbf{b}_2$ respectively, or otherwise, find the area of the triangle PA_1A_2. *E*

19 With respect to the origin O the points A, B, C have position vectors

$$a(5\mathbf{i} - \mathbf{j} - 3\mathbf{k}),\quad a(-4\mathbf{i} + 4\mathbf{j} - \mathbf{k}),\quad a(5\mathbf{i} - 2\mathbf{j} + 11\mathbf{k})$$

respectively, where a is a non-zero constant.

Find

a a vector equation for the line BC,

b a vector equation for the plane OAB,

c the cosine of the acute angle between the lines OA and OB.

Obtain, in the form $\mathbf{r.n} = p$, a vector equation for Π, the plane which passes through A and is perpendicular to BC.

Find Cartesian equations for

d the plane Π,

e the line BC. *E*

20 In a tetrahedron $ABCD$ the coordinates of the vertices B, C, D are respectively (1, 2, 3), (2, 3, 3), (3, 2, 4). Find

a the equation of the plane BCD,

b the sine of the angle between BC and the plane $x + 2y + 3z = 4$.

If AC and AD are perpendicular to BD and BC respectively and if $AB = \sqrt{26}$, find the coordinates of the two possible positions of A.

Summary of key points

1 The vector (or cross) product of the vectors **a** and **b** is defined as

$$\mathbf{a} \times \mathbf{b} = |\mathbf{a}||\mathbf{b}|\sin\theta\,\hat{\mathbf{n}},$$

where θ is the angle between **a** and **b**, and where $\hat{\mathbf{n}}$ is a unit vector perpendicular to both **a** and **b**. The direction of $\hat{\mathbf{n}}$ is that in which a right handed screw would move when turned from **a** to **b**.

2 $\mathbf{b} \times \mathbf{a} = -\mathbf{a} \times \mathbf{b}$
The vector product is not commutative. The order matters.

3 If **i**, **j** and **k** are unit vectors in the x, y and z directions respectively, then

$\mathbf{i} \times \mathbf{i} = 0$
$\mathbf{j} \times \mathbf{j} = 0$
$\mathbf{k} \times \mathbf{k} = 0$

also $\mathbf{i} \times \mathbf{j} = \mathbf{k}$ and $\mathbf{j} \times \mathbf{i} = -\mathbf{k}$
$\mathbf{j} \times \mathbf{k} = \mathbf{i}$ and $\mathbf{k} \times \mathbf{j} = -\mathbf{i}$
$\mathbf{k} \times \mathbf{i} = \mathbf{j}$ and $\mathbf{i} \times \mathbf{k} = -\mathbf{j}$

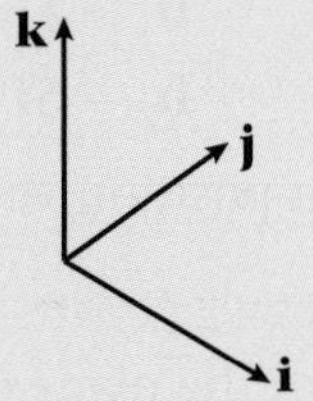

4 If $\mathbf{a} \times \mathbf{b} = 0$, then either
$\mathbf{a} = 0$ or $\mathbf{b} = 0$ or **a** and **b** are parallel.

5 In Cartesian form when $\mathbf{a} = (a_1\mathbf{i} + a_2\mathbf{j} + a_3\mathbf{k})$ and $\mathbf{b} = (b_1\mathbf{i} + b_2\mathbf{j} + b_3\mathbf{k})$

$$\mathbf{a} \times \mathbf{b} = (a_2b_3 - a_3b_2)\mathbf{i} + (a_3b_1 - a_1b_3)\mathbf{j} + (a_1b_2 - a_2b_1)\mathbf{k}$$

$$\text{i.e. } \mathbf{a} \times \mathbf{b} = \begin{vmatrix} \mathbf{i} & \mathbf{j} & \mathbf{k} \\ a_1 & a_2 & a_3 \\ b_1 & b_2 & b_3 \end{vmatrix}$$

6 After evaluating a cross product take the dot product of each of the given vectors with your answer vector. Both answers should be zero as $\mathbf{a} \times \mathbf{b}$ is perpendicular to each of **a** and **b**. **This is a useful check.**

7 Area of triangle $OAB = \frac{1}{2}|\mathbf{a} \times \mathbf{b}|$

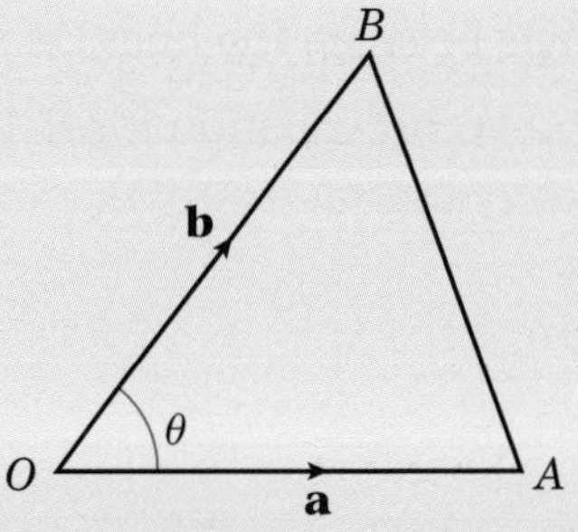

8 Area of triangle $ABC = \frac{1}{2}|\overrightarrow{AB} \times \overrightarrow{AC}| = \frac{1}{2}|(\mathbf{b} - \mathbf{a}) \times (\mathbf{c} - \mathbf{a})|$
$= \frac{1}{2}|(\mathbf{a} \times \mathbf{b}) + (\mathbf{b} \times \mathbf{c}) + (\mathbf{c} \times \mathbf{a})|$

9 Area of parallelogram $ABCD = |\overrightarrow{AB} \times \overrightarrow{AD}|$
$= |(\mathbf{b} - \mathbf{a}) \times (\mathbf{d} - \mathbf{a})|$
$= |(\mathbf{a} \times \mathbf{b}) + (\mathbf{b} \times \mathbf{d}) + (\mathbf{d} \times \mathbf{a})|$

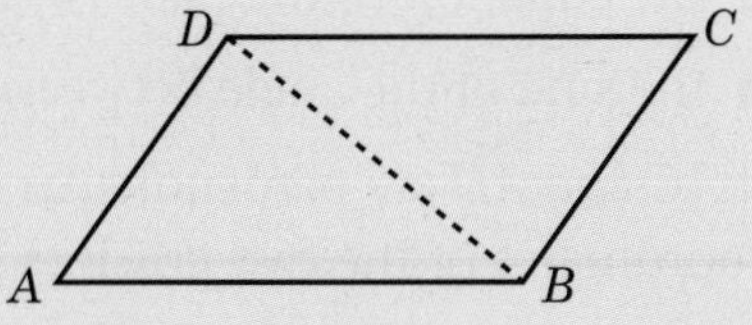

10 In Cartesian form when $\mathbf{a} = (a_1\mathbf{i} + a_2\mathbf{j} + a_3\mathbf{k})$, $\mathbf{b} = (b_1\mathbf{i} + b_2\mathbf{j} + b_3\mathbf{k})$ and $\mathbf{c} = (c_1\mathbf{i} + c_2\mathbf{j} + c_3\mathbf{k})$.

$$\mathbf{a}.(\mathbf{b} \times \mathbf{c}) = a_1(b_2c_3 - b_3c_2) + a_2(b_3c_1 - b_1c_3) + a_3(b_1c_2 - b_2c_1)$$

This can also be written as

$$\mathbf{a}.(\mathbf{b} \times \mathbf{c}) = \begin{vmatrix} a_1 & a_2 & a_3 \\ b_1 & b_2 & b_3 \\ c_1 & c_2 & c_3 \end{vmatrix}$$

11 Note that $\mathbf{a}.(\mathbf{b} \times \mathbf{c}) = \mathbf{b}.(\mathbf{c} \times \mathbf{a}) = \mathbf{c}.(\mathbf{a} \times \mathbf{b})$
Also $\mathbf{a}.(\mathbf{a} \times \mathbf{x}) = 0$ for any vector $\mathbf{x}$.

12 The volume of the parallelepiped is given by $|\mathbf{a}.(\mathbf{b} \times \mathbf{c})|$.

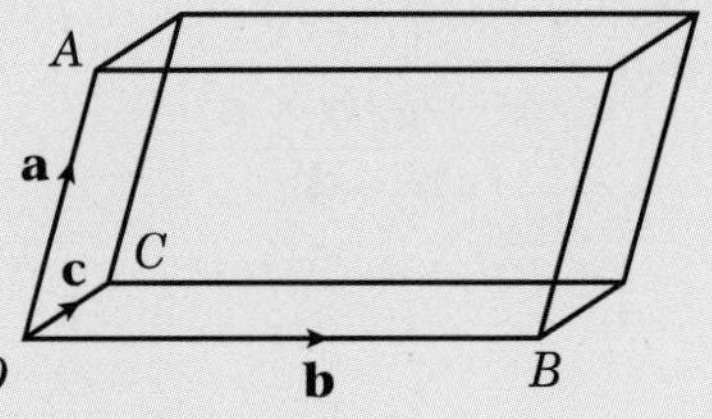

13

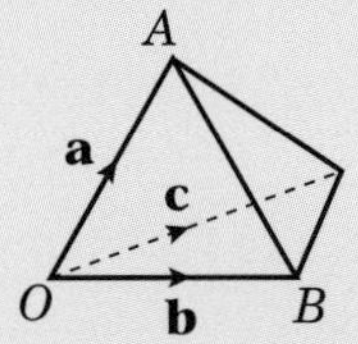

The volume of the tetrahedron is given by $|\frac{1}{6}\mathbf{a}.(\mathbf{b} \times \mathbf{c})|$.

14 $(\mathbf{r} - \mathbf{a}) \times \mathbf{b} = 0$ is an alternative form of the vector equation of a line passing through a point A with position vector $\mathbf{a}$, and parallel to the vector $\mathbf{b}$.
This may also be written $\mathbf{r} \times \mathbf{b} = \mathbf{a} \times \mathbf{b}$.

15 The general Cartesian equation of a straight line is

$$\frac{(x - x_1)}{l} = \frac{(y - y_1)}{m} = \frac{(z - z_1)}{n} = \lambda,$$

where the line passes through the point (x_1, y_1, z_1), has direction ratios $l : m : n$, and where λ is a parameter.

16 The scalar product form of the equation of a plane is $\mathbf{r}.\mathbf{n} = \mathbf{a}.\mathbf{n} = p$ where $\mathbf{n}$ is normal to the plane, $\mathbf{a}$ is the position vector of a point in the plane and $\mathbf{r}$ is the position vector of a general point on the plane. p is a scalar constant.

17 The general Cartesian equation of a plane is $ax + by + cz + d = 0$.

18 The vector equation of a plane is $\mathbf{r} = \mathbf{a} + \lambda\mathbf{b} + \mu\mathbf{c}$ where $\mathbf{a}$ is the position vector of a point in the plane, $\mathbf{b}$ and $\mathbf{c}$ are non-parallel vectors in the plane and $\mathbf{r}$ is the position vector of a general point on the plane. λ and μ are scalars and $\mathbf{b}$ and $\mathbf{c}$ are non-zero.

19 Angle between line and plane
The angle θ between the line with equation $\mathbf{r} = \mathbf{a} + \lambda\mathbf{b}$ and the plane with equation $\mathbf{r}.\mathbf{n} = p$ is given by the formula

$$\sin\theta = \left|\frac{\mathbf{b}.\mathbf{n}}{|\mathbf{b}||\mathbf{n}|}\right|$$

20 Angle between two planes

The angle θ between the plane with equation $\mathbf{r.n}_1 = p_1$ and the plane with equation $\mathbf{r.n}_2 = p_2$ is given by the formula

$$\cos\theta = \left|\frac{\mathbf{n}_1.\mathbf{n}_2}{|\mathbf{n}_1||\mathbf{n}_2|}\right|$$

21 When the equation of plane Π is written in the form $\mathbf{r}.\hat{\mathbf{n}} = d$, where $\hat{\mathbf{n}}$ is a unit vector perpendicular to Π, then d is the length of the perpendicular from the origin to the plane.

22 The shortest distance between the two skew lines with equations $\mathbf{r} = \mathbf{a} + \lambda\mathbf{b}$ and $\mathbf{r} = \mathbf{c} + \mu\mathbf{d}$, where λ and μ are scalars, is given by the formula

$$\left|\frac{(\mathbf{a} - \mathbf{c}).(\mathbf{b} \times \mathbf{d})}{|(\mathbf{b} \times \mathbf{d})|}\right|$$

After completing this chapter you should be able to:

- find transposes, determinants and inverses of 3×3 matrices
- represent linear transformations by 2×2 and 3×3 matrices
- find eigenvalues and eigenvectors of 2×2 and 3×3 matrices
- reduce symmetric matrices to diagonal form.

6

Further matrix algebra

This chapter extends the work on matrices which you learnt in the FP1 unit. Matrix algebra is used in many branches of mathematics, especially when large amounts of data are involved, as the rules for manipulating matrices can be efficiently implemented on computers. Eigenvalues and eigenvectors have many scientific applications. For example, they can be used in analysing population trends, atomic structures, stress and vibrations in mechanics and glacial sediments in geology.

6.1 You can find the transpose of a matrix.

- Given a matrix **A**, you form the **transpose** of the matrix $\mathbf{A}^T$, by interchanging the rows and the columns of **A**. You take the first row of **A** and write it as the first column of $\mathbf{A}^T$, you take the second row of **A** and write it as the second column of $\mathbf{A}^T$, and so on.

  If $\mathbf{A} = \begin{pmatrix} 2 & 4 \\ 0 & -3 \\ 1 & 5 \end{pmatrix}$, then $\mathbf{A}^T = \begin{pmatrix} 2 & 0 & 1 \\ 4 & -3 & 5 \end{pmatrix}$.

- The transpose of a matrix of dimension $n \times m$ is a matrix of dimension $m \times n$.

- The transpose of a square matrix is another square matrix with the same dimensions. For example, the transpose of a 2×2 matrix is another 2×2 matrix.

- If $\mathbf{A} = \mathbf{A}^T$, the matrix **A** is **symmetric**.

- A 2×2 matrix is symmetric if it has the form $\begin{pmatrix} a & b \\ b & c \end{pmatrix}$. Interchanging the rows and columns leaves the matrix unchanged.

- A 3×3 matrix is symmetric if it has the form $\begin{pmatrix} a & b & c \\ b & d & e \\ c & e & f \end{pmatrix}$. Interchanging the rows and columns leaves the matrix unchanged.

- The identity 3×3 matrix is $\mathbf{I} = \begin{pmatrix} 1 & 0 & 0 \\ 0 & 1 & 0 \\ 0 & 0 & 1 \end{pmatrix}$. When a matrix or vector is multiplied by the identity matrix, the matrix or vector is unchanged.

- The zero 3×3 matrix is $\mathbf{0} = \begin{pmatrix} 0 & 0 & 0 \\ 0 & 0 & 0 \\ 0 & 0 & 0 \end{pmatrix}$.

Example 1

Write down the transposes of the following matrices. State which of the matrices is symmetric.

a $\mathbf{A} = \begin{pmatrix} 4 & 3 \\ 2 & 0 \end{pmatrix}$, **b** $\mathbf{B} = \begin{pmatrix} 7 & 0 & 0 \\ 3 & -1 & 3 \end{pmatrix}$, **c** $\mathbf{C} = \begin{pmatrix} 1 & 0 & -1 \\ 0 & 2 & 0 \\ -1 & 0 & 3 \end{pmatrix}$, **d** $\mathbf{D} = \begin{pmatrix} 4 & -7 & 1 \\ 0 & 3 & -5 \\ 2 & 4 & -2 \end{pmatrix}$.

a $\mathbf{A}^T = \begin{pmatrix} 4 & 2 \\ 3 & 0 \end{pmatrix}$

The first row of **A**, (4 3), becomes the first column of $\mathbf{A}^T$, $\begin{pmatrix} 4 \\ 3 \end{pmatrix}$.

The second row of **A**, (2 0), becomes the second column of $\mathbf{A}^T$, $\begin{pmatrix} 2 \\ 0 \end{pmatrix}$.

b $\mathbf{B}^T = \begin{pmatrix} 7 & 3 \\ 0 & -1 \\ 0 & 3 \end{pmatrix}$

The first row of **B**, (7 0 0), becomes the first column of $\mathbf{B}^T$, $\begin{pmatrix} 7 \\ 0 \\ 0 \end{pmatrix}$.

The second row of **B**, (3 −1 3), becomes the second column of $\mathbf{B}^T$, $\begin{pmatrix} 3 \\ -1 \\ 3 \end{pmatrix}$.

c $\mathbf{C}^T = \begin{pmatrix} 1 & 0 & -1 \\ 0 & 2 & 0 \\ -1 & 0 & 3 \end{pmatrix}$, the matrix **C** is symmetric.

When you interchange the rows and columns of **C**, you obtain the same matrix. The matrix **C** is symmetric.

d $\mathbf{D}^T = \begin{pmatrix} 4 & 0 & 2 \\ -7 & 3 & 4 \\ 1 & -5 & -2 \end{pmatrix}$

The first row of **D** becomes the first column of $\mathbf{D}^T$. The second row of **D** becomes the second column of $\mathbf{D}^T$, and so on.

Example 2

The matrix **M** is given by

$$\mathbf{M} = \begin{pmatrix} 3 & 2 \\ 1 & -2 \\ 4 & 0 \end{pmatrix}$$

Find **a** $\mathbf{M}^T$ **b** $\mathbf{M}^T\mathbf{M}$ **c** $\mathbf{M}\mathbf{M}^T$

In each case state the dimension of your answer.

a $\mathbf{M}^T = \begin{pmatrix} 3 & 1 & 4 \\ 2 & -2 & 0 \end{pmatrix}$

The dimension of $\mathbf{M}^T$ is 2×3.

The first row of **M** becomes the first column of $\mathbf{M}^T$. The second row of **M** becomes the second column of $\mathbf{M}^T$ and the third row of **M** becomes the third column of $\mathbf{M}^T$.

b $\mathbf{M}^T\mathbf{M} = \begin{pmatrix} 3 & 1 & 4 \\ 2 & -2 & 0 \end{pmatrix}\begin{pmatrix} 3 & 2 \\ 1 & -2 \\ 4 & 0 \end{pmatrix}$

$= \begin{pmatrix} 26 & 4 \\ 4 & 8 \end{pmatrix}$

The dimension of $\mathbf{M}^T\mathbf{M}$ is 2×2.

First row times first column
$3 \times 3 + 1 \times 1 + 4 \times 4 = 26$

First row times second column
$3 \times 2 + 1 \times (-2) + 4 \times 0 = 4$

Second row times second column
$2 \times 2 + (-2) \times (-2) + 0 \times 0 = 8$

Second row times first column
$2 \times 3 + (-2) \times 1 + 0 \times 4 = 4$

c $\mathbf{MM}^{\mathrm{T}} = \begin{pmatrix} 3 & 2 \\ 1 & -2 \\ 4 & 0 \end{pmatrix}\begin{pmatrix} 3 & 1 & 4 \\ 2 & -2 & 0 \end{pmatrix}$

$$= \begin{pmatrix} 3 \times 3 + 2 \times 2 & 3 \times 1 + 2 \times (-2) & 3 \times 4 + 2 \times 0 \\ 1 \times 3 + (-2) \times 2 & 1 \times 1 + (-2) \times (-2) & 1 \times 4 + (-2) \times 0 \\ 4 \times 3 + 0 \times 2 & 4 \times 1 + 0 \times (-2) & 4 \times 4 + 0 \times 0 \end{pmatrix}$$

$$= \begin{pmatrix} 13 & -1 & 12 \\ -1 & 5 & 4 \\ 12 & 4 & 16 \end{pmatrix}$$

The dimension of $\mathbf{MM}^{\mathrm{T}}$ is 3×3.

For example, the element in the second row and third column is the second row of **M** multiplied by the third column of $\mathbf{M}^{\mathrm{T}}$.

You learnt in book FP1 how to multiply matrices and that, in general, matrix multiplication is not **commutative**, that is, in general, the matrix product **AB** is not equal to **BA**. Here $\mathbf{M}^{\mathrm{T}}\mathbf{M}$ and $\mathbf{MM}^{\mathrm{T}}$ are different and have different dimensions. You will notice, however, that both $\mathbf{M}^{\mathrm{T}}\mathbf{M}$ and $\mathbf{MM}^{\mathrm{T}}$ are symmetric. This property of a matrix and its transpose is always true.

Example 3

The matrix **A** is given by $\mathbf{A} = \begin{pmatrix} 2 & 2 & -1 \\ -1 & 2 & a \\ 2 & b & 2 \end{pmatrix}$, where a and b are constants.

Given that $\mathbf{AA}^{\mathrm{T}} = k\mathbf{I}$, where k is a constant, find the values of k, a and b.

$$\mathbf{A}^{\mathrm{T}} = \begin{pmatrix} 2 & -1 & 2 \\ 2 & 2 & b \\ -1 & a & 2 \end{pmatrix}$$

You take the first row of **A** and write it as the first column of $\mathbf{A}^{\mathrm{T}}$, you take the second row of **A** and write it as the second column of $\mathbf{A}^{\mathrm{T}}$, and so on.

$$\mathbf{AA}^{\mathrm{T}} = \begin{pmatrix} 2 & 2 & -1 \\ -1 & 2 & a \\ 2 & b & 2 \end{pmatrix}\begin{pmatrix} 2 & -1 & 2 \\ 2 & 2 & b \\ -1 & a & 2 \end{pmatrix}$$

$$= \begin{pmatrix} 4+4+1 & -2+4-a & 4+2b-2 \\ \cdots & \cdots & \cdots \\ \cdots & \cdots & \cdots \end{pmatrix}$$

You have to find three unknowns and, in this case, three elements of $\mathbf{AA}^{\mathrm{T}}$ will give you three equations to find the unknowns. You need not work out all nine elements of the matrix.

$$k\mathbf{I} = k\begin{pmatrix} 1 & 0 & 0 \\ 0 & 1 & 0 \\ 0 & 0 & 1 \end{pmatrix} = \begin{pmatrix} k & 0 & 0 \\ 0 & k & 0 \\ 0 & 0 & k \end{pmatrix}$$

When you multiply a matrix by a scalar k, you multiply all of the elements in the matrix by k. In this case, as $k \times 1 = k$ and $k \times 0 = 0$, the result is a simple matrix.

As $\mathbf{AA}^{\mathrm{T}} = k\mathbf{I}$

$$\begin{pmatrix} 9 & 2-a & 2b+2 \\ \cdots & \cdots & \cdots \\ \cdots & \cdots & \cdots \end{pmatrix} = \begin{pmatrix} k & 0 & 0 \\ 0 & k & 0 \\ 0 & 0 & k \end{pmatrix}$$

For two 3×3 matrices to be equal, all nine of the elements in the matrices must be individually equal. In principle, there are nine equations available but you only need three of them to solve this problem.

Equating the first element in the first row

$k = 9$

Equating the second element in the first row

$2 - a = 0 \Rightarrow a = 2$

Equating the third element in the first row

$2b + 2 = 0 \Rightarrow b = -1$

$k = 9$, $a = 2$ and $b = -1$.

The second element in the first row of the left hand matrix is $2 - a$. The second element in the first row of the right hand matrix is 0. So $2 - a = 0$, which is an easy equation for a.

Example 4

The matrix $\mathbf{A} = \begin{pmatrix} 3 & 0 & 2 \\ -2 & 1 & 0 \\ 1 & -2 & 4 \end{pmatrix}$ and the matrix $\mathbf{B} = \begin{pmatrix} 1 & 0 & 4 \\ 0 & 2 & 0 \\ 2 & 0 & 1 \end{pmatrix}$

a Write down $\mathbf{A}^{\mathrm{T}}$ and $\mathbf{B}^{\mathrm{T}}$. **b** Find $\mathbf{AB}$. **c** Verify that $(\mathbf{AB})^{\mathrm{T}} = \mathbf{B}^{\mathrm{T}}\mathbf{A}^{\mathrm{T}}$.

a $\mathbf{A}^{\mathrm{T}} = \begin{pmatrix} 3 & -2 & 1 \\ 0 & 1 & -2 \\ 2 & 0 & 4 \end{pmatrix}$

$\mathbf{B}^{\mathrm{T}} = \begin{pmatrix} 1 & 0 & 2 \\ 0 & 2 & 0 \\ 4 & 0 & 1 \end{pmatrix}$

You form the transposes by interchanging the rows and columns of the matrices.

b $\mathbf{AB} = \begin{pmatrix} 3 & 0 & 2 \\ -2 & 1 & 0 \\ 1 & -2 & 4 \end{pmatrix}\begin{pmatrix} 1 & 0 & 4 \\ 0 & 2 & 0 \\ 2 & 0 & 1 \end{pmatrix}$

$= \begin{pmatrix} 7 & 0 & 14 \\ -2 & 2 & -8 \\ 9 & -4 & 8 \end{pmatrix}$

You find the element in the first row and first column by multiplying the first row by the first column. $3 \times 1 + 0 \times 0 + 2 \times 2 = 7$.

You repeat this process throughout the matrix. For example, you find the element in the third row and the second column by multiplying the third row by the second column. $1 \times 0 + (-2) \times 2 + 4 \times 0 = -4$.

c $\mathbf{B}^{\mathrm{T}}\mathbf{A}^{\mathrm{T}} = \begin{pmatrix} 1 & 0 & 2 \\ 0 & 2 & 0 \\ 4 & 0 & 1 \end{pmatrix}\begin{pmatrix} 3 & -2 & 1 \\ 0 & 1 & -2 \\ 2 & 0 & 4 \end{pmatrix}$

$= \begin{pmatrix} 7 & -2 & 9 \\ 0 & 2 & -4 \\ 14 & -8 & 8 \end{pmatrix}$

Using part **b**

$(\mathbf{AB})^{\mathrm{T}} = \begin{pmatrix} 7 & -2 & 9 \\ 0 & 2 & -4 \\ 14 & -8 & 8 \end{pmatrix}$

Hence $(\mathbf{AB})^{\mathrm{T}} = \mathbf{B}^{\mathrm{T}}\mathbf{A}^{\mathrm{T}}$, as required.

To verify the relation $(\mathbf{AB})^{\mathrm{T}} = \mathbf{B}^{\mathrm{T}}\mathbf{A}^{\mathrm{T}}$, you show that it is satisfied by the specific matrices given in the question. You work out $\mathbf{B}^{\mathrm{T}}\mathbf{A}^{\mathrm{T}}$ and $(\mathbf{AB})^{\mathrm{T}}$ separately and show that they are equal.

This relation is true for any matrices **A** and **B** that can be multiplied together.

- If **A** and **B** are matrices with dimensions $n \times m$ and $m \times p$, then $(\mathbf{AB})^{\mathrm{T}} = \mathbf{B}^{\mathrm{T}}\mathbf{A}^{\mathrm{T}}$.

Exercise 6A

1 Write down the transposes of the following matrices. In each case give the dimensions of the transposed matrix.

a $\begin{pmatrix} 3 & 1 & 2 \\ -1 & 0 & 4 \end{pmatrix}$ **b** $\begin{pmatrix} 0 & 2 \\ -2 & 0 \end{pmatrix}$ **c** $\begin{pmatrix} 0 & 2 & -1 \\ -2 & 0 & 3 \\ 1 & -3 & 0 \end{pmatrix}$ **d** $\begin{pmatrix} 1 \\ 2 \\ 4 \end{pmatrix}$

2 The matrix $\mathbf{A} = \begin{pmatrix} 2 & 4 \\ -3 & 6 \end{pmatrix}$.

a Write down $\mathbf{A}^{\mathrm{T}}$. **b** Find $\mathbf{AA}^{\mathrm{T}}$. **c** Find $\mathbf{A}^{\mathrm{T}}\mathbf{A}$.

3 The matrix $\mathbf{A} = \begin{pmatrix} 3 & 2 \\ -2 & 1 \end{pmatrix}$ and the matrix $\mathbf{B} = \begin{pmatrix} 1 & 6 \\ 0 & -4 \end{pmatrix}$.

a Find **BA**. **b** Verify that $\mathbf{A}^{\mathrm{T}}\mathbf{B}^{\mathrm{T}} = (\mathbf{BA})^{\mathrm{T}}$.

4 The matrix $\mathbf{A} = \begin{pmatrix} 1 & -4 & 8 \\ 4 & -7 & -4 \\ 8 & 4 & 1 \end{pmatrix}$.

a Write down $\mathbf{A}^{\mathrm{T}}$. **b** Show that $\mathbf{AA}^{\mathrm{T}} = 81\mathbf{I}$.

5 The matrix $\mathbf{A} = \begin{pmatrix} 0 & 3 & 5 \\ -3 & 0 & -1 \\ -5 & 1 & 0 \end{pmatrix}$ and the matrix $\mathbf{B} = \begin{pmatrix} -4 & 1 & -1 \\ 1 & 5 & 2 \\ -3 & 0 & 3 \end{pmatrix}$.

Given that $\mathbf{C} = \mathbf{AB}$,

a find **C**, **b** verify that the matrix **C** is symmetric.

6 The matrix $\mathbf{A} = \begin{pmatrix} 0 & 3 & 5 \\ 2 & 0 & -1 \\ 1 & 1 & 0 \end{pmatrix}$ and the matrix $\mathbf{B} = \begin{pmatrix} 1 & 1 & -1 \\ 0 & 1 & 0 \\ -1 & 0 & 3 \end{pmatrix}$.

a Find **AB**. **b** Verify that $(\mathbf{AB})^{\mathrm{T}} = \mathbf{B}^{\mathrm{T}}\mathbf{A}^{\mathrm{T}}$.

6.2 You can find the determinant of a 3 × 3 matrix.

- In book FP1, you learnt that the determinant of a 2 × 2 matrix **A**, written det (**A**) or |**A**|, is given by the formula

$$\det(\mathbf{A}) = \begin{vmatrix} a & b \\ c & d \end{vmatrix} = ad - bc.$$

- You find the determinant of a 3 × 3 matrix by reducing the 3 × 3 determinant to 2 × 2 determinants using the formula

$$\begin{vmatrix} a & b & c \\ d & e & f \\ g & h & i \end{vmatrix} = a\begin{vmatrix} e & f \\ h & i \end{vmatrix} - b\begin{vmatrix} d & f \\ g & i \end{vmatrix} + c\begin{vmatrix} d & e \\ g & h \end{vmatrix}.$$

Notice that, in the middle expression in this formula, there is a negative sign before the b.

The 2×2 determinant associated with the element a in the first row of the determinant is found by crossing out the row and column in which a lies.

$$\begin{vmatrix} a & b & c \\ d & e & f \\ g & h & i \end{vmatrix} \rightarrow \begin{vmatrix} e & f \\ h & i \end{vmatrix}$$

The 2×2 determinant associated with the element b in the first row of the determinant is found by crossing out the row and column in which b lies.

$$\begin{vmatrix} a & b & c \\ d & e & f \\ g & h & i \end{vmatrix} \rightarrow \begin{vmatrix} d & f \\ g & i \end{vmatrix}$$

The 2×2 determinant associated with the element c in the first row of the determinant is found by crossing out the row and column in which c lies.

$$\begin{vmatrix} a & b & c \\ d & e & f \\ g & h & i \end{vmatrix} \rightarrow \begin{vmatrix} d & e \\ g & h \end{vmatrix}$$

- **As with 2×2 matrices, with 3×3 matrices, if det ($\mathbf{A}$) = 0, then $\mathbf{A}$ is a singular matrix, if det ($\mathbf{A}$) $\neq$ 0, then $\mathbf{A}$ is a non-singular matrix,**

Example 5

Find the value of $\begin{vmatrix} 1 & 2 & 4 \\ 3 & 2 & 1 \\ -1 & 4 & 3 \end{vmatrix}$.

$$\begin{vmatrix} 1 & 2 & 4 \\ 3 & 2 & 1 \\ -1 & 4 & 3 \end{vmatrix} = 1\begin{vmatrix} 2 & 1 \\ 4 & 3 \end{vmatrix} - 2\begin{vmatrix} 3 & 1 \\ -1 & 3 \end{vmatrix} + 4\begin{vmatrix} 3 & 2 \\ -1 & 4 \end{vmatrix}$$

$$= 1(6 - 4) - 2(9 + 1) + 4(12 + 2)$$

$$= 1 \times 2 - 2 \times 10 + 4 \times 14$$

$$= 2 - 20 + 56 = 38$$

This determinant is formed by crossing out the row and column in which 1 lies.

$$\begin{vmatrix} 1 & 2 & 4 \\ 3 & 2 & 1 \\ -1 & 4 & 3 \end{vmatrix}$$

This determinant is formed by crossing out the row and column in which 2 lies.

$$\begin{vmatrix} 1 & 2 & 4 \\ 3 & 2 & 1 \\ -1 & 4 & 3 \end{vmatrix}$$

This determinant is formed by crossing out the row and column in which 4 lies.

$$\begin{vmatrix} 1 & 2 & 4 \\ 3 & 2 & 1 \\ -1 & 4 & 3 \end{vmatrix}$$

Each 2×2 determinant is found using the formula $\begin{vmatrix} a & b \\ c & d \end{vmatrix} = ad - bc$.

So $\begin{vmatrix} 2 & 1 \\ 4 & 3 \end{vmatrix} = 2 \times 3 - 1 \times 4 = 6 - 4 = 2$,

$\begin{vmatrix} 3 & 1 \\ -1 & 3 \end{vmatrix} = 3 \times 3 - 1 \times (-1) = 9 + 1 = 10$,

and $\begin{vmatrix} 3 & 2 \\ -1 & 4 \end{vmatrix} = 3 \times 4 - 2 \times (-1) = 12 + 2 = 14$.

Example 6

The matrix $\mathbf{A} = \begin{pmatrix} 2 & -1 & 3 \\ 8 & -2 & 7 \\ 4 & 2 & -4 \end{pmatrix}$.

Show that $\mathbf{A}$ is singular.

$$\begin{vmatrix} 2 & -1 & 3 \\ 8 & -2 & 7 \\ 4 & 2 & -4 \end{vmatrix} = 2\begin{vmatrix} -2 & 7 \\ 2 & -4 \end{vmatrix} - (-1)\begin{vmatrix} 8 & 7 \\ 4 & -4 \end{vmatrix} + 3\begin{vmatrix} 8 & -2 \\ 4 & 2 \end{vmatrix}$$

Each 2×2 determinant is formed by crossing out the row and column in which the element in the first row lies.

$$= 2(8 - 14) + 1(-32 - 28) + 3(16 + 8)$$

In evaluating the 2×2 determinants using the formula $\begin{vmatrix} a & b \\ c & d \end{vmatrix} = ad - bc$, you need to be careful with the signs.

$$= 2 \times (-6) + 1 \times (-60) + 3 \times 24$$

$$= -12 - 60 + 72 = 0$$

As $\det(\mathbf{A}) = 0$, you conclude that $\mathbf{A}$ is singular.

Hence the matrix $\mathbf{A}$ is singular.

Example 7

The matrix $\mathbf{A} = \begin{pmatrix} 3 & k & 0 \\ -2 & 1 & 2 \\ 5 & 0 & k+3 \end{pmatrix}$, where k is a constant.

a Find $\det(\mathbf{A})$ in terms of k.

Given that $\mathbf{A}$ is singular,

b find the possible values of k.

a $$\begin{vmatrix} 3 & k & 0 \\ -2 & 1 & 2 \\ 5 & 0 & k+3 \end{vmatrix} = 3\begin{vmatrix} 1 & 2 \\ 0 & k+3 \end{vmatrix} - k\begin{vmatrix} -2 & 2 \\ 5 & k+3 \end{vmatrix} + 0\begin{vmatrix} -2 & 1 \\ 5 & 0 \end{vmatrix}$$

$$= 3(k + 3) - k(-2(k + 3) - 10)$$

Part **b** will require you to solve $\det(\mathbf{A}) = 0$, so multiply this expression out, collect together terms and express the result as a quadratic.

$$= 3k + 9 + 2k^2 + 16k$$

$$= 2k^2 + 19k + 9$$

b As $\mathbf{A}$ is singular

$$2k^2 + 19k + 9 = 0$$

As $\mathbf{A}$ is singular, its determinant is 0. This gives a quadratic equation, which you solve, giving two possible values of k.

$$(2k + 1)(k + 9) = 0$$

$$k = -\tfrac{1}{2}, -9$$

Example 8

The matrix $\mathbf{A} = \begin{pmatrix} 2 & 1 & -1 \\ 1 & 0 & 4 \\ -4 & 2 & 1 \end{pmatrix}$ and the matrix $\mathbf{B} = \begin{pmatrix} 3 & 1 & 2 \\ k & 4 & 5 \\ 0 & 2 & 3 \end{pmatrix}$, where k is a constant.

a Evaluate the determinant of **A**.

Given that the determinant of **B** is 2,

b find the value of k.

Using the value of k found in part **b**,

c find **AB**,

d verify that det (**AB**) = det (**A**) det (**B**).

a $\begin{vmatrix} 2 & 1 & -1 \\ 1 & 0 & 4 \\ -4 & 2 & 1 \end{vmatrix} = 2\begin{vmatrix} 0 & 4 \\ 2 & 1 \end{vmatrix} - 1\begin{vmatrix} 1 & 4 \\ -4 & 1 \end{vmatrix} + (-1)\begin{vmatrix} 1 & 0 \\ -4 & 2 \end{vmatrix}$

$= 2(0 - 8) - 1(1 + 16) + (-1)(2 - 0)$

$= -16 - 17 - 2 = -35$

b $\begin{vmatrix} 3 & 1 & 2 \\ k & 4 & 5 \\ 0 & 2 & 3 \end{vmatrix} = 3\begin{vmatrix} 4 & 5 \\ 2 & 3 \end{vmatrix} - 1\begin{vmatrix} k & 5 \\ 0 & 3 \end{vmatrix} + 2\begin{vmatrix} k & 4 \\ 0 & 2 \end{vmatrix}$

$= 3(12 - 10) - 1(3k - 0) + 2(2k - 0)$

$= 6 - 3k + 4k = k + 6$

$\Rightarrow k + 6 = 2 \Rightarrow k = -4$

As you are given the determinant is 2, you find an expression for det (**B**) in terms of k and then equate this expression to 2. You then solve the resulting linear equation to find k.

c $\mathbf{AB} = \begin{pmatrix} 2 & 1 & -1 \\ 1 & 0 & 4 \\ -4 & 2 & 1 \end{pmatrix}\begin{pmatrix} 3 & 1 & 2 \\ -4 & 4 & 5 \\ 0 & 2 & 3 \end{pmatrix}$

With $k = -4$, $\mathbf{B} = \begin{pmatrix} 2 & 1 & 2 \\ -4 & 4 & 5 \\ 0 & 2 & 3 \end{pmatrix}$.

$= \begin{pmatrix} 6 - 4 + 0 & 2 + 4 - 2 & 4 + 5 - 3 \\ 3 + 0 + 0 & 1 + 0 + 8 & 2 + 0 + 12 \\ -12 - 8 + 0 & -4 + 8 + 2 & -8 + 10 + 3 \end{pmatrix}$

$= \begin{pmatrix} 2 & 4 & 6 \\ 3 & 9 & 14 \\ -20 & 6 & 5 \end{pmatrix}$

d $\det(\mathbf{AB}) = \begin{vmatrix} 2 & 4 & 6 \\ 3 & 9 & 14 \\ -20 & 6 & 5 \end{vmatrix}$

$= 2\begin{vmatrix} 9 & 14 \\ 6 & 5 \end{vmatrix} - 4\begin{vmatrix} 3 & 14 \\ -20 & 5 \end{vmatrix} + 6\begin{vmatrix} 3 & 9 \\ -20 & 6 \end{vmatrix}$

$= 2(45 - 84) - 4(15 + 280) + 6(18 + 180)$

$= -78 - 1180 + 1188$

$= -70$

$= (-35) \times 2$

$= \det(\mathbf{A})\det(\mathbf{B})$

To verify the formula, you calculate the determinant of **AB** and show that it is equal to the determinant of **A** multiplied by the determinant of **B**. You worked out the determinant of **A** in part **a** and you were given the determinant of **B** for part **b**.

The formula det (**AB**) = det (**A**) det (**B**) is true for square matrices of any size.

Exercise 6B

1 Find the values of the determinants.

a $\begin{vmatrix} 1 & 0 & 0 \\ 0 & 2 & 0 \\ 0 & 0 & 3 \end{vmatrix}$ **b** $\begin{vmatrix} 0 & 4 & 0 \\ 5 & -2 & 3 \\ 2 & 1 & 4 \end{vmatrix}$ **c** $\begin{vmatrix} 1 & 0 & 1 \\ 2 & 4 & 1 \\ 3 & 5 & 2 \end{vmatrix}$ **d** $\begin{vmatrix} 2 & -3 & 4 \\ 2 & 2 & 2 \\ 5 & 5 & 5 \end{vmatrix}$

2 Find the values of the determinants.

a $\begin{vmatrix} 4 & 3 & -1 \\ 2 & -2 & 0 \\ 0 & 4 & -2 \end{vmatrix}$ **b** $\begin{vmatrix} 3 & -2 & 1 \\ 4 & 1 & -3 \\ 7 & 2 & -4 \end{vmatrix}$ **c** $\begin{vmatrix} 5 & -2 & -3 \\ 6 & 4 & 2 \\ -2 & -4 & -3 \end{vmatrix}$

3 The matrix $\mathbf{A} = \begin{pmatrix} 2 & 1 & -4 \\ 2k+1 & 3 & k \\ 1 & 0 & 1 \end{pmatrix}$.

Given that **A** is singular, find the value of the constant k.

4 The matrix $\mathbf{A} = \begin{pmatrix} 2 & -1 & 3 \\ k & 2 & 4 \\ -2 & 1 & k+3 \end{pmatrix}$, where k is a constant.

Given that the determinant of **A** is 8, find the possible values of k.

5 The matrix $\mathbf{A} = \begin{pmatrix} 2 & 5 & 3 \\ -2 & 0 & 4 \\ 3 & 10 & 8 \end{pmatrix}$ and the matrix $\mathbf{B} = \begin{pmatrix} 1 & 1 & 0 \\ 1 & 2 & 2 \\ 0 & -2 & -1 \end{pmatrix}$.

a Show that **A** is singular.

b Find **AB**.

c Show that **AB** is also singular.

6 The matrix $\mathbf{A} = \begin{pmatrix} 4 & 5 & -2 \\ 2 & -3 & 2 \\ 2 & -4 & 3 \end{pmatrix}$.

a Find det (**A**).

b Write down $\mathbf{A}^{\mathrm{T}}$

c Verify that $\det(\mathbf{A}^{\mathrm{T}}) = \det(\mathbf{A})$.

7 **a** Show that, for all values of a, b and c, the matrix $\begin{pmatrix} 0 & a & -b \\ -a & 0 & c \\ b & -c & 0 \end{pmatrix}$ is singular.

b Show that, for all real values of x, the matrix $\begin{pmatrix} 2 & -2 & 4 \\ 3 & x & -2 \\ -1 & 3 & x \end{pmatrix}$ is non-singular.

8 Find all the values of x for which the matrix $\begin{pmatrix} x-3 & -2 & 0 \\ 1 & x & -2 \\ -2 & -1 & x+1 \end{pmatrix}$ is singular.

6.3 You can find the inverse of a 3 × 3 matrix where it exists.

- **In book FP1 you learnt how to find the inverse of a 2 × 2 matrix. The rule for inverting a 2 × 2 matrix is that if $\mathbf{A} = \begin{pmatrix} a & b \\ c & d \end{pmatrix}$, then $\mathbf{A}^{-1} = \frac{1}{\det(\mathbf{A})}\begin{pmatrix} d & -b \\ -c & a \end{pmatrix}$.**

- **If $\det(\mathbf{A}) = 0$, the matrix $\mathbf{A}$ is singular and, as you cannot divide by zero, you cannot find an inverse. Similarly, with 3 × 3 matrices, you cannot find the inverse of a matrix if its determinant is zero.**

- **If the inverse of a matrix $\mathbf{A}$ is $\mathbf{A}^{-1}$, then $\mathbf{AA}^{-1} = \mathbf{A}^{-1}\mathbf{A} = \mathbf{I}$.**

- **The minor of an element of a 3 × 3 matrix is the determinant of the elements which remain when the row and the column containing the element are crossed out.**

Example 9

Find the minors of the elements 5 and 7 in the matrix

$$\begin{pmatrix} 5 & 0 & 2 \\ -1 & 8 & 1 \\ 6 & 7 & 3 \end{pmatrix}.$$

$$\begin{pmatrix} 5 & 0 & 2 \\ -1 & 8 & 1 \\ 6 & 7 & 3 \end{pmatrix}$$

To find the minor of 5, you begin by crossing out the row and the column containing 5.

$$\begin{vmatrix} 8 & 1 \\ 7 & 3 \end{vmatrix} = 8 \times 3 - 7 \times 1 = 24 - 7 = 17.$$

When you have crossed out the row and the column containing 5, you are left with the elements $\begin{pmatrix} 8 & 1 \\ 7 & 3 \end{pmatrix}$ and you evaluate the determinant of the matrix formed by these elements.

The minor of 5 is 17.

$$\begin{pmatrix} 5 & 0 & 2 \\ -1 & 8 & 1 \\ 6 & 7 & 3 \end{pmatrix}$$

To find the minor of 7, you begin by crossing out the row and the column containing 7.

$$\begin{vmatrix} 5 & 2 \\ -1 & 1 \end{vmatrix} = 5 \times 1 - 2 \times (-1) = 5 + 2 = 7$$

When you have crossed out the row and the column containing 7, you are left with the elements $\begin{pmatrix} 5 & 2 \\ -1 & 1 \end{pmatrix}$ and you evaluate the determinant of the matrix formed by these elements.

The minor of 7 is 7.

- **Finding the inverse of a 3 × 3 matrix $\mathbf{A}$ usually consists of the following 5 steps.**

  Step 1 Find the determinant of $\mathbf{A}$, $\det(\mathbf{A})$.

  Step 2 Form the matrix of the minors of $\mathbf{A}$. In this chapter, the symbol $\mathbf{M}$ is used for the matrix of the minors unless this causes confusion with another matrix in the question.

  In forming the matrix of minors $\mathbf{M}$, each of the nine elements of the matrix $\mathbf{A}$ is replaced by its minor.

Step 3 From the matrix of minors, form the matrix of **cofactors** by changing the signs of some elements of the matrix of minors according to the **rule of alternating signs** illustrated by the pattern

$$\begin{pmatrix} + & - & + \\ - & + & - \\ + & - & + \end{pmatrix}.$$

You leave the elements of the matrix of minors corresponding to the + signs in this pattern unchanged. You change the signs of the elements corresponding to the − signs. A cofactor is a minor with its appropriate sign.

In this chapter, the symbol **C** is used for the matrix of the cofactors unless this causes confusion with another matrix in the question.

Step 4 Write down the transpose, $\mathbf{C}^{\mathrm{T}}$, of the matrix of cofactors.

Step 5 The inverse of the matrix **A** is given by the formula

$$\mathbf{A}^{-1} = \frac{1}{\det(\mathbf{A})}\mathbf{C}^{\mathrm{T}}.$$

Each element of the matrix $\mathbf{C}^{\mathrm{T}}$ is divided by the determinant of **A**.

Example 10

The matrix $\mathbf{A} = \begin{pmatrix} 1 & 3 & 1 \\ 0 & 4 & 1 \\ 2 & -1 & 0 \end{pmatrix}$. Find $\mathbf{A}^{-1}$.

Step 1

$$\det(\mathbf{A}) = 1\begin{vmatrix} 4 & 1 \\ -1 & 0 \end{vmatrix} - 3\begin{vmatrix} 0 & 1 \\ 2 & 0 \end{vmatrix} + 1\begin{vmatrix} 0 & 4 \\ 2 & -1 \end{vmatrix}$$

$$= 1(0 + 1) - 3(0 - 2) + 1(0 - 8)$$

$$= 1 + 6 - 8 = -1$$

The first step of finding the inverse of a matrix is to evaluate its determinant. If the determinant is 0, the matrix does not have an inverse.

Step 2

$$\mathbf{M} = \begin{bmatrix} \begin{vmatrix} 4 & 1 \\ -1 & 0 \end{vmatrix} & \begin{vmatrix} 0 & 1 \\ 2 & 0 \end{vmatrix} & \begin{vmatrix} 0 & 4 \\ 2 & -1 \end{vmatrix} \\ \begin{vmatrix} 3 & 1 \\ -1 & 0 \end{vmatrix} & \begin{vmatrix} 1 & 1 \\ 2 & 0 \end{vmatrix} & \begin{vmatrix} 1 & 3 \\ 2 & -1 \end{vmatrix} \\ \begin{vmatrix} 3 & 1 \\ 4 & 1 \end{vmatrix} & \begin{vmatrix} 1 & 1 \\ 0 & 1 \end{vmatrix} & \begin{vmatrix} 1 & 3 \\ 0 & 4 \end{vmatrix} \end{bmatrix}$$

$$= \begin{pmatrix} 1 & -2 & -8 \\ 1 & -2 & -7 \\ -1 & 1 & 4 \end{pmatrix}$$

The second step is to form the matrix of minors. The minor of an element is found by deleting the row and the column in which the element lies.

For example, to find the minor of 4 in $\begin{pmatrix} 1 & 3 & 1 \\ 0 & 4 & 1 \\ 2 & -1 & 0 \end{pmatrix}$, delete the row and column containing 4, $\begin{pmatrix} 1 & \not{3} & 1 \\ \not{0} & \not{4} & \not{1} \\ 2 & \not{-1} & 0 \end{pmatrix}$. The minor is the determinant of the elements left, $\begin{vmatrix} 1 & 1 \\ 2 & 0 \end{vmatrix} = -2$.

Step 3

$$\mathbf{C} = \begin{pmatrix} 1 & 2 & -8 \\ -1 & -2 & 7 \\ -1 & -1 & 4 \end{pmatrix}$$

You find the matrix of cofactors by adjusting the signs of the minors using the pattern $\begin{pmatrix} + & - & + \\ - & + & - \\ + & - & + \end{pmatrix}$. Here you leave the elements $\begin{pmatrix} 1 & & -8 \\ & -2 & \\ -1 & & 4 \end{pmatrix}$ unchanged but change the signs of $\begin{pmatrix} & -2 & \\ 1 & & -7 \\ & 1 & \end{pmatrix}$.

Step 4

$$\mathbf{C}^{\mathrm{T}} = \begin{pmatrix} 1 & -1 & -1 \\ 2 & -2 & -1 \\ -8 & 7 & 4 \end{pmatrix}$$

Step 5

$$\mathbf{A}^{-1} = \frac{1}{\det(\mathbf{A})}\mathbf{C}^{\mathrm{T}} = \frac{1}{-1}\begin{pmatrix} 1 & -1 & -1 \\ 2 & -2 & -1 \\ -8 & 7 & 4 \end{pmatrix}$$

$$= \begin{pmatrix} -1 & 1 & 1 \\ -2 & 2 & 1 \\ 8 & -7 & -4 \end{pmatrix}$$

You divide each term of the matrix of cofactors, $\mathbf{C}^{\mathrm{T}}$, by the determinant of **A**, -1.

Some calculators will find inverse matrices and you may wish to use your calculator to check your answer. You may be asked to find the inverse of a matrix in algebraic form.

Example 11

The matrix $\mathbf{A} = \begin{pmatrix} 3 & 2 & -2 \\ -2 & k & 0 \\ -1 & -3 & 3 \end{pmatrix}$, $k \neq 0$. Find $\mathbf{A}^{-1}$.

Step 1

$$\det(\mathbf{A}) = 3\begin{vmatrix} k & 0 \\ -3 & 3 \end{vmatrix} - 2\begin{vmatrix} -2 & 0 \\ -1 & 3 \end{vmatrix} + (-2)\begin{vmatrix} -2 & k \\ -1 & -3 \end{vmatrix}$$

$$= 3(3k - 0) - 2(-6 - 0) - 2(6 + k)$$

$$= 9k + 12 - 12 - 2k = 7k$$

As you are given that $k \neq 0$, the matrix is non-singular and the inverse can be found.

Step 2

$$\mathbf{M} = \begin{pmatrix} \begin{vmatrix} k & 0 \\ -3 & 3 \end{vmatrix} & \begin{vmatrix} -2 & 0 \\ -1 & 3 \end{vmatrix} & \begin{vmatrix} -2 & k \\ -1 & -3 \end{vmatrix} \\ \begin{vmatrix} 2 & -2 \\ -3 & 3 \end{vmatrix} & \begin{vmatrix} 3 & -2 \\ -1 & 3 \end{vmatrix} & \begin{vmatrix} 3 & 2 \\ -1 & -3 \end{vmatrix} \\ \begin{vmatrix} 2 & -2 \\ k & 0 \end{vmatrix} & \begin{vmatrix} 3 & -2 \\ -2 & 0 \end{vmatrix} & \begin{vmatrix} 3 & 2 \\ -2 & k \end{vmatrix} \end{pmatrix}$$

$$= \begin{pmatrix} 3k & -6 & k+6 \\ 0 & 7 & -7 \\ 2k & -4 & 3k+4 \end{pmatrix}$$

The second step is to find the matrix of the minors in terms of k.

Step 3

$$C = \begin{pmatrix} 3k & 6 & k+6 \\ 0 & 7 & 7 \\ 2k & 4 & 3k+4 \end{pmatrix}$$

You obtain the matrix of the cofactors from the matrix of the minors by changing the signs of the elements corresponding to the $-$ signs in the pattern $\begin{pmatrix} + & - & + \\ - & + & - \\ + & - & + \end{pmatrix}$.

Step 4

$$C^T = \begin{pmatrix} 3k & 0 & 2k \\ 6 & 7 & 4 \\ k+6 & 7 & 3k+4 \end{pmatrix}$$

Step 5

$$A^{-1} = \frac{1}{\det(A)} C^T = \frac{1}{7k}\begin{pmatrix} 3k & 0 & 2k \\ 6 & 7 & 4 \\ k+6 & 7 & 3k+4 \end{pmatrix}$$

You can leave the answer in this form or write the inverse matrix as $\begin{pmatrix} \frac{3}{7} & 0 & \frac{2}{7} \\ \frac{6}{7k} & \frac{1}{k} & \frac{4}{7k} \\ \frac{k+6}{7k} & \frac{1}{k} & \frac{3k+4}{7k} \end{pmatrix}$.

Example 12

A and **B** are non-singular matrices. Prove that $(\mathbf{AB})^{-1} = \mathbf{B}^{-1}\mathbf{A}^{-1}$.

Let $P = (AB)^{-1}$,

then

$(AB)P = \mathbf{I}$

Use the definition of the inverse $\mathbf{XX}^{-1} = \mathbf{I}$ with $\mathbf{X} = \mathbf{AB}$.

$A^{-1}ABP = A^{-1}\mathbf{I}$

Multiply both sides of the previous equation on the left by $\mathbf{A}^{-1}$.

$(A^{-1}A)BP = A^{-1}$

As matrix multiplication is associative you can multiply any two of the matrices together first provided the order is kept.

$\mathbf{I}BP = A^{-1}$

$BP = A^{-1}$

Using $\mathbf{A}^{-1}\mathbf{A} = \mathbf{I}$ and $\mathbf{IB} = \mathbf{B}$.

$B^{-1}BP = B^{-1}A^{-1}$

Multiply both sides of the previous equation on the left by $\mathbf{B}^{-1}$.

$\mathbf{I}P = B^{-1}A^{-1}$

$P = B^{-1}A^{-1}$

Using $\mathbf{B}^{-1}\mathbf{B} = \mathbf{I}$ and $\mathbf{IP} = \mathbf{P}$.

Hence

$(AB)^{-1} = B^{-1}A^{-1}$

■ **If A and B are non-singular matrices then $(\mathbf{AB})^{-1} = \mathbf{B}^{-1}\mathbf{A}^{-1}$.**

In Section 6.1, you learnt a very similar formula for transposes, $(\mathbf{AB})^T = \mathbf{B}^T\mathbf{A}^T$. The formula for transposes is, however, true if **A** and **B** are singular.

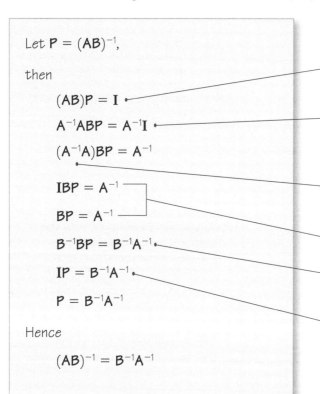

Example 13

The matrix $\mathbf{A} = \begin{pmatrix} -2 & 3 & -3 \\ 0 & 1 & 0 \\ 1 & -1 & 2 \end{pmatrix}$ and the matrix $\mathbf{B}$ is such that $(\mathbf{AB})^{-1} = \begin{pmatrix} 8 & -17 & 9 \\ -5 & 10 & -6 \\ -3 & 5 & -4 \end{pmatrix}$.

a Show that $\mathbf{A}^{-1} = \mathbf{A}$.

b Find $\mathbf{B}^{-1}$.

a $$A^2 = \begin{pmatrix} -2 & 3 & -3 \\ 0 & 1 & 0 \\ 1 & -1 & 2 \end{pmatrix}\begin{pmatrix} -2 & 3 & -3 \\ 0 & 1 & 0 \\ 1 & -1 & 2 \end{pmatrix}$$

$$= \begin{pmatrix} 4+0-3 & -6+3+3 & 6+0-6 \\ 0+0+0 & 0+1+0 & 0+0+0 \\ -2+0+2 & 3-1-2 & -3+0+4 \end{pmatrix}$$

$$= \begin{pmatrix} 1 & 0 & 0 \\ 0 & 1 & 0 \\ 0 & 0 & 1 \end{pmatrix} = \mathbf{I}$$

Comparing $A^2 = AA = \mathbf{I}$ with the definition of an inverse $AA^{-1} = \mathbf{I}$, then

$A^{-1} = A$, as required.

Given that $\mathbf{A}^{-1} = \mathbf{A}$, then multiplying both sides of the equation by $\mathbf{A}$,

$$\mathbf{AA}^{-1} = \mathbf{A}^2$$
$$\mathbf{I} = \mathbf{A}^2.$$

$\mathbf{A}^2 = \mathbf{I}$ and $\mathbf{A}^{-1} = \mathbf{A}$ are equivalent statements. If you prove one of them, the other follows.

b $(AB)^{-1} = B^{-1}A^{-1}$

$(AB)^{-1}A = B^{-1}A^{-1}A = B^{-1}\mathbf{I} = B^{-1}$

Multiply both sides of this formula on the right by $\mathbf{A}$ and use $\mathbf{A}^{-1}\mathbf{A} = \mathbf{I}$ to obtain an expression for $\mathbf{B}^{-1}$ in terms of $(\mathbf{AB})^{-1}$ and $\mathbf{A}$, both of which you already know.

$B^{-1} = (AB)^{-1}A$

$$= \begin{pmatrix} 8 & -17 & 9 \\ -5 & 10 & -6 \\ -3 & 5 & -4 \end{pmatrix}\begin{pmatrix} -2 & 3 & -3 \\ 0 & 1 & 0 \\ 1 & -1 & 2 \end{pmatrix}$$

$$= \begin{pmatrix} -16+0+9 & 24-17-9 & -24+0+18 \\ 10+0-6 & -15+10+6 & 15+0-12 \\ 6+0-4 & -9+5+4 & 9+0-8 \end{pmatrix}$$

$$= \begin{pmatrix} -7 & -2 & -6 \\ 4 & 1 & 3 \\ 2 & 0 & 1 \end{pmatrix}$$

Finding the inverse of a matrix using the five steps given earlier can be a lengthy process. For particular matrices, other methods may be available and this example illustrates two possibilities.

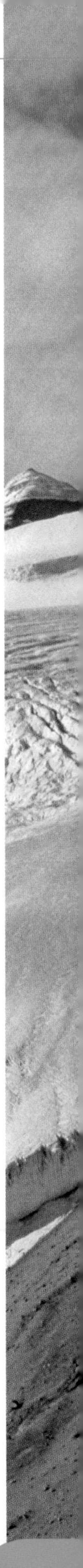

Exercise 6C

1 Find the inverses of these matrices.

a $\begin{pmatrix} 1 & 0 & 0 \\ 0 & 2 & 1 \\ 0 & 1 & 2 \end{pmatrix}$ **b** $\begin{pmatrix} 1 & 0 & 0 \\ 0 & 2 & 0 \\ 0 & 0 & 3 \end{pmatrix}$ **c** $\begin{pmatrix} 1 & 0 & 0 \\ 0 & \frac{3}{5} & -\frac{4}{5} \\ 0 & \frac{4}{5} & \frac{3}{5} \end{pmatrix}$

2 Find the inverses of these matrices.

a $\begin{pmatrix} 1 & -3 & 2 \\ 0 & -2 & 1 \\ 3 & 0 & 2 \end{pmatrix}$ **b** $\begin{pmatrix} 2 & 3 & 2 \\ 3 & -2 & 1 \\ 2 & 1 & 1 \end{pmatrix}$ **c** $\begin{pmatrix} 3 & 2 & -7 \\ 1 & -3 & 1 \\ 0 & 2 & -2 \end{pmatrix}$

3 The matrix $\mathbf{A} = \begin{pmatrix} 1 & 0 & 1 \\ 0 & 1 & 0 \\ 2 & 0 & 1 \end{pmatrix}$ and the matrix $\mathbf{B} = \begin{pmatrix} 2 & 1 & -1 \\ 1 & 0 & 1 \\ 1 & 2 & 1 \end{pmatrix}$.

a Find $\mathbf{A}^{-1}$.

b Find $\mathbf{B}^{-1}$.

Given that $(\mathbf{AB})^{-1} = \begin{pmatrix} -\frac{2}{3} & \frac{1}{2} & \frac{1}{2} \\ 1 & -\frac{1}{2} & -\frac{1}{2} \\ \frac{2}{3} & \frac{1}{2} & -\frac{1}{2} \end{pmatrix}$,

c verify that $\mathbf{B}^{-1}\mathbf{A}^{-1} = (\mathbf{AB})^{-1}$.

4 The matrix $\mathbf{A} = \begin{pmatrix} 2 & 0 & 3 \\ k & 1 & 1 \\ 1 & 1 & 4 \end{pmatrix}$.

a Show that $\det(\mathbf{A}) = 3(k + 1)$

b Given that $k \neq -1$, find $\mathbf{A}^{-1}$.

5 The matrix $\mathbf{A} = \begin{pmatrix} 5 & a & 4 \\ b & -7 & 8 \\ 2 & -2 & c \end{pmatrix}$.

Given that $\mathbf{A} = \mathbf{A}^{-1}$, find the values of the constants a, b and c.

6 The matrix $\mathbf{A} = \begin{pmatrix} 2 & -1 & 1 \\ 4 & -3 & 0 \\ -3 & 3 & 1 \end{pmatrix}$.

a Show that $\mathbf{A}^3 = \mathbf{I}$.

b Hence find $\mathbf{A}^{-1}$.

7 The matrix $\mathbf{A} = \begin{pmatrix} 1 & 1 & 0 \\ 3 & -3 & 1 \\ 0 & 3 & 2 \end{pmatrix}$.

a Show that $\mathbf{A}^3 = 13\mathbf{A} - 15\mathbf{I}$.

b Deduce that $15\mathbf{A}^{-1} = 13\mathbf{I} - \mathbf{A}^2$.

c Hence find $\mathbf{A}^{-1}$.

8 The matrix $\mathbf{A} = \begin{pmatrix} 2 & 0 & 1 \\ 4 & 3 & -2 \\ 0 & 3 & -4 \end{pmatrix}$.

a Show that $\mathbf{A}$ is singular.

The matrix $\mathbf{C}$ is the matrix of the cofactors of $\mathbf{A}$.

b Find $\mathbf{C}$.

c Show that $\mathbf{AC}^{\mathrm{T}} = \mathbf{0}$.

6.4 You can use matrices to represent linear transformations in 3 dimensions.

- A linear transformation T in three dimensions is a mapping which transforms a point with position vector $\begin{pmatrix} x \\ y \\ z \end{pmatrix}$ to another point according to a rule with the following properties.

$$T\begin{pmatrix} kx \\ ky \\ kz \end{pmatrix} = kT\begin{pmatrix} x \\ y \\ z \end{pmatrix}$$

$$T\begin{pmatrix} x_1 + x_2 \\ y_1 + y_2 \\ z_1 + z_2 \end{pmatrix} = T\begin{pmatrix} x_1 \\ y_1 \\ z_1 \end{pmatrix} + T\begin{pmatrix} x_2 \\ y_2 \\ z_2 \end{pmatrix}.$$

- In book FP1, you learnt that linear transformations in two dimensions can be represented by 2 × 2 matrices. In this chapter, you will extend this work by representing linear transformations in three dimensions by 3 × 3 matrices.

- The new point to which the point $\begin{pmatrix} x \\ y \\ z \end{pmatrix}$ is moved is called the **image** of $\begin{pmatrix} x \\ y \\ z \end{pmatrix}$.

- To identify the matrix representing a particular transformation you consider the effect of the matrix or the transformation on three simple vectors; $\begin{pmatrix} 1 \\ 0 \\ 0 \end{pmatrix}$ (sometimes denoted as **i**), $\begin{pmatrix} 0 \\ 1 \\ 0 \end{pmatrix}$ (sometimes denoted as **j**) and $\begin{pmatrix} 0 \\ 0 \\ 1 \end{pmatrix}$ (sometimes denoted as **k**).

- Given any matrix $\mathbf{M} = \begin{pmatrix} a & b & c \\ d & e & f \\ g & h & i \end{pmatrix}$, then

$$\mathbf{M}\begin{pmatrix} 1 \\ 0 \\ 0 \end{pmatrix} = \begin{pmatrix} a \\ d \\ g \end{pmatrix}, \ \mathbf{M}\begin{pmatrix} 0 \\ 1 \\ 0 \end{pmatrix} = \begin{pmatrix} b \\ e \\ h \end{pmatrix} \text{ and } \mathbf{M}\begin{pmatrix} 0 \\ 0 \\ 1 \end{pmatrix} = \begin{pmatrix} c \\ f \\ i \end{pmatrix}.$$

So the image of $\begin{pmatrix} 1 \\ 0 \\ 0 \end{pmatrix}$ is the first column of **M**, the image of $\begin{pmatrix} 0 \\ 1 \\ 0 \end{pmatrix}$ is the second column of **M** and the image of $\begin{pmatrix} 0 \\ 0 \\ 1 \end{pmatrix}$ is the third column of **M**.

- If the transformation T is represented by the matrix **T** and the transformation U is represented by the matrix **U**, then the matrix **UT** represents the combined transformation of the transformation of T followed by the transformation U.

- The symbol $\mathbb{R}^3$ is used to represent three-dimensional space. You read $T: \mathbb{R}^3 \rightarrow \mathbb{R}^3$ as 'the transformation T transforms points in three-dimensional space to points in three-dimensional space'.

Example 14

Given that $T: \begin{pmatrix} x \\ y \\ z \end{pmatrix} \mapsto \begin{pmatrix} x + z \\ y \\ x + 2y + z \end{pmatrix}$ and $U: \begin{pmatrix} x \\ y \\ z \end{pmatrix} \mapsto \begin{pmatrix} x - y + z \\ 3x - 2z \\ 3x - 4y - z \end{pmatrix}$, find matrices representing

a T **b** U **c** UT **d** TU.

a $T: \begin{pmatrix} 1 \\ 0 \\ 0 \end{pmatrix} \mapsto \begin{pmatrix} 1 + 0 \\ 0 \\ 1 + 0 + 0 \end{pmatrix} = \begin{pmatrix} 1 \\ 0 \\ 1 \end{pmatrix}$

You find the first column of the matrix by finding the image of $\begin{pmatrix} 1 \\ 0 \\ 0 \end{pmatrix}$ under T.

You find this image by substituting $x = 1$, $y = 0$ and $z = 0$ into the rule for T.

$T: \begin{pmatrix} 0 \\ 1 \\ 0 \end{pmatrix} \mapsto \begin{pmatrix} 0 + 0 \\ 1 \\ 0 + 2 + 0 \end{pmatrix} = \begin{pmatrix} 0 \\ 1 \\ 2 \end{pmatrix}$

This is the second column of the matrix.

$T: \begin{pmatrix} 0 \\ 0 \\ 1 \end{pmatrix} \mapsto \begin{pmatrix} 0 + 1 \\ 0 \\ 0 + 0 + 1 \end{pmatrix} = \begin{pmatrix} 1 \\ 0 \\ 1 \end{pmatrix}$

This is the third column of the matrix.

The matrix representing T is $\begin{pmatrix} 1 & 0 & 1 \\ 0 & 1 & 0 \\ 1 & 2 & 1 \end{pmatrix}$.

b $U: \begin{pmatrix} 1 \\ 0 \\ 0 \end{pmatrix} \mapsto \begin{pmatrix} 1 - 0 + 0 \\ 3 - 0 \\ 3 - 0 - 0 \end{pmatrix} = \begin{pmatrix} 1 \\ 3 \\ 3 \end{pmatrix}$

$U: \begin{pmatrix} 0 \\ 1 \\ 0 \end{pmatrix} \mapsto \begin{pmatrix} 0 - 1 + 0 \\ 0 - 0 \\ 0 - 4 - 0 \end{pmatrix} = \begin{pmatrix} -1 \\ 0 \\ -4 \end{pmatrix}$

$U: \begin{pmatrix} 0 \\ 0 \\ 1 \end{pmatrix} \mapsto \begin{pmatrix} 0 - 0 + 1 \\ 0 - 2 \\ 0 - 0 - 1 \end{pmatrix} = \begin{pmatrix} 1 \\ -2 \\ -1 \end{pmatrix}$

The matrix representing U is $\begin{pmatrix} 1 & -1 & 1 \\ 3 & 0 & -2 \\ 3 & -4 & -1 \end{pmatrix}$.

With practice, you should be able to write down such a matrix without showing intermediate working.

$\begin{pmatrix} x - y + z \\ 3x - 2z \\ 3x - 4y - z \end{pmatrix}$ can just be recognised as $\begin{pmatrix} 1 & -1 & 1 \\ 3 & 0 & -2 \\ 3 & -4 & -1 \end{pmatrix} \begin{pmatrix} x \\ y \\ z \end{pmatrix}$.

c The matrix representing UT is

$$\begin{pmatrix} 1 & -1 & 1 \\ 3 & 0 & -2 \\ 3 & -4 & -1 \end{pmatrix} \begin{pmatrix} 1 & 0 & 1 \\ 0 & 1 & 0 \\ 1 & 2 & 1 \end{pmatrix}$$

The matrix representing UT is found by multiplying the matrix representing U by the matrix representing T in that order. **Remember**, the transformation UT applies T first and U second.

$$= \begin{pmatrix} 1 + 0 + 1 & 0 - 1 + 2 & 1 + 0 + 1 \\ 3 + 0 - 2 & 0 + 0 - 4 & 3 + 0 - 2 \\ 3 + 0 - 1 & 0 - 4 - 2 & 3 + 0 - 1 \end{pmatrix}$$

$$= \begin{pmatrix} 2 & 1 & 2 \\ 1 & -4 & 1 \\ 2 & -6 & 2 \end{pmatrix}$$

d The matrix representing TU is

$$\begin{pmatrix} 1 & 0 & 1 \\ 0 & 1 & 0 \\ 1 & 2 & 1 \end{pmatrix}\begin{pmatrix} 1 & -1 & 1 \\ 3 & 0 & -2 \\ 3 & -4 & -1 \end{pmatrix}$$

$$= \begin{pmatrix} 1+0+3 & -1+0-4 & 1+0-1 \\ 0+3+0 & 0+0+0 & 0-2+0 \\ 1+6+3 & -1+0-4 & 1-4-1 \end{pmatrix}$$

$$= \begin{pmatrix} 4 & -5 & 0 \\ 3 & 0 & -2 \\ 10 & -5 & -4 \end{pmatrix}$$

The transformation TU applies U first and T second.

Example 15

The transformation $T: \mathbb{R}^3 \to \mathbb{R}^3$ is represented by the matrix $\mathbf{T}$.

The point with position vector $\begin{pmatrix} 1 \\ 0 \\ 0 \end{pmatrix}$ is transformed by T to the point with position vector $\begin{pmatrix} 3 \\ 4 \\ 2 \end{pmatrix}$.

The point with position vector $\begin{pmatrix} 1 \\ 1 \\ 0 \end{pmatrix}$ is transformed by T to the point with position vector $\begin{pmatrix} 6 \\ 1 \\ 5 \end{pmatrix}$.

The point with position vector $\begin{pmatrix} 2 \\ 1 \\ -4 \end{pmatrix}$ is transformed by T to the point with position vector $\begin{pmatrix} 1 \\ 1 \\ -1 \end{pmatrix}$.

a Find $\mathbf{T}$.

b Find the image of the point with position vector $\begin{pmatrix} -1 \\ 3 \\ 0 \end{pmatrix}$.

a Let $\mathbf{T} = \begin{pmatrix} a & b & c \\ d & e & f \\ g & h & i \end{pmatrix}$

$$\begin{pmatrix} a & b & c \\ d & e & f \\ g & h & i \end{pmatrix}\begin{pmatrix} 1 \\ 0 \\ 0 \end{pmatrix} = \begin{pmatrix} 3 \\ 4 \\ 2 \end{pmatrix}$$

If T transforms the column vector $\mathbf{x}_1$ to the column vector $\mathbf{x}_2$, then $\mathbf{T}\mathbf{x}_1 = \mathbf{x}_2$.

$$\begin{pmatrix} a \\ d \\ g \end{pmatrix} = \begin{pmatrix} 3 \\ 4 \\ 2 \end{pmatrix}$$

Equating the elements
$a = 3, d = 4, g = 2$

If two vectors or matrices are equal, then the corresponding elements of the vectors or matrices must be individually equal.

$$\begin{pmatrix} 3 & b & c \\ 4 & e & f \\ 2 & h & i \end{pmatrix}\begin{pmatrix} 1 \\ 1 \\ 0 \end{pmatrix} = \begin{pmatrix} 6 \\ 1 \\ 5 \end{pmatrix}$$

As you now know the values of a, d and g, you can substitute these values into **T**.

$$\begin{pmatrix} 3+b \\ 4+e \\ 2+h \end{pmatrix} = \begin{pmatrix} 6 \\ 1 \\ 5 \end{pmatrix}$$

Equating the top elements

$3 + b = 6 \Rightarrow b = 3$

Equating the middle elements

$4 + e = 1 \Rightarrow e = -3$

Equating the lowest elements

$2 + h = 5 \Rightarrow h = 3$

Equating the three elements enables you to find the values in the second column of **T**.

$$\begin{pmatrix} 3 & 3 & c \\ 4 & -3 & f \\ 2 & 3 & i \end{pmatrix}\begin{pmatrix} 2 \\ 1 \\ -4 \end{pmatrix} = \begin{pmatrix} 1 \\ 1 \\ -1 \end{pmatrix}$$

$$\begin{pmatrix} 9-4c \\ 5-4f \\ 7-4i \end{pmatrix} = \begin{pmatrix} 1 \\ 1 \\ -1 \end{pmatrix}$$

Equating the top elements

$9 - 4c = 1 \Rightarrow c = 2$

Equating the middle elements

$5 - 4f = 1 \Rightarrow f = 1$

Equating the lowest elements

$7 - 4i = -1 \Rightarrow i = 2$

$$\mathbf{T} = \begin{pmatrix} 3 & 3 & 2 \\ 4 & -3 & 1 \\ 2 & 3 & 2 \end{pmatrix}$$

b $$\mathbf{T}\begin{pmatrix} -1 \\ 3 \\ 0 \end{pmatrix} = \begin{pmatrix} 3 & 3 & 2 \\ 4 & -3 & 1 \\ 2 & 3 & 2 \end{pmatrix}\begin{pmatrix} -1 \\ 3 \\ 0 \end{pmatrix}$$

To find the image of the column vector **x** under T, you evaluate **Tx**.

$$= \begin{pmatrix} -3+9+0 \\ -4-9+0 \\ -2+9+0 \end{pmatrix} = \begin{pmatrix} 6 \\ -13 \\ 7 \end{pmatrix}$$

The image of $\begin{pmatrix} -1 \\ 3 \\ 0 \end{pmatrix}$ is $\begin{pmatrix} 6 \\ -13 \\ 7 \end{pmatrix}$.

Example 16

The transformation $T: \mathbb{R}^3 \to \mathbb{R}^3$ is represented by the matrix $\mathbf{T}$ where $\mathbf{T} = \begin{pmatrix} 3 & -2 & 1 \\ 1 & 3 & 4 \\ 2 & -1 & 1 \end{pmatrix}$. The line l_1 is transformed by T to the line l_2. The line l_1 has vector equation $\mathbf{r} = \begin{pmatrix} 2 \\ 0 \\ -3 \end{pmatrix} + t\begin{pmatrix} 3 \\ -2 \\ 1 \end{pmatrix}$, where t is a real parameter.

Find a vector equation of l_2.

$$\mathbf{r} = \begin{pmatrix} 2 \\ 0 \\ -3 \end{pmatrix} + t\begin{pmatrix} 3 \\ -2 \\ 1 \end{pmatrix} = \begin{pmatrix} 2+3t \\ -2t \\ -3+t \end{pmatrix}$$

$\begin{pmatrix} 2+3t \\ -2t \\ -3+t \end{pmatrix}$ is a general form of a point on l_1. When investigating transformations, it is often a good start to express the coordinates of a general point on a line or plane in parametric form.

The image of l_1 is given by

$$\mathbf{r} = \begin{pmatrix} 3 & -2 & 1 \\ 1 & 3 & 4 \\ 2 & -1 & 1 \end{pmatrix}\begin{pmatrix} 2+3t \\ -2t \\ -3+t \end{pmatrix} = \begin{pmatrix} 3(2+3t) + 4t - 3 + t \\ 2 + 3t - 6t + 4(-3+t) \\ 2(2+3t) + 2t - 3 + t \end{pmatrix}$$

$$= \begin{pmatrix} 14t+3 \\ t-10 \\ 9t+1 \end{pmatrix} = \begin{pmatrix} 3 \\ -10 \\ 1 \end{pmatrix} + t\begin{pmatrix} 14 \\ 1 \\ 9 \end{pmatrix}$$

A vector equation of l_2 is

$$\mathbf{r} = \begin{pmatrix} 3 \\ -10 \\ 1 \end{pmatrix} + t\begin{pmatrix} 14 \\ 1 \\ 9 \end{pmatrix}$$

There are an infinite number of possible answers to this question but, in any equation, the vector giving the direction of l_2 must be parallel to $\begin{pmatrix} 14 \\ 1 \\ 9 \end{pmatrix}$.

Example 17

The transformation $T: \mathbb{R}^3 \to \mathbb{R}^3$ is represented by the matrix $\mathbf{T}$ where $\mathbf{T} = \begin{pmatrix} 2 & 5 & -1 \\ -6 & 0 & 2 \\ 0 & 4 & 3 \end{pmatrix}$.

The plane Π_1 is transformed by T to the plane Π_2. The plane Π_1 has vector equation

$\mathbf{r} = \begin{pmatrix} 2 \\ 1 \\ -3 \end{pmatrix} + s\begin{pmatrix} 1 \\ -2 \\ 3 \end{pmatrix} + t\begin{pmatrix} -3 \\ 1 \\ -1 \end{pmatrix}$, where s and t are real parameters.

Find a vector equation of Π_2.

$$\mathbf{r} = \begin{pmatrix}2\\1\\-3\end{pmatrix} + s\begin{pmatrix}1\\-2\\3\end{pmatrix} + t\begin{pmatrix}-3\\1\\-1\end{pmatrix} = \begin{pmatrix}2+s-3t\\1-2s+t\\-3+3s-t\end{pmatrix}$$

$\begin{pmatrix}2+s-3t\\1-2s+t\\-3+3s-t\end{pmatrix}$ is general form of a point on Π_1. When investigating transformations it is often a good start to express the coordinates of a general point on a line or plane in parametric form.

$$\begin{pmatrix}2&5&-1\\-6&0&2\\0&4&3\end{pmatrix}\begin{pmatrix}2+s-3t\\1-2s+t\\-3+3s-t\end{pmatrix}$$

To find the image of the column vector **x** under T, you work out **Tx**.

$$= \begin{pmatrix}2(2+s-3t)+5(1-2s+t)-1(-3+3s-t)\\-6(2+s-3t)+0(1-2s+t)+2(-3+3s-t)\\0(2+s-3t)+4(1-2s+t)+3(-3+3s-t)\end{pmatrix}$$

$$= \begin{pmatrix}12-11s\\-18+16t\\-5+s+t\end{pmatrix} = \begin{pmatrix}12\\-18\\-5\end{pmatrix} + s\begin{pmatrix}-11\\0\\1\end{pmatrix} + t\begin{pmatrix}0\\16\\1\end{pmatrix}$$

Here, the simplest equation of a plane to find is one of the form $\mathbf{r} = \mathbf{a} + s\mathbf{b} + t\mathbf{c}$, so you separate out the terms in s and the terms in t.

A vector equation of Π_2 is $\mathbf{r} = \begin{pmatrix}12\\-18\\-5\end{pmatrix} + s\begin{pmatrix}-11\\0\\1\end{pmatrix} + t\begin{pmatrix}0\\16\\1\end{pmatrix}$.

Example 18

The transformation $T: \mathbb{R}^3 \to \mathbb{R}^3$ is represented by the matrix **T** where $\mathbf{T} = \begin{pmatrix}2&-1&3\\-1&4&-2\\3&2&4\end{pmatrix}$.

The plane Π has equation $2x - y + 3z = -6$. Show that the image of Π under T is a line and find Cartesian equations of this line.

$2x - y + 3z = -6$

Let $x = s$ and $z = t$, then $y = 6 + 2s + 3t$

Change the equation of Π into parametric form by putting two of the variables equal to s and t and then finding the third variable in terms of s and t.

The general point on Π is $\begin{pmatrix}s\\6+2s+3t\\t\end{pmatrix}$

$$\begin{pmatrix}2&-1&3\\-1&4&-2\\3&2&4\end{pmatrix}\begin{pmatrix}s\\6+2s+3t\\t\end{pmatrix}$$

$$= \begin{pmatrix}2s-6-2s-3t+3t\\-s+24+8s+12t-2t\\3s+12+4s+6t+4t\end{pmatrix}$$

$$= \begin{pmatrix}-6\\24+7s+10t\\12+7s+10t\end{pmatrix}$$

Let $\begin{pmatrix} x \\ y \\ z \end{pmatrix} = \begin{pmatrix} -6 \\ 24 + 7s + 10t \\ 12 + 7s + 10t \end{pmatrix}$

$x = -6$

$y = 24 + 7s + 10t$ ①

$z = 12 + 7s + 10t$ ②

Subtract ② from ①

$y - z = 12$

Cartesian equations of the image of Π are

$x = -6, y = z + 12$

Let $y = z + 12 = \lambda$

Then, as $x = -6$ can be written as $x + 6 = 0\lambda$,

the Cartesian equations can be written as

$$\frac{x+6}{0} = \frac{y}{1} = \frac{z+12}{1} = \lambda$$

The image of Π under T is a line.

$x = -6$ and $y - z = 12$ are both planes and the image of Π is the intersection of these planes, which is a line. In general, under linear transformations, points are transformed to points, lines to lines and planes to planes. However, this is not necessarily true when, as here, the matrix representing the transformation is singular.

In Chapter 5, you learnt that the general form of the Cartesian equation of a straight line is $\frac{x - x_1}{l} = \frac{y - y_1}{m} = \frac{z - z_1}{n}$. Anything in this form is a straight line.

Exercise 6D

1 Given that $T: \begin{pmatrix} x \\ y \\ z \end{pmatrix} \mapsto \begin{pmatrix} x - y \\ y + z \\ 2x - 3z \end{pmatrix}$ and $U: \begin{pmatrix} x \\ y \\ z \end{pmatrix} \mapsto \begin{pmatrix} 2x - 3y - z \\ 2y + 3z \\ 5z \end{pmatrix}$, find matrices representing

a T **b** U **c** TU.

2 The point with position vector $\begin{pmatrix} 1 \\ 3 \\ a \end{pmatrix}$ is transformed by the linear transformation represented by the matrix $\begin{pmatrix} 4 & -1 & 0 \\ -2 & 2 & 3 \\ 5 & -2 & 1 \end{pmatrix}$ to the point with position vector $\begin{pmatrix} b \\ -5 \\ c \end{pmatrix}$.

Find the values of the constants a, b and c.

3 The transformation $T: \mathbb{R}^3 \to \mathbb{R}^3$ is represented by the matrix $\mathbf{T}$.

The vector $\begin{pmatrix} 2 \\ 0 \\ 0 \end{pmatrix}$ is transformed by T to the vector $\begin{pmatrix} 6 \\ 2 \\ 4 \end{pmatrix}$.

The vector $\begin{pmatrix} 3 \\ 0 \\ -1 \end{pmatrix}$ is transformed by T to the vector $\begin{pmatrix} -2 \\ 3 \\ 5 \end{pmatrix}$.

The vector $\begin{pmatrix} 0 \\ 1 \\ -1 \end{pmatrix}$ is transformed by T to the vector $\begin{pmatrix} 2 \\ -1 \\ -2 \end{pmatrix}$.

Find $\mathbf{T}$.

4 The transformation $T: \mathbb{R}^3 \to \mathbb{R}^3$ is represented by the matrix $\mathbf{T}$ where $\mathbf{T} = \begin{pmatrix} 0 & -1 & 2 \\ 2 & 5 & -4 \\ 3 & 2 & 1 \end{pmatrix}$.

The line l_1 is transformed by T to the line l_2. The line l_1 has vector equation

$\mathbf{r} = \begin{pmatrix} 2 \\ 4 \\ 1 \end{pmatrix} + t\begin{pmatrix} -1 \\ -2 \\ 3 \end{pmatrix}$, where t is a real parameter.

Find a vector equation of l_2.

5 The points A and B have position vectors $\begin{pmatrix} 2 \\ 1 \\ 0 \end{pmatrix}$ and $\begin{pmatrix} -2 \\ 3 \\ 4 \end{pmatrix}$ respectively. The points A and B are transformed by the linear transformation T to the points A' and B' respectively.

The transformation T is represented by the matrix $\mathbf{T}$, where $\mathbf{T} = \begin{pmatrix} 1 & -3 & 4 \\ 2 & 3 & -2 \\ 0 & 2 & 5 \end{pmatrix}$.

a Find the position vectors of A' and B'.

b Hence find a vector equation of the line $A'B'$.

6 The transformation $T: \mathbb{R}^3 \to \mathbb{R}^3$ is represented by the matrix $\mathbf{T}$ where $\mathbf{T} = \begin{pmatrix} 3 & -2 & -2 \\ -2 & -8 & 4 \\ -2 & 4 & 0 \end{pmatrix}$.

The plane Π_1 is transformed by T to the plane Π_2. The plane Π_1 has Cartesian equation $x - 2y + z = 0$.

Find a Cartesian equation of Π_2.

7 The transformation $T: \mathbb{R}^3 \to \mathbb{R}^3$ is represented by the matrix $\mathbf{T}$ where $\mathbf{T} = \begin{pmatrix} 4 & 5 & -3 \\ -1 & 2 & 1 \\ 1 & 0 & 1 \end{pmatrix}$.

The plane Π_1 is transformed by T to the plane Π_2. The plane Π_1 has vector equation

$\mathbf{r} = \begin{pmatrix} 0 \\ 1 \\ 1 \end{pmatrix} + s\begin{pmatrix} 1 \\ -1 \\ 2 \end{pmatrix} + t\begin{pmatrix} 3 \\ 0 \\ 4 \end{pmatrix}$, where s and t are real parameters.

Find an equation of Π_2 in the form $\mathbf{r.n} = p$.

8 The transformation $T: \mathbb{R}^3 \to \mathbb{R}^3$ is represented by the matrix $\mathbf{T}$ where $\mathbf{T} = \begin{pmatrix} 4 & 1 & -2 \\ -2 & 3 & 4 \\ -1 & 0 & 2 \end{pmatrix}$.

There is a line through the origin for which every point on the line is mapped onto itself under T.

Find a vector equation of this line.

6.5 You can use inverse matrices to reverse the effect of a linear transformation.

- **If the column vector $\mathbf{x}_1$ is transformed to the column vector $\mathbf{x}_2$ by the linear transformation represented by the matrix $\mathbf{T}$ then**

  $$\mathbf{T}\mathbf{x}_1 = \mathbf{x}_2$$

  Multiplying throughout on the left by $\mathbf{T}^{-1}$

  $$\mathbf{T}^{-1}\mathbf{T}\mathbf{x}_1 = \mathbf{T}^{-1}\mathbf{x}_2$$

  As $\mathbf{T}^{-1}\mathbf{T} = \mathbf{I}$ and $\mathbf{I}\mathbf{x}_1 = \mathbf{x}_1$

  $$\mathbf{x}_1 = \mathbf{T}^{-1}\mathbf{x}_2$$

  You can use this relation to find $\mathbf{x}_1$ when you know the image of $\mathbf{x}_1$.

Example 19

The transformation $T: \mathbb{R}^3 \to \mathbb{R}^3$ is represented by the matrix $\mathbf{T}$ where $\mathbf{T} = \begin{pmatrix} 1 & 0 & 2 \\ 0 & 2 & 0 \\ 1 & 0 & 1 \end{pmatrix}$.

a Find $\mathbf{T}^{-1}$.

The vector $\begin{pmatrix} a \\ b \\ c \end{pmatrix}$ is transformed by T to the vector $\begin{pmatrix} -3 \\ 4 \\ 2 \end{pmatrix}$.

b Find the values of the constants a, b and c.

a **Step 1**

$$\det(\mathrm{T}) = 1\begin{vmatrix} 2 & 0 \\ 0 & 1 \end{vmatrix} - 0\begin{vmatrix} 0 & 0 \\ 1 & 1 \end{vmatrix} + 2\begin{vmatrix} 0 & 2 \\ 1 & 0 \end{vmatrix}$$

$$= 2 - 4 = -2$$

Step 2

The matrix of minors **M** is given by

$$\mathrm{M} = \begin{pmatrix} \begin{vmatrix} 2 & 0 \\ 0 & 1 \end{vmatrix} & \begin{vmatrix} 0 & 0 \\ 1 & 1 \end{vmatrix} & \begin{vmatrix} 0 & 2 \\ 1 & 0 \end{vmatrix} \\ \begin{vmatrix} 0 & 2 \\ 0 & 1 \end{vmatrix} & \begin{vmatrix} 1 & 2 \\ 1 & 1 \end{vmatrix} & \begin{vmatrix} 1 & 0 \\ 1 & 0 \end{vmatrix} \\ \begin{vmatrix} 0 & 2 \\ 2 & 0 \end{vmatrix} & \begin{vmatrix} 1 & 2 \\ 0 & 0 \end{vmatrix} & \begin{vmatrix} 1 & 0 \\ 0 & 2 \end{vmatrix} \end{pmatrix}$$

$$= \begin{pmatrix} 2 & 0 & -2 \\ 0 & -1 & 0 \\ -4 & 0 & 2 \end{pmatrix}$$

Step 3

The matrix of cofactors is given by

$$\mathrm{C} = \begin{pmatrix} 2 & 0 & -2 \\ 0 & -1 & 0 \\ -4 & 0 & 2 \end{pmatrix}$$

All of the elements of **M** corresponding to the negative signs in the pattern $\begin{pmatrix} + & - & + \\ - & + & - \\ + & - & + \end{pmatrix}$ are 0, so in this case the matrix of minors and the matrix of cofactors are identical.

Step 4

$$C^T = \begin{pmatrix} 2 & 0 & -4 \\ 0 & -1 & 0 \\ -2 & 0 & 2 \end{pmatrix}$$

Step 5

$$T^{-1} = \frac{1}{\det(T)}C^T = \frac{1}{-2}\begin{pmatrix} 2 & 0 & -4 \\ 0 & -1 & 0 \\ -2 & 0 & 2 \end{pmatrix}$$

$$= \begin{pmatrix} -1 & 0 & 2 \\ 0 & \frac{1}{2} & 0 \\ 1 & 0 & -1 \end{pmatrix}$$

b $$\begin{pmatrix} a \\ b \\ c \end{pmatrix} = \begin{pmatrix} -1 & 0 & 2 \\ 0 & \frac{1}{2} & 0 \\ 1 & 0 & -1 \end{pmatrix}\begin{pmatrix} -3 \\ 4 \\ 2 \end{pmatrix}$$

$$= \begin{pmatrix} 3+4 \\ 2 \\ -3-2 \end{pmatrix} = \begin{pmatrix} 7 \\ 2 \\ -5 \end{pmatrix}$$

$a = 7, b = 2, c = -5$

As $\begin{pmatrix} -3 \\ 4 \\ 2 \end{pmatrix}$ is the image of $\begin{pmatrix} a \\ b \\ c \end{pmatrix}$ then $\mathbf{T}\begin{pmatrix} a \\ b \\ c \end{pmatrix} = \begin{pmatrix} -3 \\ 4 \\ 2 \end{pmatrix}$. You find $\begin{pmatrix} a \\ b \\ c \end{pmatrix}$ by reversing the transformation using the inverse matrix, $\begin{pmatrix} a \\ b \\ c \end{pmatrix} = \mathbf{T}^{-1}\begin{pmatrix} -3 \\ 4 \\ 2 \end{pmatrix}$.

Example 20

The matrix $\mathbf{A} = \begin{pmatrix} 1 & 3 & -1 \\ 0 & 2 & 1 \\ -1 & -2 & 1 \end{pmatrix}$ and the matrix $\mathbf{B} = \begin{pmatrix} -4 & 1 & -5 \\ 1 & 0 & 1 \\ -2 & 1 & -2 \end{pmatrix}$.

a Show that $\mathbf{AB} = \mathbf{I}$.

The transformation $T: \mathbb{R}^3 \to \mathbb{R}^3$ is represented by the matrix **A**. The line l_1 is transformed by T to the line l_2. The line l_2 has vector equation $\mathbf{r} = \begin{pmatrix} 3 \\ 4 \\ -1 \end{pmatrix} + t\begin{pmatrix} -1 \\ 2 \\ 2 \end{pmatrix}$, where t is a real parameter.

b Find a vector equation of l_1.

a $$\mathbf{AB} = \begin{pmatrix} 1 & 3 & -1 \\ 0 & 2 & 1 \\ -1 & -2 & 1 \end{pmatrix}\begin{pmatrix} -4 & 1 & -5 \\ 1 & 0 & 1 \\ -2 & 1 & -2 \end{pmatrix}$$

$$= \begin{pmatrix} -4+3+2 & 1+0-1 & -5+3+2 \\ 0+2-2 & 0+0+1 & 0+2-2 \\ 4-2-2 & -1+0+1 & 5-2-2 \end{pmatrix}$$

$$= \begin{pmatrix} 1 & 0 & 0 \\ 0 & 1 & 0 \\ 0 & 0 & 1 \end{pmatrix} = \mathbf{I}, \text{ as required}$$

As **AB** = **I**, **B** = $\mathbf{A}^{-1}$ and you can use **B** to reverse the effect of T in part **b**.

b The general point on l_2 is

$$\begin{pmatrix} 3 \\ 4 \\ -1 \end{pmatrix} + t\begin{pmatrix} -1 \\ 2 \\ 2 \end{pmatrix} = \begin{pmatrix} 3-t \\ 4+2t \\ -1+2t \end{pmatrix}$$

$$\mathbf{B}\begin{pmatrix} 3-t \\ 4+2t \\ -1+2t \end{pmatrix} = \begin{pmatrix} -4 & 1 & -5 \\ 1 & 0 & 1 \\ -2 & 1 & -2 \end{pmatrix}\begin{pmatrix} 3-t \\ 4+2t \\ -1+2t \end{pmatrix}$$

$$= \begin{pmatrix} -12+4t+4+2t+5-10t \\ 3-t-1+2t \\ -6+2t+4+2t+2-4t \end{pmatrix}$$

Simplify this column vector and rearrange it into the form $\mathbf{a} + t\mathbf{b}$.

$$= \begin{pmatrix} -3-4t \\ 2+t \\ 0 \end{pmatrix} = \begin{pmatrix} -3 \\ 2 \\ 0 \end{pmatrix} + t\begin{pmatrix} -4 \\ 1 \\ 0 \end{pmatrix}$$

A vector equation of l_1 is

$$\mathbf{r} = \begin{pmatrix} -3 \\ 2 \\ 0 \end{pmatrix} + t\begin{pmatrix} -4 \\ 1 \\ 0 \end{pmatrix}$$

■ **Finding the inverse of a matrix can be a lengthy process and if, in a particular question, you are not asked to find the inverse or given a clue that enables you to find it quickly, it is possible to reverse the effect of a transformation using simultaneous equations.**

Example 21 illustrates this method. If no method is specified in a question, you are free to choose any appropriate method.

Example 21

The transformation $T: \mathbb{R}^3 \rightarrow \mathbb{R}^3$ is represented by the matrix $\mathbf{T}$ where $\mathbf{T} = \begin{pmatrix} 2 & 4 & -1 \\ 3 & -2 & 1 \\ 1 & -3 & 2 \end{pmatrix}$.

The vector $\begin{pmatrix} a \\ b \\ c \end{pmatrix}$ is transformed by T to the vector $\begin{pmatrix} -13 \\ 17 \\ 21 \end{pmatrix}$.

Find the values of the constants a, b and c.

$$\begin{pmatrix} 2 & 4 & -1 \\ 3 & -2 & 1 \\ 1 & -3 & 2 \end{pmatrix}\begin{pmatrix} a \\ b \\ c \end{pmatrix} = \begin{pmatrix} -13 \\ 17 \\ 21 \end{pmatrix}$$

$$\begin{pmatrix} 2a+4b-c \\ 3a-2b+c \\ a-3b+2c \end{pmatrix} = \begin{pmatrix} -13 \\ 17 \\ 21 \end{pmatrix}$$

Equating the elements

$2a + 4b - c = -13$ ①

$3a - 2b + c = 17$ ②

$a - 3b + 2c = 21$ ③

① + ②

$5a + 2b = 4$ ④

2 × ① + ③

$5a + 5b = -5$ ⑤

⑤ − ④

$3b = -9 \Rightarrow b = -3$

Substituting $b = -3$ into ④

$5a - 6 = 4 \Rightarrow a = 2$

Substituting $a = 2$ and $b = -3$ into ②

$6 + 6 + c = 17 \Rightarrow c = 5$

$a = 2$, $b = -3$ and $c = 5$.

Equating the elements gives you 3 equations in 3 unknowns. You solve these by eliminating one variable, here c, between the equations. This leaves 2 equations in 2 unknowns, which you can solve by any appropriate method.

Exercise 6E

1 A transformation $T: \mathbb{R}^3 \rightarrow \mathbb{R}^3$ is represented by the matrix $\mathbf{T}$ where $\mathbf{T}^{-1} = \begin{pmatrix} 2 & 3 & 3 \\ -1 & 4 & 5 \\ 2 & 1 & 1 \end{pmatrix}$.

The point with position vector $\begin{pmatrix} a \\ b \\ c \end{pmatrix}$ is transformed by T to the point with position vector $\begin{pmatrix} -12 \\ -7 \\ 8 \end{pmatrix}$.

a Find the values of the constants a, b and c.

A line l_1 which passes through the origin is transformed by T to the line l_2.

A vector equation of l_1 is $\mathbf{r} = t\begin{pmatrix} 2 \\ -2 \\ 1 \end{pmatrix}$.

b Find a vector equation of l_2.

2 The transformation $T: \mathbb{R}^3 \rightarrow \mathbb{R}^3$ is represented by the matrix $\mathbf{T}$ where $\mathbf{T} = \begin{pmatrix} 2 & 0 & -3 \\ 0 & 1 & 2 \\ -3 & 2 & 8 \end{pmatrix}$.

a Find $\mathbf{T}^{-1}$.

The vector $\begin{pmatrix} a \\ b \\ c \end{pmatrix}$ is transformed by T to the vector $\begin{pmatrix} -5 \\ 5 \\ 16 \end{pmatrix}$.

b Find the values of the constants a, b and c.

3 The transformation $T: \mathbb{R}^3 \rightarrow \mathbb{R}^3$ is represented by the matrix $\mathbf{T}$ where $\mathbf{T} = \begin{pmatrix} 1 & 1 & 2 \\ 0 & 2 & 2 \\ -3 & 0 & -4 \end{pmatrix}$.

a Find $\mathbf{T}^{-1}$.

The line l_1 is transformed by T to the line l_2. The line l_2 has vector equation

$\mathbf{r} = \begin{pmatrix} 2 \\ 4 \\ 1 \end{pmatrix} + t\begin{pmatrix} -1 \\ 0 \\ 1 \end{pmatrix}$, where t is a real parameter.

b Find a vector equation of l_1.

4 The matrix $\mathbf{T} = \begin{pmatrix} a & 1 & 2 \\ 4 & 0 & 0 \\ 0 & 0 & -1 \end{pmatrix}$, where a is a constant.

a Find $\mathbf{T}^{-1}$, in terms of a.

The transformation $T: \mathbb{R}^3 \rightarrow \mathbb{R}^3$ is represented by the matrix $\mathbf{T}$. The point with position vector $\begin{pmatrix} p \\ q \\ r \end{pmatrix}$ is transformed by T to the point with position vector $\begin{pmatrix} 2 \\ 3 \\ -1 \end{pmatrix}$.

b Find the values of the constants p, q and r.

5 The matrix $\mathbf{S} = \begin{pmatrix} 1 & -\sqrt{2} & 1 \\ \sqrt{2} & 0 & -\sqrt{2} \\ 1 & \sqrt{2} & 1 \end{pmatrix}$.

a Show that $\mathbf{SS}^{\mathrm{T}} = k\mathbf{I}$, stating the value of k.

The transformation $S: \mathbb{R}^3 \rightarrow \mathbb{R}^3$ is represented by the matrix $\mathbf{S}$.

The vector $\begin{pmatrix} a \\ b \\ c \end{pmatrix}$ is transformed by S to the vector $\begin{pmatrix} 2\sqrt{2} \\ \sqrt{2} \\ -2\sqrt{2} \end{pmatrix}$.

b Find the values of the constants a, b and c.

6 The matrix $\mathbf{A} = \begin{pmatrix} 3 & 5 & 1 \\ -2 & 3 & 0 \\ 4 & 3 & 1 \end{pmatrix}$ and the matrix $\mathbf{B} = \begin{pmatrix} 3 & a & -3 \\ b & -1 & -2 \\ -18 & 11 & c \end{pmatrix}$. Given that $\mathbf{AB} = \mathbf{I}$,

a find the values of the constants a, b and c.

The transformation $A: \mathbb{R}^3 \rightarrow \mathbb{R}^3$ is represented by the matrix $\mathbf{A}$.

The plane Π_1 is transformed by A to the plane Π_2. The plane Π_2 has vector equation

$\mathbf{r} = \begin{pmatrix} 1 \\ 1 \\ 0 \end{pmatrix} + s\begin{pmatrix} -1 \\ 0 \\ 2 \end{pmatrix} + t\begin{pmatrix} 0 \\ 1 \\ 1 \end{pmatrix}$, where s and t are real parameters.

b Find a vector equation of the plane Π_1.

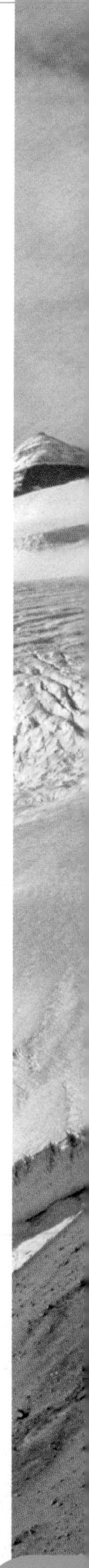

7 The transformation $T: \mathbb{R}^3 \to \mathbb{R}^3$ is represented by the matrix $\mathbf{T}$ where $\mathbf{T} = \begin{pmatrix} -1 & 3 & 6 \\ 1 & 4 & 2 \\ 2 & -5 & 1 \end{pmatrix}$.

The vector $\begin{pmatrix} a \\ b \\ c \end{pmatrix}$ is transformed by T to the vector $\begin{pmatrix} -8 \\ 0 \\ 3 \end{pmatrix}$.

Find the values of the constants a, b and c.

8 The matrix $\mathbf{S} = \begin{pmatrix} 2 & -1 & 2 \\ 0 & 2 & 1 \\ 1 & 0 & 1 \end{pmatrix}$ and the matrix $\mathbf{T} = \begin{pmatrix} 3 & 4 & 4 \\ -6 & -7 & -6 \\ 4 & 4 & 3 \end{pmatrix}$.

a Find $\mathbf{S}^{-1}$.

b Show that $\mathbf{T}^2 = \mathbf{I}$.

The transformation $S: \mathbb{R}^3 \to \mathbb{R}^3$ is represented by the matrix $\mathbf{S}$ and the transformation $T: \mathbb{R}^3 \to \mathbb{R}^3$ is represented by the matrix $\mathbf{T}$.

The transformation U is the transformation T followed by the transformation S.

The point $\begin{pmatrix} a \\ b \\ c \end{pmatrix}$ is transformed by U to the point $\begin{pmatrix} 6 \\ -3 \\ 2 \end{pmatrix}$.

c Find the values of the constants a, b and c.

6.6 You can find the eigenvalues and eigenvectors of 2 × 2 and 3 × 3 matrices.

- An **eigenvector** of a matrix **A** is a non-zero column vector $\mathbf{x}$ which satisfies the equation

  $\mathbf{Ax} = \lambda\mathbf{x}$, where λ is a scalar.

  The value of the scalar λ is the **eigenvalue** of the matrix corresponding to the eigenvector $\mathbf{x}$.

  The word **eigen** is German and means particular or special. Eigenvectors are also known as characteristic or latent vectors.

- The magnitude of an eigenvector may be changed by the linear transformation represented by the matrix but the direction of the eigenvector is unchanged or **invariant**. The eigenvalue can be interpreted as the magnification factor of the eigenvector under the transformation.

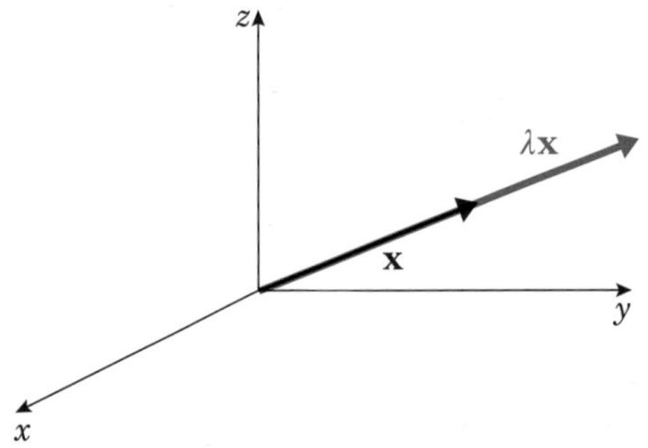

Under the transformation, the eigenvector $\mathbf{x}$ maps to the vector $\lambda\mathbf{x}$.

- If $\mathbf{x}$ is an eigenvector of the matrix **A** then, by definition

  $$\mathbf{Ax} = \lambda\mathbf{x} = \lambda\mathbf{Ix}.$$

  Rearranging

  $$\mathbf{Ax} - \lambda\mathbf{Ix} = (\mathbf{A} - \lambda\mathbf{I})\mathbf{x} = 0.$$

  As by definition $\mathbf{x}$ is non-zero, the matrix $(\mathbf{A} - \lambda\mathbf{I})$ is singular and has determinant zero, that is

  $$\det(\mathbf{A} - \lambda\mathbf{I}) = 0$$

- The equation $\det(\mathbf{A} - \lambda\mathbf{I}) = 0$ is called the **characteristic equation** of **A**.

  You solve the characteristic equation of a matrix to find its eigenvalues.

  If the matrix is a 2×2 matrix, then the characteristic equation is a quadratic equation.

  If the matrix is a 3×3 matrix, then the characteristic equation is a cubic equation. Often questions will give you a hint which enables you to factorise the cubic. However, if a hint is not given, you may have to search for one of the eigenvalues using the factor theorem you learnt in book C2.

  By definition, an eigenvector is non-zero, but zero can be an eigenvalue of a matrix. Although complex eigenvalues are possible and have important applications in Physics, only real eigenvalues are used in this specification.

- A **normalised vector** is a vector of unit magnitude. In three dimensions, you normalise the vector $\begin{pmatrix} a \\ b \\ c \end{pmatrix}$ by dividing each of the elements by the magnitude of the vector, which is $\sqrt{(a^2 + b^2 + c^2)}$.

  Any vector can be normalised but in this chapter you will be mainly concerned with **normalised eigenvectors**.

  If $\begin{pmatrix} a \\ b \end{pmatrix}$ is an eigenvector of a 2×2 matrix, then $\begin{pmatrix} \frac{a}{\sqrt{(a^2 + b^2)}} \\ \frac{b}{\sqrt{(a^2 + b^2)}} \end{pmatrix}$ is the corresponding normalised eigenvector.

  If $\begin{pmatrix} a \\ b \\ c \end{pmatrix}$ is an eigenvector of a 3×3 matrix, then $\begin{pmatrix} \frac{a}{\sqrt{(a^2 + b^2 + c^2)}} \\ \frac{b}{\sqrt{(a^2 + b^2 + c^2)}} \\ \frac{c}{\sqrt{(a^2 + b^2 + c^2)}} \end{pmatrix}$ is the corresponding normalised eigenvector.

Example 22

Find the eigenvalues and corresponding eigenvectors of the matrix $\mathbf{A} = \begin{pmatrix} 2 & 5 \\ -1 & -4 \end{pmatrix}$.

$$\mathbf{A} - \lambda\mathbf{I} = \begin{pmatrix} 2 & 5 \\ -1 & -4 \end{pmatrix} - \lambda\begin{pmatrix} 1 & 0 \\ 0 & 1 \end{pmatrix}$$

$$= \begin{pmatrix} 2 & 5 \\ -1 & -4 \end{pmatrix} - \begin{pmatrix} \lambda & 0 \\ 0 & \lambda \end{pmatrix} = \begin{pmatrix} 2-\lambda & 5 \\ -1 & -4-\lambda \end{pmatrix}$$

$$\det(\mathbf{A} - \lambda\mathbf{I}) = \begin{vmatrix} 2-\lambda & 5 \\ -1 & -4-\lambda \end{vmatrix}$$

$$= (2-\lambda)(-4-\lambda) - 5 \times (-1)$$

$$= -8 - 2\lambda + 4\lambda + \lambda^2 + 5$$

$$= \lambda^2 + 2\lambda - 3$$

The eigenvalues are the solutions of $\det(\mathbf{A} - \lambda\mathbf{I}) = 0$. You begin by finding $\mathbf{A} - \lambda\mathbf{I}$ and finding its determinant as a polynomial in λ.

$$\det(\mathbf{A} - \lambda\mathbf{I}) = 0 \Rightarrow \lambda^2 + 2\lambda - 3 = 0$$

$$(\lambda - 1)(\lambda + 3) = 0$$

$$\lambda = 1, -3$$

This equation is the **characteristic equation of A**.

The eigenvalues of A are 1 and -3.

To find an eigenvector of A corresponding to the eigenvalue 1

$$\begin{pmatrix} 2 & 5 \\ -1 & -4 \end{pmatrix}\begin{pmatrix} x \\ y \end{pmatrix} = 1\begin{pmatrix} x \\ y \end{pmatrix}$$

An eigenvector is a solution of $\mathbf{Ax} = \lambda\mathbf{x}$. In this case, you have to find a column vector $\mathbf{x} = \begin{pmatrix} x \\ y \end{pmatrix}$ satisfying the equation when $\lambda = 1$.

$$\begin{pmatrix} 2x + 5y \\ -x - 4y \end{pmatrix} = \begin{pmatrix} x \\ y \end{pmatrix}$$

Equating the upper elements

$$2x + 5y = x$$

$$x = -5y$$

Equating the lower elements gives $-x - 4y = y$, which leads to $x = -5y$. This is the same equation as you obtained from the upper elements and so gives you no extra information. With 2×2 matrices, one equation gives sufficient information to find an eigenvector.

Let $y = 1$, then $x = -5 \times 1 = -5$

Here you have a free choice of one variable. You can choose any non-zero value of y and then evaluate x. It is sensible to choose a simple number that avoids fractions.

An eigenvector corresponding to 1 is $\begin{pmatrix} -5 \\ 1 \end{pmatrix}$.

Any non-zero multiple of this vector is also a correct eigenvector of the matrix. For example, $\begin{pmatrix} 5 \\ -1 \end{pmatrix}$ is also correct.

To find an eigenvector of A corresponding to the eigenvalue -3

$$\begin{pmatrix} 2 & 5 \\ -1 & -4 \end{pmatrix}\begin{pmatrix} x \\ y \end{pmatrix} = -3\begin{pmatrix} x \\ y \end{pmatrix}$$

You repeat the procedure used for $\lambda = 1$ with $\lambda = -3$.

$$\begin{pmatrix} 2x + 5y \\ -x - 4y \end{pmatrix} = \begin{pmatrix} -3x \\ -3y \end{pmatrix}$$

Equating the upper elements

$$2x + 5y = -3x$$

$$5x + 5y = 0 \Rightarrow y = -x$$

The lower elements would give $-x - 4y = -3y$ which is equivalent to $y = -x$ so, again, this gives you no additional information.

Let $x = 1$, then $y = -1$

An eigenvector corresponding to -3 is $\begin{pmatrix} 1 \\ -1 \end{pmatrix}$.

Any multiple of this vector is also correct. The normalised eigenvector $\begin{pmatrix} \frac{1}{\sqrt{2}} \\ -\frac{1}{\sqrt{2}} \end{pmatrix}$ is sometimes asked for.

Example 23

Find the eigenvalues and corresponding eigenvectors of the matrix $\mathbf{A} = \begin{pmatrix} 2 & 1 & -3 \\ 0 & 2 & 1 \\ 0 & -4 & -3 \end{pmatrix}$.

$$\mathbf{A} - \lambda\mathbf{I} = \begin{pmatrix} 2 & 1 & -3 \\ 0 & 2 & 1 \\ 0 & -4 & -3 \end{pmatrix} - \lambda\begin{pmatrix} 1 & 0 & 0 \\ 0 & 1 & 0 \\ 0 & 0 & 1 \end{pmatrix}$$

$$= \begin{pmatrix} 2 & 1 & -3 \\ 0 & 2 & 1 \\ 0 & -4 & -3 \end{pmatrix} - \begin{pmatrix} \lambda & 0 & 0 \\ 0 & \lambda & 0 \\ 0 & 0 & \lambda \end{pmatrix} = \begin{pmatrix} 2-\lambda & 1 & -3 \\ 0 & 2-\lambda & 1 \\ 0 & -4 & -3-\lambda \end{pmatrix}$$

$$\det(\mathbf{A} - \lambda\mathbf{I}) = \begin{vmatrix} 2-\lambda & 1 & -3 \\ 0 & 2-\lambda & 1 \\ 0 & -4 & -3-\lambda \end{vmatrix}$$

As with 2 × 2 matrices, the eigenvalues are the solutions of det $(\mathbf{A} - \lambda\mathbf{I}) = 0$. You begin by finding $\mathbf{A} - \lambda\mathbf{I}$ and finding its determinant. With a 3 × 3 matrix the characteristic equation is a cubic which can have 3 real roots and, hence, 3 eigenvalues.

$$= (2-\lambda)\begin{vmatrix} 2-\lambda & 1 \\ -4 & -3-\lambda \end{vmatrix} - 1\begin{vmatrix} 0 & 1 \\ 0 & -3-\lambda \end{vmatrix} + (-3)\begin{vmatrix} 0 & 2-\lambda \\ 0 & -4 \end{vmatrix}$$

$$= (2-\lambda)((2-\lambda)(-3-\lambda)+4) - 0 + 0$$

$$= (2-\lambda)(-6-2\lambda+3\lambda+\lambda^2+4)$$

$$= (2-\lambda)(\lambda^2+\lambda-2) = (2-\lambda)(\lambda+2)(\lambda-1)$$

$$\det(\mathbf{A} - \lambda\mathbf{I}) = 0 \Rightarrow (2-\lambda)(\lambda+2)(\lambda-1) = 0$$

$$\lambda = 2, -2, 1$$

The eigenvalues of $\mathbf{A}$ are -2, 1 and 2.

To find an eigenvector of A corresponding to the eigenvalue −2

$$\begin{pmatrix} 2 & 1 & -3 \\ 0 & 2 & 1 \\ 0 & -4 & -3 \end{pmatrix}\begin{pmatrix} x \\ y \\ z \end{pmatrix} = -2\begin{pmatrix} x \\ y \\ z \end{pmatrix}$$

An eigenvector is a solution of $\mathbf{Ax} = \lambda\mathbf{x}$. In this case, you have to find a column vector $\mathbf{x} = \begin{pmatrix} x \\ y \\ z \end{pmatrix}$ satisfying the equation when $\lambda = -2$.

$$\begin{pmatrix} 2x+y-3z \\ 2y+z \\ -4y-3z \end{pmatrix} = \begin{pmatrix} -2x \\ -2y \\ -2z \end{pmatrix}$$

Equating the middle elements

$$2y + z = -2y \Rightarrow z = -4y$$

Let $y = 1$, then $z = -4$

Here you have a free choice of one variable. You can choose any non-zero value for y or x and then evaluate the other variable.

Equating the top elements and substituting $y = 1$ and $z = -4$

$$2x + y - 3z = -2x$$

$$4x = -y + 3z = -1 - 12 = -13 \Rightarrow x = -\tfrac{13}{4}$$

An eigenvector corresponding to -2 is $\begin{pmatrix} -\frac{13}{4} \\ 1 \\ -4 \end{pmatrix}$.

Equating the lowest elements gives an equivalent equation to the one you obtained from the middle elements and so gives you no extra information. With 3 × 3 matrices usually two equations will give you all the information you need to find an eigenvector.

To find an eigenvector of A corresponding to the eigenvalue 1

$$\begin{pmatrix} 2 & 1 & -3 \\ 0 & 2 & 1 \\ 0 & -4 & -3 \end{pmatrix}\begin{pmatrix} x \\ y \\ z \end{pmatrix} = 1\begin{pmatrix} x \\ y \\ z \end{pmatrix}$$

You repeat the procedure used for $\lambda = -2$ with $\lambda = 1$.

$$\begin{pmatrix} 2x + y - 3z \\ 2y + z \\ -4y - 3z \end{pmatrix} = \begin{pmatrix} x \\ y \\ z \end{pmatrix}$$

Equating the middle elements

$$2y + z = y \Rightarrow y = -z$$

Let $z = 1$, the $y = -1$

Equating the top elements and substituting $y = -1$ and $z = 1$

$$2x + y - 3z = x$$

$$x = -y + 3z = 1 + 3 = 4$$

An eigenvector corresponding to 1 is $\begin{pmatrix} 4 \\ -1 \\ 1 \end{pmatrix}$.

Any non-zero multiple of this eigenvector is also a correct eigenvector.

To find an eigenvector of A corresponding to the eigenvalue 2

$$\begin{pmatrix} 2 & 1 & -3 \\ 0 & 2 & 1 \\ 0 & -4 & -3 \end{pmatrix}\begin{pmatrix} x \\ y \\ z \end{pmatrix} = 2\begin{pmatrix} x \\ y \\ z \end{pmatrix}$$

$$\begin{pmatrix} 2x + y - 3z \\ 2y + z \\ -4y - 3z \end{pmatrix} = \begin{pmatrix} 2x \\ 2y \\ 2z \end{pmatrix}$$

Equating the middle elements

$$2y + z = 2y \Rightarrow z = 0$$

This calculation differs from the calculation for the other two eigenvalues in that these two equations give you that $y = z = 0$ and there is no choice of values.

Equating the lowest elements and using $z = 0$

$$-4y - 3z = 2z \Rightarrow 4y = -5z = 0 \Rightarrow y = 0$$

Equating the top elements

$$2x + y - 3z = 2x \Rightarrow y = 3z$$

It is sensible now to equate the top elements to attempt to find out something about x but the terms in x cancel out.

Let $x = 1$

The variable x appears in no equation and so can take any value. 1 is the simplest value to take.

An eigenvector corresponding to 2 is $\begin{pmatrix} 1 \\ 0 \\ 0 \end{pmatrix}$.

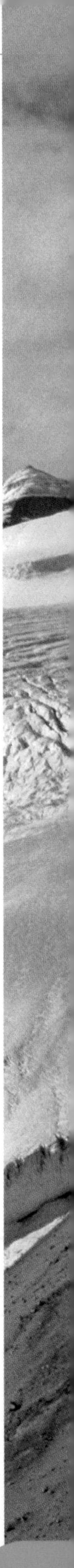

Example 24

The matrix $\mathbf{A} = \begin{pmatrix} 2 & -1 & 1 \\ 0 & 3 & 5 \\ 2 & 1 & 0 \end{pmatrix}$.

a Show that -2 is the only real eigenvalue of **A**.

b Find a normalised eigenvector of **A** corresponding to the eigenvalue -2.

a $\mathbf{A} - \lambda\mathbf{I} = \begin{pmatrix} 2 & -1 & 1 \\ 0 & 3 & 5 \\ 2 & 1 & 0 \end{pmatrix} - \begin{pmatrix} \lambda & 0 & 0 \\ 0 & \lambda & 0 \\ 0 & 0 & \lambda \end{pmatrix} = \begin{pmatrix} 2-\lambda & -1 & 1 \\ 0 & 3-\lambda & 5 \\ 2 & 1 & -\lambda \end{pmatrix}$

$$\det(\mathbf{A} - \lambda\mathbf{I}) = \begin{vmatrix} 2-\lambda & -1 & 1 \\ 0 & 3-\lambda & 5 \\ 2 & 1 & -\lambda \end{vmatrix}$$

$$= (2-\lambda)\begin{vmatrix} 3-\lambda & 5 \\ 1 & -\lambda \end{vmatrix} - (-1)\begin{vmatrix} 0 & 5 \\ 2 & -\lambda \end{vmatrix} + 1\begin{vmatrix} 0 & 3-\lambda \\ 2 & 1 \end{vmatrix}$$

$$= (2-\lambda)(-3\lambda + \lambda^2 - 5) - 10 - 2(3-\lambda)$$

$$= -6\lambda + 2\lambda^2 - 10 + 3\lambda^2 - \lambda^3 + 5\lambda - 10 - 6 + 2\lambda$$

$$= -\lambda^3 + 5\lambda^2 + \lambda - 26$$

$\det(\mathbf{A} - \lambda\mathbf{I}) = 0 \Rightarrow -\lambda^3 + 5\lambda^2 + \lambda - 26 = 0$

$\lambda^3 - 5\lambda^2 - \lambda + 26 = 0$

$(\lambda + 2)(\lambda^2 + k\lambda + 13) = 0$

The question implies that $\lambda = -2$ is a root of the characteristic equation and so $(\lambda + 2)$ must be a factor of the cubic. Here equating a coefficient has been used to complete the factorisation but you can use any appropriate method.

Equating coefficients of λ^2

$-5 = 2 + k \Rightarrow k = -7$

$(\lambda + 2)(\lambda^2 - 7\lambda + 13) = 0$

The discriminant of $\lambda^2 - 7\lambda + 13 = 0$ is

$b^2 - 4ac = 49 - 52 = -3 < 0$

To show that there is only one real root of the cubic, you show that the discriminant of the quadratic factor is negative.

The equation $\lambda^2 - 7\lambda + 13 = 0$ has no real solutions.

Hence -2 is the only real eigenvalue of **A**.

b $\begin{pmatrix} 2 & -1 & 1 \\ 0 & 3 & 5 \\ 2 & 1 & 0 \end{pmatrix}\begin{pmatrix} x \\ y \\ z \end{pmatrix} = -2\begin{pmatrix} x \\ y \\ z \end{pmatrix}$

$$\begin{pmatrix} 2x - y + z \\ 3y + 5z \\ 2x + y \end{pmatrix} = \begin{pmatrix} -2x \\ -2y \\ -2z \end{pmatrix}$$

Equating the middle elements

$$3y + 5z = -2y \Rightarrow y = -z$$

Let $z = 1$, then $y = -1$

Equating the lowest elements

$$2x + y = -2z \Rightarrow x = \frac{-y - 2z}{2}$$

Substituting $y = -1$ and $z = 1$

$$x = \frac{1 - 2}{2} = -\frac{1}{2}$$

An eigenvector of **A** is $2\begin{pmatrix} -\frac{1}{2} \\ -1 \\ 1 \end{pmatrix} = \begin{pmatrix} -1 \\ -2 \\ 2 \end{pmatrix}$

The working gives $\begin{pmatrix} -\frac{1}{2} \\ -1 \\ 1 \end{pmatrix}$ as the eigenvector but as any multiple of this is also an eigenvector, it is sensible to multiply this by 2, or -2, to avoid working in fractions.

The magnitude of this eigenvector is

$$\sqrt{((-1)^2 + (-2)^2 + 2^2)} = 3$$

A normalised eigenvector is found by dividing all of the terms by the magnitude of the original eigenvector.

A normalised eigenvector of **A** is

$$\frac{1}{3}\begin{pmatrix} -1 \\ -2 \\ 2 \end{pmatrix} = \begin{pmatrix} -\frac{1}{3} \\ -\frac{2}{3} \\ \frac{2}{3} \end{pmatrix}$$

$\begin{pmatrix} \frac{1}{3} \\ \frac{2}{3} \\ -\frac{2}{3} \end{pmatrix}$ is also correct. If a column vector $\mathbf{x}$ is a normalised eigenvector, then $-\mathbf{x}$ is also a normalised eigenvector.

Example 25

A transformation $T: \mathbb{R}^2 \rightarrow \mathbb{R}^2$ is represented by the matrix

$$\mathbf{A} = \begin{pmatrix} 4 & -5 \\ 1 & -2 \end{pmatrix}.$$

a Find the eigenvalues of **A**.

b Find Cartesian equations of the two lines passing through the origin which are invariant under T.

a $\mathbf{A} - \lambda\mathbf{I} = \begin{pmatrix} 4 & -5 \\ 1 & -2 \end{pmatrix} - \begin{pmatrix} \lambda & 0 \\ 0 & \lambda \end{pmatrix} = \begin{pmatrix} 4-\lambda & -5 \\ 1 & -2-\lambda \end{pmatrix}$

$\det(\mathbf{A} - \lambda\mathbf{I}) = \begin{vmatrix} 4-\lambda & -5 \\ 1 & -2-\lambda \end{vmatrix}$

With practice, you can write down this line without the previous working.

$= (4-\lambda)(-2-\lambda) + 5$

$= -8 - 4\lambda + 2\lambda + \lambda^2 + 5$

$= \lambda^2 - 2\lambda - 3 = (\lambda - 3)(\lambda + 1)$

$\det(\mathbf{A} - \lambda\mathbf{I}) = 0 \Rightarrow \lambda = 3, -1$

The eigenvalues of **A** are 3 and −1.

b $\begin{pmatrix} 4 & -5 \\ 1 & -2 \end{pmatrix}\begin{pmatrix} x \\ y \end{pmatrix} = 3\begin{pmatrix} x \\ y \end{pmatrix}$

$\begin{pmatrix} 4x - 5y \\ x - 2y \end{pmatrix} = \begin{pmatrix} 3x \\ 3y \end{pmatrix}$

Equating the lower elements

$x - 2y = 3y \Rightarrow y = \frac{1}{5}x$

An eigenvector is a vector whose direction is unchanged or invariant under a transformation. The line of action of the eigenvector is invariant under the transformation and a Cartesian equation for an eigenvector is an equation of an invariant line.

$\begin{pmatrix} 4 & -5 \\ 1 & -2 \end{pmatrix}\begin{pmatrix} x \\ y \end{pmatrix} = -1\begin{pmatrix} x \\ y \end{pmatrix}$

$\begin{pmatrix} 4x - 5y \\ x - 2y \end{pmatrix} = \begin{pmatrix} -x \\ -y \end{pmatrix}$

Equating the lower elements

$x - 2y = -y \Rightarrow y = x$

The equations of the invariant lines are

$y = x$ and $y = \frac{1}{5}x$

■ **An invariant line is one where any point on the line is mapped to another point on the same line. Except for the origin, the image point will usually be different from the original point as the distance of the point from the origin will be changed by a scale factor which is the eigenvalue.**

However if the eigenvalue is 1, then every point on the line of action of the corresponding eigenvector is mapped to itself. This gives a line of invariant points.

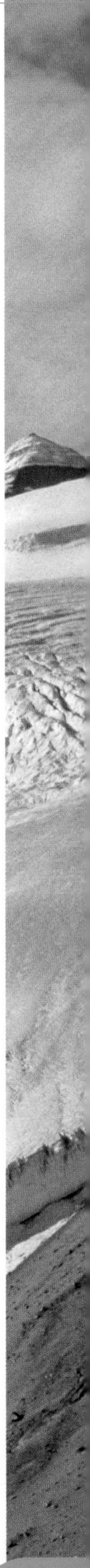

Example 26

The matrix $\mathbf{A} = \begin{pmatrix} 2 & 1 & 1 \\ 1 & 2 & 1 \\ 1 & 1 & 2 \end{pmatrix}$

a Show that 1 is an eigenvalue of **A** and that there is only one other distinct eigenvalue.

b Find an eigenvector corresponding to the eigenvalue 1.

a $$\mathbf{A} - \lambda\mathbf{I} = \begin{pmatrix} 2-\lambda & 1 & 1 \\ 1 & 2-\lambda & 1 \\ 1 & 1 & 2-\lambda \end{pmatrix}$$

$$\det(\mathbf{A} - \lambda\mathbf{I}) = \begin{vmatrix} 2-\lambda & 1 & 1 \\ 1 & 2-\lambda & 1 \\ 1 & 1 & 2-\lambda \end{vmatrix}$$

$$= (2-\lambda)\begin{vmatrix} 2-\lambda & 1 \\ 1 & 2-\lambda \end{vmatrix} - 1\begin{vmatrix} 1 & 1 \\ 1 & 2-\lambda \end{vmatrix} + 1\begin{vmatrix} 1 & 2-\lambda \\ 1 & 1 \end{vmatrix}$$

$$= (2-\lambda)((2-\lambda)^2 - 1) - (1-\lambda) + (\lambda - 1)$$

$$= (2-\lambda)(\lambda^2 - 4\lambda + 3) + 2\lambda - 2$$

$$= (2-\lambda)(\lambda - 3)(\lambda - 1) + 2(\lambda - 1)$$

$$= (\lambda - 1)(2\lambda - 6 - \lambda^2 + 3\lambda + 2)$$

$$= -(\lambda - 1)(\lambda^2 - 5\lambda + 4) = -(\lambda - 1)^2(\lambda - 4)$$

There are a number of ways of factorising the cubic, but as you know that 1 is a root of the cubic, it is sensible to look for the factor $(\lambda - 1)$.

The solutions of $\det(\mathbf{A} - \lambda\mathbf{I}) = 0$ are 1 repeated and 4.

1 is an eigenvalue and the only other distinct eigenvalue is 4.

b $$\begin{pmatrix} 2x + y + z \\ x + 2y + z \\ x + y + 2z \end{pmatrix} = \begin{pmatrix} x \\ y \\ z \end{pmatrix}$$

Equating the top elements

$$2x + y + z = x \Rightarrow x + y + z = 0$$

Equating the middle and the lowest elements both give you the same equation, $x + y + z = 0$. So the elements of the eigenvector only need to satisfy this one equation. You can choose any value you like for two of the values and then work the third one out. This extra element of choice has arisen because of the repeated root. However, not every case of a repeated root gives this extra choice.

Let $y = 1$ and $z = 1$, then $x = -2$

An eigenvector corresponding to the eigenvalue 1 is

$$\begin{pmatrix} -2 \\ 1 \\ 1 \end{pmatrix}.$$

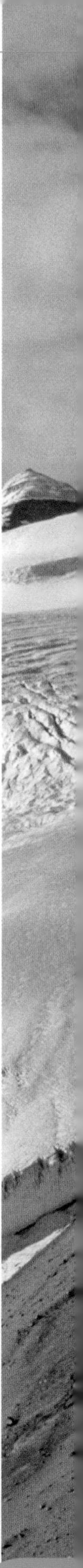

Exercise 6F

1 Find the eigenvalues and corresponding eigenvectors of the matrices

a $\begin{pmatrix} 2 & 4 \\ 1 & 5 \end{pmatrix}$ **b** $\begin{pmatrix} 4 & -1 \\ -1 & 4 \end{pmatrix}$ **c** $\begin{pmatrix} 3 & -2 \\ 0 & 4 \end{pmatrix}$.

2 A transformation $T: \mathbb{R}^2 \to \mathbb{R}^2$ is represented by the matrix

$$\mathbf{A} = \begin{pmatrix} 3 & 4 \\ -2 & 9 \end{pmatrix}$$

a Find the eigenvalues of **A**.

b Find Cartesian equations of the two lines passing through the origin which are invariant under T.

3 Find the eigenvalues and corresponding eigenvectors of the matrices

a $\begin{pmatrix} 3 & 0 & 0 \\ 2 & 4 & 2 \\ -2 & 0 & 1 \end{pmatrix}$ **b** $\begin{pmatrix} 4 & -2 & -4 \\ 2 & 3 & 0 \\ 2 & -5 & -4 \end{pmatrix}$.

4 The matrix $\mathbf{A} = \begin{pmatrix} 2 & 2 & -2 \\ -3 & 2 & 0 \\ 1 & 4 & -3 \end{pmatrix}$.

a Show that -1 is the only real eigenvalue of **A**.

b Find an eigenvector corresponding to the eigenvalue -1.

5 The matrix $\mathbf{A} = \begin{pmatrix} 2 & -1 & 3 \\ 0 & 2 & 4 \\ 0 & 2 & 0 \end{pmatrix}$.

a Show that 4 is an eigenvalue of **A** and find the other two eigenvalues of **A**.

b Find an eigenvector corresponding to the eigenvalue 4.

6 The matrix $\mathbf{A} = \begin{pmatrix} 1 & 1 & 3 \\ 2 & 4 & -1 \\ 4 & 4 & 3 \end{pmatrix}$.

Given that 3 is an eigenvalue of **A**,

a find the other two eigenvalues of **A**,

b find eigenvectors corresponding to each of the eigenvalues of **A**.

7 The matrix $\mathbf{A} = \begin{pmatrix} 2 & 2 & 1 \\ -2 & 4 & 0 \\ 4 & 2 & 5 \end{pmatrix}$.

a Show that 2 is an eigenvalue of **A**.

b Find the other two eigenvalues of **A**.

c Find a normalised eigenvector of **A** corresponding to the eigenvalue 2.

8 The matrix $\mathbf{A} = \begin{pmatrix} 4 & 2 & 1 \\ -2 & 0 & 5 \\ 0 & 3 & 4 \end{pmatrix}$.

a Show that -2 is an eigenvalue of $\mathbf{A}$ and that there is only one other distinct eigenvalue.

b Find an eigenvector corresponding to each of the eigenvalues.

9 The matrix $\mathbf{A} = \begin{pmatrix} 1 & -1 & 0 \\ -1 & 0 & 1 \\ 1 & 2 & 1 \end{pmatrix}$.

Given that 2 is an eigenvalue of $\mathbf{A}$,

a find the other two eigenvalues of $\mathbf{A}$,

b find eigenvectors corresponding to each of the eigenvalues of $\mathbf{A}$.

10 Given that $\begin{pmatrix} 2 \\ 2 \\ -1 \end{pmatrix}$ is an eigenvector of the matrix $\mathbf{A}$ where

$$\mathbf{A} = \begin{pmatrix} 4 & 1 & 2 \\ 1 & a & 0 \\ -1 & 1 & b \end{pmatrix},$$

a find the eigenvalue of $\mathbf{A}$ corresponding to $\begin{pmatrix} 2 \\ 2 \\ -1 \end{pmatrix}$,

b find the value of a and the value of b,

c show that $\mathbf{A}$ has only one real eigenvalue.

6.7 You can reduce a symmetric matrix to diagonal form.

- **If $\mathbf{M}$ is a square matrix such that $\mathbf{MM}^\mathrm{T} = \mathbf{I}$, then $\mathbf{M}$ is called an orthogonal matrix.**

- **If $\mathbf{M}$ is an orthogonal matrix, then $\mathbf{M}^{-1} = \mathbf{M}^\mathrm{T}$.**

- **Two eigenvectors $\mathbf{x}_1$ and $\mathbf{x}_2$ are orthogonal if their scalar product $\mathbf{x}_1.\mathbf{x}_2 = 0$. You learnt in book C4 that if non-zero vectors have scalar product zero, they are perpendicular. Perpendicular and orthogonal have the same meaning in this context but it is customary to use the word orthogonal when referring to eigenvectors.**

- **If $\mathbf{M}$ is an orthogonal matrix consisting of the normalised column vectors $\mathbf{x}_1$, $\mathbf{x}_2$ and $\mathbf{x}_3$, then $\mathbf{x}_1.\mathbf{x}_2 = \mathbf{x}_2.\mathbf{x}_3 = \mathbf{x}_3.\mathbf{x}_1 = 0$. The three vectors are mutually orthogonal.**

To show that a matrix $\mathbf{M}$ is orthogonal, you can either show that $\mathbf{MM}^\mathrm{T} = \mathbf{I}$ or that it consists of 3 mutually orthogonal normalised vectors.

■ A **diagonal matrix** is a square matrix in which all of the elements which are not on the diagonal from the top left to the bottom right of the matrix are zero. The diagonal from the top left to the bottom right of the matrix is called the **leading diagonal**.

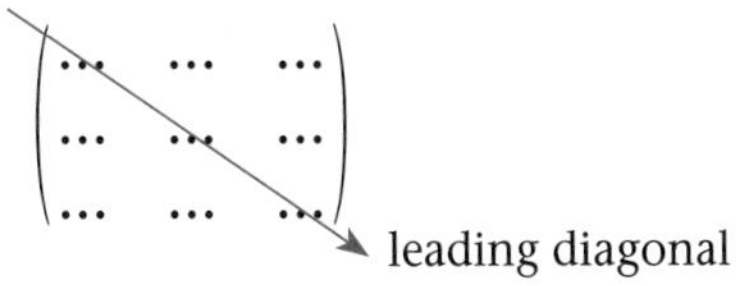

The general 2 × 2 diagonal matrix is $\begin{pmatrix} a & 0 \\ 0 & b \end{pmatrix}$.

The general 3 × 3 diagonal matrix is $\begin{pmatrix} a & 0 & 0 \\ 0 & b & 0 \\ 0 & 0 & c \end{pmatrix}$.

It is possible for some of the elements on the leading diagonal to be 0.

■ You reduce a symmetric matrix **A** to a diagonal matrix **D** using the following procedure.

1. Find normalised eigenvectors of **A**.
2. Form a matrix **P** with columns consisting of the normalised eigenvectors of **A**.
3. Write down $\mathbf{P}^{\mathrm{T}}$, the transpose of the matrix **P**.
4. A diagonal matrix **D** is given by $\mathbf{P}^{\mathrm{T}}\mathbf{AP} = \mathbf{D}$.

■ When you reduce a symmetric matrix **A** to a diagonal matrix **D**, the elements on the diagonal are the eigenvalues of **A**.

■ For any symmetric matrix **A**, the matrix **P** is an orthogonal matrix and so $\mathbf{P}^{\mathrm{T}} = \mathbf{P}^{-1}$. It follows that $\mathbf{P}^{\mathrm{T}}\mathbf{AP}$ and $\mathbf{P}^{-1}\mathbf{AP}$ are identical expressions.

Example 27

The matrix $\mathbf{M} = \begin{pmatrix} a & \frac{2}{3} & \frac{2}{3} \\ -\frac{2}{3} & b & c \\ -\frac{2}{3} & -\frac{1}{3} & \frac{2}{3} \end{pmatrix}$.

Given that $\mathbf{MM}^{\mathrm{T}} = \mathbf{I}$,

a find the values of the constants a, b and c.

Given that $\mathbf{x}_1 = \begin{pmatrix} a \\ -\frac{2}{3} \\ -\frac{2}{3} \end{pmatrix}$, $\mathbf{x}_2 = \begin{pmatrix} \frac{2}{3} \\ b \\ -\frac{1}{3} \end{pmatrix}$ and $\mathbf{x}_3 = \begin{pmatrix} \frac{2}{3} \\ c \\ \frac{2}{3} \end{pmatrix}$, using the values of a, b and c found in part **a**,

b show that each of the vectors $\mathbf{x}_1$, $\mathbf{x}_2$ and $\mathbf{x}_3$ is orthogonal to the other two.

a $MM^T = \begin{pmatrix} a & \frac{2}{3} & \frac{2}{3} \\ -\frac{2}{3} & b & c \\ -\frac{2}{3} & -\frac{1}{3} & \frac{2}{3} \end{pmatrix}\begin{pmatrix} a & -\frac{2}{3} & -\frac{2}{3} \\ \frac{2}{3} & b & -\frac{1}{3} \\ \frac{2}{3} & c & \frac{2}{3} \end{pmatrix}$

$= \begin{pmatrix} \ldots & -\frac{2}{3}a + \frac{2}{3}b + \frac{2}{3}c & -\frac{2}{3}a - \frac{2}{9} + \frac{4}{9} \\ \ldots & \ldots & \frac{4}{9} - \frac{1}{3}b + \frac{2}{3}c \\ \ldots & \ldots & \ldots \end{pmatrix} = \begin{pmatrix} 1 & 0 & 0 \\ 0 & 1 & 0 \\ 0 & 0 & 1 \end{pmatrix}$

As you only need three equations to find three variables, there is no need to work all of the matrix product out.

It is sensible not to use the elements on the leading diagonal as two of these will contain squared terms which lead to ambiguous signs.

Equating the third elements in the first row

$-\frac{2}{3}a - \frac{2}{9} + \frac{4}{9} = 0 \Rightarrow \frac{2}{3}a = \frac{2}{9} \Rightarrow a = \frac{1}{3}$

Equating the second elements in the first row and substituting $a = \frac{1}{3}$

$-\frac{2}{9} + \frac{2}{3}b + \frac{2}{3}c = 0$

$\frac{2}{3}b + \frac{2}{3}c = \frac{2}{9}$ ①

Equating the third elements in the second row

$\frac{4}{9} - \frac{1}{3}b + \frac{2}{3}c = 0$

$-\frac{1}{3}b + \frac{2}{3}c = -\frac{4}{9}$ ②

① − ②

$b = \frac{2}{9} + \frac{4}{9} = \frac{2}{3}$

Substituting $b = \frac{2}{3}$ into ①

$\frac{4}{9} + \frac{2}{3}c = \frac{2}{9} \Rightarrow \frac{2}{3}c = \frac{2}{9} - \frac{4}{9} = -\frac{2}{9} \Rightarrow c = -\frac{1}{3}$

$a = \frac{1}{3}, b = \frac{2}{3}, c = -\frac{1}{3}$

Although you are not asked to state it explicitly, part **a** establishes that the matrix $\begin{pmatrix} \frac{1}{3} & \frac{2}{3} & \frac{2}{3} \\ -\frac{2}{3} & \frac{2}{3} & -\frac{1}{3} \\ -\frac{2}{3} & -\frac{1}{3} & \frac{2}{3} \end{pmatrix}$ is an orthogonal matrix.

b $\mathbf{x}_1.\mathbf{x}_2 = \begin{pmatrix} \frac{1}{3} \\ -\frac{2}{3} \\ -\frac{2}{3} \end{pmatrix}.\begin{pmatrix} \frac{2}{3} \\ \frac{2}{3} \\ -\frac{1}{3} \end{pmatrix} = \frac{1}{3} \times \frac{2}{3} + (-\frac{2}{3}) \times \frac{2}{3} + (-\frac{2}{3}) \times (-\frac{1}{3})$

$= \frac{2}{9} - \frac{4}{9} + \frac{2}{9} = 0$

Hence $\mathbf{x}_1$ and $\mathbf{x}_2$ are orthogonal.

$\mathbf{x}_2.\mathbf{x}_3 = \begin{pmatrix} \frac{2}{3} \\ \frac{2}{3} \\ -\frac{1}{3} \end{pmatrix}.\begin{pmatrix} \frac{2}{3} \\ -\frac{1}{3} \\ \frac{2}{3} \end{pmatrix} = \frac{2}{3} \times \frac{2}{3} + \frac{2}{3} \times (-\frac{1}{3}) + (-\frac{1}{3}) \times \frac{2}{3}$

$= \frac{4}{9} - \frac{2}{9} - \frac{2}{9} = 0$

Hence $\mathbf{x}_2$ and $\mathbf{x}_3$ are orthogonal.

$$\mathbf{x}_1.\mathbf{x}_3 = \begin{pmatrix} \frac{1}{3} \\ -\frac{2}{3} \\ -\frac{2}{3} \end{pmatrix} . \begin{pmatrix} \frac{2}{3} \\ -\frac{1}{3} \\ \frac{2}{3} \end{pmatrix} = \tfrac{1}{3} \times \tfrac{2}{3} + (-\tfrac{2}{3}) \times (-\tfrac{1}{3}) + (-\tfrac{2}{3}) \times \tfrac{2}{3}$$

$$= \tfrac{2}{9} + \tfrac{2}{9} - \tfrac{4}{9} = 0$$

Hence $\mathbf{x}_2$ and $\mathbf{x}_3$ are orthogonal.

Each of the vectors $\mathbf{x}_1$, $\mathbf{x}_2$ and $\mathbf{x}_3$ is orthogonal to the other two.

Part **b** illustrates the general property that the thee column vectors making up a 3 × 3 orthogonal matrix are orthogonal to each other.

Example 28

The matrix $\mathbf{A} = \begin{pmatrix} 2 & -1 \\ -1 & 2 \end{pmatrix}$. Reduce **A** to a diagonal matrix.

$$\mathbf{A} - \lambda\mathbf{I} = \begin{pmatrix} 2 & -1 \\ -1 & 2 \end{pmatrix} - \begin{pmatrix} \lambda & 0 \\ 0 & \lambda \end{pmatrix} = \begin{pmatrix} 2-\lambda & -1 \\ -1 & 2-\lambda \end{pmatrix}$$

$$\begin{vmatrix} 2-\lambda & -1 \\ -1 & 2-\lambda \end{vmatrix} = (2-\lambda)(2-\lambda) - 1$$

$$= \lambda^2 - 4\lambda + 3 = (\lambda - 1)(\lambda - 3)$$

$$\det(\mathbf{A} - \lambda\mathbf{I}) = 0 \Rightarrow (\lambda - 1)(\lambda - 3) = 0 \Rightarrow \lambda = 1, 3$$

To diagonalise a symmetric matrix, you find normalised eigenvectors of the matrix. You begin by finding the eigenvalues.

For $\lambda = 1$

$$\begin{pmatrix} 2 & -1 \\ -1 & 2 \end{pmatrix}\begin{pmatrix} x \\ y \end{pmatrix} = 1\begin{pmatrix} x \\ y \end{pmatrix}$$

$$\begin{pmatrix} 2x - y \\ -x + 2y \end{pmatrix} = \begin{pmatrix} x \\ y \end{pmatrix}$$

Equating the upper elements

$$2x - y = x \Rightarrow y = x$$

Let $x = 1$, then $y = 1$

An eigenvector corresponding to the eigenvalue 1 is $\begin{pmatrix} 1 \\ 1 \end{pmatrix}$.

The magnitude of $\begin{pmatrix} 1 \\ 1 \end{pmatrix}$ is $\sqrt{(1^2 + 1^2)} = \sqrt{2}$.

A normalised eigenvector corresponding to the eigenvalue 1 is

$$\begin{pmatrix} \frac{1}{\sqrt{2}} \\ \frac{1}{\sqrt{2}} \end{pmatrix}.$$

To convert an eigenvector **x** to a normalised eigenvector, you divide each of the elements of **x** by the magnitude of **x**.

For $\lambda = 3$

$$\begin{pmatrix} 2 & -1 \\ -1 & 2 \end{pmatrix}\begin{pmatrix} x \\ y \end{pmatrix} = 3\begin{pmatrix} x \\ y \end{pmatrix}$$

$$\begin{pmatrix} 2x - y \\ -x + 2y \end{pmatrix} = \begin{pmatrix} 3x \\ 3y \end{pmatrix}$$

Equating the upper elements

$$2x - y = 3x \Rightarrow y = -x$$

Let $x = 1$, then $y = -1$

An eigenvector corresponding to the eigenvalue 3 is $\begin{pmatrix} 1 \\ -1 \end{pmatrix}$.

The magnitude of $\begin{pmatrix} 1 \\ -1 \end{pmatrix}$ is $\sqrt{(1^2 + (-1)^2)} = \sqrt{2}$.

A normalised eigenvector corresponding to the eigenvalue 3 is

$$\begin{pmatrix} \frac{1}{\sqrt{2}} \\ -\frac{1}{\sqrt{2}} \end{pmatrix}.$$

The negative of this vector $\begin{pmatrix} -\frac{1}{\sqrt{2}} \\ \frac{1}{\sqrt{2}} \end{pmatrix}$ is also correct and would be just as appropriate for diagonalising the matrix.

$$\mathbf{P} = \begin{pmatrix} \frac{1}{\sqrt{2}} & \frac{1}{\sqrt{2}} \\ \frac{1}{\sqrt{2}} & -\frac{1}{\sqrt{2}} \end{pmatrix}$$

You form the orthogonal matrix **P** from the normalised eigenvectors by using the eigenvectors as the columns of the matrix.

$$\mathbf{P}^{\mathrm{T}} = \begin{pmatrix} \frac{1}{\sqrt{2}} & \frac{1}{\sqrt{2}} \\ \frac{1}{\sqrt{2}} & -\frac{1}{\sqrt{2}} \end{pmatrix}$$

In this case, as **P** is symmetric, $\mathbf{P}^{\mathrm{T}} = \mathbf{P}$.

$$\mathbf{P}^{\mathrm{T}}\mathbf{AP} = \begin{pmatrix} \frac{1}{\sqrt{2}} & \frac{1}{\sqrt{2}} \\ \frac{1}{\sqrt{2}} & -\frac{1}{\sqrt{2}} \end{pmatrix}\begin{pmatrix} 2 & -1 \\ -1 & 2 \end{pmatrix}\begin{pmatrix} \frac{1}{\sqrt{2}} & \frac{1}{\sqrt{2}} \\ \frac{1}{\sqrt{2}} & -\frac{1}{\sqrt{2}} \end{pmatrix}$$

$$= \begin{pmatrix} \frac{1}{\sqrt{2}} & \frac{1}{\sqrt{2}} \\ \frac{1}{\sqrt{2}} & -\frac{1}{\sqrt{2}} \end{pmatrix}\begin{pmatrix} \frac{2}{\sqrt{2}} - \frac{1}{\sqrt{2}} & \frac{2}{\sqrt{2}} + \frac{1}{\sqrt{2}} \\ -\frac{1}{\sqrt{2}} + \frac{2}{\sqrt{2}} & -\frac{1}{\sqrt{2}} - \frac{2}{\sqrt{2}} \end{pmatrix} = \begin{pmatrix} \frac{1}{\sqrt{2}} & \frac{1}{\sqrt{2}} \\ \frac{1}{\sqrt{2}} & -\frac{1}{\sqrt{2}} \end{pmatrix}\begin{pmatrix} \frac{1}{\sqrt{2}} & \frac{3}{\sqrt{2}} \\ \frac{1}{\sqrt{2}} & -\frac{3}{\sqrt{2}} \end{pmatrix}$$

$$= \begin{pmatrix} \frac{1}{2} + \frac{1}{2} & \frac{3}{2} - \frac{3}{2} \\ \frac{1}{2} - \frac{1}{2} & \frac{3}{2} + \frac{3}{2} \end{pmatrix} = \begin{pmatrix} 1 & 0 \\ 0 & 3 \end{pmatrix}$$

The diagonal matrix is given by

$$\mathbf{D} = \begin{pmatrix} 1 & 0 \\ 0 & 3 \end{pmatrix}.$$

The non-zero number in the first column, 1, is the eigenvalue corresponding to the eigenvector $\begin{pmatrix} \frac{1}{\sqrt{2}} \\ \frac{1}{\sqrt{2}} \end{pmatrix}$ used as the first column of **P**.

The non-zero number in the second column, 3 is the eigenvalue corresponding to the eigenvector $\begin{pmatrix} \frac{1}{\sqrt{2}} \\ -\frac{1}{\sqrt{2}} \end{pmatrix}$ used as the first column of **P**. A similar result is true for 3×3 matrices.

If you take **P** as $\begin{pmatrix} \frac{1}{\sqrt{2}} & \frac{1}{\sqrt{2}} \\ -\frac{1}{\sqrt{2}} & \frac{1}{\sqrt{2}} \end{pmatrix}$, which is a valid choice, then $\mathbf{D} = \begin{pmatrix} 3 & 0 \\ 0 & 1 \end{pmatrix}$.

Example 29

The matrix $\mathbf{A} = \begin{pmatrix} 2 & 0 & 1 \\ 0 & -2 & 0 \\ 1 & 0 & 2 \end{pmatrix}$. Reduce $\mathbf{A}$ to a diagonal matrix.

$$\mathbf{A} - \lambda\mathbf{I} = \begin{pmatrix} 2 & 0 & 1 \\ 0 & -2 & 0 \\ 1 & 0 & 2 \end{pmatrix} - \begin{pmatrix} \lambda & 0 & 0 \\ 0 & \lambda & 0 \\ 0 & 0 & \lambda \end{pmatrix} = \begin{pmatrix} 2-\lambda & 0 & 1 \\ 0 & -2-\lambda & 0 \\ 1 & 0 & 2-\lambda \end{pmatrix}$$

$$\begin{vmatrix} 2-\lambda & 0 & 1 \\ 0 & -2-\lambda & 0 \\ 1 & 0 & 2-\lambda \end{vmatrix} = (2-\lambda)\begin{vmatrix} -2-\lambda & 0 \\ 0 & 2-\lambda \end{vmatrix} - 0\begin{vmatrix} 0 & 0 \\ 1 & 2-\lambda \end{vmatrix} + 1\begin{vmatrix} 0 & -2-\lambda \\ 1 & 0 \end{vmatrix}$$

$$= (2-\lambda)(-2-\lambda)(2-\lambda) + 1(2+\lambda)$$

$$= (2+\lambda)(-(2-\lambda)^2 + 1) = -(2+\lambda)((2-\lambda)^2 - 1)$$

$$= -(\lambda+2)(\lambda^2 - 4\lambda + 3) = -(\lambda+2)(\lambda-1)(\lambda-3)$$

$\det(\mathbf{A} - \lambda\mathbf{I}) = 0 \Rightarrow -(\lambda+2)(\lambda-1)(\lambda-3) = 0 \Rightarrow \lambda = -2, 1, 3$

For $\lambda = -2$

$$\begin{pmatrix} 2 & 0 & 1 \\ 0 & -2 & 0 \\ 1 & 0 & 2 \end{pmatrix}\begin{pmatrix} x \\ y \\ z \end{pmatrix} = -2\begin{pmatrix} x \\ y \\ z \end{pmatrix}$$

The orthogonal matrix **P** is formed with normalised eigenvectors, so you begin by finding these.

$$\begin{pmatrix} 2x + z \\ -2y \\ x + 2z \end{pmatrix} = \begin{pmatrix} -2x \\ -2y \\ -2z \end{pmatrix}$$

Equating the top elements

$2x + z = -2x \Rightarrow z = -4x$

Equating the lowest elements and using $z = -4x$

$x + 2z = -2z \Rightarrow x = -4z = 16x \Rightarrow x = 0$

As $z = -4x$, $z = 0$

Equating the middle elements

$-2y = -2y$, an identity

As the only equation in y is an identity then y can take any non-zero value. The simplest value to take is 1.

Let $y = 1$

An eigenvector corresponding to -2 is $\begin{pmatrix} 0 \\ 1 \\ 0 \end{pmatrix}$.

As this vector has magnitude 1, it is already normalised and can be used to form the orthogonal matrix **P** without modification.

For $\lambda = 1$

$$\begin{pmatrix} 2 & 0 & 1 \\ 0 & -2 & 0 \\ 1 & 0 & 2 \end{pmatrix}\begin{pmatrix} x \\ y \\ z \end{pmatrix} = 1\begin{pmatrix} x \\ y \\ z \end{pmatrix}$$

$$\begin{pmatrix} 2x + z \\ -2y \\ x + 2z \end{pmatrix} = \begin{pmatrix} x \\ y \\ z \end{pmatrix}$$

Equating the top elements

$$2x + z = x \Rightarrow z = -x$$

Let $x = 1$, then $z = -1$

Equating the middle elements

$$-2y = y \Rightarrow y = 0$$

An eigenvector corresponding to 1 is $\begin{pmatrix} 1 \\ 0 \\ -1 \end{pmatrix}$.

The magnitude of $\begin{pmatrix} 1 \\ 0 \\ -1 \end{pmatrix}$ is $\sqrt{(1^2 + 0^2 + (-1)^2)} = \sqrt{2}$.

To convert an eigenvector **x** to a normalised eigenvector, you divide each of the elements of **x** by the magnitude of **x**.

A normalised eigenvector corresponding to 1 is

$$\begin{pmatrix} \frac{1}{\sqrt{2}} \\ 0 \\ -\frac{1}{\sqrt{2}} \end{pmatrix}.$$

For $\lambda = 3$

$$\begin{pmatrix} 2 & 0 & 1 \\ 0 & -2 & 0 \\ 1 & 0 & 2 \end{pmatrix}\begin{pmatrix} x \\ y \\ z \end{pmatrix} = 3\begin{pmatrix} x \\ y \\ z \end{pmatrix}$$

$$\begin{pmatrix} 2x + z \\ -2y \\ x + 2z \end{pmatrix} = \begin{pmatrix} 3x \\ 3y \\ 3z \end{pmatrix}$$

Equating the top elements

$$2x + z = 3x \Rightarrow z = x$$

Let $x = 1$, then $z = 1$

Equating the middle elements

$$-2y = 3y \Rightarrow y = 0$$

An eigenvector corresponding to 3 is $\begin{pmatrix} 1 \\ 0 \\ 1 \end{pmatrix}$.

The magnitude of $\begin{pmatrix} 1 \\ 0 \\ 1 \end{pmatrix}$ is $\sqrt{(1^2 + 0^2 + 1^2)} = \sqrt{2}$.

A normalised eigenvector corresponding to 3 is

$$\begin{pmatrix} \frac{1}{\sqrt{2}} \\ 0 \\ \frac{1}{\sqrt{2}} \end{pmatrix}.$$

If you have carried out the calculation correctly, the normalised eigenvectors of a symmetric matrix are orthogonal and, as a check on your work, it is worth checking that this is so. In this case

$$\begin{pmatrix} \frac{1}{\sqrt{2}} \\ 0 \\ -\frac{1}{\sqrt{2}} \end{pmatrix} \cdot \begin{pmatrix} \frac{1}{\sqrt{2}} \\ 0 \\ \frac{1}{\sqrt{2}} \end{pmatrix} = \frac{1}{\sqrt{2}} \times \frac{1}{\sqrt{2}} + 0 \times 0 + \left(-\frac{1}{\sqrt{2}}\right) \times \frac{1}{\sqrt{2}} = 0,$$

which confirms that the vectors are orthogonal and that the working is correct.

$$\mathbf{P} = \begin{pmatrix} 0 & \frac{1}{\sqrt{2}} & \frac{1}{\sqrt{2}} \\ 1 & 0 & 0 \\ 0 & -\frac{1}{\sqrt{2}} & \frac{1}{\sqrt{2}} \end{pmatrix}$$

You form the orthogonal matrix **P** from the normalised eigenvectors by using the eigenvectors as the columns of the matrix.

$$\mathbf{P}^{\mathrm{T}} = \begin{pmatrix} 0 & 1 & 0 \\ \frac{1}{\sqrt{2}} & 0 & -\frac{1}{\sqrt{2}} \\ \frac{1}{\sqrt{2}} & 0 & \frac{1}{\sqrt{2}} \end{pmatrix}$$

$$\mathbf{P}^{\mathrm{T}}\mathbf{AP} = \begin{pmatrix} 0 & 1 & 0 \\ \frac{1}{\sqrt{2}} & 0 & -\frac{1}{\sqrt{2}} \\ \frac{1}{\sqrt{2}} & 0 & \frac{1}{\sqrt{2}} \end{pmatrix} \begin{pmatrix} 2 & 0 & 1 \\ 0 & -2 & 0 \\ 1 & 0 & 2 \end{pmatrix} \begin{pmatrix} 0 & \frac{1}{\sqrt{2}} & \frac{1}{\sqrt{2}} \\ 1 & 0 & 0 \\ 0 & -\frac{1}{\sqrt{2}} & \frac{1}{\sqrt{2}} \end{pmatrix}$$

$$= \begin{pmatrix} 0 & 1 & 0 \\ \frac{1}{\sqrt{2}} & 0 & -\frac{1}{\sqrt{2}} \\ \frac{1}{\sqrt{2}} & 0 & \frac{1}{\sqrt{2}} \end{pmatrix} \begin{pmatrix} 0 & \frac{2}{\sqrt{2}} - \frac{1}{\sqrt{2}} & \frac{2}{\sqrt{2}} + \frac{1}{\sqrt{2}} \\ -2 & 0 & 0 \\ 0 & \frac{1}{\sqrt{2}} - \frac{2}{\sqrt{2}} & \frac{1}{\sqrt{2}} + \frac{2}{\sqrt{2}} \end{pmatrix}$$

$$= \begin{pmatrix} 0 & 1 & 0 \\ \frac{1}{\sqrt{2}} & 0 & -\frac{1}{\sqrt{2}} \\ \frac{1}{\sqrt{2}} & 0 & \frac{1}{\sqrt{2}} \end{pmatrix} \begin{pmatrix} 0 & \frac{1}{\sqrt{2}} & \frac{3}{\sqrt{2}} \\ -2 & 0 & 0 \\ 0 & -\frac{1}{\sqrt{2}} & \frac{3}{\sqrt{2}} \end{pmatrix}$$

$$= \begin{pmatrix} -2 & 0 & 0 \\ 0 & \frac{1}{2} + \frac{1}{2} & 0 \\ 0 & 0 & \frac{3}{2} + \frac{3}{2} \end{pmatrix} = \begin{pmatrix} -2 & 0 & 0 \\ 0 & 1 & 0 \\ 0 & 0 & 3 \end{pmatrix}$$

$$\mathbf{D} = \begin{pmatrix} -2 & 0 & 0 \\ 0 & 1 & 0 \\ 0 & 0 & 3 \end{pmatrix}$$

The non-zero elements in the diagonal matrix are the eigenvalues of the matrix **A** in the order corresponding to the order in which you used the normalised eigenvectors to form the orthogonal matrix **P**.

Example 30

The matrix $\mathbf{A} = \begin{pmatrix} 7 & 5 & 5 \\ 5 & -2 & 4 \\ 5 & 4 & -2 \end{pmatrix}$.

a Verify that $\begin{pmatrix} 2 \\ 1 \\ 1 \end{pmatrix}$ is an eigenvector of **A** and find the corresponding eigenvalue.

b Show that −6 is another eigenvalue of **A** and find the corresponding eigenvector.

c Given that the third eigenvector of **A** is $\begin{pmatrix} 1 \\ -1 \\ -1 \end{pmatrix}$, find a matrix **P** and a diagonal matrix **D** such that $\mathbf{P}^{-1}\mathbf{AP} = \mathbf{D}$.

a $\begin{pmatrix} 7 & 5 & 5 \\ 5 & -2 & 4 \\ 5 & 4 & -2 \end{pmatrix}\begin{pmatrix} 2 \\ 1 \\ 1 \end{pmatrix} = \begin{pmatrix} 14+5+5 \\ 10-2+4 \\ 10+4-2 \end{pmatrix} = \begin{pmatrix} 24 \\ 12 \\ 12 \end{pmatrix} = 12\begin{pmatrix} 2 \\ 1 \\ 1 \end{pmatrix}$

To show that a column vector **x** is an eigenvector of **A**, you have to find a constant such that $\mathbf{Ax} = \lambda\mathbf{x}$.

Hence $\begin{pmatrix} 2 \\ 1 \\ 1 \end{pmatrix}$ is an eigenvector of A corresponding to the eigenvalue 12.

b $\mathbf{A} - \lambda\mathbf{I} = \begin{pmatrix} 7 & 5 & 5 \\ 5 & -2 & 4 \\ 5 & 4 & -2 \end{pmatrix} - \begin{pmatrix} \lambda & 0 & 0 \\ 0 & \lambda & 0 \\ 0 & 0 & \lambda \end{pmatrix} = \begin{pmatrix} 7-\lambda & 5 & 5 \\ 5 & -2-\lambda & 4 \\ 5 & 4 & -2-\lambda \end{pmatrix}$

When $\lambda = -6$

$$\det(\mathbf{A} - \lambda\mathbf{I}) = \begin{vmatrix} 7-(-6) & 5 & 5 \\ 5 & -2-(-6) & 4 \\ 5 & 4 & -2-(-6) \end{vmatrix} = \begin{vmatrix} 13 & 5 & 5 \\ 5 & 4 & 4 \\ 5 & 4 & 4 \end{vmatrix}$$

$$= 13\begin{vmatrix} 4 & 4 \\ 4 & 4 \end{vmatrix} - 5\begin{vmatrix} 5 & 4 \\ 5 & 4 \end{vmatrix} + 5\begin{vmatrix} 5 & 4 \\ 5 & 4 \end{vmatrix}$$

$$= 13(16-16) - 5(20-20) + 5(20-20) = 0$$

Hence −6 is an eigenvalue of A.

To show that −6 is an eigenvalue, it is sufficient to show that substituting $\lambda = -6$ into the determinant of $\mathbf{A} - \lambda\mathbf{I}$ gives 0. You do not have to solve the cubic characteristic equation completely.

To find an eigenvector corresponding to −6

$$\begin{pmatrix} 7 & 5 & 5 \\ 5 & -2 & 4 \\ 5 & 4 & -2 \end{pmatrix}\begin{pmatrix} x \\ y \\ z \end{pmatrix} = -6\begin{pmatrix} x \\ y \\ z \end{pmatrix}$$

$$\begin{pmatrix} 7x+5y+5z \\ 5x-2y+4z \\ 5x+4y-2z \end{pmatrix} = \begin{pmatrix} -6x \\ -6y \\ -6z \end{pmatrix}$$

Equating the top elements

$7x + 5y + 5z = -6x \Rightarrow 5y + 5z = -13x$

$y + z = -\frac{13}{5}x$ ①

Equating the middle elements

$$5x - 2y + 4z = -6y \Rightarrow 4y + 4z = -5x$$

$$y + z = -\tfrac{5}{4}x \qquad ②$$

From ① and ②

$$-\tfrac{13}{5}x = -\tfrac{5}{4}x \Rightarrow x = 0$$

Substituting $x = 0$ into ②

$$4y + 4z = 0 \Rightarrow z = -y$$

Let $y = 1$, then $z = -1$

An eigenvector corresponding to the eigenvalue -6 is $\begin{pmatrix} 0 \\ 1 \\ -1 \end{pmatrix}$.

c To find the eigenvalue corresponding to $\begin{pmatrix} 0 \\ -1 \\ -1 \end{pmatrix}$

> You will need the eigenvalue corresponding to this eigenvector for the third non-zero element of the diagonal matrix **D**. You already know that the other two elements are 12 and −6.

$$\begin{pmatrix} 7 & 5 & 5 \\ 5 & -2 & 4 \\ 5 & 4 & -2 \end{pmatrix}\begin{pmatrix} 1 \\ -1 \\ -1 \end{pmatrix} = \begin{pmatrix} 7-5-5 \\ 5+2-4 \\ 5-4+2 \end{pmatrix} = \begin{pmatrix} -3 \\ 3 \\ 3 \end{pmatrix} = -3\begin{pmatrix} 1 \\ -1 \\ -1 \end{pmatrix}$$

The corresponding eigenvalue is -3.

The magnitude of $\begin{pmatrix} 2 \\ 1 \\ 1 \end{pmatrix}$ is $\sqrt{(2^2 + 1^2 + 1^2)} = \sqrt{6}$.

A normalised eigenvector corresponding to 12 is $\begin{pmatrix} \frac{2}{\sqrt{6}} \\ \frac{1}{\sqrt{6}} \\ \frac{1}{\sqrt{6}} \end{pmatrix}$.

> The matrix **P** is made up of columns of normalised eigenvalues. **P** is an orthogonal matrix and so $\mathbf{P}^{\mathrm{T}} = \mathbf{P}^{-1}$. Hence there is no difference between the expression $\mathbf{P}^{-1}\mathbf{AP}$, used to diagonalise **A** in this example and the expression $\mathbf{P}^{\mathrm{T}}\mathbf{AP}$, used in Examples 27 and 28.

The magnitude of $\begin{pmatrix} 0 \\ 1 \\ -1 \end{pmatrix}$ is $\sqrt{(0^2 + 1^2 + (-1)^2)} = \sqrt{2}$.

A normalised eigenvector corresponding to -6 is $\begin{pmatrix} 0 \\ \frac{1}{\sqrt{2}} \\ -\frac{1}{\sqrt{2}} \end{pmatrix}$.

The magnitude of $\begin{pmatrix} 1 \\ 1 \\ -1 \end{pmatrix}$ is $\sqrt{(1^2 + (-1)^2 + (-1)^2)} = \sqrt{3}$.

A normalised eigenvector corresponding to -3 is $\begin{pmatrix} \frac{1}{\sqrt{3}} \\ -\frac{1}{\sqrt{3}} \\ -\frac{1}{\sqrt{3}} \end{pmatrix}$.

$$\mathbf{P} = \begin{pmatrix} \frac{2}{\sqrt{6}} & 0 & \frac{1}{\sqrt{3}} \\ \frac{1}{\sqrt{6}} & \frac{1}{\sqrt{2}} & -\frac{1}{\sqrt{3}} \\ \frac{1}{\sqrt{6}} & -\frac{1}{\sqrt{2}} & -\frac{1}{\sqrt{3}} \end{pmatrix}$$

$$\mathbf{D} = \begin{pmatrix} 12 & 0 & 0 \\ 0 & -6 & 0 \\ 0 & 0 & -3 \end{pmatrix}$$

> You know that **P** is a matrix made up with normalised eigenvectors as its columns and that **D** is the diagonal matrix with corresponding eigenvalues as the elements of the leading diagonals. Multiplying the matrices out is a laborious process and you should not do this unless the question requires it.

Exercise 6G

1 Reduce the following matrices to diagonal matrices.

a $\begin{pmatrix} 1 & 3 \\ 3 & 1 \end{pmatrix}$ **b** $\begin{pmatrix} 1 & -2 \\ -2 & 4 \end{pmatrix}$

2 The matrix $\mathbf{A} = \begin{pmatrix} 3 & \sqrt{2} \\ \sqrt{2} & 4 \end{pmatrix}$.

a Find the eigenvalues of **A**.

b Find normalised eigenvectors of **A** corresponding to each of the two eigenvalues of **A**.

c Write down a matrix **P** and a diagonal matrix **D** such that $\mathbf{P}^\mathrm{T}\mathbf{AP} = \mathbf{D}$.

3 The matrix $\mathbf{P} = \begin{pmatrix} \frac{1}{\sqrt{6}} & -\frac{1}{\sqrt{3}} & \frac{1}{\sqrt{2}} \\ \frac{1}{\sqrt{6}} & -\frac{1}{\sqrt{3}} & -\frac{1}{\sqrt{2}} \\ \frac{2}{\sqrt{6}} & \frac{1}{\sqrt{3}} & 0 \end{pmatrix}$.

a Show that **P** is an orthogonal matrix.

The matrix $\mathbf{A} = \begin{pmatrix} \frac{3}{2} & -\frac{3}{2} & 1 \\ -\frac{3}{2} & \frac{3}{2} & 1 \\ 1 & 1 & 1 \end{pmatrix}$.

b Show that $\mathbf{P}^\mathrm{T}\mathbf{AP}$ is a diagonal matrix.

4 The matrix $\mathbf{A} = \begin{pmatrix} 2 & 0 & 2 \\ 0 & 2 & 0 \\ 2 & 0 & 2 \end{pmatrix}$. Reduce **A** to a diagonal matrix.

5 The matrix $\mathbf{A} = \begin{pmatrix} 5 & 3 & 3 \\ 3 & 1 & 1 \\ 3 & 1 & 1 \end{pmatrix}$.

The eigenvalues of **A** are 0, −1 and 8.

a Find a normalised eigenvector corresponding to the eigenvalue 0.

Given that $\begin{pmatrix} -1 \\ 1 \\ 1 \end{pmatrix}$ is an eigenvector of **A** corresponding to the eigenvalue −1 and that $\begin{pmatrix} 2 \\ 1 \\ 1 \end{pmatrix}$ is an eigenvector of **A** corresponding to the eigenvalue 8,

b find a matrix **P** and a diagonal matrix **D** such that $\mathbf{P}^{-1}\mathbf{AP} = \mathbf{D}$.

6 The matrix $\mathbf{A} = \begin{pmatrix} 7 & 0 & 2 \\ 0 & 5 & -2 \\ -2 & -2 & 6 \end{pmatrix}$.

a Given that 9 is an eigenvalue of **A**, find the other two eigenvalues of **A**.

b Find eigenvectors of **A** corresponding to each of the three eigenvalues of **A**.

c Find a matrix **P** and a diagonal matrix **D** such that $\mathbf{P}^\mathrm{T}\mathbf{AP} = \mathbf{D}$.

7 The matrix $\mathbf{A} = \begin{pmatrix} 1 & 2 & 0 \\ 2 & 1 & \sqrt{5} \\ 0 & \sqrt{5} & 1 \end{pmatrix}$.

a Show that 4 is an eigenvalue of **A** and find the other two eigenvalues of **A**.

b Find a normalised eigenvector of **A** corresponding to the eigenvalue 4.

Given that $\begin{pmatrix} -2 \\ 3 \\ -\sqrt{5} \end{pmatrix}$ and $\begin{pmatrix} \sqrt{5} \\ 0 \\ -2 \end{pmatrix}$ are eigenvectors of **A**,

c find a matrix **P** and a diagonal matrix **D** such that $\mathbf{P}^{-1}\mathbf{AP} = \mathbf{D}$.

8 The eigenvalues of the matrix

$$\mathbf{A} = \begin{pmatrix} 2 & 2 & -3 \\ 2 & 2 & 3 \\ -3 & 3 & 3 \end{pmatrix}$$

are λ_1, λ_2, λ_3, where $\lambda_1 > \lambda_2 > \lambda_3$.

a Show that $\lambda_1 = 6$ and find the other two eigenvalues λ_2 and λ_3.

b Verify that $\det(\mathbf{A}) = \lambda_1\lambda_2\lambda_3$.

c Find an eigenvector corresponding to the value $\lambda_1 = 6$.

Given that $\begin{pmatrix} 1 \\ 1 \\ 0 \end{pmatrix}$ and $\begin{pmatrix} 1 \\ -1 \\ 1 \end{pmatrix}$ are eigenvectors corresponding to λ_2 and λ_3 respectively,

d write down a matrix **P** such that $\mathbf{P}^{\mathrm{T}}\mathbf{AP}$ is a diagonal matrix. E

Mixed exercise 6H

1 $\mathbf{A} = \begin{pmatrix} 1 & 0 & 2 \\ t & 3 & 1 \\ -2 & -1 & 1 \end{pmatrix}$

Given that **A** is singular, find the value of t. E

2 $\mathbf{M} = \begin{pmatrix} 1 & 0 & 0 \\ x & 2 & 0 \\ 3 & 1 & 1 \end{pmatrix}$

Find $\mathbf{M}^{-1}$ in terms of x. E

3 The matrix **M** has eigenvalues $\lambda_1 = 5$ and $\lambda_2 = -15$ and $\mathbf{M} = \begin{pmatrix} 1 & 8 \\ 8 & -11 \end{pmatrix}$.

a For each eigenvalue, find a corresponding eigenvector.

b Find a matrix **P** such that $\mathbf{P}^{\mathrm{T}}\mathbf{AP} = \begin{pmatrix} 5 & 0 \\ 0 & -15 \end{pmatrix}$. E

4 The matrix $\mathbf{A} = \begin{pmatrix} 5 & 2 \\ 2 & 1 \end{pmatrix}$ and the matrix $\mathbf{B} = \begin{pmatrix} 2 & -1 \\ -4 & 2 \end{pmatrix}$.

a Find $\mathbf{AB}$.

b Verify that $\mathbf{B}^{\mathrm{T}}\mathbf{A}^{\mathrm{T}} = (\mathbf{AB})^{\mathrm{T}}$.

5 A transformation $T: \mathbb{R}^2 \to \mathbb{R}^2$ is represented by the matrix

$$\mathbf{A} = \begin{pmatrix} -5 & 8 \\ 3 & -7 \end{pmatrix}.$$

a Find the eigenvalues of $\mathbf{A}$.

b Find Cartesian equations of the two lines passing through the origin which are invariant under T.

6 Given that 1 is an eigenvalue of the matrix

$$\begin{pmatrix} 3 & 1 & 0 \\ 2 & 4 & 0 \\ 1 & 0 & 1 \end{pmatrix},$$

a find a corresponding eigenvector,

b find the other eigenvalues of the matrix.

7 The transformation $T: \mathbb{R}^3 \to \mathbb{R}^3$ is represented by the matrix $\mathbf{T}$ where $\mathbf{T} = \begin{pmatrix} 4 & 3 & 0 \\ 0 & -2 & 1 \\ 3 & 1 & -2 \end{pmatrix}$.

The line l_1 is transformed by T to the line l_2. The line l_1 has vector equation

$\mathbf{r} = \begin{pmatrix} 1 \\ 0 \\ 2 \end{pmatrix} + t\begin{pmatrix} 2 \\ -3 \\ 0 \end{pmatrix}$, where t is a real parameter.

Find Cartesian equations of l_2.

8 $\mathbf{A} = \begin{pmatrix} 3 & 4 & -4 \\ 4 & 5 & 0 \\ -4 & 0 & 1 \end{pmatrix}$

a Show that 3 is an eigenvalue of $\mathbf{A}$ and find the other two eigenvalues.

b Find an eigenvector corresponding to the eigenvalue 3.

Given that the vectors $\begin{pmatrix} 2 \\ 2 \\ -1 \end{pmatrix}$ and $\begin{pmatrix} 2 \\ -1 \\ 2 \end{pmatrix}$ are eigenvectors corresponding to the other two eigenvalues,

c find a matrix $\mathbf{P}$ such that $\mathbf{P}^{\mathrm{T}}\mathbf{AP}$ is a diagonal matrix.

9 $\mathbf{A} = \begin{pmatrix} 2 & -2 & 0 \\ -2 & 1 & 2 \\ 0 & 2 & 5 \end{pmatrix}$

a Show that $\begin{pmatrix} 2 \\ 3 \\ -1 \end{pmatrix}$ and $\begin{pmatrix} 2 \\ -1 \\ 1 \end{pmatrix}$ are eigenvectors of $\mathbf{A}$, giving their corresponding eigenvalues.

b Given that 6 is the third eigenvalue of **A**, find a corresponding eigenvector.

c Hence write down a matrix such that $\mathbf{P}^{-1}\mathbf{AP}$ is a diagonal matrix. *E*

10 **a** Calculate the inverse of the matrix

$$\mathbf{A}(x) = \begin{pmatrix} 1 & x & -1 \\ 3 & 0 & 2 \\ 1 & 1 & 0 \end{pmatrix}, x \neq \tfrac{5}{2}.$$

The image of the vector $\begin{pmatrix} a \\ b \\ c \end{pmatrix}$ when it is transformed by the matrix $\begin{pmatrix} 1 & 3 & -1 \\ 3 & 0 & 2 \\ 1 & 1 & 0 \end{pmatrix}$ is the vector $\begin{pmatrix} 4 \\ 3 \\ 5 \end{pmatrix}$.

b Find the values of a, b and c. *E*

11 **a** Show that for all values of the constant α, an eigenvalue of the matrix **A** is 1, where

$$\mathbf{A} = \begin{pmatrix} \alpha & 0 & 2 \\ 4 & 3 & 0 \\ -2 & -1 & 1 \end{pmatrix}.$$

An eigenvector of the matrix **A** is $\begin{pmatrix} 2 \\ -2 \\ 1 \end{pmatrix}$ and the corresponding eigenvalue is β ($\beta \neq 1$).

b Find the value of α and the value of β.

c For your value of α, find the third eigenvalue of **A**. *E*

12 The matrix **A** is defined by $\mathbf{A} = \begin{pmatrix} 1 & -1 & 3 \\ 2 & 1 & u \\ 0 & 1 & 1 \end{pmatrix}$.

a Find $\mathbf{A}^{-1}$ in terms of u, stating the condition for which **A** is non-singular.

The image vector of $\begin{pmatrix} a \\ b \\ c \end{pmatrix}$ when transformed by the matrix $\mathbf{A} = \begin{pmatrix} 1 & -1 & 3 \\ 2 & 1 & 4 \\ 0 & 1 & 1 \end{pmatrix}$ is $\begin{pmatrix} -2.8 \\ 5.3 \\ 2.3 \end{pmatrix}$.

b Find the values of a, b and c. *E*

13 $$\mathbf{M} = \begin{pmatrix} 3 & 0 & 0 \\ 1 & 1 & 1 \\ 4 & -1 & 3 \end{pmatrix}$$

a Show that the matrix **M** has only two distinct eigenvalues.

b Find an eigenvector corresponding to each of these eigenvalues. *E*

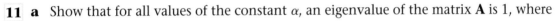

14 The matrix $\mathbf{P} = \begin{pmatrix} \frac{1}{2} & -\frac{1}{2} & \frac{1}{\sqrt{2}} \\ \frac{1}{2} & -\frac{1}{2} & -\frac{1}{\sqrt{2}} \\ \frac{1}{\sqrt{2}} & \frac{1}{\sqrt{2}} & 0 \end{pmatrix}$.

a Show that the matrix **P** is orthogonal.

The transformation $P: \mathbb{R}^3 \rightarrow \mathbb{R}^3$ is represented by the matrix **P**.

The plane Π_1 is transformed by A to the plane Π_2. The plane Π_2 has Cartesian equation $x + y - \sqrt{2}z = 0$.

b Find a Cartesian equation of the plane Π_1.

15 **a** Determine the eigenvalues of the matrix

$$\mathbf{A} = \begin{pmatrix} 3 & -3 & 6 \\ 0 & 2 & -8 \\ 0 & 0 & -2 \end{pmatrix}$$

b Show that $\begin{pmatrix} 3 \\ 1 \\ 0 \end{pmatrix}$ is an eigenvector of **A**.

$$\mathbf{B} = \begin{pmatrix} 7 & -6 & 2 \\ 1 & 2 & 3 \\ 1 & -3 & 2 \end{pmatrix}$$

c Show that $\begin{pmatrix} 3 \\ 1 \\ 0 \end{pmatrix}$ is an eigenvector of **B** and write down the corresponding eigenvalue.

d Hence, or otherwise, write down an eigenvector of the matrix **AB**, and state the corresponding eigenvalue.

E

16 $$\mathbf{A} = \begin{pmatrix} 1 & 0 & 1 \\ 3 & 1 & 1 \\ 4 & 2 & 7 \end{pmatrix}$$

a Showing your working, find $\mathbf{A}^{-1}$.

The transformation $T: \mathbb{R}^3 \rightarrow \mathbb{R}^3$ is represented by the matrix **A**.

b Find Cartesian equations of the line which is mapped by T onto the line

$$x = \frac{y}{4} = \frac{z}{3}.$$

E

Summary of key points

1 The **transpose** of a matrix, $\mathbf{A}^{\mathrm{T}}$**,** is obtained by interchanging the rows and columns of the matrix **A**.

2 If $\mathbf{A} = \mathbf{A}^{\mathrm{T}}$, the matrix **A** is **symmetric.**

3 The identity 3 × 3 matrix is $\mathbf{I} = \begin{pmatrix} 1 & 0 & 0 \\ 0 & 1 & 0 \\ 0 & 0 & 1 \end{pmatrix}$.

4 The zero 3 × 3 matrix is $\mathbf{0} = \begin{pmatrix} 0 & 0 & 0 \\ 0 & 0 & 0 \\ 0 & 0 & 0 \end{pmatrix}$.

5 If **A** and **B** are matrices with dimensions $n \times m$ and $m \times p$, then $(\mathbf{AB})^{\mathrm{T}} = \mathbf{B}^{\mathrm{T}}\mathbf{A}^{\mathrm{T}}$.

6 $\begin{vmatrix} a & b & c \\ d & e & f \\ g & h & i \end{vmatrix} = a\begin{vmatrix} e & f \\ h & i \end{vmatrix} - b\begin{vmatrix} d & f \\ g & i \end{vmatrix} + c\begin{vmatrix} d & e \\ g & h \end{vmatrix}$.

7 If $\det(\mathbf{A}) = 0$,then **A** is a **singular** matrix.
If $\det(\mathbf{A}) \neq 0$, then **A** is a **non-singular** matrix.

8 If the matrix **A** is non-singular then it has an inverse $\mathbf{A}^{-1}$ and $\mathbf{AA}^{-1} = \mathbf{A}^{-1}\mathbf{A} = \mathbf{I}$.

9 The **minor** of an element of a 3 × 3 matrix is the determinant of the elements which remain when the row and the column containing the element are crossed out.

10 To find the inverse of a non-singular 3 × 3 matrix **A**:

1 Find the determinant of **A**, det (**A**).

2 Form **M**, the matrix of the minors of **A**.

3 Form **C**, the matrix of cofactors, by changing the signs of some elements of **M** according to the rule of alternating signs.

4 Write down the transpose, $\mathbf{C}^{\mathrm{T}}$, of the matrix of cofactors.

5 The inverse of the matrix **A** is given by the formula $\mathbf{A}^{-1} = \dfrac{1}{\det(\mathbf{A})}\mathbf{C}^{\mathrm{T}}$.

11 If **A** and **B** are non-singular matrices then $(\mathbf{AB})^{-1} = \mathbf{B}^{-1}\mathbf{A}^{-1}$.

12 If the transformation T is represented by the matrix **T** and the transformation U is represented by the matrix **U**, then the matrix **UT** represents the combined transformation of the transformation T followed by the transformation U.

13 An **eigenvector** of a matrix **A** is a non-zero column vector **x** which satisfies the equation $\mathbf{Ax} = \lambda\mathbf{x}$, where λ is a scalar which is the corresponding **eigenvalue** of the matrix.

14 The equation det $(\mathbf{A} - \lambda\mathbf{I}) = 0$ is the **characteristic equation** of **A**. You solve this equation of a matrix to find the eigenvalues of the matrix.

15 If $\begin{pmatrix} a \\ b \\ c \end{pmatrix}$ is an eigenvector of a matrix, then $\begin{pmatrix} \frac{a}{\sqrt{(a^2+b^2+c^2)}} \\ \frac{b}{\sqrt{(a^2+b^2+c^2)}} \\ \frac{c}{\sqrt{(a^2+b^2+c^2)}} \end{pmatrix}$ is the corresponding **normalised eigenvector**.

16 If **M** is a square matrix such that $\mathbf{MM}^{\mathrm{T}} = \mathbf{I}$, then **M** is called an **orthogonal matrix**.

17 If **M** is an orthogonal matrix, then $\mathbf{M}^{-1} = \mathbf{M}^{\mathrm{T}}$.

18 Two eigenvectors $\mathbf{x}_1$ and $\mathbf{x}_2$ are **orthogonal** if their scalar product $\mathbf{x}_1.\mathbf{x}_2 = 0$.

19 If **M** is an orthogonal matrix consisting of the normalised column vectors $\mathbf{x}_1$, $\mathbf{x}_2$ and $\mathbf{x}_3$, then $\mathbf{x}_1.\mathbf{x}_2 = \mathbf{x}_2.\mathbf{x}_3 = \mathbf{x}_3.\mathbf{x}_1 = 0$.

20 A **diagonal matrix** is a square matrix in which all of the elements which are not on the diagonal from the top left to the bottom right of the matrix are zero. $\begin{pmatrix} a & 0 \\ 0 & b \end{pmatrix}$ and $\begin{pmatrix} d & 0 & 0 \\ 0 & e & 0 \\ 0 & 0 & f \end{pmatrix}$ are diagonal matrices.

21 To reduce a symmetric matrix **A** to a diagonal matrix **D**:

1 Find normalised eigenvectors of **A**.

2 Form an orthogonal matrix **P** with columns consisting of the normalised eigenvectors of **A**.

3 Write down $\mathbf{P}^{\mathrm{T}}$, the transpose of the matrix **P**.

4 The diagonal matrix **D** is given by $\mathbf{P}^{\mathrm{T}}\mathbf{AP} = \mathbf{D}$.

22 When symmetric matrix **A** is reduced to a diagonal matrix **D**, the elements on the diagonal are the eigenvalues of **A**.

Review Exercise

1 Find the magnitude of the vector

$$(-\mathbf{i} - \mathbf{j} + \mathbf{k}) \times (-\mathbf{i} + \mathbf{j} - \mathbf{k}).$$ E

2 Given that $\mathbf{p} = 3\mathbf{i} + \mathbf{k}$ and $\mathbf{q} = \mathbf{i} + 3\mathbf{j} + c\mathbf{k}$, find the value of the constant c for which the vector $(\mathbf{p} \times \mathbf{q}) + \mathbf{p}$ is parallel to the vector $\mathbf{k}$. E

3 Referred to a fixed origin O, the position vectors of three non-linear points A, B and C are $\mathbf{a}$, $\mathbf{b}$ and $\mathbf{c}$ respectively. By considering $\overrightarrow{AB} \times \overrightarrow{AC}$, prove that the area of $\triangle ABC$ can be expressed in the form $\frac{1}{2}|\mathbf{a} \times \mathbf{b} + \mathbf{b} \times \mathbf{c} + \mathbf{c} \times \mathbf{a}|$. E

4 The figure shows a right prism with triangular ends ABC and DEF, and parallel edges AD, BE, CF.

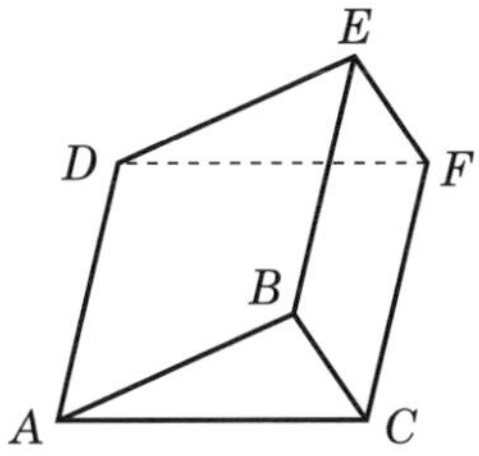

Given that

A is $(2, 7, -1)$, B is $(5, 8, 2)$, C is $(6, 7, 4)$ and D is $(12, 1, -9)$,

a find $\overrightarrow{AB} \times \overrightarrow{AC}$,

b find $\overrightarrow{AD}.(\overrightarrow{AB} \times \overrightarrow{AC})$.

c Calculate the volume of the prism. E

5 The plane Π_1 has vector equation
$\mathbf{r} = (5\mathbf{i} + \mathbf{j}) + u(-4\mathbf{i} + \mathbf{j} + 3\mathbf{k}) + v(\mathbf{j} + 2\mathbf{k})$,
where u and v are parameters.

a Find a vector $\mathbf{n}_1$ normal to Π_1.

The plane Π_2 has equation $3x + y - z = 3$.

b Write down a vector $\mathbf{n}_2$ normal to Π_2.

c Show that $4\mathbf{i} + 13\mathbf{j} + 25\mathbf{k}$ is perpendicular to both $\mathbf{n}_1$ and $\mathbf{n}_2$.

Given that the point $(1, 1, 1)$ lies on both Π_1 and Π_2,

d write down an equation of the line of intersection of Π_1 and Π_2 in the form $\mathbf{r} = \mathbf{a} + t\mathbf{b}$, where t is a parameter. E

6 The points A, B and C lie on the plane Π and, relative to a fixed origin O, they have position vectors

$\mathbf{a} = 3\mathbf{i} - \mathbf{j} + 4\mathbf{k}$, $\mathbf{b} = -\mathbf{i} + 2\mathbf{j}$,
$\mathbf{c} = 5\mathbf{i} - 3\mathbf{j} + 7\mathbf{k}$

respectively.

a Find $\overrightarrow{AB} \times \overrightarrow{AC}$.

b Obtain the equation of Π in the form $\mathbf{r.n} = p$.

The point D has position vector $5\mathbf{i} + 2\mathbf{j} + 3\mathbf{k}$.

c Calculate the volume of the tetrahedron $ABCD$. E

7 The points A and B have position vectors $4\mathbf{i} + \mathbf{j} - 7\mathbf{k}$ and $2\mathbf{i} + 6\mathbf{j} + 2\mathbf{k}$ respectively relative to a fixed origin O.

a Show that angle AOB is a right angle.

b Find a vector equation for the median AM of the triangle OAB.

c Find a vector equation of the plane OAB, giving your answer in the form $\mathbf{r.n} = p$. **E**

8 Referred to a fixed origin O, the point A has position vector $a(4\mathbf{i} + \mathbf{j} + 2\mathbf{k})$ and the plane Π has equation

$\mathbf{r}.(\mathbf{i} - 5\mathbf{j} + 3\mathbf{k}) = 5a$,

where a is a scalar constant.

a Show that A lies in the plane Π.

The point B has position vector $a(2\mathbf{i} + 11\mathbf{j} - 4\mathbf{k})$.

b Show that $\overrightarrow{BA}$ is perpendicular to the plane Π.

c Calculate, to the nearest one tenth of a degree, $\angle OBA$. **E**

9 The points A, B, C and D have coordinates $(3, 1, 2)$, $(5, 2, -1)$, $(6, 4, 5)$ and $(-7, 6, -3)$ respectively.

a Find $\overrightarrow{AC} \times \overrightarrow{AD}$.

b Find a vector equation of the line through A which is perpendicular to $\overrightarrow{AC}$ and $\overrightarrow{AD}$.

c Verify that B lies on this line.

d Find the volume of the tetrahedron $ABCD$. **E**

10 The line l_1 has equation

$$\mathbf{r} = \mathbf{i} + 6\mathbf{j} - \mathbf{k} + \lambda(2\mathbf{i} + 3\mathbf{k})$$

and the line l_2 has equation

$$\mathbf{r} = 3\mathbf{i} + p\mathbf{j} + \mu(\mathbf{i} - 2\mathbf{j} + \mathbf{k}),$$

where p is a constant.

The plane Π_1 contains l_1 and l_2.

a Find a vector which is normal to Π_1.

b Show that an equation for Π_1 is $6x + y - 4z = 16$.

c Find the value of p.

The plane Π_2 has equation $\mathbf{r}.(\mathbf{i} + 2\mathbf{j} + \mathbf{k}) = 2$.

d Find an equation for the line of intersection of Π_1 and Π_2, giving your answer in the form

$(\mathbf{r} - \mathbf{a}) \times \mathbf{b} = \mathbf{0}$. **E**

11 The plane Π passes through the points $A(-2, 3, 5)$, $B(1, -3, 1)$ and $C(4, -6, -7)$.

a Find $\overrightarrow{AC} \times \overrightarrow{BC}$.

b Hence, or otherwise, find the equation of the plane Π in the form $\mathbf{r.n} = p$.

The perpendicular from the point $(25, 5, 7)$ to Π meets the plane at the point F.

c Find the coordinates of F. **E**

12 The plane Π passes through the points $P(-1, 3, -2)$, $Q(4, -1, -1)$ and $R(3, 0, c)$, where c is a constant.

a Find, in terms of c, $\overrightarrow{RP} \times \overrightarrow{RQ}$.

Given that $\overrightarrow{RP} \times \overrightarrow{RQ} = 3\mathbf{i} + d\mathbf{j} + \mathbf{k}$, where d is a constant,

b find the value of c and show that $d = 4$.

c Find an equation of Π in the form $\mathbf{r.n} = p$, where p is a constant.

The point S has position vector $\mathbf{i} + 5\mathbf{j} + 10\mathbf{k}$. The point S' is the image of S under reflection in Π.

d Find the position vector of S'. **E**

13 The points A, B and C lie on the plane Π_1 and, relative to a fixed origin O, they have position vectors

$$\mathbf{a} = \mathbf{i} + 3\mathbf{j} - \mathbf{k},\ \mathbf{b} = 3\mathbf{i} + 3\mathbf{j} - 4\mathbf{k},$$
$$\mathbf{c} = 5\mathbf{i} - 2\mathbf{j} - 2\mathbf{k}$$

respectively.

a Find $(\mathbf{b} - \mathbf{a}) \times (\mathbf{c} - \mathbf{a})$.

b Find an equation of Π_1, giving your answer in the form $\mathbf{r.n} = p$.

The plane Π_2 has Cartesian equation $x + z = 3$ and Π_1 and Π_2 intersect in the line l.

c Find an equation of l in the form $(\mathbf{r} - \mathbf{p}) \times \mathbf{q} = \mathbf{0}$.

The point P is the point on l that is nearest to the origin O.

d Find the coordinates of P. *E*

14 The points $A(2, 0, -1)$ and $B(4, 3, 1)$ have position vectors $\mathbf{a}$ and $\mathbf{b}$ respectively with respect to a fixed origin O.

a Find $\mathbf{a} \times \mathbf{b}$.

The plane Π_1 contains the points O, A and B.

b Verify that an equation of Π_1 is $x - 2y + 2z = 0$.

The plane Π_2 has equation $\mathbf{r}.\mathbf{n} = d$ where $\mathbf{n} = 3\mathbf{i} + \mathbf{j} - \mathbf{k}$ and d is a constant. Given that B lies on Π_2,

c find the value of d.

The planes Π_1 and Π_2 intersect in the line L.

d Find an equation of L in the form $\mathbf{r} = \mathbf{p} + t\mathbf{q}$, where t is a parameter.

e Find the position vector of the point X on L where OX is perpendicular to L. *E*

15 The points A, B and C have position vectors, relative to a fixed origin O,

$$\mathbf{a} = 2\mathbf{i} - \mathbf{j},\ \mathbf{b} = \mathbf{i} + 2\mathbf{j} + 3\mathbf{k},$$
$$\mathbf{c} = 2\mathbf{i} + 3\mathbf{j} + 2\mathbf{k},$$

respectively. The plane Π passes through A, B and C.

a Find $\overrightarrow{AB} \times \overrightarrow{AC}$.

b Show that a Cartesian equation of Π is $3x - y + 2z = 7$.

The line l has equation $(\mathbf{r} - 5\mathbf{i} - 5\mathbf{j} - 3\mathbf{k}) \times (2\mathbf{i} - \mathbf{j} - 2\mathbf{k}) = \mathbf{0}$. The line l and the plane Π intersect at the point T.

c Find the coordinates of T.

d Show that A, B and T lie on the same straight line. *E*

16 The plane Π passes through the points $A(-1, -1, 1)$, $B(4, 2, 1)$ and $C(2, 1, 0)$.

a Find a vector equation of the line perpendicular to Π which passes through the point $D(1, 2, 3)$.

b Find the volume of the tetrahedron $ABCD$.

c Obtain the equation of Π in the form $\mathbf{r}.\mathbf{n} = p$.

The perpendicular from D to the plane Π meets Π at the point E.

d Find the coordinates of E.

e Show that $DE = \dfrac{11\sqrt{35}}{35}$.

The point D' is the reflection of D in Π.

f Find the coordinates of D'. *E*

17 The points A, B and C have position vectors $(\mathbf{j} + 2\mathbf{k})$, $(2\mathbf{i} + 3\mathbf{j} + \mathbf{k})$ and $(\mathbf{i} + \mathbf{j} + 3\mathbf{k})$, respectively, relative to the origin O. The plane Π contains the points A, B and C.

a Find a vector which is perpendicular to Π.

b Find the area of $\triangle ABC$.

c Find a vector equation of Π in the form $\mathbf{r}.\mathbf{n} = p$.

d Hence, or otherwise, obtain a Cartesian equation of Π.

e Find the distance of the origin O from Π.

The point D has position vector $(3\mathbf{i} + 4\mathbf{j} + \mathbf{k})$. The distance of D from Π is $\dfrac{1}{\sqrt{17}}$.

f Using this distance, or otherwise, calculate the acute angle between the line AD and Π, giving your answer in degrees to one decimal place. *E*

18 Relative to a fixed origin O the lines l_1 and l_2 have equations

$$l_1 : \mathbf{r} = -\mathbf{i} + 2\mathbf{j} - 4\mathbf{k} + s(-2\mathbf{i} + \mathbf{j} + 3\mathbf{k}),$$
$$l_2 : \mathbf{r} = -\mathbf{j} + 7\mathbf{k} + t(-\mathbf{i} + \mathbf{j} - \mathbf{k}),$$

where s and t are variable parameters.

a Show that the lines intersect and are perpendicular to each other.

b Find a vector equation of the straight line l_3 which passes through the point of intersection of l_1 and l_2 and the point with position vector $4\mathbf{i} + \lambda\mathbf{j} - 3\mathbf{k}$, where λ is a real number.

The line l_3 makes an angle θ with the plane containing l_1 and l_2.

c Find $\sin\theta$ in terms of λ.

Given that l_1, l_2 and l_3 are coplanar,

d find the value of λ. **E**

19 Referred to a fixed origin O, the planes Π_1 and Π_2 have equations $\mathbf{r}.(2\mathbf{i} - \mathbf{j} + 2\mathbf{k}) = 9$ and $\mathbf{r}.(4\mathbf{i} + 3\mathbf{j} - \mathbf{k}) = 8$ respectively.

a Determine the shortest distance from O to the line of intersection of Π_1 and Π_2.

b Find, in vector form, an equation of the plane Π_3 which is perpendicular to Π_1 and Π_2 and passes through the point with position vector $2\mathbf{j} + \mathbf{k}$.

c Find the position vector of the point that lies in Π_1, Π_2 and Π_3. **E**

20 Vector equations of the two straight lines l and m are respectively

$$\mathbf{r} = \mathbf{j} + 3\mathbf{k} + t(2\mathbf{i} + \mathbf{j} - \mathbf{k}),$$
$$\mathbf{r} = \mathbf{i} + \mathbf{j} - \mathbf{k} + u(-2\mathbf{i} + \mathbf{j} + \mathbf{k}).$$

a Show that these lines do not intersect.

The point A with parameter t_1 lies on l and the point B with parameter u_1 lies on m.

b Write down the vector $\overrightarrow{AB}$ in terms of $\mathbf{i}$, $\mathbf{j}$, $\mathbf{k}$, t_1 and u_1.

Given that the line AB is perpendicular to both l and m,

c find the values of t_1 and u_1 and show that, in this case, the length of AB is $\frac{7}{\sqrt{5}}$. **E**

21 $$\mathbf{A} = \begin{pmatrix} 1 & 1 & 2 \\ 0 & 1 & 1 \\ 0 & 0 & 1 \end{pmatrix}$$

Prove by induction, that for all positive integers n,

$$\mathbf{A}^n = \begin{pmatrix} 1 & n & \frac{1}{2}(n^2 + 3n) \\ 0 & 1 & n \\ 0 & 0 & 1 \end{pmatrix}.$$ **E**

22 $$\mathbf{A} = \begin{pmatrix} k & 1 & -2 \\ 0 & -1 & k \\ 9 & 1 & 0 \end{pmatrix},$$

where k is a real constant.

a Find the values of k for which $\mathbf{A}$ is singular.

Given that $\mathbf{A}$ is non-singular,

b find, in terms of k, $\mathbf{A}^{-1}$. **E**

23 The matrix $\mathbf{M}$ is given by

$$\mathbf{M} = \begin{pmatrix} 1 & 4 & -1 \\ 3 & 0 & p \\ a & b & c \end{pmatrix},$$

where p, a, b and c are constants and $a > 0$.

Given that $\mathbf{MM}^{\mathrm{T}} = k\mathbf{I}$ for some constant k, find

a the value of p,

b the value of k,

c the values of a, b and c,

d $\det\mathbf{M}$. **E**

24 **a** Given that $\mathbf{A} = \begin{pmatrix} 1 & 1 & 2 \\ 0 & 2 & 1 \\ 1 & 0 & 2 \end{pmatrix}$, find $\mathbf{A}^2$.

b Using $\mathbf{A}^3 = \begin{pmatrix} 10 & 9 & 23 \\ 5 & 9 & 14 \\ 9 & 5 & 19 \end{pmatrix}$, show that

$$\mathbf{A}^3 - 5\mathbf{A}^2 + 6\mathbf{A} - \mathbf{I} = \mathbf{0}.$$

c Deduce that $\mathbf{A}(\mathbf{A} - 2\mathbf{I})(\mathbf{A} - 3\mathbf{I}) = \mathbf{I}$.

d Hence find $\mathbf{A}^{-1}$. **E**

25 Given that $\mathbf{A} = \begin{pmatrix} 1 & 0 & 0 \\ 0 & 2 & 1 \\ 0 & 0 & 1 \end{pmatrix}$, use matrix multiplication to find

a $\mathbf{A}^2$,

b $\mathbf{A}^3$.

c Prove by induction that

$$\mathbf{A}^n = \begin{pmatrix} 1 & 0 & 0 \\ 0 & 2^n & 2^n - 1 \\ 0 & 0 & 1 \end{pmatrix}, n \geqslant 1.$$

d Find the inverse of $\mathbf{A}^n$. **E**

26 $$\mathbf{A} = \begin{pmatrix} 3 & 1 & -1 \\ 1 & 1 & 1 \\ 5 & 3 & u \end{pmatrix}, u \neq 1$$

a Show that $\det \mathbf{A} = 2(u - 1)$.

b Find the inverse of $\mathbf{A}$.

The image of the vector $\begin{pmatrix} a \\ b \\ c \end{pmatrix}$ when transformed by the matrix $\begin{pmatrix} 3 & 1 & -1 \\ 1 & 1 & 1 \\ 5 & 3 & 6 \end{pmatrix}$ is $\begin{pmatrix} 3 \\ 1 \\ 6 \end{pmatrix}$.

c Find the values of a, b and c. **E**

27 The transformation R is represented by the matrix $\mathbf{M}$, where

$$\mathbf{M} = \begin{pmatrix} 3 & a & 0 \\ 2 & b & 0 \\ c & 0 & 1 \end{pmatrix},$$

and where a, b and c are constants.

Given that $\mathbf{M} = \mathbf{M}^{-1}$,

a find the values of a, b and c,

b evaluate the determinant of $\mathbf{M}$,

c find an equation satisfied by all the points which remain invariant under R. **E**

28 The transformation $T: \mathbb{R}^3 \to \mathbb{R}^3$ is represented by the matrix $\mathbf{M}$.

The vector $\begin{pmatrix} 2 \\ -1 \\ 0 \end{pmatrix}$ is transformed by T to $\begin{pmatrix} -5 \\ -1 \\ 0 \end{pmatrix}$, the vector $\begin{pmatrix} 0 \\ -1 \\ 2 \end{pmatrix}$ is transformed to $\begin{pmatrix} -1 \\ 9 \\ 0 \end{pmatrix}$ and the vector $\begin{pmatrix} \alpha \\ 0 \\ 1 \end{pmatrix}$ is transformed to $\begin{pmatrix} -\alpha + 1 \\ 5 \\ 2\alpha + 2 \end{pmatrix}$, where α ($\alpha \neq -1$) is a constant.

a Find $\mathbf{M}$.

The plane Π_1 has equation

$$\mathbf{r} = \begin{pmatrix} 3 \\ 0 \\ 1 \end{pmatrix} + \lambda \begin{pmatrix} 2 \\ -1 \\ 0 \end{pmatrix} + \mu \begin{pmatrix} 0 \\ -1 \\ 2 \end{pmatrix},$$

where λ and μ are parameters, and T transforms Π_1 to the plane Π_2.

b Find a Cartesian equation of Π_2. **E**

29 The transformation $S: \mathbb{R}^3 \to \mathbb{R}^3$ maps the point $\begin{pmatrix} x \\ y \\ z \end{pmatrix}$ onto the point $\begin{pmatrix} a \\ b \\ c \end{pmatrix}$ where

$$\begin{aligned} a &= x + y - z \\ b &= \quad\;\; y + z \\ c &= \qquad\quad z, \end{aligned}$$

The matrix of this transformation is $\mathbf{A}$.

a By solving the given equations for x, y and z in terms of a, b and c, or otherwise, write down the matrix $\mathbf{A}^{-1}$.

The transformation $T: \mathbb{R}^3 \to \mathbb{R}^3$ has matrix

$$\mathbf{B} = \begin{pmatrix} 1 & -2 & 2 \\ 2 & -1 & -2 \\ 2 & 2 & 1 \end{pmatrix}$$

b Given that $\mathbf{BB}^{\mathrm{T}} = k\mathbf{I}$, find the value of k.

U is the composite transformation consisting of T followed by S.

c Find the point whose image under U is $\begin{pmatrix} 1 \\ 0 \\ 1 \end{pmatrix}$. **E**

30 $\mathbf{M} = \begin{pmatrix} 4 & -5 \\ 6 & -9 \end{pmatrix}$

a Find the eigenvalues of **M**.

A transformation $T : \mathbb{R}^2 \to \mathbb{R}^2$ is represented by the matrix **M**. There is a line through the origin for which every point on the line is mapped onto itself under T.

b Find the Cartesian equation of this line. *E*

31 A transformation $T : \mathbb{R}^2 \to \mathbb{R}^2$ is represented by the matrix

$\mathbf{A} = \begin{pmatrix} k & 2 \\ 6 & -1 \end{pmatrix}$, where k is a constant.

For the case $k = -4$,

a find the image under T of the line with equation $y = 2x + 1$.

For the case $k = 2$, find

b the two eigenvalues of **A**,

c a Cartesian equation of the two lines passing through the origin which are invariant under T. *E*

32 The eigenvalues of the matrix **M**, where

$\mathbf{M} = \begin{pmatrix} 4 & -2 \\ 1 & 1 \end{pmatrix}$,

are λ_1 and λ_2, where $\lambda_1 < \lambda_2$.

a Find the value of λ_1 and the value of λ_2.

b Find $\mathbf{M}^{-1}$.

c Verify that the eigenvalues of $\mathbf{M}^{-1}$ are λ_1^{-1} and λ_2^{-1}.

A transformation $T : \mathbb{R}^2 \to \mathbb{R}^2$ is represented by the matrix **M**. There are two lines, passing through the origin, each of which is mapped onto itself under the transformation T.

d Find Cartesian equations for each of these lines. *E*

33 Find the eigenvalues and corresponding eigenvectors for the matrix

$\begin{pmatrix} 2 & -3 & 1 \\ 3 & 1 & 3 \\ -5 & 2 & -4 \end{pmatrix}$ *E*

34 Given that $\begin{pmatrix} 0 \\ 1 \\ -1 \end{pmatrix}$ is an eigenvector of the matrix **A** where

$\mathbf{A} = \begin{pmatrix} 3 & 4 & p \\ -1 & q & -4 \\ 1 & 1 & 3 \end{pmatrix}$,

a find the eigenvalue of **A** corresponding to $\begin{pmatrix} 0 \\ 1 \\ -1 \end{pmatrix}$,

b find the value of p and the value of q.

The image of the vector $\begin{pmatrix} l \\ m \\ n \end{pmatrix}$ when transformed by **A** is $\begin{pmatrix} 10 \\ -4 \\ 3 \end{pmatrix}$.

c Using the values of p and q from part **b**, find the values of the constants l, m and n. *E*

35 $\mathbf{A} = \begin{pmatrix} 5 & 1 & -2 \\ -1 & 6 & 1 \\ 0 & 1 & 3 \end{pmatrix}$

a Show that 3 is an eigenvalue of **A**.

b Find the other two eigenvalues of **A**.

c Find also a normalised eigenvector corresponding to the eigenvalue 3. *E*

36 $\mathbf{A} = \begin{pmatrix} 3 & 2 & 4 \\ 2 & 0 & 2 \\ 4 & 2 & k \end{pmatrix}$

a Show that $\det \mathbf{A} = 20 - 4k$.

b Find $\mathbf{A}^{-1}$.

Given that $k = 3$ and that $\begin{pmatrix} 0 \\ 2 \\ -1 \end{pmatrix}$ is an eigenvector of **A**,

c find the corresponding eigenvalue.

Given that the only other distinct eigenvalue of **A** is 8,

d find a corresponding eigenvector. *E*

37 $\mathbf{A} = \begin{pmatrix} 1 & 0 & 4 \\ 0 & 5 & 4 \\ 4 & 4 & 3 \end{pmatrix}$

a Verify that $\begin{pmatrix} 2 \\ -2 \\ 1 \end{pmatrix}$ is an eigenvector of $\mathbf{A}$ and find the corresponding eigenvalue.

b Show that 9 is another eigenvalue of $\mathbf{A}$ and find the corresponding eigenvector.

c Given that the third eigenvector of $\mathbf{A}$ is $\begin{pmatrix} 2 \\ 1 \\ -2 \end{pmatrix}$, find a matrix $\mathbf{P}$ and a diagonal matrix $\mathbf{D}$ such that $\mathbf{P}^{\mathrm{T}}\mathbf{AP} = \mathbf{D}$. **E**

38 $\mathbf{A} = \begin{pmatrix} 6 & 2 & -3 \\ 2 & 0 & 0 \\ -3 & 0 & 2 \end{pmatrix}$

Given that $\lambda = -1$ and $\lambda = 8$ are two eigenvalues of $\mathbf{A}$,

a find the third eigenvalue of $\mathbf{A}$.

b Find the normalised eigenvector corresponding to the eigenvalue $\lambda = 8$.

Given that $\begin{pmatrix} \frac{1}{\sqrt{14}} \\ \frac{2}{\sqrt{14}} \\ \frac{3}{\sqrt{14}} \end{pmatrix}$ and $\begin{pmatrix} \frac{1}{\sqrt{6}} \\ \frac{-2}{\sqrt{6}} \\ \frac{1}{\sqrt{6}} \end{pmatrix}$ are normalised eigenvectors corresponding to the other two eigenvalues,

c find a matrix $\mathbf{P}$ such that $\mathbf{P}^{\mathrm{T}}\mathbf{AP}$ is a diagonal matrix.

d Find $\mathbf{P}^{\mathrm{T}}\mathbf{AP}$. **E**

39 $\mathbf{M} = \begin{pmatrix} 1 & 0 & 1 \\ 0 & 2 & 0 \\ 4 & 3 & 1 \end{pmatrix}$

a Find the eigenvalues and corresponding eigenvectors of $\mathbf{M}$.

The transformation $T : \mathbb{R}^3 \rightarrow \mathbb{R}^3$ is represented by the matrix $\mathbf{M}$.

b Find Cartesian equations of the image of the line

$$\frac{x}{2} = y = \frac{z}{-1}$$

under this transformation. **E**

40 **a** Show that 9 is an eigenvalue of the matrix $\begin{pmatrix} 6 & -2 & 2 \\ -2 & 5 & 0 \\ 2 & 0 & 7 \end{pmatrix}$.

b Find the other two eigenvalues of the matrix.

c Find also normalised eigenvectors $\mathbf{x}_1$, $\mathbf{x}_2$ and $\mathbf{x}_3$ corresponding to each of these eigenvalues.

d Verify that the matrix $\mathbf{P}$ with columns $\mathbf{x}_1$, $\mathbf{x}_2$ and $\mathbf{x}_3$ is an orthogonal matrix. **E**

Examination style paper

1 An ellipse E has a focus at (6, 0) and the corresponding directrix has equation $x = 12$, find

a the exact value of the eccentricity of E, (4)

b a Cartesian equation of E. (2)

(Total 6 marks)

2 $$\text{f}(x) = \frac{\cosh 2x}{\sqrt{1 + \sinh 2x}}, \; x > 0$$

Find the x-coordinate of the stationary point of f(x), giving your answer to 3 significant figures.

(Total 7 marks)

3 **a** Find $\displaystyle\int \frac{1 + 6x}{\sqrt{1 - 9x^2}}\,\text{d}x$ (5)

b Find the exact value of $\displaystyle\int_0^{\frac{1}{6}} \frac{1 + 6x}{\sqrt{1 - 9x^2}}\,\text{d}x$ (3)

(Total 8 marks)

4 $$I_n = \int x^n \text{e}^{3x}\,\text{d}x, \; n \geqslant 0$$

a Prove that, for $n \geqslant 1$,

$$I_n = \tfrac{1}{3}(x^n \text{e}^{3x} - nI_{n-1})$$ (3)

b Find, in terms of e, the exact value of

$$\int_0^2 x^3 \text{e}^{3x}\,\text{d}x$$ (5)

(Total 8 marks)

5 The line l_1 has Cartesian equations $x - 2 = 4y = z + 3$ and the line l_2 has equation

$$\mathbf{r} = \begin{pmatrix} 4 \\ 5 \\ 1 \end{pmatrix} + s\begin{pmatrix} -1 \\ 2 \\ 0 \end{pmatrix}$$

The plane Π_1 contains l_1 and l_2.

a Find a vector which is normal to Π_1. (3)

b Show that an equation of Π_1 is $8x + 4y - 9z = 43$ (2)

c Find the shortest distance of the point $D(1, 1, 1)$ from Π_1. (3)

(Total 8 marks)

6 Figure 1 shows a sketch of the curve with parametric equations

$$x = a\cos^3 t, \quad y = a\sin^3 t, \quad 0 \leqslant t \leqslant \frac{\pi}{2}$$

where a is a positive constant.

The curve cuts the x-axis at the point P and the y-axis at the point Q.

Find the perimeter of the shaded region bounded by the arc PQ and the chord PQ.

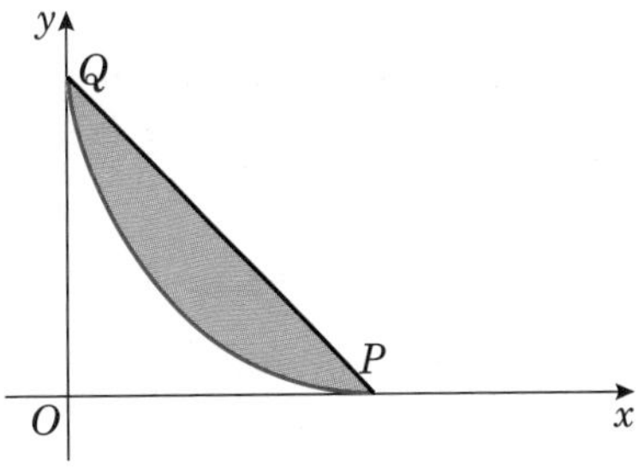

Figure 1

(Total 8 marks)

7 The point $P(ap^2, 2ap)$ lies on the parabola M with equation $y^2 = 4ax$, where a is a positive constant.

a Show that an equation of the tangent to M at P is

$$py = x + ap^2$$ (3)

The point $Q(9ap^2, 6ap)$ also lies on M.

b Write down an equation of the tangent to M at Q. (2)

The tangent at P and the tangent at Q intersect at the point V.

c Find, as p varies, the locus of V. (4)

(Total 9 marks)

8 **a** Using the definition of $\sinh x$ or $\operatorname{cosech} x$ in terms of exponentials, show that, for $x \geqslant 0$

$$\operatorname{arcosech} x = \ln\left(\frac{1 + \sqrt{1 + x^2}}{x}\right).$$ (5)

b Solve the equation

$$3\coth^2 x = 7\operatorname{cosech} x + 1$$

giving your answers in terms of natural logarithms. (5)

(Total 10 marks)

9 $\mathbf{A} = \begin{pmatrix} 3 & 0 & 0 \\ k & 2 & 5 \\ l & 2 & -1 \end{pmatrix}$ where k and l are constants

a Show that $\begin{pmatrix} 0 \\ 5 \\ 2 \end{pmatrix}$ is an eigenvector of $\mathbf{A}$ and find the corresponding eigenvalue. (2)

Given that -3 is also an eigenvalue of $\mathbf{A}$

b find the corresponding eigenvector. (4)

Given that $\begin{pmatrix} 1 \\ 1 \\ 1 \end{pmatrix}$ is also an eigenvector of $\mathbf{A}$

c find the corresponding eigenvalue, the value of k and the value of l. (5)

(Total 11 marks)

Answers

Exercise 1A

1 a 27.29 (2 d.p.) b 1.13 (2 d.p.)
c −0.96 (2 d.p.) d 0.01 (2 d.p.)

2 a $\frac{e - e^{-1}}{2}$ b $\frac{e^4 + e^{-4}}{2}$
c $\frac{e - 1}{e + 1}$ d $\frac{2}{e^{-1} + e}$

3 a $\frac{3}{4}$ b $\frac{5}{3}$
c $\frac{3}{5}$ d $\frac{2\pi}{\pi^2 - 1}$

4 $x = 1.32$ (2 d.p.)
$x = -1.32$ (2 d.p.)

5 $x = 0.88$ (2 d.p.)

6 $x = -0.55$ (2 d.p.)

7 $x = 0.10$ (2 d.p.)

8 $x = 2.77$ (2 d.p.)
$x = -2.77$ (2 d.p.)

Exercise 1B

1

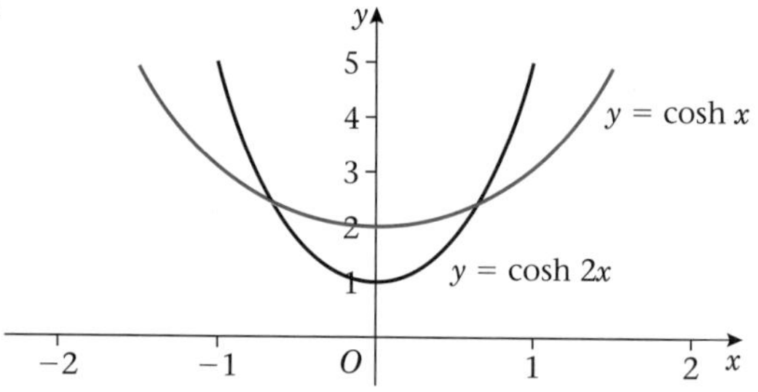

2 a

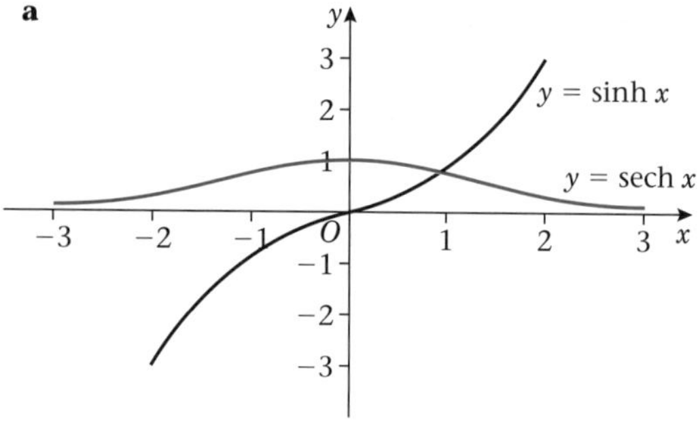

3 a $f(x) \in \mathbb{R}$ (All real numbers.)
b $f(x) \geqslant 1$
c $-1 < f(x) < 1$
$|f(x)| < 1$
d $0 < f(x) \leqslant 1$
e $f(x) \in \mathbb{R}, f(x) \neq 0$
(All real numbers except zero.)
f $f(x) < -1, f(x) > 1$
$|f(x)| > 1$

4 a

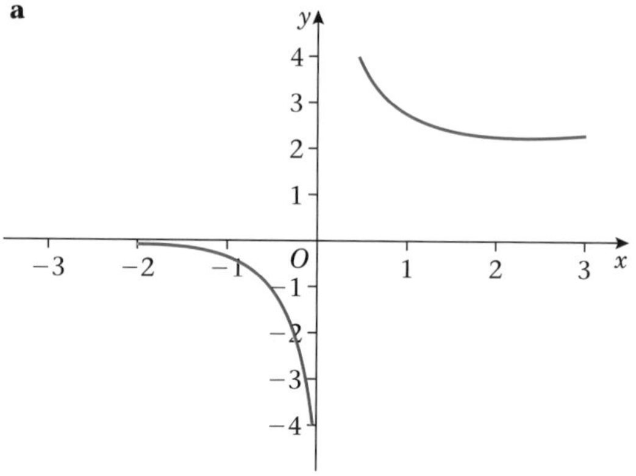

b $x = 0$
$y = 2$
$y = 0$

5

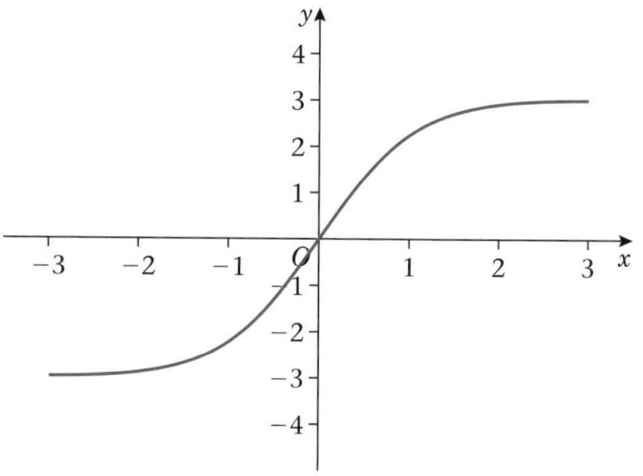

b $y = -3$
$y = 3$

Exercise 1C

1 R.H.S. $= 2\sinh A\cosh A$

$$= 2\left(\frac{e^A - e^{-A}}{2}\right)\left(\frac{e^A + e^{-A}}{2}\right)$$
$$= \tfrac{1}{2}(e^{2A} - 1 + 1 - e^{-2A})$$
$$= \frac{e^{2A} - e^{-2A}}{2}$$
$$= \sinh 2A = \text{L.H.S.}$$

2 R.H.S. $= \cosh A\cosh B - \sinh A\sinh B$

$$= \left(\frac{e^A + e^{-A}}{2}\right)\left(\frac{e^B + e^{-B}}{2}\right) - \left(\frac{e^A - e^{-A}}{2}\right)\left(\frac{e^B - e^{-B}}{2}\right)$$
$$= \frac{e^{A+B} + e^{-A+B} + e^{A-B} + e^{-A-B}}{4}$$
$$- \frac{e^{A+B} - e^{-A+B} - e^{A-B} - e^{-A-B}}{4}$$

$$= \frac{2(e^{-A+B} + e^{A-B})}{4}$$
$$= \frac{e^{A-B} + e^{-(A-B)}}{2}$$
$$= \cosh(A - B) = \text{L.H.S.}$$

3 R.H.S. $= 4\cosh^3 A - 3\cosh A$

$$= 4\left(\frac{e^A + e^{-A}}{2}\right)^3 - 3\left(\frac{e^A + e^{-A}}{2}\right)$$

$$(e^A + e^{-A})^3 = e^{3A} + 3e^{2A}e^{-A} + 3e^Ae^{-2A} + e^{-3A}$$
$$= e^{3A} + 3e^A + 3e^{-A} + e^{-3A}$$

$$\text{R.H.S.} = \frac{e^{3A} + 3e^A + 3e^{-A} + e^{-3A}}{2} - \frac{3(e^A + e^{-A})}{2}$$
$$= \frac{e^{3A} + e^{-3A}}{2}$$
$$= \cosh 3A = \text{L.H.S.}$$

4 R.H.S. $= 2\sinh\left(\frac{A - B}{2}\right)\cosh\left(\frac{A + B}{2}\right)$

$$= 2\left(\frac{e^{\frac{A-B}{2}} - e^{\frac{-A+B}{2}}}{2}\right)\left(\frac{e^{\frac{A+B}{2}} + e^{\frac{-A-B}{2}}}{2}\right)$$
$$= \frac{1}{2}\left(e^{\frac{A-B}{2}+\frac{A+B}{2}} - e^{\frac{-A+B}{2}+\frac{A+B}{2}} + e^{\frac{A-B}{2}+\frac{-A-B}{2}} - e^{\frac{-A+B}{2}+\frac{-A-B}{2}}\right)$$
$$= \frac{1}{2}(e^A - e^B + e^{-B} - e^{-A})$$
$$= \frac{1}{2}(e^A - e^{-A}) - \frac{1}{2}(e^B - e^{-B})$$
$$= \sinh A - \sinh B$$
$$= \text{L.H.S.}$$

5 L.H.S. $= \coth A - \tanh A$

$$= \frac{e^{2A} + 1}{e^{2A} - 1} - \frac{e^{2A} - 1}{e^{2A} + 1}$$
$$= \frac{(e^{2A} + 1)^2 - (e^{2A} - 1)^2}{(e^{2A} - 1)(e^{2A} + 1)}$$
$$= \frac{e^{4A} + 2e^{2A} + 1 - e^{4A} + 2e^{2A} - 1}{e^{4A} - 1}$$
$$= \frac{4e^{2A}}{e^{4A} - 1}$$
$$= \frac{4}{e^{2A} - e^{-2A}} = 2\left(\frac{2}{e^{2A} - e^{-2A}}\right)$$
$$= 2\,\text{cosech}\,2A = \text{R.H.S.}$$

6 $\sinh(A - B) = \sinh A\cosh B - \cosh A\sinh B$

7 $\sinh 3A = 3\sinh A + 4\sinh^3 A$

8 $\cosh A + \cosh B = 2\cosh\left(\frac{A + B}{2}\right)\cosh\left(\frac{A - B}{2}\right)$

9 $\cosh 2A = \frac{1 + \tanh^2 A}{1 - \tanh^2 A}$

10 $\cosh 2A = \cosh^4 A - \sinh^4 A$

11 **a** $\sinh x = \pm\sqrt{3}$

b $\tanh x = \pm\frac{\sqrt{3}}{2}$

c $\cosh 2x = 7$

12 **a** $\cosh x = \sqrt{2}$

b $\sinh 2x = -2\sqrt{2}$

c $\tanh 2x = -\frac{2\sqrt{2}}{3}$

Exercise 1D

1

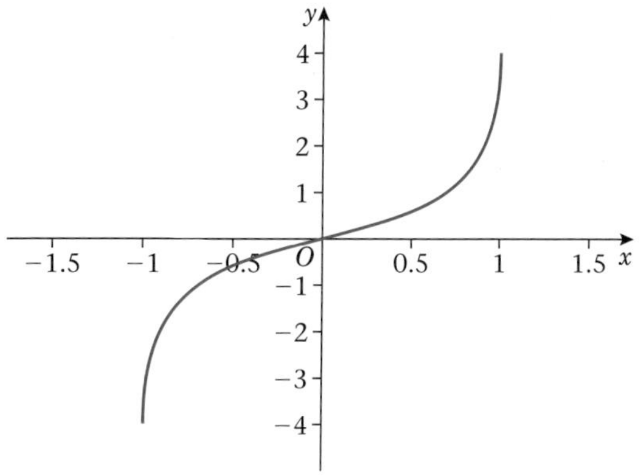

$y = \text{artanh}\,x,\ |x| < 1$

2

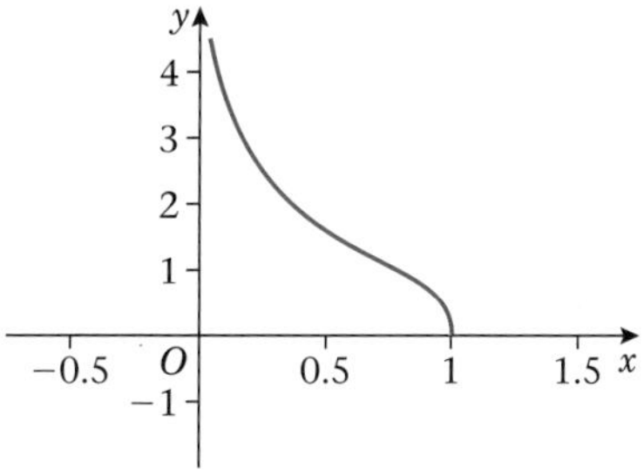

$y = \text{arsech}\,x,\ 0 < x \leqslant 1$

3

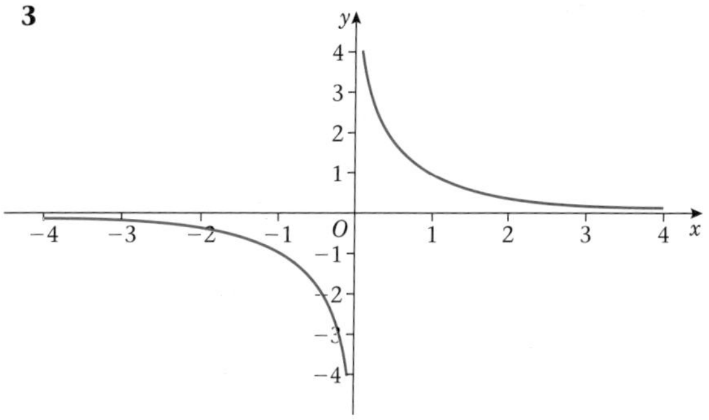

$y = \text{arcosech}\,x,\ x \neq 0$

4

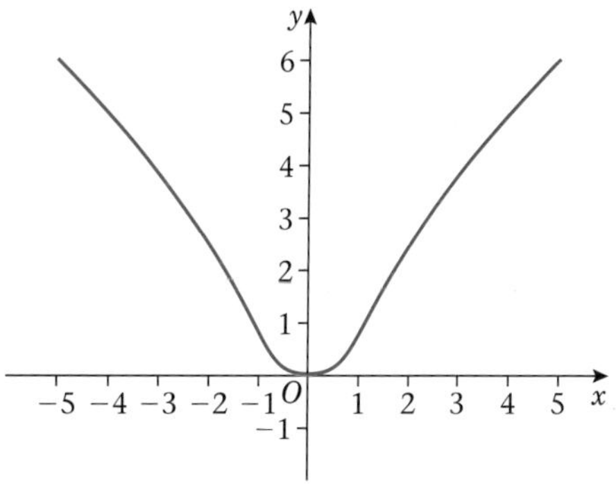

$y = (\text{arsinh}\,x)^2$

7 **a** $\ln(2 + \sqrt{5})$

b $\ln(3 + 2\sqrt{2})$

c $\frac{1}{2}\ln 3$

8 **a** $\ln(\sqrt{2} + \sqrt{3})$

b $\ln(2 + \sqrt{5})$

c $\frac{1}{2}\ln\left(\frac{11}{9}\right)$

9 **a** $\ln(-3+\sqrt{10})$

b $\ln\left(\frac{3+\sqrt{5}}{2}\right)$

c $\frac{1}{2}\ln(2+\sqrt{3})$

Exercise 1E

1 $x = \ln\left(\frac{1}{7}\right), x = 0$

2 $x = \ln 3$

3 $x = \ln\left(\frac{7}{2}\right), x = \ln 4$

4 $x = \ln\left(\frac{5}{3}\right)$

5 $x = \ln\left(\frac{-3+\sqrt{13}}{2}\right)$

$x = \ln(4+\sqrt{17})$

6 $x = \ln(2 \pm \sqrt{3})$

7 $x = \ln(4 \pm \sqrt{15})$

8 $x = 0, x = \ln\left(\frac{7 \pm 3\sqrt{5}}{2}\right)$

9 $x = \ln\left(\frac{5}{2}\right), x = \ln 3$

10 $x = \ln(1+\sqrt{2})$

Mixed Exercise 1F

1 **a** $\frac{4}{3}$ **b** $\frac{13}{5}$ **c** $-\frac{15}{17}$

2 **a**

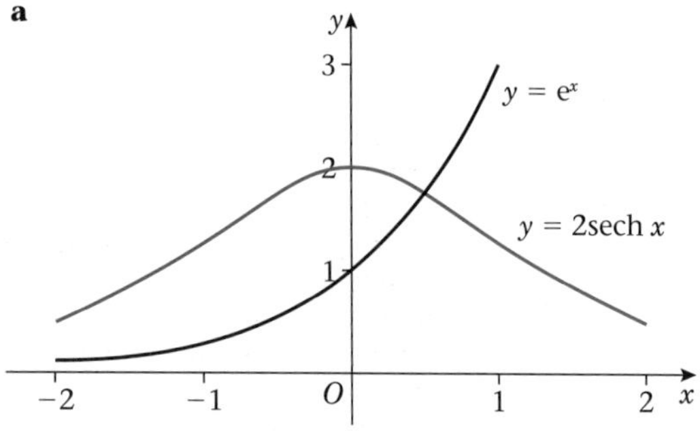

b $x = \frac{1}{2}\ln 3$

3 R.H.S. $= \sinh A\cosh B - \cosh A\sinh B$

$$= \left(\frac{e^{A}-e^{-A}}{2}\right)\left(\frac{e^{B}+e^{-B}}{2}\right) - \left(\frac{e^{A}+e^{-A}}{2}\right)\left(\frac{e^{B}-e^{-B}}{2}\right)$$

$$= \frac{e^{A+B}-e^{-A+B}+e^{A-B}-e^{-A-B}}{4}$$

$$- \frac{e^{A+B}+e^{-A+B}-e^{A-B}-e^{-A-B}}{4}$$

$$= \frac{2(e^{A-B}-e^{-A+B})}{4}$$

$$= \frac{e^{A-B}-e^{-(A-B)}}{2}$$

$= \sinh(A-B) =$ L.H.S.

4 R.H.S. $= \dfrac{2\tanh\frac{1}{2}x}{1-\tanh^2\frac{1}{2}x}$

$$2\tanh\tfrac{1}{2}x = \frac{2(e^x-1)}{e^x+1}$$

$$1-\tanh^2\tfrac{1}{2}x = 1-\left(\frac{e^x-1}{e^x+1}\right)^2$$

$$= \frac{(e^x+1)^2-(e^x-1)^2}{(e^x+1)^2}$$

$$= \frac{4e^x}{(e^x+1)^2}$$

So R.H.S. $= \dfrac{2(e^x-1)}{e^x+1} \times \dfrac{(e^x+1)^2}{4e^x}$

$$= \frac{(e^x-1)(e^x+1)}{2e^x}$$

$$= \frac{e^{2x}-1}{2e^x}$$

$$= \frac{e^x-e^{-x}}{2}$$

$= \sinh x =$ L.H.S.

5 **a** $R = 12$

$\alpha = 0.405$

b 12

6 **b** $\ln\left(\frac{1+\sqrt{10}}{3}\right)$

7 $x = \ln\left(\frac{1}{2}\right), x = \ln 7$

8 $x = \ln\left(\frac{5}{3}\right)$

9 $x = \ln\left(\frac{-14+\sqrt{205}}{3}\right)$

$x = \ln(1+\sqrt{2})$

10 $x = \ln 4$

12 **a**

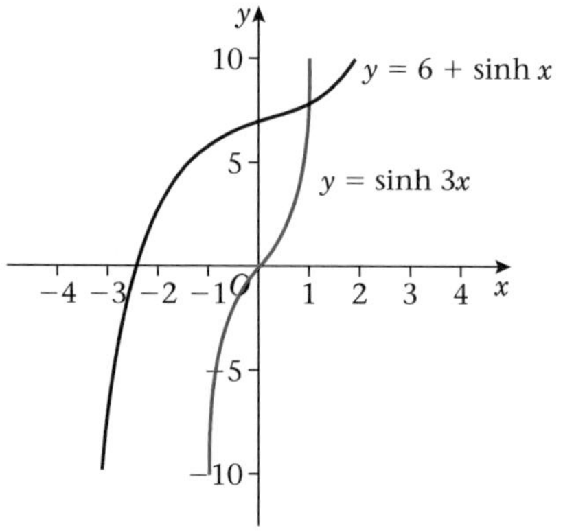

b $(\ln(1+\sqrt{2}), 7)$

13 $y = \dfrac{12-13x}{12x-13}$

14 **a** $R = 4$

$\alpha = 0.693$

$4\sinh(x+0.693)$

b $x = 0.75$ (2 d.p.)

c 0.75 (2 d.p.)

Exercise 2A

1 **a** **i**

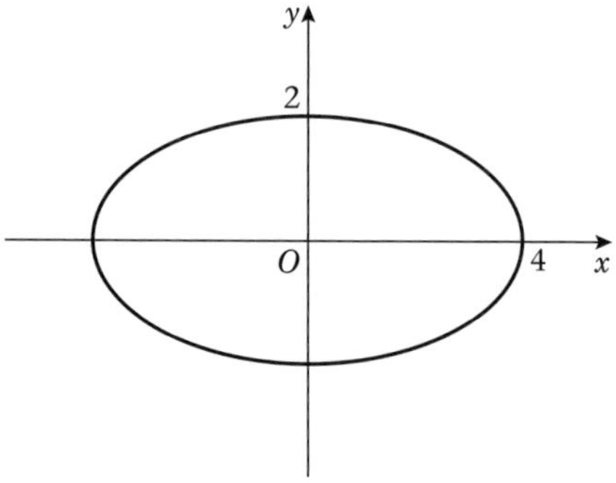

ii $x = 4\cos\theta, y = 2\sin\theta$

b i

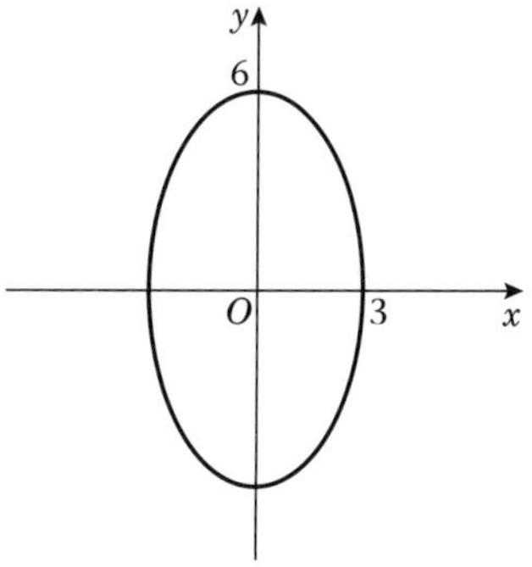

ii $x = 3\cos\theta, y = 6\sin\theta$

c i

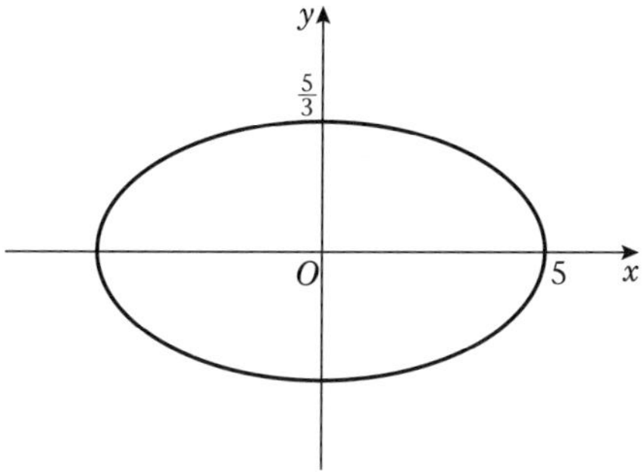

ii $x = 5\cos\theta, y = \frac{5}{3}\sin\theta$

2 a i

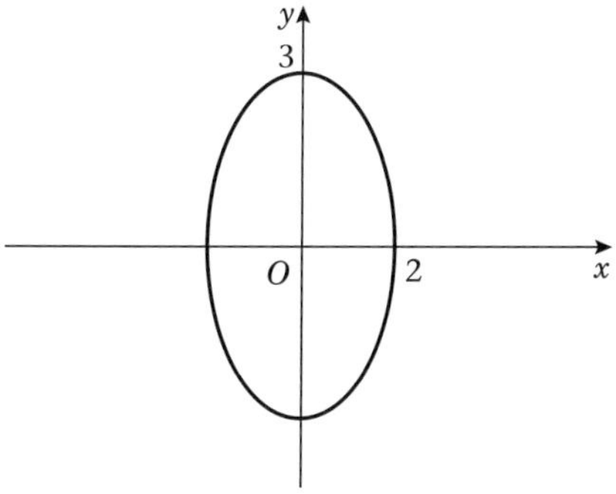

ii $\frac{x^2}{2^2} + \frac{y^2}{3^2} = 1$

b i

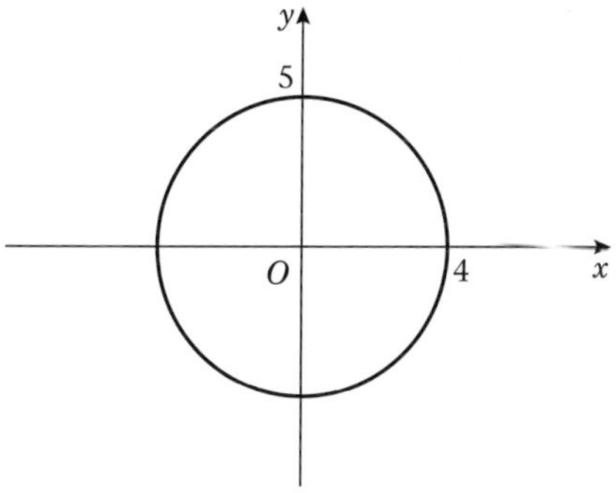

ii $\frac{x^2}{4^2} + \frac{y^2}{5^2} = 1$

c i

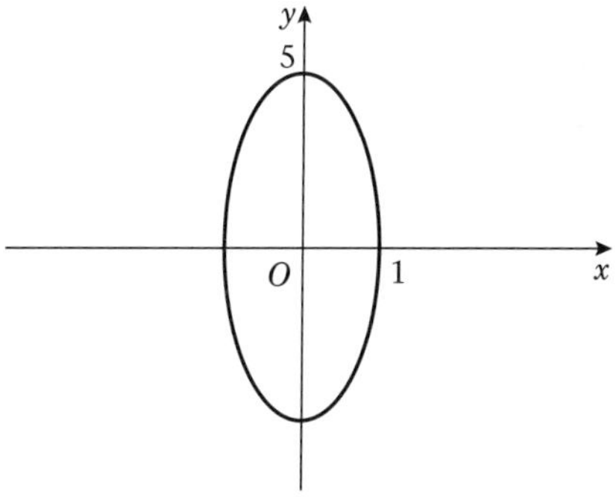

ii $x^2 + \frac{y^2}{5^2} = 1$

d i

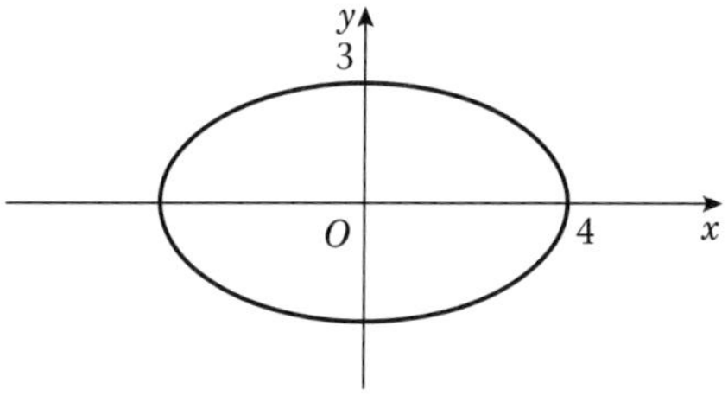

ii $\frac{x^2}{4^2} + \frac{y^2}{3^2} = 1$

Exercise 2B

1 Equation of tangent is: $ay\sin\theta + bx\cos\theta = ab$
Equation of normal is:
$by\cos\theta - ax\sin\theta = (b^2 - a^2)\sin\theta\cos\theta$
- **a** So equation of tangent is: $2y\sin\theta + x\cos\theta = 2$
  equation of normal is:
  $y\cos\theta - 2x\sin\theta = -3\sin\theta\cos\theta$
- **b** So equation of tangent is: $5y\sin\theta + 3x\cos\theta = 15$
  equation of normal is:
  $3y\cos\theta - 5x\sin\theta = -16\sin\theta\cos\theta$

2 a Tangent $6y + \sqrt{5}x = 9$
Normal $3\sqrt{5}y = 18x - 16\sqrt{5}$

b Tangent $2\sqrt{3}y - x = 8$
Normal y `+ $2\sqrt{3}x = -3\sqrt{3}$

4 b $\left(-\frac{4}{5}\sqrt{5}, \frac{1}{5}\sqrt{5}\right)$

5 a $2y\cos\theta - 3\sin\theta x = -5\sin\theta\cos\theta$

b P is $\left(-\frac{3}{2}, \sqrt{3}\right)$ or $\left(-\frac{3}{2}, -\sqrt{3}\right)$

6 $c = \pm 2\sqrt{2}$

7 $m = \pm 2$

8 a $m = 2$ **b** P is $\left(-\frac{3}{2}, 1\right)$

c $A\left(0, \frac{1}{4}\right)$ **d** $\left(\frac{45}{16}\right)$

9 c $\frac{1}{2}$

d $\left(\frac{9}{10}\sqrt{10}, \frac{2}{10}\sqrt{10}\right)$

10 $m = \pm 2, c = \pm 8$

Exercise 2C

1 a

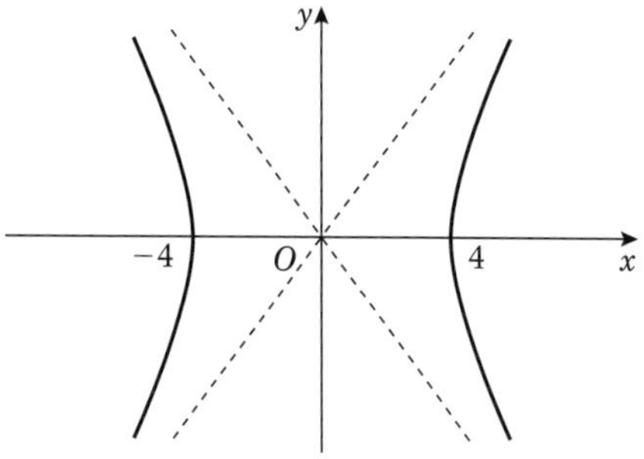

Asymptote $y = \pm 2x$

b

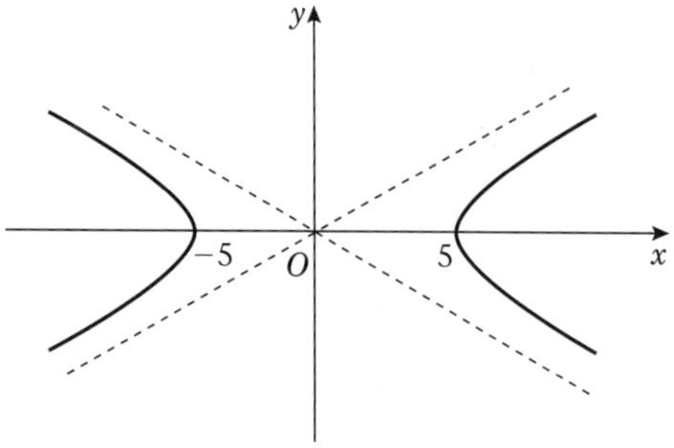

Asymptote $y = \pm\frac{2}{5}x$

c

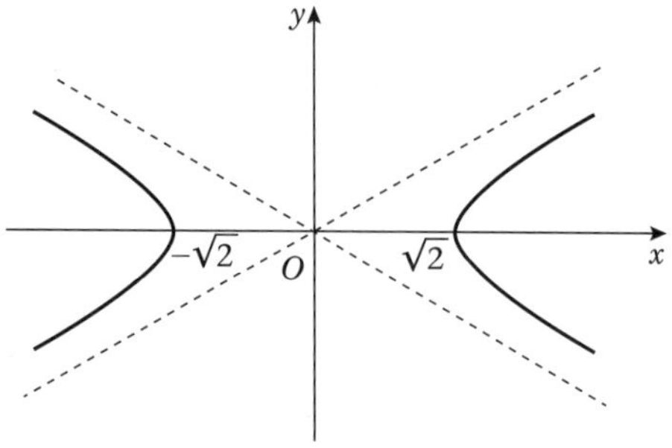

Asymptote $y = \pm\frac{1}{2}x$

2 a i

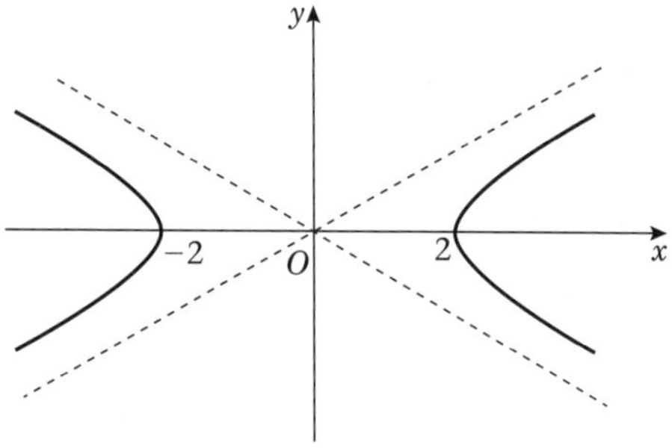

Asymptote $y = \pm\frac{3}{2}x$

ii $\dfrac{x^2}{a^2} - \dfrac{y^2}{b^2} = 1 \Rightarrow \dfrac{x^2}{4} - \dfrac{y^2}{9} = 1$

b i

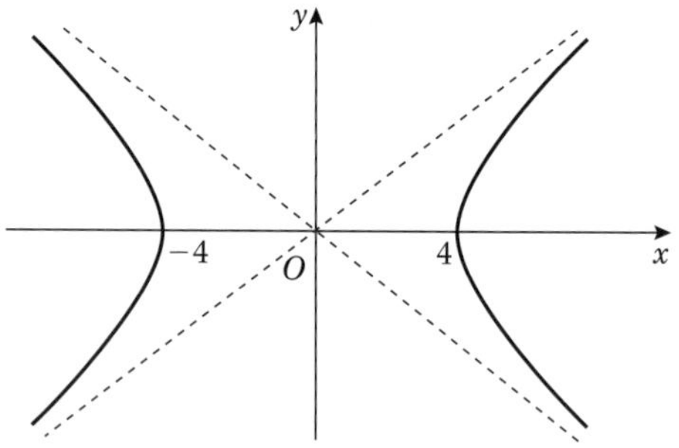

Asymptote $y = \pm\frac{3}{4}x$

ii $\dfrac{x^2}{16} - \dfrac{y^2}{9} = 1$

c i

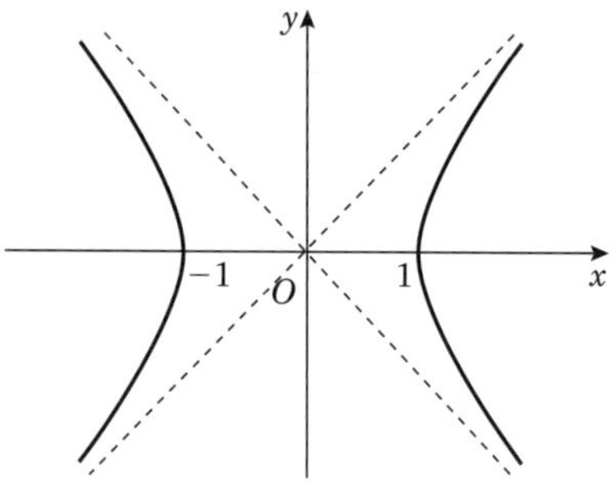

Asymptote $y = \pm 2x$

ii $x^2 - \dfrac{y^2}{4} = 1$

d i

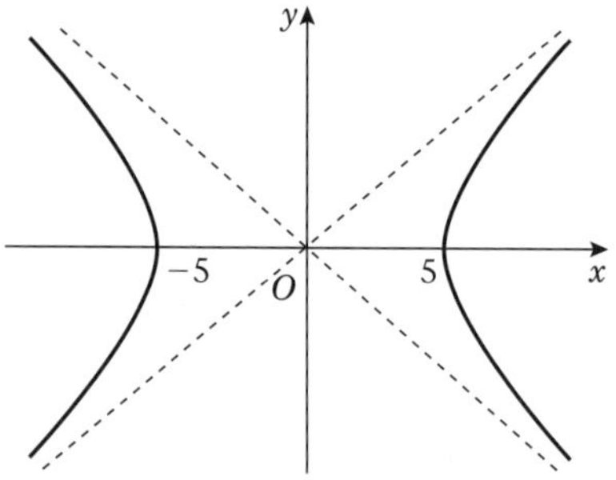

Asymptote $y = \pm\frac{7}{5}x$

ii $\dfrac{x^2}{25} - \dfrac{y^2}{49} = 1$

Exercise 2D

1 a Tangent $8y = 3x - 4$
Normal $3y + 8x = 108$
b Tangent $3y = 2x - 6$
Normal $2y + 3x = 48$
c Tangent $5y = 2x - 5$
Normal $2y + 5x = 56$

2 a Tangent $5y \sinh t + 10 = 2x \cosh t$
Normal $2y \cosh t + 5x \sinh t = 29 \cosh t \sinh t$
b Tangent $y \tan t + 3 = 3 \sec tx$
Normal $3y \sec t + x \tan t = 10 \sec t \tan t$

5 a A is $\left(0, -\dfrac{3}{\sinh t}\right)$
b B is $\left(0, \frac{25}{3}\sinh t\right)$
c $\frac{2}{3}(25 \sinh^2 t + 9) \coth t$

6 P and Q are $(4, 3\sqrt{3})$ and $(4, -3\sqrt{3})$
7 $c = \pm 6$
8 $m = \pm \frac{13}{7}$
9 **a** $c = 3$
b P is $\left(\frac{25}{3}, -\frac{16}{3}\right)$
10 $m = \pm 4$ and $c = \pm 7$

Exercise 2E

1 **a** $e = \frac{2}{3}$
b $e = \frac{\sqrt{7}}{4}$
c $e = \frac{1}{\sqrt{2}}$
2 **a** Focus $= (\pm 1, 0)$; directrix $x = \pm 4$
b Focus $= (\pm 3, 0)$; directrix $x = \pm \frac{16}{3}$
c Focus $= (0, \pm 2)$; directrix $y = \pm \frac{9}{2}$
3 **a** $e = \frac{1}{2}$
b $\frac{x^2}{36} + \frac{y^2}{27} = 1$
4 **a** $e = \frac{1}{2}$
b $\frac{x^2}{16} + \frac{y^2}{12} = 1$
5 **a** $e = \frac{2\sqrt{2}}{\sqrt{5}} = \frac{2\sqrt{10}}{5}$
b $e = \frac{4}{3}$
c $e = \frac{5}{3}$
6 **a**

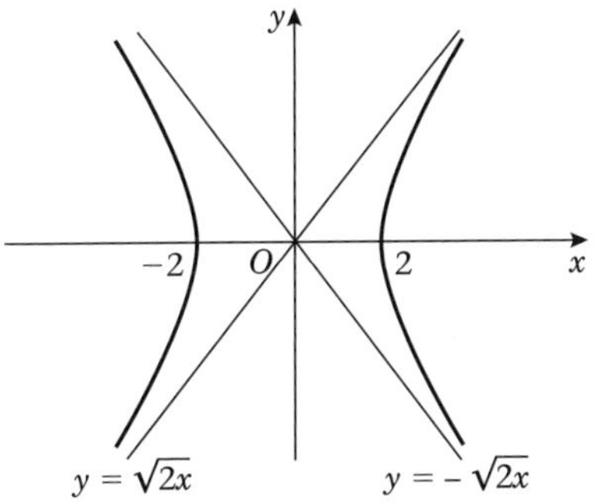

Asymptotes $y = \pm\sqrt{2}x$

b

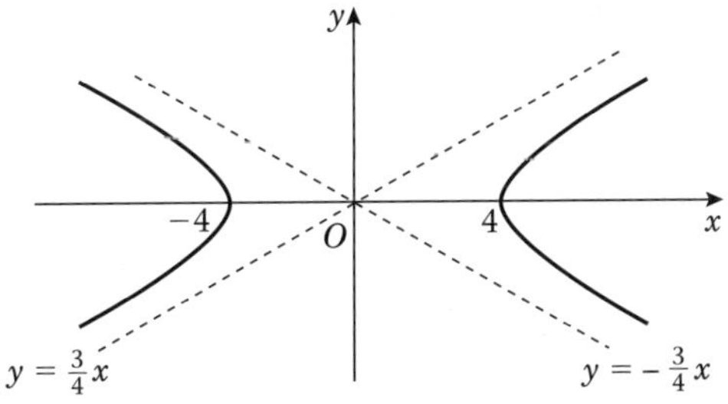

Asymptotes $y = \pm\frac{3}{4}x$

c

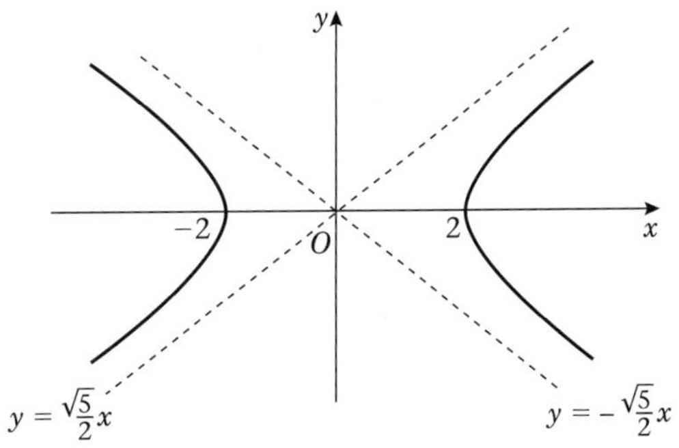

Asymptotes $y = \pm\frac{\sqrt{5}}{2}x$

Exercise 2F

1 **a** $(apq, a(p + q))$
c $y = a$
2 $\frac{a^2}{4x^2} = 1 + \frac{b^2}{4y^2}$
3 $4a^2x^2 = (a^2 + b^2)^2 + 4b^2y^2$
4 $4b^2y^2 + 4a^2x^2 = (a^2 - b^2)^2$
5

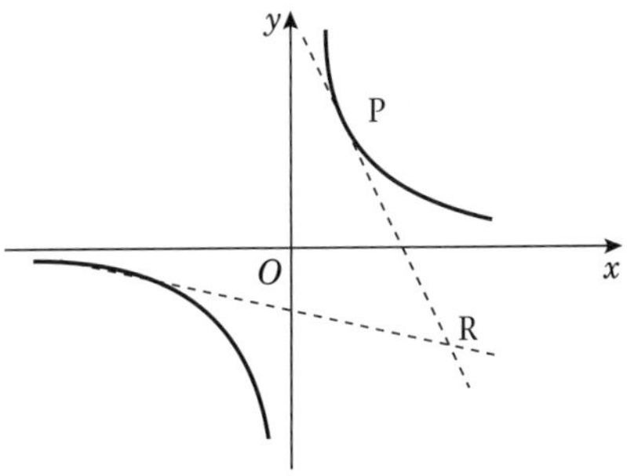

Equation of tangent at P is: $x + p^2y = 2cp$
c **i** $y = -2x$ **ii** $y = 2c^2$ **iii** $x = 2c^2$
6 $y = \frac{1}{2}$

Mixed Exercise 2G

1 **a** $\frac{x^2}{a^2} - \frac{y^2}{a^2m^2} = 1$
3 **b** $\left(-\frac{4}{3}, -12\right)$ and $\left(12, \frac{4}{3}\right)$
6 **a** $\frac{1}{t}$
d $X = a + \frac{at^2}{2} \Rightarrow at^2 = 2(X - a)$

$Y = \frac{at}{2} \quad \Rightarrow 2at = 4Y$

$\therefore (4Y)^2 = 4a \cdot 2(X - a)$ or $2Y^2 = a(X - a)$

7

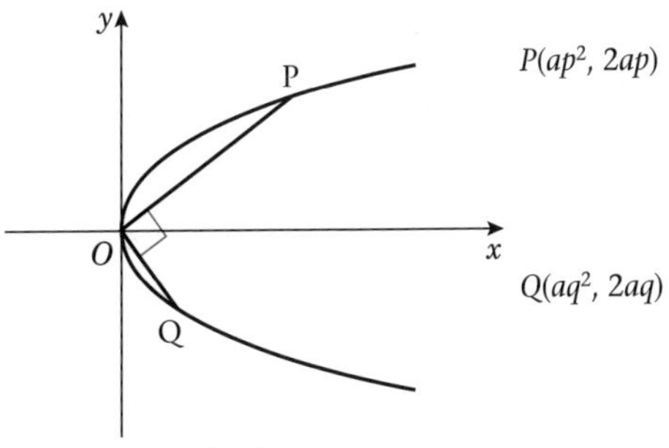

b $y + xq = aq^3 + 2aq$

Exercise 3A

1 $2\cosh 2x$
2 $5\sinh 5x$
3 $2\text{sech}^2 2x$
4 $3\cosh 3x$
5 $4\text{cosech}^2 4x$
6 $-2\tanh 2x \text{ sech } 2x$
7 $e^{-x}(\cosh x - \sinh x)$
8 $\cosh 3x + 3x \sinh 3x$
9 $\dfrac{x\cosh x - \sinh x}{3x^2}$
10 $x(2\cosh 3x + 3x \sinh 3x)$
11 $2\cosh 2x \cosh 3x + 3\sinh 2x \sinh 3x$
12 $\tanh x$
13 $3x^2 \cosh x^3$
14 $4\cosh 2x \sinh 2x$
15 $\sinh x \, e^{\cosh x}$
16 $-\coth x \text{ cosec} x$
18 $\tanh^{-1}\frac{1}{12}$
19 $\dfrac{dy}{dx} = 3\sinh 3x \sinh x + \cosh 3x \cosh x$

$\dfrac{d^2y}{dx^2} = 2(5\cosh 3x \sinh x + 3\sinh 3x \cosh x)$

20 $4y \sinh q - x \cosh q = -16$
$x \cosh q - 4y \sinh q = 16$
$4x \sinh q - y \cosh q = 63\sinh q \cosh q$

Exercise 3B

1 a $\dfrac{2}{\sqrt{4x^2 - 1}}$ b $\dfrac{1}{\sqrt{(x + 1)^2 + 1}}$

c $\dfrac{3}{1 - 9x^2}$ d $\dfrac{-1}{x(1 - x^2)^{\frac{1}{2}}}$

e $\dfrac{2x}{\sqrt{x^4 - 1}}$ f $\dfrac{3}{\sqrt{9x^2 - 1}}$

g $2x \text{ arcosh} x + \dfrac{x^2}{\sqrt{x^2 - 1}}$

h $y = \text{arsinh}\dfrac{x}{2}$

Let $t = \dfrac{x}{2}$ $y = \text{arsinh } t$

$\dfrac{dt}{dx} = \dfrac{1}{2}$ $\dfrac{dy}{dt} = \dfrac{1}{\sqrt{t^2 + 1}}$

$\dfrac{dy}{dx} = \dfrac{1}{2\sqrt{\left(\dfrac{x}{2}\right)^2 + 1}}$

$= \dfrac{1}{\sqrt{x^2 + 4}}$

i $y = e^{x^3} \text{arsinh } x$

$\dfrac{dy}{dx} = 3x^2 e^{x^3} \text{arsinh } x + \dfrac{e^{x^3}}{\sqrt{x^2 + 1}}$

j $y = \text{arsinh } x \text{ arcosh } x$

$\dfrac{dy}{dx} = \dfrac{1}{\sqrt{x^2 + 1}} \text{arcosh } x + \dfrac{1}{\sqrt{x^2 - 1}} \text{arsinh } x$

k $y = \text{arcosh } x \text{ sech } x$

$\dfrac{dy}{dx} = \dfrac{1}{\sqrt{x^2 + 1}} \text{sech } x - \text{arcosh } x \tanh x \text{ sech } x$

$= \text{sech } x\left(\dfrac{1}{\sqrt{x^2 + 1}} 2 \text{ arcosh } x \tanh x\right)$

l $y = x \text{ arcosh } 3x$

$\dfrac{dy}{dx} = \text{arcosh } 3x + x \cdot \dfrac{3}{\sqrt{9x^2 - 1}}$

5 $-\dfrac{2x \text{ arcosh} x}{(x^2 - 1)^{\frac{3}{2}}}$

6 $25y - 25\ln 5 = 169x - 156$

Exercise 3C

2 a $-\dfrac{2}{\sqrt{1 - 4x^2}}$

b Let $y = \arctan \dfrac{x}{2}$

Let $t = \dfrac{x}{2}$ $y = \arctan t$

$\dfrac{dt}{dx} = \dfrac{1}{2}$ $\dfrac{dy}{dt} = \dfrac{1}{1 + t^2}$

$\dfrac{dy}{dx} = \dfrac{1}{1 + t^2} \cdot \dfrac{1}{2} = \dfrac{1}{2\left(1 + \dfrac{x^2}{4}\right)} = \dfrac{2}{4 + x^2}$ or $\dfrac{2}{x^2 + 4}$

c $\dfrac{3}{\sqrt{1 - 9x^2}}$ d $-\dfrac{1}{1 + x^2}$

e $\dfrac{1}{x\sqrt{x^2 - 1}}$ f $-\dfrac{1}{x\sqrt{x^2 - 1}}$

g $-\dfrac{1}{(x - 1)\sqrt{1 - 2x}}$ h $-\dfrac{2x}{\sqrt{1 - x^4}}$

i $e^x \arccos x - \dfrac{1}{\sqrt{1 - x^2}}$ j $\dfrac{\cos x}{\sqrt{1 - x^2}} - \sin x \arcsin x$

k $x\left(2\arccos x - \dfrac{x}{\sqrt{1 - x^2}}\right)$ l $\dfrac{e^{\arctan x}}{1 + x^2}$

3 $\dfrac{1}{1 + x^2(\arctan x)^2}\left(\arctan x + \dfrac{x}{1 + x^2}\right)$

5 $\sqrt{3}y - \dfrac{\pi\sqrt{3}}{6} = 4x - 1$

Exercise 3D

1 $2\sinh 2x$

2 a $\dfrac{3}{\sqrt{9x^2 + 1}}$ b $\dfrac{2x}{\sqrt{x^4 + 1}}$

c $\dfrac{1}{\sqrt{x^2 - 4}}$ d $2x\left(\text{arcosh } 2x + \dfrac{x}{\sqrt{4x^2 - 1}}\right)$

5 $\ln 2$

7 $x = \text{arcosh}(\sinh 2x)$
Let $t = \sinh 2x$ $x = \text{arcosh } t$

$\dfrac{dt}{dx} = 2\cosh 2x$ $\dfrac{dx}{dt} = \dfrac{1}{\sqrt{t^2 - 1}}$

$\dfrac{dy}{dx} = \dfrac{1}{\sqrt{t^2 - 1}} \times 2\cosh 2x$

$= \dfrac{2\cosh 2x}{\sqrt{\sinh^2 2x - 1}}$

9 $\dfrac{1}{x^2 + 1}$

11 tangent
$ay \sinh q - xb \cosh q + ab = 0$
normal
$ax \sinh q + by \cosh q - \sinh q \cosh q (a^2 + b^2) = 0$

Exercise 4A

1 **a** $\cosh x + 3\sinh x + C$
b $5\tanh x + C$
c $-\coth x + C$
d $\sinh x - \tanh x + C$
e $-\operatorname{sech} x + C$
f $-3\operatorname{cosech} x + C$
g $\tanh x - \operatorname{sech} x + C$
h $\tanh x + \coth x + C$

2 **a** $\frac{1}{2}\cosh 2x + c$
b $3\sinh\left(\frac{x}{3}\right) + C$
c $\frac{1}{2}\tanh(2x - 1) + C$
d $-\frac{1}{5}\coth 5x + C$
e $-\frac{1}{2}\operatorname{cosech} 2x + c$
f $-\frac{1}{\left(\frac{1}{\sqrt{2}}\right)}\operatorname{sech}\left(\frac{x}{\sqrt{2}}\right) + C = -\sqrt{2}\operatorname{sech}\left(\frac{x}{\sqrt{2}}\right) + C$
g $\cosh 5x - \sinh 4x + 6\tanh\left(\frac{x}{2}\right) + C$

3 **a** $\arctan x + C$ **b** $\operatorname{arsinh} x + C$
c $\ln|1 + x| + C$ **d** $\ln(1 + x^2) + C$
e $\arcsin x + C$ **f** $\operatorname{arcosh} x + C$
g $3\sqrt{x^2 - 1} + C$ **h** $-\frac{3}{(1 + x)} + C$

4 **a** $-2\sqrt{(1 - x^2)} + \arcsin x + C$
b $\operatorname{arcosh} x + \sqrt{(x^2 - 1)} + C$
c $\sqrt{(1 + x^2)} - 3\operatorname{arsinh} x + C$

5 **b** $x - \arctan x + C$

Exercise 4B

1 **a** $\frac{1}{4}\sinh^4 x + C$
b $\frac{1}{4}\ln\cosh 4x + C$
c $\frac{1}{6}\tanh^6 x + C$
d $-\frac{1}{7}\operatorname{cosech}^7 x + C$
e $\frac{1}{3}(\cosh 2x)^{\frac{3}{2}} + C$
f $-\frac{1}{30}\operatorname{sech}^{10} 3x + C$

2 **a** $\frac{1}{3}\ln(2 + 3\cosh x) + C$
b $\tanh x + \frac{1}{2}\tanh^2 x + C$ or $\tanh x - \frac{1}{2}\operatorname{sech}^2 x + C$
c $5x + 2\ln\cosh x + C$

4 **a** $\frac{1}{3}x\cosh 3x - \frac{1}{9}\sinh 3x + C$
b $x\tanh x - \ln\cosh x + C$

5 **a** $\frac{1}{4}e^{2x} + \frac{1}{2}x + C$
b $\frac{1}{2}e^{x} + \frac{1}{10}e^{-5x} + C$
c $\frac{1}{16}e^{4x} - \frac{1}{16}e^{-4x} + \frac{1}{8}e^{2x} - \frac{1}{8}e^{-2x} + C$
or $\frac{1}{8}\sinh 4x + \frac{1}{4}\sinh 2x + C$

6 $\int\cosh^2 3x\,dx = \frac{1}{4}\int(e^{3x} + e^{-3x})^2\,dx$
$= \frac{1}{4}\int(e^{6x} + 2 + e^{-6x})\,dx$
$= \frac{1}{24}e^{6x} - \frac{1}{24}e^{-6x} + \frac{1}{2}x + C$
$= \frac{1}{12}\sinh 6x + \frac{1}{2}x + C$ which agrees with result in Example **5b**

7 $1 - \frac{1}{e}$

8 **a** $\frac{1}{4}\sinh 2x - \frac{1}{2}x + C$
b $x + 2\operatorname{sech} x + C$
c $x - \frac{1}{3}\coth 3x + C$
d $-\frac{1}{8}x + \frac{1}{32}\sinh 4x + C$
e $\sinh x + \frac{2}{3}\sinh^3 x + \frac{1}{5}\sinh^5 x + C$
f $\frac{1}{2}\ln\cosh 2x - \frac{1}{4}\tanh^2 2x + C$

11 **a** $4\arctan(e^{x}) + C$
b $\arctan(e^{2x}) + C$
c $4\arctan\left(e^{\frac{x}{2}}\right) + C$

12 **a** $\frac{1}{8}\sinh(2x^2) + \frac{x^2}{4} + C$
b $\frac{1}{2}\tanh(x^2) + C$

Exercise 4C

3 **a** $3\arcsin\left(\frac{x}{2}\right) + C$ **b** $\operatorname{arcosh}\left(\frac{x}{3}\right) + C$
c $\frac{4\sqrt{5}}{5}\arctan\left(\frac{x}{\sqrt{5}}\right) + C$ **d** $\frac{1}{2}\operatorname{arsinh}\left(\frac{2x}{5}\right) + C$

4 **a** $\arcsin\left(\frac{x}{5}\right) + C$ **b** $3\operatorname{arsinh}\left(\frac{x}{3}\right) + C$
c $\operatorname{arcosh}\left(\frac{x}{\sqrt{2}}\right) + C$ **d** $\frac{1}{2}\arctan\left(\frac{x}{4}\right) + C$

5 **a** $\frac{1}{2}\operatorname{arcosh}\left(\frac{x}{\sqrt{3}}\right) + C$ **b** $\frac{\sqrt{3}}{6}\arctan\left(\frac{\sqrt{3}x}{2}\right) + C$
c $\frac{1}{3}\operatorname{arsinh}\left(\frac{3x}{4}\right) + C$ **d** $\frac{1}{2}\arcsin\left(\frac{2x}{\sqrt{3}}\right) + C$

6 **a** 0.927 (3 s.f.) **b** 0.977 (3 s.f.)
c 0.719 (3 s.f.)

7 **a** $\ln\{1 + \sqrt{2}\}$ **b** $\ln\left(\frac{4}{3}\right)$
c $\left(\frac{\pi}{12}\right)$

8 **a** 2.27 {s.f.} **b** 4.13 (s.f.)

10 **a** $\frac{x}{9} - \frac{2}{27}\arctan\frac{3x}{2} + C$
b $\sqrt{x}\sqrt{1 + x} - \operatorname{arsinh}(\sqrt{x}) + C$

11 **a** $\sqrt{x^2 - 4} - 2\operatorname{arcosh}\left(\frac{x}{2}\right) + C$
b $-2\sqrt{2 - x^2} - \arcsin\left(\frac{x}{\sqrt{2}}\right) + C$
c $\frac{2\sqrt{3}}{3}\arctan(\sqrt{3}x) + \frac{1}{2}\ln(1 + 3x^2) + C$

12 $2\ln x + \frac{4}{\sqrt{5}}\arctan\left(\frac{x}{\sqrt{5}}\right) - \frac{1}{2}\ln(x^2 + 5) + C$

14 0.824 (3 s.f.)

16 **b** 12.9 (s.f.)

17 **b** $\frac{2}{\sqrt{3}}\arctan\left(\frac{e^{x}}{\sqrt{3}}\right) + C$

18 0.360 (3 s.f.)

19 **a** **i** Using partial fractions

$$\frac{1}{a^2 - x^2} = \frac{1}{2a}\left\{\frac{1}{a - x} + \frac{1}{a + x}\right\}$$

So $\int\frac{dx}{a^2 - x^2} = \frac{1}{2a}\int\left\{\frac{1}{a - x} + \frac{1}{a + x}\right\}dx$

$= \frac{1}{2a}[-\ln a - x + \ln a + x] + C$

$= \frac{1}{2a}\ln\left|\frac{a + x}{a - x}\right| + C$

ii $\frac{1}{a}\operatorname{artanh}\left(\frac{x}{a}\right) + D$

b $\frac{1}{2}\ln\left|\frac{a+x}{a-x}\right|$

20 a $\text{arcsec}\,x + C$

b $\sqrt{x^2-1} - \text{arcsec}\,x + C$

Exercise 4D

1 a $\arcsin\left(\frac{x+2}{3}\right) + C$ **b** $\text{arcosh}\left(\frac{x-2}{4}\right) + C$

c $\text{arsinh}\,(x+3) + C$ **d** $\text{arcosh}\,(x-1) + C$

e $\frac{\sqrt{10}}{10}\arctan\left(\frac{\sqrt{2}\,(x+1)}{\sqrt{5}}\right) + C$

f $\frac{1}{2}\arcsin\left(\frac{2x+3}{3}\right) + C$

g $\frac{1}{\sqrt{2}}\arcsin\left(\frac{x+3}{4}\right) + C$

h $\frac{1}{3}\text{arcosh}\left(\frac{9x-4}{\sqrt{7}}\right) + C$

2 a $\frac{1}{2}\text{arsinh}\,(2x-3) + C$

b $\frac{1}{2}\text{arcosh}\left(\frac{2x-3}{\sqrt{5}}\right) + C$

3 a 0.400 (3 s.f.) **b** 0.325 (3 s.f.) **c** 0.597 (3 s.f.)

4 a $\ln\{2+\sqrt{5}\}$ **b** $\frac{\pi}{3\sqrt{3}}$

6 a $\text{arsinh}\,(x+2) + C$

b $\arcsin\left(\frac{x-2}{3}\right) + C$

7 $\frac{\pi\sqrt{3}}{90}$

8 $\ln(4-\sqrt{7})$

10 Using the substitution $x = 2\sin\theta - 1$, $dx = 2\cos\theta\, d\theta$ and
$$3 - 2x - x^2 = 3 - 2(2\sin\theta - 1) - (4\sin^2\theta - 4\sin\theta + 1) = 4 - 4\sin^2\theta = 4\cos^2\theta$$

So
$$\int\frac{x}{\sqrt{3-2x-x^2}}\,dx = \int\frac{2\sin\theta - 1}{2\cos\theta}\times 2\cos\theta\, d\theta$$
$$= \int(2\sin\theta - 1)\, d\theta$$
$$= -2\cos\theta - \theta + C$$
$$= -2\sqrt{1-\left(\frac{x+1}{2}\right)^2} - \theta + C$$
$$= -\sqrt{3-2x-x^2} - \arcsin\left(\frac{x+1}{2}\right) + C$$

Exercise 4E

1 b 0.467 (3 s.f.)

c $\frac{1}{2}[(2x+1)\,\text{arsinh}\,(2x+1) - \sqrt{4x^2+4x+2} + C$

4 c 4.23 (3 s.f.)

5 a $\frac{\sqrt{2}}{8}\pi - 1 + \frac{\sqrt{2}}{2}$ **b** $\frac{\pi-2}{4}$

Exercise 4F

1 b $2x^3e^{\frac{x}{2}} - 12x^2e^{\frac{x}{2}} + 48xe^{\frac{x}{2}} - 96e^{\frac{x}{2}} + C$

3 $\frac{16}{7}$

4 b $-x^3e^{-x} - 3x^2e^{-x} - 6xe^{-x} - 6e^{-x} + K$

c $24 - 65e^{-1}$ or $\frac{24e - 65}{e}$

5 b $\ln\cosh x - \frac{1}{2}\tanh^2 x - \frac{1}{4}\tanh^4 x + C$

6 a $\frac{1}{3}\tan^3 x - \tan x + x + C$

b $\ln\sqrt{2} - \frac{1}{4}$

7 b $2(\ln 2)^3 - 6(\ln 2)^2 + 12(\ln 2) - 6$

8 a $\frac{16}{35}$ **b** $\frac{\pi}{32}$ **c** $\frac{8}{105}$ **d** $\frac{35\pi}{768}$

9 a $I_{n+1} = \int\frac{\sin^{2n+2}x}{\cos x}\,dx$

b $\int\frac{\sin^4 x}{\cos x}\,dx = I_2$

Substituting $n = 1$ in reduction formula gives
$$I_2 = I_1 - \frac{\sin^3 x}{3} = \left(I_0 - \frac{\sin x}{1}\right) - \frac{\sin^3 x}{3}$$
$$I_0 = \int\frac{1}{\cos x}\,dx = \int\sec x\,dx = \ln(\sec x + \tan x) + C$$

So
$$\int\frac{\sin^4 x}{\cos x}\,dx = \ln[(\sec x + \tan x)] - \sin x - \frac{\sin^3 x}{3} + C$$

Applying the given limits gives
$$\int_0^{\frac{\pi}{4}}\frac{\sin^4 x}{\cos x}\,dx = \left[\ln|(\sec x + \tan x)| - \sin x - \frac{\sin^3 x}{3}\right]_0^{\frac{\pi}{4}}$$
$$= \ln(1+\sqrt{2}) - \frac{\sqrt{2}}{2} - \frac{\left(\frac{\sqrt{2}}{2}\right)^3}{3}$$
$$= \ln(1+\sqrt{2}) - \frac{\sqrt{2}}{2} - \frac{\sqrt{2}}{12}$$
$$= \ln(1+\sqrt{2}) - \frac{7\sqrt{2}}{12}$$

10 b $\frac{243}{1540}$

11 b i $\frac{128}{315}$ **ii** $\frac{34\,992}{35}$ **iii** π

c Use substitution $x = 2\sin\theta$

12 a Integrating by parts with $u = x^n$ and $\frac{dv}{dx} = \sqrt{4-x}$
$$\frac{du}{dx} = nx^{n-1}, \quad v = -\frac{2}{3}(4-x)^{\frac{3}{2}}$$

So
$$\int_0^4 x^n\sqrt{4-x}\,dx = \left[-\frac{2}{3}x^n(4-x)^{\frac{3}{2}}\right]_0^4 - \int_0^4 -\frac{2}{3}nx^{n-1}(4-x)^{\frac{3}{2}}\,dx$$
$$= [0-0] + \frac{2}{3}n\int_0^4 x^{n-1}(4-x)^{\frac{3}{2}}\,dx \;(n>0)$$
$$= \frac{2}{3}n\int_0^4 x^{n-1}\{(4-x)\sqrt{4-x}\}\,dx$$
$$= \frac{2}{3}n\int_0^4 x^{n-1}4\sqrt{4-x}\,dx + \frac{2}{3}n\int_0^4 x^{n-1}\{-x\sqrt{4-x}\}\,dx$$
$$= \frac{8}{3}n\int_0^4 x^{n-1}\sqrt{4-x}\,dx - \frac{2}{3}n\int_0^4 x^n\sqrt{4-x}\,dx$$

So $I_n = \frac{8}{3}nI_{n-1} - \frac{2}{3}nI_n$

$$(2n+3)I_n = 8nI_{n-1} \Rightarrow I_n = \frac{8n}{2n+3}I_{n-1},\; n \geqslant 1$$

b 52.0 (3 s.f.)

13 a $I_n = \int\cos^n x\,dx = \int\cos^{n-1}x\cos x\,dx$

Integrating by parts with $u = \cos^{n-1}x$ and $\frac{dv}{dx} = \cos x$
$$\frac{du}{dx} = (n-1)\cos^{n-2}x(-\sin x),\; v = \sin x$$

So
$$I_n = \int\cos^n x\,dx = \cos^{n-1}x\sin x - \int-(n-1)\cos^{n-2}x\sin^2 x\,dx$$

$= \cos^{n-1}x\sin x + (n-1)\int\cos^{n-2}x(1 - 1\cos^2 x)\,dx$

$= \cos^{n-1}x\sin x + (n-1)\int\cos^{n-2}x\,dx$

$\quad - (n-1)\int\cos^n x\,dx$

Giving $I_n = \cos^{n-1}x\sin x + (n-1)I_{n-2} - (n-1)I_n$

So $nI_n = \cos^{n-1}x\sin x + (n-1)I_{n-2}$

b $nJ_n = (n-1)J_{n-2}$

c **i** $\frac{3\pi}{4}$ **ii** $\frac{35\pi}{64}$

14 **b** $\frac{16}{315}$

15 **b** $(x^4 + 12x^2 + 24)\sinh x - (4x^3 + 24x)\cosh x + C$

c $6 - e - 8e^{-1}$ or $\frac{6e - e^2 - 8}{e}$

16 **a** $I_{n-2} = \int\frac{\sin(n-2)x}{\sin x}\,dx$

b **i** $2\sin x + \frac{2\sin 3x}{3} + C$ **ii** $\frac{\pi}{6} - \frac{\sqrt{3}}{6}$

17 **b** **i** $\frac{752}{1215}$

Exercise 4G

1 $\frac{56}{3}$ or $18\frac{2}{3}$

2 $\ln(2 + \sqrt{3})$

3 $\frac{3}{2}$

4 $4\frac{2}{3}$

5 6.82 (s.f.)

7 1.5 They represent the same curve.

8 $\frac{1}{2}\ln(4 + \sqrt{17}) + 2\sqrt{17}$

10 $3a$

Total length of curve $= 4 \times 3a = 12a$ (symmetry)

11 $2\arctan(e) - \frac{\pi}{2}$ or 0.866 (3 s.f.)

12 $4a$

14 $\sqrt{2}\,[e^{\frac{\pi}{4}} - 1]$ or 1.69 (3 s.f.)

Exercise 4H

1 **a** 45π

2 $\frac{\pi}{27}[10\sqrt{10} - 1]$ or 3.56 (3 s.f.)

3 $\frac{2\pi}{3}[5\sqrt{5} - 1]$

4 $\frac{592}{3}\pi$

5 **a** 8.84 (3 s.f.)

6 **b** $23\frac{1}{9}\pi$

7 $\frac{384\pi}{5}$ (241 (3 s.f.))

8 **a** $4\pi R^2$

11 **b** $\frac{24\pi}{5}[25\sqrt{5} + 1]$

12 $\frac{11\pi}{9}$

13 $\frac{93\pi a^2}{80}$

Mixed Exercise 4I

2 **a** $a = 2$

$b = 1$

$c = 16$

b $\frac{\pi}{32}$

3 **a** $\frac{1}{20}\cosh 10x - \frac{1}{4}\cosh 2x + C$

b $-\frac{1}{2}\ln(1 + 2\operatorname{sech}x) + C$

c $\frac{1}{4}e^{2x} - \frac{1}{2}x + C$

4 960 (2 s.f.)

5 **a** $\frac{1}{2}\arctan 2x + \frac{1}{4}\ln(1 + 4x^2) + C$

b $\frac{1}{8}[\pi + 2\ln 2]$

6 594 (3 s.f.)

8 **a** **i** 1 **ii** $\frac{\pi}{2} - 1$

d $\frac{\pi^4}{16} - 3\pi^2 + 24$

9 **a** $\operatorname{arsinh}\left(\frac{x-1}{3}\right) + C$

b $\frac{1}{3}\arctan\left(\frac{x-1}{3}\right) + C$

c Using the substitution $x = \sin\theta$, so $dx = \cos\theta\,d\theta$

$$\int_0^{\frac{1}{2}}\frac{x^4\,dx}{\sqrt{(1-x^2)}} = \int_0^{\frac{\pi}{6}}\frac{\sin^4\theta\cos\theta\,d\theta}{\cos\theta}$$

$$= \int_0^{\frac{\pi}{6}}\sin^4\theta\,d\theta$$

$$= \frac{1}{4}\int_0^{\frac{\pi}{6}}(1 - 2\cos 2\theta + \cos^2 2\theta)\,d\theta$$

$$= \frac{1}{4}\int_0^{\frac{\pi}{6}}\left(1 - 2\cos 2\theta + \frac{1 + \cos 4\theta}{2}\right)d\theta$$

$$= \frac{1}{4}\left[\frac{3\theta}{2} - \sin 2\theta + \frac{\sin 4\theta}{8}\right]_0^{\frac{\pi}{6}}$$

$$= \frac{1}{4}\left(\frac{\pi}{4} - \frac{\sqrt{3}}{2} + \frac{\sqrt{3}}{16}\right)$$

$$= \frac{(4\pi - 7\sqrt{3})}{64}$$

10 **b** $\frac{39}{70}$

11 **b** $\frac{160\pi}{3}$

13 **a** $\frac{\pi}{8}$

b **i** $\arcsin\left(\frac{x-2}{2}\right) + C$

ii $2(4x - x^2)^{\frac{1}{2}} + C$

iii $\frac{\pi}{3} - 2\sqrt{3}$

14 $y = 2\sqrt{x}$ represents the section of curve for $x \geqslant 0$, $y \geqslant 0$, so $\frac{dy}{dx} = \frac{1}{\sqrt{x}}$

b $\frac{8\pi}{3}(2\sqrt{2} - 1)$

15 **b** $\frac{1}{2}(2x - 1)\operatorname{arcosh}\sqrt{x} - \frac{1}{2}\sqrt{x}\sqrt{x - 1} + C$

16 **b** $\frac{\sin 10x}{5} + \frac{\sin 8x}{4} + \frac{\sin 6x}{3} + \frac{\sin 4x}{2} + \sin 2x + x + C$

17 **b** $\frac{\pi}{3}$

18 **a** $\frac{2}{\sqrt{3}}\arctan(\sqrt{3}e^x) + C$

19 **b** $\frac{1}{4}\sec^3 x\tan x + \frac{3}{8}\sec x\tan x + \frac{3}{8}\ln|\sec x + \tan x| + C$

Review Exercise 1

1 $\frac{1}{2}\ln 3$

2 $\ln\left(\frac{1}{3}\right)$, $\ln 3$

3 $p = 3$, $q = \frac{20}{3}$

4 $\ln\frac{1}{3}, \ln 7$

5 $\frac{1}{3}, \frac{3}{5}$

6 **a** $k \geqslant \sqrt{3}$
b $0, -\ln 3$

7 **b** $k = -1, a = 2$

8 **b** $\pm\ln(3 + \sqrt{8})$

9 **b** $\ln(\sqrt{2} \pm 1)$.

13 $x = -\ln 2, y = \ln\frac{3}{2}$

14 **a**

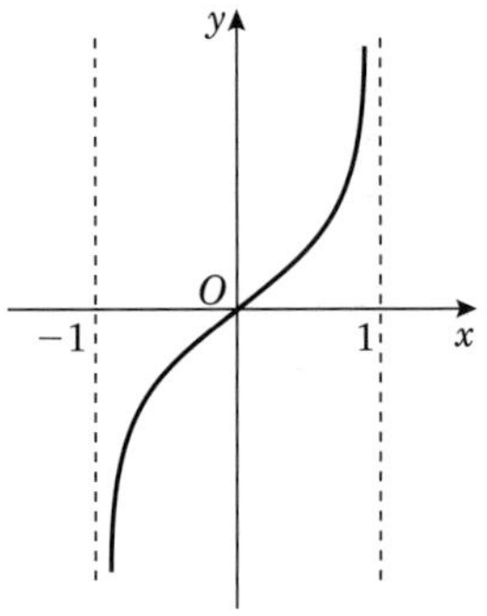

Graph of $y = \text{artanh}\,x$.

b $\frac{1}{2}, \frac{1}{3}$

c $\pm\ln\left(\frac{3 + \sqrt{5}}{2}\right)$

16 **a** $16\cosh^5\theta - 20\cosh^3\theta + 5\cosh\theta$
b ± 0.96

17 **a**

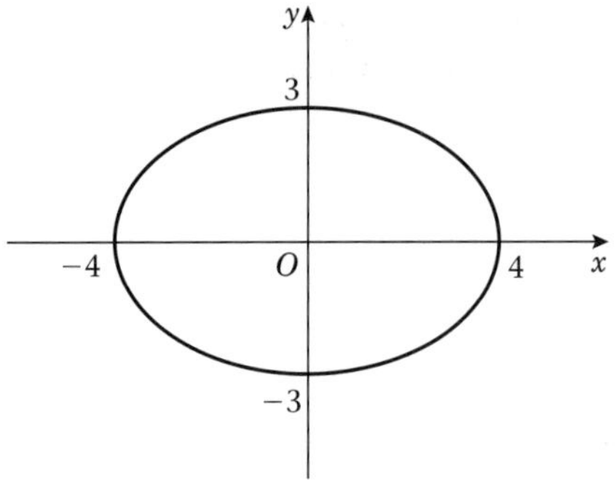

b $\frac{\sqrt{7}}{4}$ **c** $(\pm\sqrt{7}, 0)$

18 **a** $\frac{\sqrt{5}}{2}$
b $4\sqrt{5}$
c

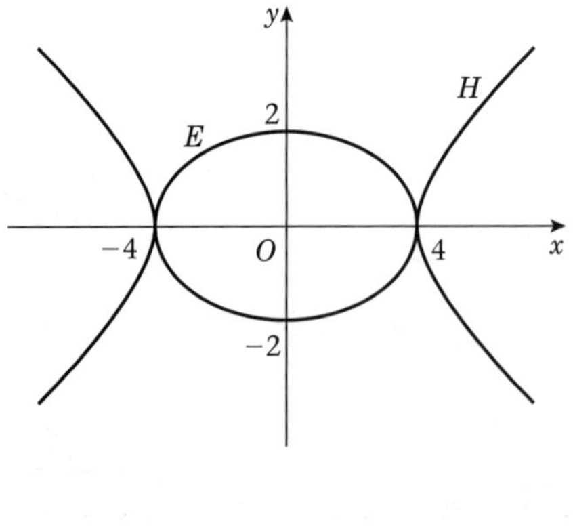

19 **a**

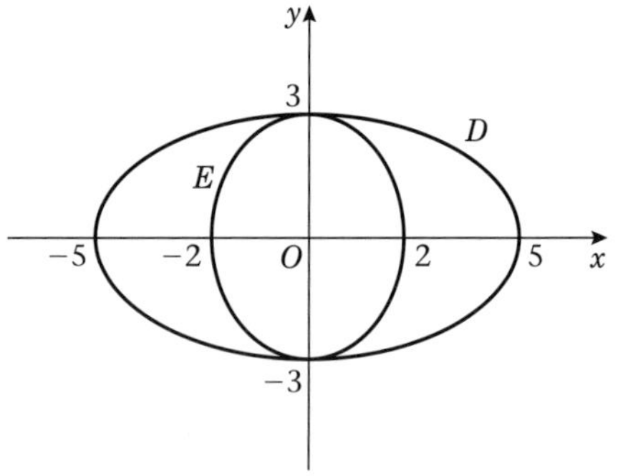

b $\sqrt{21}$

20 **a** $(\pm\sqrt{5}, 0)$

21 **a** $\frac{1}{2}$ **b** $y = -\frac{1}{2}x + 2$ **c** 2

23 **b** $\frac{\pi}{3}, \frac{2\pi}{3}, \frac{4\pi}{3}, \frac{5\pi}{3}$

24 **a** $ay\sin t + bx\cos t = ab$
b $ax\sin t - by\cos t = (a^2 - b^2)\sin t\cos t$
c $\left(\frac{a^2 - b^2}{2a}\cos t, \frac{b}{2\sin t}\right)$

25 **a** $x^2 + 4y^2 = a^2$ **b** $x = \pm\frac{2a}{\sqrt{3}}$ **c** $b = \frac{a}{2}$

27 **b** $y = -3x + 13$ and $y = -\frac{3}{7}x + \frac{37}{7}$

28 **c** $\frac{b^2 + a^2m^2}{2m}$
e $-\frac{a}{\sqrt{2}}$

29 **a** $\frac{\sqrt{5}}{3}$
b $(\pm\sqrt{5}, 0)$
$x = \pm\frac{9}{\sqrt{5}}$

30 **b** $(a\sqrt{2}, 0), x = \frac{a\sqrt{2}}{2}$
c The coordinates of P are $\left(\frac{a\sqrt{2}}{2}, \frac{a\sqrt{2}}{2}\right)$.
The coordinates of Q are $\left(\frac{a\sqrt{2}}{2}, -\frac{a\sqrt{2}}{2}\right)$.

31 **c** $\frac{4a^2x^2}{(2a^2 - b^2)^2} + \frac{4y^2}{b^2} = 1$

32 **a** tangent at P
$x\cosh t - y\sin t = 1$
normal at P
$x\sinh t + y\cosh t = 2\sinh t\cosh t$

33 **a** $bx - ay\sin\theta = ab\cos\theta$
$ax\sin\theta + by = (a^2 + b^2)\tan\theta$

36 **b** $\frac{128}{289}$

37 **a** $\frac{1}{4}\ln(2 + \sqrt{3})$

38 **b**

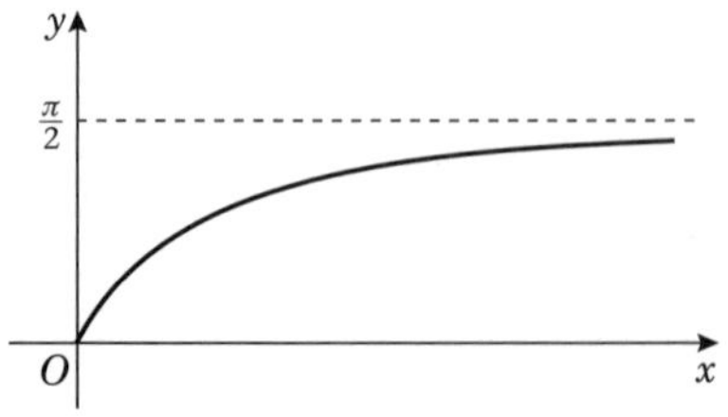

c $\frac{1}{3}(\pi - \sqrt{3}\ln 2)$

39 $\ln 2$

40 $\ln 3$

42 **b** $x\,\text{artanh}\,x + \frac{1}{2}\ln(1 - x^2) + A$

43 **a** $\frac{1}{2}\arcsin 2x - \frac{1}{4}\sqrt{(1 - 4x^2)} + C$

b 0.372 (3 d.p.)

45 **d** $\ln(1 + \sqrt{2}) - \sqrt{2} + 1$

46 **a** $2\arctan(e^x) + A$

b

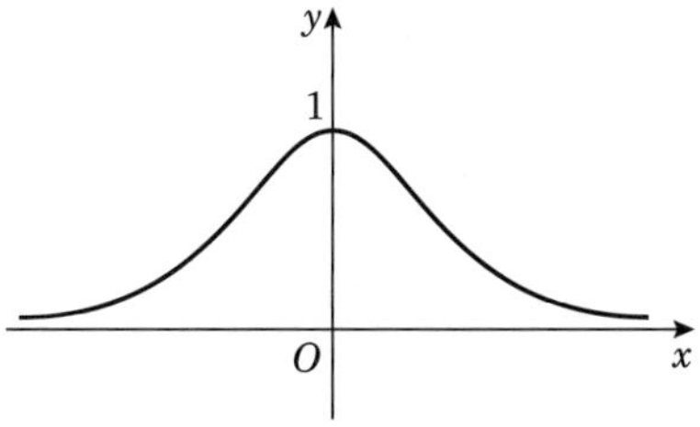

c 2.604 (3 d.p.)

47 **b** **i** (1.732, −0.902), (−1.732, 0.902).

ii (1.732, −0.902) is a minimum point and (−1.732, 0.902) is a maximum point.

iii

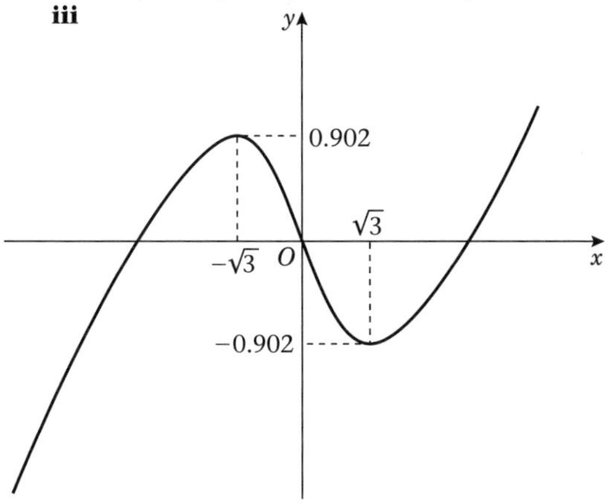

c 1.302 (3 d.p.)

48 $\frac{1}{2}\arctan\left(\frac{5e^x + 3}{4}\right) + A$

50 **a** $p = 2, q = 1, r = 4$

b $\frac{1}{4}\arctan\left(\frac{2x + 1}{2}\right) + C$

51 $\frac{3\sqrt{2}}{4} - \frac{1}{4}\ln(\sqrt{2} + 1)$

52 **b** $\frac{2}{\sqrt{(1 - 4x^2)}}$

53 **c** $\frac{\pi}{4} - \frac{\sqrt{2}}{2}\ln(1 + \sqrt{2})$

54 **a** $\frac{\sqrt{5}}{20}$

b $k = \frac{9}{2}$

55 **b** $\left(\frac{\pi}{2}\right)^6 - 30\left(\frac{\pi}{2}\right)^4 + 360\left(\frac{\pi}{2}\right)^2 - 720$

56 **b** $\frac{2048}{105}$

57 **c** $\frac{1}{8}(3\ln(1 + \sqrt{2}) - \sqrt{2})$

58 **b** $\frac{2016}{5}$

59 **b** $\frac{4}{5}\sqrt{3} - \frac{17}{15}\sqrt{2}$

60 **b** $J_n = -e^{-1} + nJ_{n-1}$

e $\frac{1}{2}\left(e - \frac{5}{e}\right)$

61 **b** $\sqrt{3} + \frac{1}{2}\ln(2 + \sqrt{3})$

63 $2\sqrt{2}$

65 **b** $(a\ln(4 + \sqrt{17}), a\sqrt{17})$.

66 **a** $6a$

b $\frac{12}{5}\pi a^2$

67 **b** $\pi\left(\frac{15}{16} + \ln 2\right)$

Exercise 5A

1 **a** $5\mathbf{i}$ **b** $-3\mathbf{j}$
c $3\mathbf{j}$ **d** $-3\mathbf{j} - 3\mathbf{k}$
e $-6\mathbf{k} - 2\mathbf{i}$ **f** $6\mathbf{k} + 2\mathbf{i}$
g $5\mathbf{i} - 16\mathbf{j} - 7\mathbf{k}$ **h** $9\mathbf{i} - 3\mathbf{k}$
i $-9\mathbf{i}$ **j** $\mathbf{i} - 5\mathbf{j} - 3\mathbf{k}$

2 **a** $-6\mathbf{i} + (3\lambda + 1)\mathbf{j} - 2\mathbf{k}$

b $(7\lambda - 3)\mathbf{i} + \mathbf{j} + (1 - 2\lambda)\mathbf{k}$

3 $-\frac{1}{3}\mathbf{i} - \frac{2}{3}\mathbf{j} + \frac{2}{3}\mathbf{k}$ or $\frac{1}{3}\mathbf{i} + \frac{2}{3}\mathbf{j} - \frac{2}{3}\mathbf{k}$

4 $\frac{1}{7}(-\mathbf{i} + 4\sqrt{2}\mathbf{j} + 4\mathbf{k})$

5 $\frac{1}{11}(6\mathbf{i} + 6\mathbf{j} + 7\mathbf{k})$

6 $\frac{1}{9}(4\mathbf{i} + 4\mathbf{j} - 7\mathbf{k})$

7 $-\mathbf{i} - 2\sqrt{2}\mathbf{j} + 4\mathbf{k}$

8 $\sqrt{8}$ or $2\sqrt{2}$ or 2.83 (to 3 s.f.)

9 **a** −14

b $-8\mathbf{i} - 24\mathbf{j} - 8\mathbf{k}$

c $\frac{1}{\sqrt{11}}(-\mathbf{i} - 3\mathbf{j} - \mathbf{k})$

10 **a** $\frac{\sqrt{221}}{15}$ **b** 1 **c** $\frac{\sqrt{21}}{11}$

11 Any multiple of $(\mathbf{i} + \mathbf{j} - \mathbf{k})$

12 $u = -1$, $v = 4$ and $w = 11$

13 **a** $a = 1$ and $b = -1$ **b** $-\frac{5}{6}$

14 $\lambda = \frac{3}{2}$ and $\mu = -\frac{3}{2}$

Exercise 5B

1 4.5

2 $\frac{5\sqrt{2}}{2}$

3 16.5

4 $\frac{3}{2}\sqrt{3}$

5 **i** $2\sqrt{13}$ **ii** 8.5

6 $\frac{3}{2}\sqrt{2}$

7 $\frac{5}{2}\sqrt{3}$

8 $5\sqrt{2}$

9 $10\sqrt{2}$

10 $3\sqrt{2}$

11 $\frac{\sqrt{3}}{2}a^2$

12 **b** $\overrightarrow{AB}$ is parallel to $\overrightarrow{DC}$.

Exercise 5C

1 **a** 21 **b** 21 **c** 21

2 **a** is parallel to the plane containing **b** and **c**

3 17

4 18

5 $\frac{3}{2}$

6 **a** 3 **b** $\pm\frac{1}{3}(\mathbf{i} + 2\mathbf{j} - 2\mathbf{k})$ **c** $2\frac{1}{3}$

7 **b** $\frac{2}{3}\sqrt{2}$

8 **a** $\overrightarrow{AB} = -2\mathbf{i} - \mathbf{j} + 3\mathbf{k}$

$\overrightarrow{AC} = \mathbf{i} - 3\mathbf{j} + 2\mathbf{k}$

$\overrightarrow{AB} \times \overrightarrow{AC} = 7\mathbf{i} + 7\mathbf{j} + 7\mathbf{k}$

b $\dfrac{7\sqrt{3}}{2}$

c $\frac{7}{3}$

9 **a** $5\mathbf{i} - \mathbf{j} - 7\mathbf{k}$

$2\mathbf{i} - 8\mathbf{j} + \mathbf{k}$

b **i** $\frac{5}{2}\sqrt{3}$

ii $\frac{19}{6}$

10 **a** $\mathbf{i} + 2\mathbf{j}$

b $\overrightarrow{OP} = 2\sqrt{5}$

Area of $OQR = \dfrac{\sqrt{5}}{2}$

Volume of tetrahedron $= \frac{5}{3}$

c $\mathbf{a}.(\mathbf{b} \times \mathbf{c}) = 10$

This is 6 × volume of tetrahedron so verified.

Exercise 5D

1 **a** $\mathbf{r} \times (3\mathbf{i} + \mathbf{j} - 2\mathbf{k}) = -4\mathbf{i} + 10\mathbf{j} - \mathbf{k}$

b $\mathbf{r} \times (\mathbf{i} + \mathbf{j} + 5\mathbf{k}) = 3\mathbf{i} - 13\mathbf{j} + 2\mathbf{k}$

c $\mathbf{r} \times (-\mathbf{i} - 2\mathbf{j} + 3\mathbf{k}) = -4\mathbf{i} - 13\mathbf{j} - 10\mathbf{k}$

2 **a** $\dfrac{x-2}{3} = \dfrac{y-1}{1} = \dfrac{z-2}{-2} = \lambda$

b $\dfrac{x-2}{1} = \dfrac{y}{1} = \dfrac{z+3}{5} = \lambda$

c $\dfrac{x-4}{-1} = \dfrac{y+2}{-2} = \dfrac{z-1}{3} = \lambda$

3 **a** $\left[\mathbf{r} - \begin{pmatrix} 1 \\ 3 \\ 5 \end{pmatrix}\right] \times \begin{pmatrix} 5 \\ 1 \\ -3 \end{pmatrix} = 0$

b $\left[\mathbf{r} - \begin{pmatrix} 3 \\ 4 \\ 12 \end{pmatrix}\right] \times \begin{pmatrix} 1 \\ -1 \\ -7 \end{pmatrix} = 0$

c $\left[\mathbf{r} - \begin{pmatrix} -2 \\ 2 \\ 6 \end{pmatrix}\right] \times \begin{pmatrix} 5 \\ 5 \\ 5 \end{pmatrix} = 0$

d $\left[\mathbf{r} - \begin{pmatrix} 1 \\ 1 \\ 1 \end{pmatrix}\right] \times \begin{pmatrix} -3 \\ -1 \\ 5 \end{pmatrix} = 0$

4 **a** $\dfrac{x-1}{5} = \dfrac{y-3}{1} = \dfrac{z-5}{-3} = \lambda$

b $\dfrac{x-3}{1} = \dfrac{y-4}{-1} = \dfrac{z-12}{-7} = \lambda$

c $\dfrac{x+2}{5} = \dfrac{y-2}{5} = \dfrac{z-6}{5} = \lambda$ or $x + 2 = y - 2 = z - 6 = \mu$

d $\dfrac{x-4}{3} = \dfrac{y-2}{1} = \dfrac{z+4}{-5} = \lambda$

5 **a** $[\mathbf{r} - (\mathbf{i} + \mathbf{j} - 2\mathbf{k})] \times (2\mathbf{i} - \mathbf{k}) = 0$

b $[\mathbf{r} - (\mathbf{i} + 4\mathbf{j})] \times (3\mathbf{i} + \mathbf{j} - 5\mathbf{k}) = 0$

c $[\mathbf{r} - (3\mathbf{i} + 4\mathbf{j} - 4\mathbf{k})] \times (2\mathbf{i} - 2\mathbf{j} - 3\mathbf{k}) = 0$

6 **i** $\mathbf{r} \times (2\mathbf{i} + 5\mathbf{j} + \frac{3}{2}\mathbf{k}) = -9\mathbf{i} - \frac{3}{2}\mathbf{j} + 17\mathbf{k}$

ii $\mathbf{r} = 3\mathbf{i} - \mathbf{j} + \frac{3}{2}\mathbf{k} + t(2\mathbf{i} + 5\mathbf{j} + \frac{3}{2}\mathbf{k})$

or $\mathbf{r} = 3\mathbf{i} - \mathbf{j} + \frac{3}{2}\mathbf{k} + s(4\mathbf{i} + 10\mathbf{j} + 3\mathbf{k})$

7 $p = 3$ and $q = 3$

8 $\mathbf{r} = -\mathbf{j} + 2\mathbf{k} + t(\mathbf{i} + \mathbf{j} - \mathbf{k})$

Exercise 5E

1 **a** $\mathbf{r}.(2\mathbf{i} + \mathbf{j} + \mathbf{k}) = 0$

b $\mathbf{r}.(5\mathbf{i} - \mathbf{j} - 3\mathbf{k}) = 0$

c $\mathbf{r}.(\mathbf{i} + 3\mathbf{j} + 4\mathbf{k}) = -10$

d $\mathbf{r}.(4\mathbf{i} + \mathbf{j} - 5\mathbf{k}) = 9$

2 **a** $2x + y + z = 0$

b $5x - y - 3z = 0$

c $x + 3y + 4z = -10$

d $4x + y - 5z = 9$

3 **a** $\mathbf{r} = \mathbf{i} + 2\mathbf{j} + \lambda(2\mathbf{i} - \mathbf{j} - \mathbf{k}) + \mu(3\mathbf{i} + \mathbf{j} + 2\mathbf{k})$

b $\mathbf{r} = 3\mathbf{i} + 4\mathbf{j} + \mathbf{k} + \lambda(-4\mathbf{i} - 6\mathbf{j} - \mathbf{k}) + \mu(-\mathbf{i} - 3\mathbf{j} + 3\mathbf{k})$

or $\mathbf{r} = 3\mathbf{i} + 4\mathbf{j} + \mathbf{k} + \lambda'(4\mathbf{i} + 6\mathbf{j} + \mathbf{k}) + \mu(-\mathbf{i} - 3\mathbf{j} + 3\mathbf{k})$

c $\mathbf{r} = 2\mathbf{i} - \mathbf{j} - \mathbf{k} + \lambda(\mathbf{i} + 2\mathbf{j} + 3\mathbf{k}) + \mu(2\mathbf{i} + \mathbf{j} + 2\mathbf{k})$

d $\mathbf{r} = -\mathbf{i} + \mathbf{j} + 3\mathbf{k} + \lambda(\mathbf{j} + 2\mathbf{k}) + \mu(\mathbf{i} + 3\mathbf{j} + \mathbf{k})$

4 **a** $x + 7y - 5z = 15$

b $21x - 13y - 6z = 5$

c $x + 4y - 3z = 1$

d $-5x + 2y - z = 4$

5 **a** $3x + y - z = 2$

b $7x - 2y + z = 5$

c $x + 2y - z = 3$

d $2x - 6y - z = 2$

6 **a** $\mathbf{r}.(2\mathbf{i} - 9\mathbf{j} = 4\mathbf{k}) = -15$

b $\mathbf{r}.(2\mathbf{i} - \mathbf{j} + \mathbf{k}) = 2$

c $\mathbf{r}.(8\mathbf{i} - 5\mathbf{j} + \mathbf{k}) = 22$

7 $-10x - 2y + 16z = 4$

Exercise 5F

1 **a** The two lines do meet at the point (3, 1, 10)

b The lines do not meet.

c The two lines do meet at the point $(0, 1\frac{1}{2}, 4\frac{1}{2})$

2 **a** $(2\frac{2}{3}, \frac{1}{6}, 4\frac{1}{3})$

b There are no values of λ for which the line meets the plane.

The line is parallel to the plane.

c (1, 2, 0)

3 **a** $\mathbf{r} = (\frac{5}{2}\mathbf{i} + \frac{5}{2}\mathbf{k}) + \lambda(\frac{3}{2}\mathbf{i} + \mathbf{j} + \frac{5}{2}\mathbf{k})$

b $\mathbf{r} = (3\mathbf{i} - \mathbf{j}) + \lambda(\frac{2}{3}\mathbf{i} + \frac{4}{3}\mathbf{j} + \mathbf{k})$

c $\mathbf{r} = (-3\mathbf{i} - \frac{13}{3}\mathbf{j}) + \lambda(\mathbf{i} + \frac{2}{3}\mathbf{j} + \mathbf{k})$

4 $\alpha = 68.3°$ (to 3 s.f.)

5 $\alpha = 40.2°$ (to 3 s.f.)

6 $\alpha = 4.25°$ (to 3 s.f.)

7 $\alpha = 43.1°$ (to 3 s.f.)

8 $\alpha = 21.7°$ (3 s.f.)

9 **a** 3 **b** $\frac{1}{3}$ **c** $\frac{2}{3}$ **d** 4

10 **a** 3 **b** 1

11 $\frac{13}{11}$

12 $x = \dfrac{\sqrt{198}}{5}$ or 2.81 (3 s.f.)

13 **a** The lines do not meet.

Distance $= \dfrac{4\sqrt{11}}{11}$ or 1.21

b Lines do not meet.

$x = 3\sqrt{2}$ or 4.24 (3 s.f.)

c Lines do not meet.

Shortest distance = 0.196 (3 s.f.)

14 3.54 (3 s.f.)

15 **b** $\dfrac{7\sqrt{3}}{3} = 4.04$ (3 s.f.)

Mixed Exercise 5G

1 $3\sqrt{2}$ or 4.24

2 $\frac{7\sqrt{6}}{9}$ or 1.91 (3 s.f.)

3 **a** $\mathbf{i} - \mathbf{j} - \mathbf{k}$
b $\frac{2}{3}\sqrt{3}$

4 **a** $\mathbf{r} = 2\mathbf{i} - 3\mathbf{j} + \mathbf{k} + \lambda(-4\mathbf{i} + \mathbf{j} - 2\mathbf{k})$
b $\frac{5}{2}\sqrt{5}$ or 5.59 (3 s.f.)

5 **a** $5\mathbf{i} + 5\mathbf{j} - 5\mathbf{k}$
b A is $(1\frac{3}{5}, \frac{1}{5}, 1\frac{4}{5})$
B is $(2\frac{4}{15}, \frac{13}{15}, 1\frac{2}{15})$

6 **a** $\frac{1}{\sqrt{50}}(3\mathbf{i} + 5\mathbf{j} + 4\mathbf{k})$
b $3x + 5y + 4z = 30$
c $3\sqrt{2}$

7 **b** $\frac{\sqrt{2}}{2}$ or 0.707 (to 3 s.f.)
c $x + z = 1$

8 **a** $-15\mathbf{i} - 20\mathbf{j} + 10\mathbf{k}$ or a multiple of $(3\mathbf{i} + 4\mathbf{j} - 2\mathbf{k})$
b $3x + 4y - 2z - 5 = 0$
c 5

9 **a** $-6\mathbf{i} - 4\mathbf{j} + 2\mathbf{k}$
b $\mathbf{r}.(3\mathbf{i} + 2\mathbf{j} - \mathbf{k}) = 0$
c $(-1, 1, -1)$

10 **a** $-\mathbf{i} + 7\mathbf{j} + 5\mathbf{k}$
b $-x + 7y + 5z = 0$
c $(1, -2, 3)$

11 **a** 73° (nearest degree)
b $\mathbf{r} \times (\mathbf{i} + \frac{1}{2}\mathbf{j} + 3\mathbf{k}) = (-\frac{5}{2}\mathbf{i} - 16\mathbf{j} + \frac{7}{2}\mathbf{k})$

12 **a** $-\mathbf{i} + \mathbf{j} + 4\mathbf{k}$
c 27° (nearest degree)

13 $2\sqrt{6}$ or 4.90

14 **c** $\mathbf{r} = 2\mathbf{i} - 2\mathbf{j} + 3\mathbf{k} + \lambda(2\mathbf{i} - \mathbf{j} + \mathbf{k})$
d $(-1, -\frac{1}{2}, \frac{3}{2})$
e 3.67 (3 s.f.)
f $\mathbf{r}.(2\mathbf{i} - \mathbf{j} + \mathbf{k}) = 9$

15 **a** $\mathbf{r} = \mathbf{i} + 2\mathbf{j} + \mathbf{k} + \lambda(2\mathbf{i} + \mathbf{j} + 3\mathbf{k})$
b $(3, 3, 4)$
c $5\mathbf{i} - \mathbf{j} - 3\mathbf{k}$
d $\frac{\sqrt{35}}{\sqrt{34}}$
e $(5, 4, 7)$

16 **b** $\mathbf{r} = 7\mathbf{i} + 2\mathbf{j} - 6\mathbf{k}$
c $\frac{14}{15}$
d $\mathbf{r} = \mathbf{i} - \mathbf{j} + \lambda(2\mathbf{i} + \mathbf{j} - 2\mathbf{k}) + \mu(-3\mathbf{i} + 4\mathbf{k})$

17 $2x - 5y + 3z + 10 = 0$

18 **b** $-10\mathbf{i} + 10\mathbf{j} - 5\mathbf{k}$
c $+2x - 2y + z = 10$
d 15

19 **a** $\mathbf{r} = a(-4\mathbf{i} + 4\mathbf{j} - \mathbf{k}) + \lambda a(9\mathbf{i} - 6\mathbf{j} + 12\mathbf{k})$
b $\mathbf{r} = a(5\mathbf{i} - \mathbf{j} - 3\mathbf{k}) + \lambda a(5\mathbf{i} - \mathbf{j} - 3\mathbf{k}) + \mu a(-4\mathbf{i} + 4\mathbf{j} - \mathbf{k})$
c $\frac{12}{\sqrt{35}\sqrt{33}}$ or 0.353 (3 s.f.)
d $3x - 2y + 4z = 5a$
e $\frac{x + 4a}{3} = \frac{y - 4a}{-2} = \frac{z + a}{4} = \lambda'$

20 **a** $\mathbf{r}\cdot(\mathbf{i} - \mathbf{j} - 2\mathbf{k}) = -7$
$x - y - 2z + 7 = 0$
b $\frac{3}{\sqrt{2}\sqrt{14}} = 0.567$ (3 s.f.)
c $(0, 5, 7)$ and $(4, 1, -1)$

Exercise 6A

1 **a** $\begin{pmatrix} 3 & -1 \\ 1 & 0 \\ 0 & 4 \end{pmatrix}$ dimension 3×2
b $\begin{pmatrix} 0 & -2 \\ 2 & 0 \end{pmatrix}$ dimension 2×2
c $\begin{pmatrix} 0 & -2 & 1 \\ 2 & 0 & -3 \\ -1 & 3 & 0 \end{pmatrix}$ dimension 3×3
d $(1\ 2\ 4)$ dimension 1×3

2 **a** $\begin{pmatrix} 2 & -3 \\ 4 & 6 \end{pmatrix}$
b $\begin{pmatrix} 20 & 18 \\ 18 & 45 \end{pmatrix}$
c $\begin{pmatrix} 13 & -10 \\ -10 & 52 \end{pmatrix}$

3 **a** $\begin{pmatrix} -9 & 8 \\ 8 & -4 \end{pmatrix}$

4 **a** $\begin{pmatrix} 1 & 4 & 8 \\ -4 & -7 & 4 \\ 8 & -4 & 1 \end{pmatrix}$

5 **a** $\begin{pmatrix} -12 & 15 & 21 \\ 15 & -3 & 0 \\ 21 & 0 & 7 \end{pmatrix}$

6 **a** $\begin{pmatrix} -5 & 3 & 15 \\ 3 & 2 & -5 \\ 1 & 2 & -1 \end{pmatrix}$

Exercise 6B

1 **a** 6 **b** -56 **c** 1 **d** 0

2 **a** 20 **b** 17 **c** 0

3 17

4 $-8, -2$

5 **b** $\begin{pmatrix} 7 & 6 & 7 \\ -2 & -10 & -4 \\ 13 & 7 & 12 \end{pmatrix}$

6 **a** -10
b $\begin{pmatrix} 4 & 2 & 2 \\ 5 & -3 & -4 \\ -2 & 2 & 3 \end{pmatrix}$

8 $-1, 0, 3$

Exercise 6C

1 **a** $\begin{pmatrix} 1 & 0 & 0 \\ 0 & \frac{2}{3} & -\frac{1}{3} \\ 0 & -\frac{1}{3} & \frac{2}{3} \end{pmatrix}$
b $\begin{pmatrix} 1 & 0 & 0 \\ 0 & \frac{1}{2} & 0 \\ 0 & 0 & \frac{1}{3} \end{pmatrix}$
c $\begin{pmatrix} 1 & 0 & 0 \\ 0 & \frac{3}{5} & \frac{4}{5} \\ 0 & -\frac{4}{5} & \frac{3}{5} \end{pmatrix}$

2 a $\begin{pmatrix} 4 & -6 & -1 \\ -3 & 4 & 1 \\ -6 & 9 & 2 \end{pmatrix}$

b $\begin{pmatrix} -\frac{3}{5} & -\frac{1}{5} & \frac{7}{5} \\ -\frac{1}{5} & -\frac{2}{5} & \frac{4}{5} \\ \frac{7}{5} & \frac{4}{5} & -\frac{13}{5} \end{pmatrix}$

c $\begin{pmatrix} 2 & -5 & -\frac{19}{2} \\ 1 & -3 & -5 \\ 1 & -3 & -\frac{11}{2} \end{pmatrix}$

3 a $\begin{pmatrix} -1 & 0 & 1 \\ 0 & 1 & 0 \\ 2 & 0 & -1 \end{pmatrix}$

b $\begin{pmatrix} \frac{1}{3} & \frac{1}{2} & -\frac{1}{6} \\ 0 & -\frac{1}{2} & \frac{1}{2} \\ -\frac{1}{3} & \frac{1}{2} & \frac{1}{6} \end{pmatrix}$

4 b $\frac{1}{3(k+1)}\begin{pmatrix} 3 & 3 & -3 \\ 1-4k & 5 & 3k-2 \\ k-1 & -2 & 2 \end{pmatrix}$

5 $a = -4, b = 8, c = 3$

6 b $\begin{pmatrix} -3 & 4 & 3 \\ -4 & 5 & 4 \\ 3 & -3 & -2 \end{pmatrix}$

7 c $\frac{1}{15}\begin{pmatrix} 9 & 2 & -1 \\ 6 & -2 & 1 \\ -9 & 3 & 6 \end{pmatrix}$

8 b $\begin{pmatrix} -6 & 16 & 12 \\ 3 & -8 & -6 \\ -3 & 8 & 6 \end{pmatrix}$

Exercise 6D

1 a $\begin{pmatrix} 1 & -1 & 0 \\ 0 & 1 & 1 \\ 2 & 0 & -3 \end{pmatrix}$

b $\begin{pmatrix} 2 & -3 & -1 \\ 0 & 2 & 3 \\ 0 & 0 & 5 \end{pmatrix}$

c $\begin{pmatrix} 2 & -5 & -4 \\ 0 & 2 & 8 \\ 4 & -6 & -17 \end{pmatrix}$

2 $a = -3, b = 1, c = -4$

3 $\begin{pmatrix} 3 & 13 & 11 \\ 1 & -1 & 0 \\ 2 & -1 & 1 \end{pmatrix}$

4 $\mathbf{r} = \begin{pmatrix} -2 \\ 20 \\ 15 \end{pmatrix} + t\begin{pmatrix} 8 \\ -24 \\ -4 \end{pmatrix}$

5 a The position vector of A' is $\begin{pmatrix} -1 \\ 7 \\ 2 \end{pmatrix}$ and the position vector of B' is $\begin{pmatrix} 5 \\ -3 \\ 26 \end{pmatrix}$.

b $\mathbf{r} = \begin{pmatrix} -1 \\ 7 \\ 2 \end{pmatrix} + t\begin{pmatrix} 6 \\ -10 \\ 24 \end{pmatrix}$.

6 $6x + 2y + 9z = 0$

7 $\mathbf{r}.\begin{pmatrix} -10 \\ 49 \\ -7 \end{pmatrix} = 120$

8 $\mathbf{r} = t\begin{pmatrix} 1 \\ -1 \\ 1 \end{pmatrix}$

Exercise 6E

1 a $a = -21, b = 24, c = -23$

b $\mathbf{r} = t\begin{pmatrix} 1 \\ -5 \\ 3 \end{pmatrix}$

2 a $\begin{pmatrix} -4 & 6 & -3 \\ 6 & -7 & 4 \\ -3 & 4 & -2 \end{pmatrix}$

b $a = 2, b = -1, c = 3$

3 a $\begin{pmatrix} 4 & -2 & 1 \\ 3 & -1 & 1 \\ -3 & \frac{3}{2} & -1 \end{pmatrix}$

b $\mathbf{r} = \begin{pmatrix} 1 \\ 3 \\ -1 \end{pmatrix} + t\begin{pmatrix} -3 \\ -2 \\ 2 \end{pmatrix}$

4 a $\begin{pmatrix} 0 & \frac{1}{4} & 0 \\ 1 & -\frac{a}{4} & 2 \\ 0 & 0 & -1 \end{pmatrix}$

b $p = \frac{3}{4}, q = -\frac{3a}{4}, r = 1$

5 a $k = 4$

b $a = \frac{1}{2}, b = -2, c = -\frac{1}{2}$

6 a $a = -2, b = 2, c = 19$

b $\mathbf{r} = \begin{pmatrix} 1 \\ 1 \\ -7 \end{pmatrix} + s\begin{pmatrix} -9 \\ -6 \\ 56 \end{pmatrix} + t\begin{pmatrix} -5 \\ -3 \\ 30 \end{pmatrix}$

7 $a = 2, b = 0, c = -1$

8 a $\begin{pmatrix} -2 & -1 & 5 \\ -1 & 0 & 2 \\ 2 & 1 & -4 \end{pmatrix}$

c $a = -1, b = 2, c = -1$

Exercise 6F

1 a The eigenvalues are 1 and 6.
An eigenvector corresponding to the eigenvalue 1 is $\begin{pmatrix} -4 \\ 1 \end{pmatrix}$.
An eigenvector corresponding to the eigenvalue 6 is $\begin{pmatrix} 1 \\ 1 \end{pmatrix}$.

b The eigenvalues are 3 and 5.
An eigenvector corresponding to the eigenvalue 3 is $\begin{pmatrix} 1 \\ 1 \end{pmatrix}$.

An eigenvector corresponding to the eigenvalue 5 is $\begin{pmatrix} 1 \\ -1 \end{pmatrix}$.

c The eigenvalues are 3 and 4.
An eigenvector corresponding to the eigenvalue 3 is $\begin{pmatrix} 1 \\ 0 \end{pmatrix}$.
An eigenvector corresponding to the eigenvalue 4 is $\begin{pmatrix} -2 \\ 1 \end{pmatrix}$.

2 **a** 5, 7
b $y = \frac{1}{2}x, y = x$

3 **a** The eigenvalues are 1, 3 and 4.
An eigenvector corresponding to the eigenvalue 1 is $\begin{pmatrix} 0 \\ -2 \\ 3 \end{pmatrix}$.
An eigenvector corresponding to the eigenvalue 3 is $\begin{pmatrix} 1 \\ 0 \\ -1 \end{pmatrix}$.
An eigenvector corresponding to the eigenvalue 4 is $\begin{pmatrix} 0 \\ 1 \\ 0 \end{pmatrix}$.

b The eigenvalues are -1, 0 and 4.
An eigenvector corresponding to the eigenvalue -1 is $\begin{pmatrix} -2 \\ 1 \\ -3 \end{pmatrix}$.
An eigenvector corresponding to the eigenvalue 0 is $\begin{pmatrix} 3 \\ -2 \\ 4 \end{pmatrix}$.
An eigenvector corresponding to the eigenvalue 4 is $\begin{pmatrix} 1 \\ 2 \\ -1 \end{pmatrix}$.

4 **b** $\begin{pmatrix} 1 \\ 1 \\ \frac{5}{2} \end{pmatrix}$

5 **b** $\begin{pmatrix} \frac{1}{2} \\ 2 \\ 1 \end{pmatrix}$

6 **a** -1, 6.
b An eigenvector corresponding to the eigenvalue -1 is $\begin{pmatrix} -2 \\ 1 \\ 1 \end{pmatrix}$.
An eigenvector corresponding to the eigenvalue 3 is $\begin{pmatrix} 1 \\ -1 \\ 1 \end{pmatrix}$.
An eigenvector corresponding to the eigenvalue 6 is $\begin{pmatrix} 5 \\ 1 \\ 8 \end{pmatrix}$.

7 **b** 4, 5.
c $\begin{pmatrix} \frac{1}{\sqrt{6}} \\ \frac{1}{\sqrt{6}} \\ -\frac{2}{\sqrt{6}} \end{pmatrix}$

8 **b** An eigenvector corresponding to the eigenvalue -2 is $\begin{pmatrix} \frac{1}{2} \\ 2 \\ 1 \end{pmatrix}$.
An eigenvector corresponding to the eigenvalue 5 is $\begin{pmatrix} 5 \\ 1 \\ 3 \end{pmatrix}$.

9 **a** $\pm\sqrt{2}$.
b An eigenvector corresponding to the eigenvalue $\sqrt{2}$ is $\begin{pmatrix} 1 \\ 1-\sqrt{2} \\ \sqrt{2}-1 \end{pmatrix}$.
An eigenvector corresponding to the eigenvalue $-\sqrt{2}$ is $\begin{pmatrix} 1 \\ 1+\sqrt{2} \\ -1-\sqrt{2} \end{pmatrix}$.
An eigenvector corresponding to the eigenvalue 2 is $\begin{pmatrix} 1 \\ -1 \\ -1 \end{pmatrix}$.

10 **b** $a = 3$ and $b = 4$

Exercise 6G

1 **a** $\begin{pmatrix} -2 & 0 \\ 0 & 4 \end{pmatrix}$ **b** $\begin{pmatrix} 5 & 0 \\ 0 & 0 \end{pmatrix}$

2 **a** 2, 5
b A normalised eigenvector corresponding to the eigenvalue 2 is $\begin{pmatrix} -\frac{\sqrt{2}}{\sqrt{3}} \\ \frac{1}{\sqrt{3}} \end{pmatrix}$.
A normalised eigenvector corresponding to the eigenvalue 5 is $\begin{pmatrix} \frac{1}{\sqrt{3}} \\ \frac{\sqrt{2}}{\sqrt{3}} \end{pmatrix}$.
c $\mathbf{P} = \begin{pmatrix} -\frac{\sqrt{2}}{\sqrt{3}} & \frac{1}{\sqrt{3}} \\ \frac{1}{\sqrt{3}} & \frac{\sqrt{2}}{\sqrt{3}} \end{pmatrix}$ $\mathbf{D} = \begin{pmatrix} 2 & 0 \\ 0 & 5 \end{pmatrix}$

4 $\begin{pmatrix} 0 & 0 & 0 \\ 0 & 2 & 0 \\ 0 & 0 & 4 \end{pmatrix}$

5 **a** $\begin{pmatrix} 0 \\ \frac{1}{\sqrt{2}} \\ -\frac{1}{\sqrt{2}} \end{pmatrix}$
b $\mathbf{P} = \begin{pmatrix} 0 & -\frac{1}{\sqrt{3}} & \frac{2}{\sqrt{6}} \\ \frac{1}{\sqrt{2}} & \frac{1}{\sqrt{3}} & \frac{1}{\sqrt{6}} \\ -\frac{1}{\sqrt{2}} & \frac{1}{\sqrt{3}} & \frac{1}{\sqrt{6}} \end{pmatrix}$ $\mathbf{D} = \begin{pmatrix} 0 & 0 & 0 \\ 0 & -1 & 0 \\ 0 & 0 & 8 \end{pmatrix}$

6 a 3, 6

b An eigenvector corresponding to the eigenvalue 3 is $\begin{pmatrix}1\\2\\2\end{pmatrix}$.

An eigenvector corresponding to the eigenvalue 6 is $\begin{pmatrix}2\\-2\\1\end{pmatrix}$.

An eigenvector corresponding to the eigenvalue 9 is $\begin{pmatrix}2\\1\\-2\end{pmatrix}$.

c $\mathbf{P} = \begin{pmatrix}\frac{1}{3} & \frac{2}{3} & \frac{2}{3}\\ \frac{2}{3} & -\frac{2}{3} & \frac{1}{3}\\ \frac{2}{3} & \frac{1}{3} & -\frac{2}{3}\end{pmatrix}$ $\mathbf{D} = \begin{pmatrix}3 & 0 & 0\\0 & 6 & 0\\0 & 0 & 9\end{pmatrix}$

7 a −2, 1

b $\begin{pmatrix}\frac{2}{\sqrt{18}}\\ \frac{3}{\sqrt{18}}\\ \frac{\sqrt{5}}{\sqrt{18}}\end{pmatrix}$

c $\mathbf{P} = \begin{pmatrix}\frac{2}{\sqrt{18}} & -\frac{2}{\sqrt{18}} & \frac{\sqrt{5}}{3}\\ \frac{3}{\sqrt{18}} & \frac{3}{\sqrt{18}} & 0\\ \frac{\sqrt{5}}{\sqrt{18}} & -\frac{\sqrt{5}}{\sqrt{18}} & -\frac{2}{3}\end{pmatrix}$ $\mathbf{D} = \begin{pmatrix}4 & 0 & 0\\0 & -2 & 0\\0 & 0 & 1\end{pmatrix}$

8 a $\lambda_2 = 4, \lambda_3 = -3$

c $\begin{pmatrix}1\\-1\\-2\end{pmatrix}$

d $\begin{pmatrix}\frac{1}{\sqrt{6}} & \frac{1}{\sqrt{2}} & \frac{1}{\sqrt{3}}\\ -\frac{1}{\sqrt{6}} & \frac{1}{\sqrt{2}} & -\frac{1}{\sqrt{3}}\\ -\frac{2}{\sqrt{6}} & 0 & \frac{1}{\sqrt{3}}\end{pmatrix}$

Mixed Exercise 6H

1 8

2 $\frac{1}{2}\begin{pmatrix}2 & 0 & 0\\-x & 1 & 0\\x-6 & -1 & 2\end{pmatrix}$

3 a An eigenvector corresponding to the eigenvalue 5 is $\begin{pmatrix}2\\1\end{pmatrix}$.

An eigenvector corresponding to the eigenvalue −15 is $\begin{pmatrix}1\\-2\end{pmatrix}$.

b $\begin{pmatrix}\frac{2}{\sqrt{5}} & \frac{1}{\sqrt{5}}\\ \frac{1}{\sqrt{5}} & -\frac{2}{\sqrt{5}}\end{pmatrix}$

4 a $\begin{pmatrix}2 & -1\\0 & 0\end{pmatrix}$

5 a −1, −11.

b $y = \frac{1}{2}x, y = -\frac{3}{4}x$

6 a $\begin{pmatrix}0\\0\\1\end{pmatrix}$ **b** 2, 5

7 $\frac{x-4}{-1} = \frac{y-2}{6} = \frac{z+1}{3}$

8 a −3, 9 **b** $\begin{pmatrix}1\\-2\\-2\end{pmatrix}$

c $\begin{pmatrix}\frac{1}{3} & \frac{2}{3} & \frac{2}{3}\\ -\frac{2}{3} & \frac{2}{3} & -\frac{1}{3}\\ -\frac{2}{3} & -\frac{1}{3} & \frac{2}{3}\end{pmatrix}$

9 a $\begin{pmatrix}2\\3\\-1\end{pmatrix}$ is an eigenvalue of **A** corresponding to the eigenvalue −1.

$\begin{pmatrix}2\\-1\\1\end{pmatrix}$ is an eigenvalue of **A** corresponding to the eigenvalue 3.

b $\begin{pmatrix}1\\-2\\-4\end{pmatrix}$

c $\begin{pmatrix}\frac{2}{\sqrt{14}} & \frac{2}{\sqrt{6}} & \frac{1}{\sqrt{21}}\\ \frac{3}{\sqrt{14}} & -\frac{1}{\sqrt{6}} & -\frac{2}{\sqrt{21}}\\ -\frac{1}{\sqrt{14}} & \frac{1}{\sqrt{6}} & -\frac{4}{\sqrt{21}}\end{pmatrix}$

10 a $\frac{1}{2x-5}\begin{pmatrix}-2 & -1 & 2x\\2 & 1 & -5\\3 & x-1 & -3x\end{pmatrix}$

b $a = 19, b = -14, c = -27$

11 b $\alpha = -2, \beta = -1$

c 2

12 a $\frac{1}{9-u}\begin{pmatrix}1-u & 4 & -3-u\\-2 & 1 & 6-u\\2 & -1 & 3\end{pmatrix}, u \neq 9$

b $a = 2.7, b = 3.1, c = -0.8$

13 b An eigenvalue corresponding to the eigenvalue 2 is $\begin{pmatrix}0\\1\\1\end{pmatrix}$.

An eigenvalue corresponding to the eigenvalue 3 is $\begin{pmatrix}1\\4\\7\end{pmatrix}$.

14 b $y = 0$

15 d $\begin{pmatrix}3\\1\\0\end{pmatrix}$ is an eigenvector of **AB** corresponding to the eigenvalue 10.

16 a $\frac{1}{7}\begin{pmatrix}5 & 2 & -1\\-17 & 3 & 2\\2 & -2 & 1\end{pmatrix}$ **b** $\frac{x}{10} = \frac{y}{1} = \frac{z}{-3}$

Review Exercise 2

1 $2\sqrt{2}$

2 $\frac{1}{3}$

4 **a** $5\mathbf{i} - 3\mathbf{j} - 4\mathbf{k}$
b 100
c 50

5 **a** $-\mathbf{i} + 8\mathbf{j} - 4\mathbf{k}$
b $3\mathbf{i} + \mathbf{j} - \mathbf{k}$
d $\mathbf{r} = \mathbf{i} + \mathbf{j} + \mathbf{k} + t(4\mathbf{i} + 13\mathbf{j} + 25\mathbf{k})$

6 **a** $\mathbf{i} + 4\mathbf{j} + 2\mathbf{k}$
b $\mathbf{r}.(\mathbf{i} + 4\mathbf{j} + 2\mathbf{k}) = 7$
c 2

7 **b** $\mathbf{r} = 4\mathbf{i} + \mathbf{j} - 7\mathbf{k} + \lambda(-3\mathbf{i} + 2\mathbf{j} + 8\mathbf{k})$
c $\mathbf{r}.(2\mathbf{i} - \mathbf{j} + \mathbf{k}) = 0$

8 **c** 22.3° (nearest one tenth of a degree)

9 **a** $\begin{pmatrix} -30 \\ -15 \\ 45 \end{pmatrix}$
b $\mathbf{r} = \begin{pmatrix} 3 \\ 1 \\ 2 \end{pmatrix} + \lambda\begin{pmatrix} -2 \\ -1 \\ 3 \end{pmatrix}$
d 35

10 **a** $6\mathbf{i} + \mathbf{j} - 4\mathbf{k}$
c -2
d $(\mathbf{r} - (-3\mathbf{i} + 6\mathbf{j} - 7\mathbf{k})) \times (-9\mathbf{i} + 10\mathbf{j} - 11\mathbf{k}) = \mathbf{0}$

11 **a** $\begin{pmatrix} 36 \\ 12 \\ 9 \end{pmatrix}$ **b** $\mathbf{r}.\begin{pmatrix} 12 \\ 4 \\ 3 \end{pmatrix} = 3$ **c** $(1, -3, 1)$

12 **a** $\begin{pmatrix} -5 - 4c \\ -6 - 5c \\ 1 \end{pmatrix}$
b $c = -2$
c $\mathbf{r}.\begin{pmatrix} 3 \\ 4 \\ 1 \end{pmatrix} = 7$
d $\begin{pmatrix} -5 \\ -3 \\ 8 \end{pmatrix}$

13 **a** $-15\mathbf{i} - 10\mathbf{j} - 10\mathbf{k}$
b $\mathbf{r}.(3\mathbf{i} + 2\mathbf{j} + 2\mathbf{k}) = 7$
c $(\mathbf{r} - (3\mathbf{i} - \mathbf{j})) \times (-2\mathbf{i} + \mathbf{j} + 2\mathbf{k}) = \mathbf{0}$
d $\left(\frac{13}{9}, -\frac{2}{9}, \frac{14}{9}\right)$

14 **a** $3\mathbf{i} - 6\mathbf{j} + 6\mathbf{k}$
c 14
d $\mathbf{r} = 4\mathbf{i} + 3\mathbf{j} + \mathbf{k} + t(\mathbf{j} + \mathbf{k})$
e $4\mathbf{i} + \mathbf{j} - \mathbf{k}$

15 **a** $\begin{pmatrix} -6 \\ 2 \\ -4 \end{pmatrix}$
c $(-1, 8, 9)$

16 **a** $\mathbf{r} = \begin{pmatrix} 1 \\ 2 \\ 3 \end{pmatrix} + t\begin{pmatrix} -3 \\ 5 \\ 1 \end{pmatrix}$ **b** $\frac{11}{6}$
c $\mathbf{r}.\begin{pmatrix} -3 \\ 5 \\ 1 \end{pmatrix} = -1$ **d** $\left(\frac{68}{35}, \frac{15}{35}, \frac{94}{35}\right)$
f $\left(\frac{101}{35}, -\frac{40}{35}, \frac{83}{35}\right)$

17 **a** $2\mathbf{i} - 3\mathbf{j} - 2\mathbf{k}$ **b** $\frac{\sqrt{17}}{2}$
c $\mathbf{r}.(2\mathbf{i} - 3\mathbf{j} - 2\mathbf{k}) = -7$ **d** $2x - 3y - 2z = -7$
e $\frac{7}{\sqrt{17}}$ **f** 3.2° (1 d.p.)

18 **b** $\mathbf{r} = -5\mathbf{i} + 4\mathbf{j} + 2\mathbf{k} + u(9\mathbf{i} + (\lambda - 4)\mathbf{j} - 5\mathbf{k})$
c $\frac{5\lambda + 11}{\sqrt{42}\sqrt{(\lambda^2 - 8\lambda + 122)}}$
d $-\frac{11}{5}$

19 **a** $\sqrt{10}$ **b** $\mathbf{r}.(\mathbf{i} - 2\mathbf{j} - 2\mathbf{k}) = -6$
c $2\mathbf{i} + \mathbf{j} + 3\mathbf{k}$

20 **b** $(1 - 2t_1 - 2u_1)\mathbf{i} + (-t_1 + u_1)\mathbf{j} + (-4 + t_1 + u_1)\mathbf{k}$
c $u_1 = \frac{3}{5}$
$t_1 = \frac{3}{5}$

22 **a** $k = 3, 6$
b $\frac{1}{-k^2 + 9k - 18}\begin{pmatrix} -k & -2 & k - 2 \\ 9k & 18 & -k^2 \\ 9 & 9 - k & -k \end{pmatrix}$

23 **a** 3
b 18
c $a = 2\sqrt{2}$
$b = -\sqrt{2}$
$c = -2\sqrt{2}$
d $54\sqrt{2}$

24 **a** $\begin{pmatrix} 3 & 3 & 7 \\ 1 & 4 & 4 \\ 3 & 1 & 6 \end{pmatrix}$
d $\begin{pmatrix} 4 & -2 & -3 \\ 1 & 0 & -1 \\ -2 & 1 & 2 \end{pmatrix}$

25 **a** $\begin{pmatrix} 1 & 0 & 0 \\ 0 & 4 & 3 \\ 0 & 0 & 1 \end{pmatrix}$ **b** $\begin{pmatrix} 1 & 0 & 0 \\ 0 & 8 & 7 \\ 0 & 0 & 1 \end{pmatrix}$
d $\begin{pmatrix} 1 & 0 & 0 \\ 0 & 2^{-n} & 2^{-n} - 1 \\ 0 & 0 & 1 \end{pmatrix}$

26 **b** $\frac{1}{2(u - 1)}\begin{pmatrix} u - 3 & -u - 3 & 2 \\ -u + 5 & 3u + 5 & -4 \\ -2 & -4 & 2 \end{pmatrix}$
c $a = 1.2, b = -0.4, c = 0.2$

27 **a** $a = -4$
$b = -3$
$c = 0$
b -1
c $x = 2y$

28 **a** $\begin{pmatrix} -1 & 3 & 1 \\ 0 & 1 & 5 \\ 2 & 4 & 2 \end{pmatrix}$
b $z = 8$

29 **a** $\begin{pmatrix} 1 & -1 & 2 \\ 0 & 1 & -1 \\ 0 & 0 & 1 \end{pmatrix}$
b 9
c $\begin{pmatrix} \frac{1}{3} \\ -\frac{1}{3} \\ 1 \end{pmatrix}$

30 **a** $-6, 1$
b $y = \frac{3}{5}x$

31 **a** The image under T of the line with equation $y = 2x + 1$ is the point with coordinates $(2, -1)$.
b $-2, 3$
c $y = \frac{1}{2}x, y = 2x$

32 **a** $\lambda_1 = 2, \lambda_2 = 3$
b $\frac{1}{6}\begin{pmatrix} 1 & 2 \\ -1 & 4 \end{pmatrix}$
d $y = \frac{1}{2}x, y = x.$

33 The eigenvalues of the matrix are -2, 0 and 1.
An eigenvector corresponding to the eigenvalue -2 is $\begin{pmatrix} 4 \\ 3 \\ -7 \end{pmatrix}$.
An eigenvector corresponding to the eigenvalue 0 is $\begin{pmatrix} 10 \\ 3 \\ -11 \end{pmatrix}$.
An eigenvector corresponding to the eigenvalue 1 is $\begin{pmatrix} 1 \\ 0 \\ 1 \end{pmatrix}$.

34 **a** 2
b $p = 4$
$q = -2$
c $l = 2, m = 1, n = 0$

35 **b** 5, 6
c $\begin{pmatrix} \frac{1}{\sqrt{2}} \\ 0 \\ \frac{1}{\sqrt{2}} \end{pmatrix}$

36 **b** $\frac{1}{20 - 4k}\begin{pmatrix} -4 & -2k + 8 & 4 \\ -2k + 8 & 3k - 16 & 2 \\ 4 & 2 & -4 \end{pmatrix}$
c -1
d $\begin{pmatrix} 2 \\ 1 \\ 2 \end{pmatrix}$

37 **b** $\begin{pmatrix} 1 \\ 2 \\ 2 \end{pmatrix}$.
c $\mathbf{P} = \begin{pmatrix} \frac{2}{3} & \frac{1}{3} & \frac{2}{3} \\ -\frac{2}{3} & \frac{2}{3} & \frac{1}{3} \\ \frac{1}{3} & \frac{2}{3} & -\frac{2}{3} \end{pmatrix}$ $\mathbf{D} = \begin{pmatrix} 3 & 0 & 0 \\ 0 & 9 & 0 \\ 0 & 0 & -3 \end{pmatrix}$

38 **a** 1
b $\begin{pmatrix} \frac{4}{\sqrt{21}} \\ \frac{1}{\sqrt{21}} \\ \frac{-2}{\sqrt{21}} \end{pmatrix}$
c $\begin{pmatrix} \frac{1}{\sqrt{14}} & \frac{1}{\sqrt{6}} & \frac{4}{\sqrt{21}} \\ \frac{2}{\sqrt{14}} & \frac{-2}{\sqrt{6}} & \frac{1}{\sqrt{21}} \\ \frac{3}{\sqrt{14}} & \frac{1}{\sqrt{6}} & \frac{-2}{\sqrt{21}} \end{pmatrix}$
d $\begin{pmatrix} 1 & 0 & 0 \\ 0 & -1 & 0 \\ 0 & 0 & 8 \end{pmatrix}$

39 **a** The eigenvalues of $\mathbf{M}$ are -1, 2 and 3.
An eigenvector corresponding to the eigenvalue -1 is $\begin{pmatrix} 1 \\ 0 \\ -2 \end{pmatrix}$.
An eigenvector corresponding to the eigenvalue 2 is $\begin{pmatrix} 1 \\ -1 \\ 1 \end{pmatrix}$.
An eigenvector corresponding to the eigenvalue 3 is $\begin{pmatrix} 1 \\ 0 \\ 2 \end{pmatrix}$.
b $x = \frac{y}{2} = \frac{z}{10}$.

40 **b** 3, 6
c A normalised eigenvector corresponding to 3 is $\begin{pmatrix} \frac{2}{3} \\ \frac{2}{3} \\ -\frac{2}{3} \end{pmatrix}$.
A normalised eigenvector corresponding to 6 is $\begin{pmatrix} -\frac{1}{3} \\ \frac{2}{3} \\ \frac{2}{3} \end{pmatrix}$.
A normalised eigenvector corresponding to 9 is $\begin{pmatrix} \frac{2}{3} \\ -\frac{1}{3} \\ \frac{2}{3} \end{pmatrix}$.

Examination Style Paper

1 **a** $\frac{6}{\sqrt{72}} = \frac{1}{\sqrt{72}}$
b $\frac{x^2}{72} + \frac{y^2}{36} = 1$

2 0.201599... = 0.202 (3 s.f.)

3 **a** $I = \frac{1}{3}\arcsin 3x - \frac{2}{3}(1 - 9x^2)^{\frac{1}{2}} + c$
b $\frac{\pi}{18} - \frac{\sqrt{3}}{3} + \frac{2}{3}$

4 **b** $\frac{46}{27}e^6 + \frac{2}{27}$

5 **c** $\frac{40}{\sqrt{161}}$

6 $\frac{3a}{2} + a\sqrt{2}$

7 **c** $3y^2 = 16ax$

8 **b** $x = \ln\left(1 + \frac{\sqrt{5}}{2}\right)$ or $\ln(3 + \sqrt{10})$

9 **b** $p\begin{pmatrix} 0 \\ 1 \\ -1 \end{pmatrix}$, for some constant p
c the eigenvalue is 3
$k = -4$
$l = 2$

Index